REA

# MENSCHHEITSDÄMMERUNG

# MENSCHHEITSDÄMMERUNG

## Dawn of Humanity
### A Document of Expressionism

*With Biographies and Bibliographies*

*Edited by*
*Kurt Pinthus*

*Translated and with an Introduction by*

*Joanna M. Ratych*
*Ralph Ley*
*Robert C. Conard*

CAMDEN HOUSE

Published by Camden House, Inc.
Drawer 2025
Columbia, SC 29202 USA

Printed on acid-free paper.
Binding materials are chosen for strength and
durability.

Printed in the United States of America

ISBN 1-879751-48-8

**Library of Congress Cataloging-in-Publication Data**

Menschheitsdämmerung : dawn of humanity : a document of expressionism
with biographies and bibliographies / edited by Kurt Pinthus ;
translated and with an introduction by Joanna M. Ratych, Ralph Ley,
and Robert C. Conard.
    p.    cm.  -- (Studies in German literature, linguistics, and
culture)
    Includes bibliographical references and index.
    ISBN 1-879751-48-8 (alk. paper)
    1. German poetry--20th century.   I. Pinthus, Kurt, 1886-1975
    II. Ratych, Joanna M.   III. Ley, Ralph.   IV. Conard, Robert C., 1933-

    V. Series:  Studies in German literature, linguistics, and
culture (Unnumbered)
    PT1174.M45   1993
    831'.9108--dc20                                               93-2165
                                                                  CIP

# *Acknowledgments*

$F$or permission to publish a complete translation of the final revised edition (1964) of *Menschheitsdämmerung* with illustrations we wish to thank the licenser, Rowohlt Taschenbuch Verlag GmbH, Reinbek bei Hamburg, as well as the custodian of the literary estate of Kurt Pinthus, Die deutsche Schillergesellschaft, Schiller Nationalmuseum, Marbach am Neckar. For permission to publish a translation of Kurt Pinthus's essay "Die Geschichte der *Menschheitsdämmerung*" in *Gedichte der Menschheits- dämmerung. Interpretationen expressionistischer Lyrik*, edited by Horst Denkler, 1971, pp. vii-xxviii, we wish to thank the Wilhelm Fink Verlag GmbH & Co. KG, Munich.

For their help, encouragement, and good advice we are indebted to Professor Christine Cosentino, Department of German, Rutgers University, Camden, New Jersey; Professor Horst Denkler, Fachbereich Germanistik, Freie Universität Berlin; Mr. Fred Grubel, Vice President, The Leo Baeck Institute, New York City; Professor James Hardin, Department of Germanic, Slavic and Oriental Literatures, University of South Carolina, Columbia; Professor Morris A. Moskowitz, Department of Hebraic Studies, Rutgers University, New Brunswick, New Jersey; Herr Friedrich Pfäfflin, Deutsches Literaturarchiv, Schiller-Nationalmuseum, Marbach am Neckar; and Professor Guy Stern, Department of German and Slavic Languages and Literatures, Wayne State University, Detroit, Michigan.

For their financial support we are grateful to the College of Arts and Sciences, University of Dayton, and to the Research Council of Rutgers University.

# Contents

# Translators' Introduction

## 1. A Word about *Menschheitsdämmerung* and the Relevance of Expressionism.

*E*xpressionism may well be Germany's most original contribution to the arts since the Middle Ages; it is certainly its most important contribution to the cultural history of the twentieth century. It has had a worldwide impact on letters, on the figurative arts, on music and dance, on stagecraft and cinema, and even on architecture. Its best-known achievements have been in painting, drama, and poetry. The first of these is readily accessible to a non-German audience — painting speaks an international language, and Expressionist paintings hang in the major art museums of the world. As for drama, many of the key plays have been translated into English, the lingua franca of our age. Poetry is another matter. Six Expressionists (Gottfried Benn, Iwan Goll, Else Lasker-Schüler, August Stramm, Georg Trakl, and Franz Werfel) have had poems published in English translation in individual volumes, but only two of them (Lasker-Schüler and Trakl) have received adequate treatment in this respect. Otherwise the Expressionist poets are scattered about in collections of modern German poetry or do not appear anywhere in English. The earliest of these collections, the Deutsch-Yarmolinsky anthology of 1923, includes the most poets (21), but they are represented by a mere 52 poems. The most recent and most comprehensive of all the anthologies dealing exclusively with the German poets of our century, Michael Hamburger's *German Poetry 1910–1975*, contains a total of 288 poems, of which but 43 are by 11 Expressionists. Perhaps ironically, a recent anthology comprising an international array of writers, poets, and playwrights killed in the Great War, Tom Cross's *The Lost Voices of World War I* (1988), contains the largest number of Expressionist poems (64) to appear in any collection heretofore. Hence it would seem there is a certain justification for the translation into English of a comprehensive anthology of Expressionist poetry.

Of the twenty or so collections of this kind put out in Germany between 1913 and 1924, Kurt Pinthus's *Menschheitsdämmerung* is the most famous and the most widely quoted of them all. Containing as it does all the manifold styles, forms, and themes of Expressionism in its 278 poems by 23 poets, it has become the most representative literary document of this modern movement. Between November 1919, when it was rushed into print to take advantage of the Christmas season (it was antedated 1920), and the end of 1922 the book went through four press runs and sold 20,000 copies, a remarkable figure for any collection of poetry, but more so for one that defied traditional form so drastically. When the book was brought out again in 1959 as a Rowohlt paperback — it had been out of print ever since the Nazis banned it in 1933 — it again enjoyed four press runs within two years; this time the response was even more enormous: 45,000 copies sold. It has been selling steadily ever since. There can be no doubt that this new edition more than lived up to its changed subtitle, "A Document of Expressionism," for it was the decisive publication in the rediscovery of literary Expressionism which took place in the 1950s. In addition, Pinthus's introduction to the original edition of 1919 and his retrospect introduction to the edition of 1959 provided considerable impulse to the renascent scholarly interest in the movement.

What makes *Menschheitsdämmerung* unique among Expressionist anthologies is its design, which is suggested by the ambiguity of the apocalyptic title. It can mean both the twilight of the human race and the dawn of a new humanity. Pinthus knew that the destructive and the utopian elements of the movement could not be separated — that its poets were imbued with a common revolutionary mentality that was at one and the same time a protest and a plea. It was a passionate protest against the military-industrial complex of their day, against the dangers of technology and urbanization, against the stupidity of war, against the dissolution of personal autonomy in a mass society, against the abuse of the poor as mere objects of history, against the existential ineffectiveness of the "dead" God of organized religion. It was a passionate plea for the revolutionizing of the human spirit, for a renewal of everything timelessly human beyond the boundaries of tribe, of state, of class, of religion, of race, a plea for cosmic unity and universal brotherhood. Pinthus succeeded in recreating the totality of the movement, the simultaneousness of its extremes, in what he called in his original subtitle a "Symphony of the Newest Poetry" performed by a 23-piece orchestra. No one was more qualified than Pinthus to lead such an orchestra. He was a (if not the) principal literary theoretician of Expressionism and in his capacity as chief editorial reader of the leading publisher of the movement knew the poetry of the period inside out. Many of the poets whose careers he helped launch became his personal friends. It was fortunate, too, that Pinthus put the anthology together just as Expressionism had crested. Everything of any significance was in place, ready to be collated by the perfect person for the job. (A translation of the story of how *Menschheitsdämmerung* came to be, Pinthus's last essay before his death in 1975 at the age of 89, is included in the present volume).

Expressionism was not just a sociological phenomenon. It was also an artistic revolution. It advocated not only a new society, but also a new form. Never before was there and never since has there been such an intimate connection between art and social criticism and such a fanatical belief in the power of art to change society. Form was made to serve the cause; it became part of the message. For urgency's sake it was pulverized, raped, and distorted; its innovations initiated the modern style in German poetry. It was abstract and anti-mimetic, but not totally so. Total abstraction would have meant sacrificing content to form, total mimesis would have prevented the poet from expressing the essential reality behind the surface reality, the visionary rather than the merely visual. The Expressionists despised form as an end in itself; yet no other group of poets made it a motif of their poetry as often as they did. They wrote the longest and the shortest lines in German literature, the most rhetorical and the most succinct, the most naive and the most sophisticated, they wreaked havoc with syntax, created new words, gave old words new meanings, fashioned startling compounds, expressed their intuitive experiences in dynamic and daring metaphors or in the piling up of images devoid of any temporal or spatial relationship. In his "symphony of the newest poetry" Pinthus was as successful in capturing the multiplex totality of this stylistic and linguistic revolt as he was in compacting the societal themes of Expressionism.

It has been stated many times that Expressionism revolutionized the arts but failed to revolutionize society. Both its historic and its persistent relevance in the cultural sphere seem beyond dispute. Along with French Cubism and Surrealism and Italian Futurism it constitutes the heart and soul of the modernist movement; the main tendencies that superseded it in Germany, Dadaism and Neo-Factualism (*Neue Sachlichkeit*), would be inconceivable without it; Expressionism has made a tremendous contribution to the ongoing evolution of poetic language; it spawned the two dominant poets of mid-20th century Germany, Gottfried Benn and Bertolt Brecht; the faculty of the Bauhaus, the most celebrated arts and crafts school of our century, was largely made up of artists with strong ties to Expressionism; the roots of Erwin Piscator's Political Theater, which in time influenced the even more innovative Epic Theater of Brecht, were in Expressionism; it was not without its stimulus on four of America's best playwrights, Eugene O'Neill, Elmer Rice, Thornton Wilder, and Tennessee Williams; it was the catalyst that sparked, in the 1930s, the longest and most heated debate on formalism, modernism, and the emerging doctrine of Socialist Realism among leading Marxist writers and theoreticians, including Walter Benjamin, Ernst Bloch, Brecht, Georg Lukács, and Anna Seghers; Expressionism anticipated the French Theater of the Absurd of the 1940s and 1950s and it was the forerunner of the street theater and the hippy troubadour poets of the 1950s and 1960s; paintings that were labeled Abstract Expressionist and Neo-Expressionist occupied center stage in the art world after World War II and in the 1980s respectively; recently a New York art dealer advertised in *The Times* that he was willing to pay more than half a million dollars for a Kandinsky, and more than one-quarter of a million for a Dix, a Feininger, a Jawlensky, a Kirchner, a Klee, a Kokoschka, a Macke, a Marc, a Nolde, a Schiele; shortly before that announcement a stage adaptation of the Expressionist film classic, *The Cabinet of Dr. Caligari*, premiered in New York; over the past decade Stephanie Barron, curator for 20th century art at one of America's greatest museums, the Los Angeles County Museum, has mounted three highly successful exhibitions of Expressionist art (the first and most revealing, *Sculpture of Expressionism,* opened in Cologne in 1984; the second, *Expressionism — the Second Generation,* was shown in Los Angeles, Fort Worth and Düsseldorf in 1990; the third and most spectacular, *Degenerate Art — the Fate of the Avant-garde in Nazi Germany*, was a reconstruction of the horrific *Degenerate Art* exhibition put on by the Nazis in Munich in 1937 in order to ridicule leading modernist works plundered from the museums of Germany. It was shown in Los Angeles, Chicago and Washington and completed its run in the spring of 1992 in Berlin, where a quarter of a million people saw it).

If Expressionism has achieved success as a revolution in vision and language, its other central tendency, an idealistic revolt that aimed at the total regeneration of the human being, resulted in dismal failure. This failure is exemplified in the fate of the one political entity in which Expressionist writers played a prominent role, the Socialist (later: Council or Soviet) Republic of Bavaria, proclaimed four days before the armistice that ended World War I as the first republic on German soil since the Revolution of 1848. Its head of state (until his assassination by a racist nationalist) was Kurt Eisner, an Expressionist playwright and the local leader of the Independent Socialist Party. The Independents had seceded from the mainstream of German socialism in 1917 because of the latter's support of the Kaiser's war aims. Its platform of peace, pacifism, international brotherhood and effective social change generally squared with the aspirations of the Expressionists. Eisner was a Kantian rather than a Marxist socialist; he rejected violence of any sort, even in a revolutionary situation. His brand of socialism was a complement to the anarcho-socialism of his political ally, the Expressionist philosopher Gustav Landauer. The latter maintained that the just society could be established *at any time* regardless of social conditions, that its establishment was a matter of the will and not of economic laws. He categorically rejected the concepts of class warfare and of the dictatorship of the proletariat. The Independents, taking Switzerland as their political model, wanted to transform Germany into a commonwealth of free states and do away with a centralized militaristic Reich. The forces controlling the central government in Berlin (soon to be known as the Weimar Republic), a reluctant alliance between the Social Democrats and the military, succeeded rather easily and rather brutally in crushing the secessionist Bavarian Republic. Its leaders were, in the opinion of the British historian, A.J.P. Taylor, "the last and noblest of German liberals, the only Germans to escape from the worship of power. Their very virtue was their undoing."

With the self-dissolution of the Independents as a party in the early 1920s, Expressionism ceased to be any kind of cohesive political force. Some Expressionists became left-wing Social Democrats, others Communists, a few eventually turned to Nazism, but the majority joined the ranks of the "homeless left," individuals unable to endure the capitulation of the Social Democrats to capitalism or the stern dogmatism of the Communists but somehow clinging to their belief in a "socialism of the heart," defined by one of their best theoreticians, Kurt Hiller, as "not the doctrine of a party but an ethical outlook. It is nothing but the realization of brotherhood."

In the 1930s the ideological (along with the formal) aspects of Expressionism came under simultaneous attack from the left and the right. Georg Lukács, the most formidable Communist philosopher of our century, contended that Expressionism signified the ideological agony and helplessness of the middle class and that in its attempt to create an irrational utopia it had paved the way for the infamous myths of Nazism. It was an attack from which Expressionism did not begin to recover in the official Communist world until the 1950s, not long after the unmasking of Lukács as a "revisionist." Behind the Iron Curtain the gradual emergence of Expressionism as ideologically respectable, as a precursor of Marxism-Leninism in its wish to change the world for the better — despite its "credulity" (*the human being is refinable in a vacuum*) and its "moral rigorism" (*it is wrong to kill*) — was highlighted in the late 1960s by the East German publication of a fully intact edition of *Menschheitsdämmerung* in commemoration of the 50th anniversary of its original appearance, and of the most comprehensive anthology of Expressionist poetry ever put together.

The Nazis excoriated Expressionism as a product of the materialistic degeneration of the western democracies, polluted by its pacifist, left-wing, and Jewish associations, and stigmatized by its anti-patriotic stance during the Great War. Following this condemnation, Expressionism as an activism became a dead issue in Nazi Germany and continued to remain one in West Germany until the middle 1960s, when the thaw in the Cold War climate of the Adenauer "restoration period" started to set in. With the growth of the New Left, the politicizing of West German universities, and the rise of a counterculture, critics and scholars began focusing on the politically uncomfortable aspects of pre-Nazi literature and art. It was at this time that political Expressionism enjoyed a momentary high water mark in the West — the enthusiastic utopianism of the Bavarian Republic of 1918-1919 found an echo in the student uprising in the streets of Paris during May, 1968; and the communitarian aspirations of Expressionism found their exemplification in two of the most famous books of the countercultural movement: Charles A. Reich's *The Greening of America* (1970) and E.F. Schumacher's *Small Is Beautiful. Economics As If People Mattered* (1973), the latter based on the organic and decentralist economics of Tolstoy, Landauer, and Ghandi.

Like the Expressionist flare-up of the 1910s, the student idealism of the 1960s was short-lived. Our 20th century, the bloodiest in the history of humanity, is coming to a close. Of the three "isms" that were largely responsible for making it so, the one that precipitated the first of our world wars with its guns of August 1914 in the Balkans remains very much with us. Our world is still very capable of falling back into the nationalist abyss — witness the "ethnic-cleansing" guns of August 1992 at Sarajevo. Many of the problems of the planet the Expressionists were so desperately and pathologically concerned about have gotten worse: the plight of the cities and the poor and the minorities, the rapaciousness of industry and technology, world hunger, the corruption of the political process, the loss of individuality through the computerization of the already reified human being. Our century has borne witness to the indestructibility, nay, triumph of the type of mentality that is the polar opposite of the Expressionist ethos: a stodgy, unimaginative, greedy, selfish, provincial, chauvinistic philistinism. The core of this ethos was expressed best (and rather sadly) by Ernst Toller, the playwright and poet who was the last head-of-state of the "Expressionist" Republic of Bavaria. It was written at the time of Hitler's accession to power in 1933, a few years before Toller committed suicide in a New York hotel room, alone, penniless, and worn-out by his anti-fascist efforts: "The suffering that human being inflicts on human being is beyond my comprehension. Are people naturally so cruel? Have they so little imagination that they cannot realize the manifold torments that humanity endures? I do not believe in the essential weakness of the human being. I believe that the worst things are done from lack of imagination, from laziness of heart." Toller's call for generosity of spirit finds a remarkable parallel in the statements and actions of a contemporary playwright who also became the head of a state. Vaclav Havel, who helped lead the peaceful or "velvet" revolution in Czechoslovakia in 1989, said in his inaugural address as President, "Our country, if that is what we want, can now permanently radiate love, understanding, the power of spirit and ideas." He preached the need for tolerance and civility, for a society in which "no member of a single race, a single nation, a single sex, or a single religion may be endowed with basic rights that are any different from anyone else's," for conciliation between Czechs and Slovaks, for European unity; he had the courage to deplore past mistreatment of an ethnic German minority; he strongly but vainly disapproved of witch-hunting purges of former Communists; he made his erstwhile house-arrest jailers into presidential bodyguards. And he had a vision, his antidote to jingoism: the transformation of his country into a democratic federation of Czechs and Slovaks that might serve as a model of a multiethnic Central European democratic federation — not unlike Toller's dream of a peaceable Germany along Swiss lines. He was not elected to a second term, a casualty of nationalistic fervor. So much for the aspirations of Expressionist politicians *redivivi*! (In January, 1993 he became president of the new Czech Republic, but with reduced powers.)

"The salvation of this human world lies nowhere else than in the human heart," Vaclav Havel stated in a speech before the Congress of the

United States, while still president of a united Czechoslovakia. He was iterating the Expressionist contention that the truly human community can only be effected by a quantum leap inspired by the transformation of individual human beings. In the final analysis, with its vision of a world without misery, without war, and without hatred, the activistic side of Expressionism was very ephemeral and very foolish, and yet somehow in its appeal to what is noblest in us human beings it remains timelessly relevant.

## 2. A Word about Our Translation
### of *Menschheitsdämmerung*.

The present volume is a translation of the final revised edition of *Menschheitsdämmerung* (1964) in its entirety plus, as previously mentioned, Pinthus's 1971 essay on the origins of his anthology. Our project was conceived more than a dozen years ago but it lay dormant until the realization struck us in 1989 that the anthology would be celebrating its 75th birthday in November, 1994. That was the spark that lit the fire under us. Because of the very stern resistance Expressionist texts in general offer to the translator, none of us would have dared tackle such a risky undertaking alone. In order to translate almost impossible German into readable English, in order to convey the right meaning and permit the right nuance, what is ideally required is a bilingualism that commences at birth. One of us is a native of Austria with a degree in English literature, the second of us a first-generation American with a degree in German literature, and the third an American with a degree in German literature who has no ethnic background of recent vintage. So in a sense the three of us put together are fairly bilingual. Unfortunately we are academics and not poets — common wisdom has it that only poets should translate poets. Obviously in our translation something had to give and in the end we felt even more keenly the truth expressed in the lament of a German writer-in-exile dependent on translators: "The best translation is still just a hand in a glove."

For the two readerships we had in mind, our glove is much less opaque for the first group than for the second. For those whose knowledge of German is only fair, who must resort to a dictionary and plod along slowly from line to line, our translation is meant as an aid to making their burden considerably lighter as they struggle to enjoy the German text. As for the second group, readers whose knowledge of German is poor or non-existent, we beg their indulgence as we recall the words of Germany's greatest poet: "Say what you will of the inadequacy of translation, it remains one of the most important and worthiest concerns in the totality of world affairs."

Our translation attempts both to adhere to the text as closely as possible without sacrificing content, and to capture the stylistic peculiarities of the poems. The renderings are in prose but in line-by-line stanza form. Where our efforts to be faithful to imagery, rhythm, word order, and punctuation threaten comprehensibility, we usually opt for clarity, but the choices can be very painful. Thus as we write this we are still debating whether we did the right thing in changing Benn's daring "sickle-yearning" to the prosaic but clearer "harvest nostalgia;" in not substituting for Wolfenstein's tersely harsh "where gazes project crampedly" the rhythm-destroying but more English "where gazes project in confining circles"; or in intruding on the breathlessness of a Becher line by inserting a comma: "Verandas sail [,] moonflag-bedecked gondolas." Pushkin had it right when he called translators the post-horses of culture.

The language of our translation is the American idiom of the 1990s. Thus, Werfel's "Neger" becomes not "negro" but "black." However, when the ambience of a poem demands it, we opt for an older terminology. And so Stadler's lowly "Verkäuferinnen" become not "saleswomen" but "salesgirls." In striving for a gender-neutral translation, our biggest headache was what to do with the word "Mensch." From the beginning the phrases most frequently used to describe Expressionist poetry and its societal goals have been, respectively, "O Mensch Dichtung" and "der neue Mensch," invariably appearing in English as "O man poetry" and "the new man." Since the Expressionists had no intention of excluding women from their appeals — the German "Mensch" is totally gender-neutral — and since the English "man" is ambiguous (witness the changing of the "new man" of St. Paul's Epistles (King James Version) to the "new self," the "new life" and the "new nature" in contemporary renderings of the New Testament), we made the decision to translate "Mann" as "man" and "Mensch" as "human being" or "person" or "someone." We violated our rule twice. When "Mensch" seemed to refer to Christ, the Son of Man, in a Trakl poem we used a capitalized "Man" to make this clear. And we rendered the title of Werfel's *Spiegelmensch* as *Mirrorman* rather than *Mirrorperson*, since the eponymous character is male. The German "Mensch" also has a warm ring to it which is lost in translating it as "man" rather than "human being." We readily acknowledge that what we have done will, to use the vernacular, take some getting used to. But it is, we like to think, what Kurt Pinthus and his band of Expressionist poets would have wanted us to do: make form an instrument of heart and mind.

## 3. Suggested Reader-friendly Literature on Expressionism.

For readers without a working knowledge of German who might be interested in getting more information about Expressionism in general and literary Expressionism in particular we can recommend the following books, all of which are user-friendly (they cite in English): John Willett's *Expressionism* (1970), a detailed account of the movement in all its manifestations and nicely illustrated; R.S. Furness's *Expressionism* (1973), a short but very serviceable introduction; two works concentrating on a literary genre, Roy F. Allen's *German Expressionist Poetry (1979)* and J. M. Ritchie's *German Expressionist Drama* (1976); Walter H. Sokel's *The Writer in Extremis: Expressionism in Twentieth Century German Literature* (1959), a seminal study of the existential background of the Expressionists and still one of the major contributions to an understanding of the modernist features of the movement; *Passion and Rebellion: The Expressionist Heritage* (1983), a collection of articles edited by Stephen Eric Bronner and Douglas Kellner emphasizing the socio-historical, philosophical, and ideological dimensions of Expressionism; a collection of essays assembled by Ulrich Weisstein, *Expressionism As an International Literary Phenomenon* (1973); *Regression and Apocalypse: Studies in North American Literary Expressionism* (1989), Sherrill E. Graces's groundbreaking study of the considerable influence of Expressionism on American and Canadian playwrights and novelists; *The Era of German Expressionism* (1974), edited by Paul Raabe and translated by J.M. Ritchie, a collation of notes, letters, documents, and commentaries delineating the lives and ideas of the movement's leading writers, artists, publishers, and men and women of the theater; and finally, for the browser there is the richly illustrated *Phaidon Encyclopedia of Expressionism: Painting and the Graphic Arts — Sculpture — Architecture — Literature — Drama — The Expressionist Stage — Cinema — Music* (1978), edited by Lionel Richard and translated from the French by Stephen Tint.

Joanna M. Ratych
Rutgers University

Ralph Ley
Rutgers University

Robert C. Conard
University of Dayton

# After 40 Years

*E*xactly 40 years ago, at the end of 1919, the collection *Menschheits-dämmerung — Symphonie jüngster Dichtung* (Dawn of Humanity — Symphony of the Newest Poetry) appeared for the first time. Back then an explosive pioneering work, an avant-garde experiment, today regarded as "still the best," as "the most representative," as "the classical anthology of Expressionism," in fact, as "the first and only collection of this circle of poets." Those who in that decade called themselves "the newest generation" are today the generation of the old — or the dead. A young critic of literature and contemporary culture in Berlin, a friend to many friends, who passionately loved his epoch and its literature, put together this stormy, forward storming book; — a man driven out of his country, deprived of his citizenship, who as he approaches the middle of his eighth decade, is issuing anew from New York in a paperback series of classics this collection...in its old form. Why?

Is there such a great demand for this book? Is it still a living work, testifying to life; perhaps awakening life? Is it only still important as an historic document? Or is it being printed again because editor and publisher have remained friends and kept up their literary ties — certainly a very rare occurrence — for fifty years?

The three central ideas of the book were: to present the most characteristic of the many poets of the decade 1910-1920 considered Expressionist; to present them in such a way as to reveal an external and internal picture of this decade; not to have the poets march up in chronological or alphabetical order, but to group, to interweave and arrange them according to principal themes, minor themes, and minute themes, similar to the construction of a symphony in four movements.

These three central ideas were immediately recognized and acknowledged when the collection appeared. The book, which both publisher and editor modestly hoped would serve as a lane for Expressionism, suddenly opened up a broad avenue for this literary movement. It went through four printings totaling 20,000 copies in two years and found, as the editor could write at the time, "a rapid and ready acceptance by an age whose essence it depicted." No collection of poetry in our century has been quoted as often as *Menschheitsdämmerung*, and what has been said about it in print is many times greater in volume than the work itself. Many of the selections contained in the book are today considered to be the best or at least the most typical poems of Expressionism and have gone into innumerable later anthologies and school readers. Universities in Europe and America use this collection as the basis for courses in 20th-century poetry. A Dutch professor even asserts that the editor's introduction "has influenced scholarship" and he adduces such scholars as WALZEL, F.J. SCHNEIDER, HUIZINGA, CHRISTIANSEN, who have adopted the "optimistic tendency" (he means "positive tendency") in that depiction of Expressionism. But the book, equally destroyed by the Nazis and the bombs by the thousands of copies, was, after the resurrection of Germany, in greater demand and aroused more attention than before 1933. It is now almost impossible to buy the book second-hand and at auctions it commands extraordinary prices.

All of this is of course not said to extol *Menschheitsdämmerung* or the editor or Expressionism, but to justify the new edition.

Today how does one judge the Expressionism of the decade 1910-1920, now called in literary history the epoch of "early" or "high" Expressionism — as whose representative *Menschheitsdämmerung* is regarded? The most comprehensive of the more recent works on literary Expressionism up to now, edited by Professors HERMANN FRIEDMANN and OTTO MANN together with twelve other literary historians and entitled *Expressionismus — Gestalten einer literarischen Bewegung* (Expressionism — Figures of a Literary Movement) (Heidelberg, 1956) says in its preface: "This phenomenon of the history of the times [Expressionism] is again exciting for us today: how a generation of young poets confronts the decline of the European human being and his art. Its impulses and repercussions are still present for us today in the poets who were stimulated by Expressionism in their youth. But this Expressionism is at the same time more than just a movement in the history of the times, more than just a force in the history of literature. In its best works it has given us poetry whose timeless quality we are today beginning to recognize and which we must include in the canon of our classics."

But how do the Expressionist poets of the decade 1910–1920 themselves see this epoch now, in our decade 1950-1960? Let us just cite the two poets who initially were closest to one another in their crushing rejection of the world of that time and who later were furthest apart from each other politically and literarily: GOTTFRIED BENN and JOHANNES R. BECHER.

Gottfried Benn, considered a leading poet of Expressionism at least in his early period since 1912, and ever remaining an Expressionist in the rapid simultaneity and global arbitrariness of his associations, wrote in 1955, a year before his death, when he was almost seventy years old, the introduction to the anthology *Lyrik des expressionistischen Jahrzehnts* (Lyrical Poetry of the Expressionist Decade). In this introduction, after initial misgivings about a uniform definition of that poetry and about his affiliation with it, he finally burst out enthusiastically: "A revolt with eruptions, ecstasies, hate, longing for a new humanity, with the dashing of language in order to dash the world.... They [the poets] condensed, filtered, experimented so that with this expressive method they could lift themselves, their spirit, the disintegrated, tortured, deranged existence of their decades up into those spheres of form in which over sunken metropolises and decayed imperiums the artist, he alone, consecrates his epoch and his people to human immortality.... But there it is still, 1910-1920. My generation. Hammering the absolute into abstract, hard forms: image, verse, flute song.... It was an incriminated generation: ridiculed, jeered, cast out politically as degenerate — a generation precipitous, sparkling, surging, affected by calamities and wars, marked for a short life.... In other words, Expressionism and the Expressionist decade: ...It rose up, fought its battles on all the Catalaunian fields, and declined. Raised its flag over Bastille, Kremlin, Golgotha, only Olympus it could not reach nor any other classical terrain."

Johannes R. Becher, in 1957, similarly a year before his death, while he was minister of education and the arts of the German Democratic Republic, began his confessional book, *Das poetische Prinzip* (The Poetic Principle) thus: "When I speak of my own past, my own past as poet, what didn't I myself do subsequently to help correct the Expressionist rebellion, and to bring my impetuous poetic colossi into line with my present insights...." But a few pages later a sympathetic longing for that distant youth grips him too: "We may have failed to achieve what we so exuberantly and vehemently set out to do: to realize in poetry the 'coincidentia oppositorum' of Nicholas of Cusa; nonetheless, some things remain, and above all it is instructive insofar as one is willing to make the effort to think about what we attempted at that time.... Although we never realized in a classical work the idea of simultaneity, the spirit of an Expressionist pantheism, I am convinced that someday people will come back to these experiments and also rediscover, along with many, many other things that have in the meantime passed into oblivion, this-our-rebellion at the turn of the century...."

Everyone will recognize how, in the sober enthusiasm of old age, the practically identical fervid recollection of that period of their youth lives on in both poets. — Since this series of quotations began with the opinions of two West German literary historians, let them be concluded with a comment by one of the leading East German literary historians (living in the Federal Republic since 1963). Professor HANS MAYER, a generation younger than BENN and BECHER, admits, after indicating (in a book commemorating the poet RUDOLF LEONHARD) how far removed *Menschheitsdämmerung* was from his generation, the generation of "Neue Sachlichkeit" (The New Sobriety): "It was obvious: such poetry expressly belonged together, it derived from a common historical experience, a common human, social, and artistic intention.... All objections may be valid. Nevertheless: what riches, what intensity of hatred and empathy."

But what, one will now ask, does the editor himself think of *Menschheitsdämmerung* today, of Expressionism and its effects. The editor has been asked these questions time and again, in Germany as well as in America, in discussions as well as in letters; he has heard them from literary historians and students; he was interviewed and questioned about them on radio. In order to be able to answer quicker and more precisely the editor will step out of his anonymity into his individual self.

What I have to say about the Expressionist generation, as it is called, can be found in the twelve pages of the preface "Zuvor" (Before) of the original edition of 1920, and in the thirty pages of the "Nachklang" (Reverberation) of the later editions. There I laid out what this poetry was and why it was and had to be that way; I explained how it came about and what it aimed and strove for. Therefore, I beseech each person to read attentively my observations in "Zuvor" and "Nachklang," both of which are reprinted word for word following this introduction. If the style seems strange or effusive, the reason is that it is an example of how Expressionist prose style in essay form sounded around 1920, in contrast to the sober-precise style attempted in this introduction.

When the new edition was being planned, the question was raised: should the collection be brought up-to-date, obsolete, unpalatable, perhaps ridiculous materials be thrown out, and should later poems of these and other poets of Expressionism be integrated in their stead? I insisted that *Menschheitsdämmerung* had to be republished as an historical document, exactly as it appeared 40 years ago. I took the same stand back in 1922 when the 15 to 20 thousandth copy of the book was to be printed, and explained my position in the "Nachklang." The words of 1922 are even more valid today.

In this edition, then, not a letter has been changed (apart from printing errors). Not a single poem has been left out; to be sure, however, the very few poems of the initial printings that were replaced in later editions by other poems of the same poets (at their request) have been reinserted, so that therefore this new edition contains all the poems that appeared in all four printings between 1920 and 1922. For this reason one will find, e.g., IWAN GOLL's poem "Der Panamakanal" (The Panama Canal) both in the revised first version as well as in the later version of 1918, which the poet gave me for the last printings.

If one wants to know what critical views I presently have about the individual poets and poems in this collection, about the durability of Expressionism, and about a comparison between today's young generation and the generation of that time, I can only express them very hesitantly. For after German lyrical Expressionism had spent itself in the early 1920s, I turned my attention increasingly to theater, film, and radio, and, after my emigration, I became an academic teacher, a researcher, and a writer and have devoted myself fully to comparative contemporary theater, to universal theater history, and in recent years to a previously almost unknown field: the pre-history of the theater, i.e., the theater of the prehistoric and primitive human being as well as of the pre-Hellenistic advanced cultures and the pre-Columbian American civilizations. But it has been this extensive and continuous interest in the artistic expression of many groups and peoples over the last 20,000 years that has afforded me much deeper insights into the literature and art of our century than was previously possible.

Therefore I can only make a few aphoristic-suggestive comments in answer to these questions. Probably most people living today in German-speaking countries, whether old or young, would find more or less the same poems of that epoch as I do to be living, informative and effective. I am pleased that DÄUBLER and ELSE LASKER-SCHÜLER, HEYM, TRAKL, STADLER, BENN, GOLL, and WERFEL have, as it were, been elevated to the ranks of the classical authors of Expressionism who are admired and studied. I am pleased that STRAMM and the early BECHER are analyzed as linguistic phenomena. But I regret that so many of those hundreds of poets, that almost all of the dozens of journals, yearbooks, anthologies, and series-publications of Expressionist literature have disappeared completely and are

15

practically impossible to find, and that hardly anything is still known about such unique and intrinsically worthwhile poets as EHRENSTEIN and ZECH, WOLFENSTEIN and LICHTENSTEIN.

It is difficult to make clear to today's literary youth, who remain isolated as individuals, are aware of this and frequently suffer from it, that in the years 1910-1920 the young authors in Prague, Berlin, Munich, Vienna, Leipzig, across all German-speaking countries, even across all of Europe, despite many differences in basic convictions, intentions, and forms of expression, felt they were part of a unity, a community, a common effort — in their struggle against a decaying, dying past and a tradition that prevented a better future, in their struggle for a new consciousness, for new ideas and forms which, in all likelihood, they knew were not as new as they made them out to be for the sake of effect.

In contrast to earlier literary movements: Storm and Stress, Romanticism, Young Germany, not just several or a dozen or several dozen authors were involved, but actually hundreds who knew, recognized, and acknowledged one another. Only a later, comprehensive examination will show that here and there in Germany and in Europe there were not just several groups of artists and literati who were called Expressionists or used this or some similar term to describe themselves, but rather that originally from APOLLINAIRE and COCTEAU to the Surrealists in France, from the Futurists to UNGARETTI and MONTALE in Italy, from the German-writing Expressionists to MAYAKOVSKY and YESENIN in Russia, from POUND and ELIOT to AUDEN and SPENDER, from JIMENEZ and GUILLÉN to GARCÍA LORCA and finally to the younger Americans there existed a conscious worldwide community (although it gradually broke up into many, frequently oppositional groups). Yet it has to be emphasized far more strongly that the German Expressionists were among the earliest and first in this community, and that in 1920 their number was greater and their talent for expression richer in comparison with other countries.

Therefore, it is a tragic irony that some of the current young poets in Germany became acquainted with Expressionism secondhand after the Nazi period and learned about it from, e.g., ELIOT, SAINT-JOHN PERSE, AUDEN, LORCA, or the plays of THORNTON WILDER and TENNESSEE WILLIAMS; they along with many others had their beginnings later than the generation around 1910. Just a few examples: THORNTON WILDER lived in Berlin for a long time in the twenties to study theater; AUDEN and SPENDER and ISHERWOOD worked together with German Expressionists and translated them; TENNESSEE WILLIAMS was a student of PISCATOR in New York.

When German literature began to stir again after 1945, began to catch up and emulate, what was once called German Expressionism had not yet been rediscovered, not yet been reprinted, had disappeared and been forgotten almost totally. But right after the Second World War the Expressionists of the Romance and English languages were, and continue to be, frequently translated into German. If one were to translate the German Expressionists of the years 1910–1920 into English or French, one would immediately recognize interrelationships and priorities. IWAN GOLL, who grew up bilingual, was able to render his own poetry into French at an early age and was always more highly regarded in France than in Germany. For this reason, from 1930 on he wrote only in French, until on his deathbed around 1950 he again sang his most beautiful poems in the German language.

At this point the problem referred to above must be addressed, namely, that Expressionism with its deviations was not at all as new as some believed or tried to make others believe. Recently several studies, especially HUGO FRIEDRICH's *Die Struktur der modernen Lyrik* (The Structure of Modern Poetry) (rowohlts deutsche enzyklopädie Nr. 25, 1956), have attempted to show how closely Expressionism is related to or connected with the revolutionizing of French poetry through BAUDELAIRE, MALLARMÉ and RIMBAUD. The objection can be made that such a complete shattering of language, such a loud cry of awakening and of intentional arousal as was manifest in Expressionism was never present in that French literary revolution. In prose and drama reference is constantly made to LAUTRÉAMONT and JARRY as forerunners in the amassing of wildly confusing associations. Ultimately one will be led back to certain demands, formulations, and experiments of Romanticism, primarily to NOVALIS, FRIEDRICH SCHLEGEL and, of course, HÖLDERLIN. Concerning the similarity of Expressionism with the forms of the Baroque much has already been said. But the recurrence of certain exaggerated means of expression beyond the conventions of realism, logic, and causality probably has less to do with influence than it does with similar or parallel convictions and negative reactions to so-called reality. In Spain, however, what we call Expressionism has already existed for centuries in the form of those simultaneous, non-logically and non-causally coordinated associations in lyric poetry and is also dominant in the folk song, just as it is, incidentally, in the folk song of many other peoples.

A dissertation on *Menschheitsdämmerung* points out how similar the ideas of activist Expressionism are to the thoughts of LUDWIG FEUERBACH. The author identifies almost verbatim correspondences between FEUERBACH and passages in poems or in my own and others' writings of that time. I was flabbergasted, on behalf of my friends as well, since we had certainly never read FEUERBACH. — Similarly Benn asserted more than once that he did not know MALLARMÉ and got to read RIMBAUD in translation only very late in life, although the parallel between Mallarmé and Benn's later lyrical poetry is astonishing.

The same dissertation also attempts to prove that the subtitle of the original edition of *Menschheitsdämmerung*, "Symphonie jüngster Dichtung" (Symphony of the Newest Poetry) "is justified, that the editor actually succeeded in uniting, according to a definite idea, the various, often disparate currents of lyrical Expressionism into a great symphony that rises as an independent work of art above the historical realities and coincidences of that poetic movement." The author adds musical examples, among others Beethoven's so-called "Humanity Melody" from the cantata on the death of the liberal Emperor Joseph II (not discovered until 1884) with the words "Then the human beings, the human beings emerged into the light" — the very melody that Beethoven lets resound again to oboes and flutes in *Fidelio* 15 years later as Leonore releases her freed beloved from his chains.

The Humanity Melody can be designated the principal messianic theme of Expressionism. And with this observation we come upon a noteworthy relationship that has heretofore been indicated nowhere. In a book that appeared in Holland with the title *Im Schatten des Nihilismus* (In the Shadow of Nihilism), the author tries to prove that German Expressionism was, with only a very few exceptions, a nihilistic movement that prepared the way for Nazism by its destruction of all values and forms. This contention has been put forward and repeated a number of times, and a student wrote to me frankly that he wanted to prove in his dissertation that *Menschheitsdämmerung* was the work of the devil. Now it is surely easy enough to pick out a few dozen totally negative, hopelessly pessimistic, and dangerously nihilistic quotations from the thousands of poems of an entire epoch. Besides this, we live in a time of such thorough conformity both in the democratically and socialistically governed countries that any provocation, any criticism or negation of the monopolized prevailing views and values is branded as nihilism. But when the Expressionist poets were destructive, they were so because of their deep suffering in the present and because of their fanatical belief in a new beginning for the arts, for the life of the individual, and for the human community. Hence their destructive passion was not nihilistic but constructive; *Umsturz und Aufbau* (Revolution and Reconstruction) was the title of a 1919 series of poems and essays. Goethe himself formulated continuity in destruction through literature as follows in 1797: "It is a characteristic of the literary world that nothing is destroyed in it without something new arising from the destruction, and always something new of the very same kind."

The humanism of the Renaissance was also a communal movement throughout Europe; humanism also wanted to create a new age by destroying spiritually the preceding epoch of the Middle Ages; and it was humanism that was directly concerned with the human being and had recourse to the human being — like Expressionism. The Expressionists were disillusioned humanists because the reality in which they lived had nothing in common with the reality which the humanism of the academic high schools and the universities taught. It might even be said that the socialist or utopian demands of Expressionism derive not from Marx, as is assumed, but from humanism (Marx, too, probably came from the same tradition). For humanism had once created the word "utopia" and the very idea of it.

The main difference between the generation after the Second World War and the one after the First is probably that the younger generation had neither the awareness of community, the will to achieve a common effect, nor were they obsessed with the initial belief in the victory of humanitarian ideas and of liberated and liberating forms manifested in the writings of the generation of 1910–1920. The survivors of the Second World War in Germany obviously had nothing left to destroy; they found themselves in a destroyed world. They had nothing left to restore or proclaim, for the ruins were barely sufficient to create a new economy, a new private life. In comparison to the earlier pathetic or exuberant expressiveness, the lyric poetry of today seems to have a more inward direction, to be more skeptically reflective. Instead of the self-assured outburst: "Lit by the morrow, we are the promised illumined ones" (E.W. LOTZ), the uneasy question sounded: "With timid voice I speak to you: will you hear me?" (K. KROLOW). In contrast to the entreating, screaming titles of the Expressionist poets, the most successful anthologies of the postwar period have titles like *Ergriffenes Dasein* (Deeply Affected Existence) (HOLTHUSEN and KEMP) or simply and modestly *Transit, Lyrikbuch der Jahrhundertmitte* (Transit, Book of Poems of the Middle of the Century) (HÖLLERER).

Today's poetry obviously feeds off the past more than the preceding literary movements did. The Expressionism in existence around 1920 had produced many imitators, too. At the time one joked: there is a lot of bechering, werfeling, and zeching going on; one could just as easily say today: there is a lot of trakling, benning, and golling going on. The melody

19

of Hölderlin runs through this poetry like an unending theme. A new classicism, a new romanticism, even a new Biedermeier can be heard.

Nothing is gained by posing the question: has Expressionism stayed alive? or: is it being revived? The fact is that it is alive, and, it goes without saying, not just as a much researched and discussed literary movement, not just in the large number of poems already recognized as classics, but above and beyond any historical considerations, in a way that no one ever expected. No matter that accusation and scream, trombone blast and fanfare flourish expressive of the demands of the day have died away and disappeared and mean little to today's youth — precisely the element that was once most violently condemned and ridiculed: exploded, exploding language, non-form or mis-form, tumultuous or dreamy sequencing of alogical, acausal associations — at the time weapon of the fighting spirit —, all of this has become actual form, unconscious or taken-for-granted heritage, common property of later generations. And thus German poetry is once again united with the contemporary poetry of world literature in its adherence to the imperative on which, remarkably, the enlightener DIDEROT and the romanticists NOVALIS and FRIEDRICH SCHLEGEL found themselves in agreement, and which was carried out in the revolutionary or modern poetry of the Romance- and, later, the English-speaking peoples: poetry must be dark and chaotic.

But just as science makes the effort not only to penetrate the unconscious, the unknown, but also to clarify it so that it becomes self-awareness and knowledge, so too — and this I have said for forty years — a future poetry of celestial clarity, of the brightest knowledge and understanding will be possible.

Whatever form this development may take, one will have to admit that Expressionism was the last common, general, and conscious effort of an entire generation to create anew and to develop further art, music, and literature — and, as it initially hoped, humanity as well. Thus we must admit and accept the fact that in its visions and forms Expressionist poetry was, to a far greater degree than any other precursory generation, a seismograph registering in advance the tremors of our century, not only in its horrible forebodings of the First World War and of the collapse of every existing order and value caused by it, but also far beyond the Second World War and the first half of our century right up to our helplessness in the face of the present-day self-destructibility of humanity. Decades ago, in a spectacular ballad PAUL ZECH celebrated the ascent and crash of a space rocket on a Pacific island in all of its irradiating destructiveness, and the opening line of GOTTFRIED BENN's *Verlorenes Ich* (Lost Self) can stand for his many poems dealing with the consciousness of being destroyed: "Lost self, fragmented by stratospheres." But the Expressionist poets were at the same time pioneers in the discovery of unknown processes of consciousness and of those associations (already characterized a number of times) that swarm through the external and internal cosmos, as well as in the — today actually even of more pressing importance — demands for peace and for mutual assistance among the nations.

Nevertheless I do not advise the grandchildren of the Expressionists to imitate what was offered or reoffered in the book *Menschheitsdämmerung*. I do not think, as some members of the younger generation advise, that the poetry of today should consciously build a bridge back to what was salvaged from the "destruction of German literature" (described by MUSCHG). Rather I simply wish these grandchildren the courage of the generation of 1910–1920: the courage to love the human being of the present and the future and the courage to experiment perpetually in life and poetry.

Explication and critical judgment of what has been pointed out here should be left to a literary history that has up to now come to grips in such a thorough and friendly (or hostile) fashion with the kind of poetry to be found in *Menschheitsdämmerung*. Precisely because so much has already been written about Expressionism and its poets, I have decided not to utilize the space allotted to me beyond the poems for yet another detailed essay but to utilize it for something completely different that I hope will prove useful. Namely for a painstaking undertaking that has not been attempted heretofore: to add to the few already known biographies and bibliographies by compiling concise, fact-filled vitas and above all lists of book publications by the authors that are as complete as possible, inserting this material in the appendix entitled "Poets and Works."

For the Nazis had succeeded in branding the 23 poets of *Menschheitsdämmerung* — both those who were still alive as well as those who were already dead, were killed or killed themselves — as degenerate or at least as undesirable and in proscribing, burning, and eradicating their works to such an extent that their lives are frequently shrouded in darkness. It is practically or completely impossible to locate many of their books, and even the titles of their publications can be ascertained only with the greatest effort. As far as I know, there is no reference work that offers biographical data on and bibliographies of these poets which are to some degree reliable or complete, and even individual treatments, dissertations, and collected works show mistakes and gaps. The scholarly compilation *Expressionismus, Gestalten einer literarischen Bewegung* (Expressionism, Figures of a Literary Movement) admits: "The usual biographical sources are in large measure contradictory." And although it declares "that the greatest possible effort has been made to be reliable," nevertheless in several instances the biographical and above all the bibliographical data concerning even very well-known poets are not accurate or complete — they cannot be — and bio-bibliographical information on lesser-known, neglected, and forgotten poets can be even less accurate and complete, regardless of the source. Even relatives and friends of the poets are frequently unable to provide reliable information, for they live scattered all over the world, and things left behind by the deceased as well as memories of them have in large part vanished.

As one of the last survivors of that generation, one who knew all these poets well, insofar as they were still living in 1919, and knows those close to them, I began a project as far back as fifteen years ago to compile a bibliography of all the poets who were exiled and who have died and to investigate their fates; thanks to time-consuming searches I have now completed the project as far as the poets of *Menschheitsdämmerung* are concerned. This painstaking research grew into a labor of love. I hope it will serve as an act of thanksgiving and as a memorial to these poets, so that they may live on or live again.

And so the bio-bibliographical appendix has grown quite large — to the detriment of this introduction. But even though in 1920 some of these authors wished for anonymity, as was often the case in those days, I think that now those friends of literature who knew and loved these poets and their works prior to 1933, and especially the younger generation that came to know them after 1945, have a right to know: where and how did they live, when and how did they die, what did they publish before 1920, after 1920, after 1933, and in exile?

From the bibliographies one can gather how extensive the work of some of these poets is in terms of numbers, themes, and genres, and at the same time one must bear in mind that many of their manuscripts have been lost or remain unpublished. The literary remains of some poets have been preserved, but they are scattered over many lands. Therefore, to the extent possible, I have also listed the location and nature of their unpublished works.

Perhaps there are still lacunae and mistakes in these bio-bibliographies; but as far as I know, these are the first complete bibliographies, at least readily available in book form, for BECHER, EHRENSTEIN, GOLL, HASEN-

CLEVER, HEYM, HEYNICKE, KLEMM, ELSE LASKER-SCHÜLER, LEONHARD, OTTEN, RUBINER, STRAMM, WERFEL, WOLFENSTEIN, and ZECH. Even readers and scholars familiar with Expressionism will find in this new edition some new information. Even anonymous and illegally disseminated writings, publications which had very small printings, and such that were destroyed are listed, e.g., a collection of political poems by RUDOLF LEONHARD which was smuggled into Germany disguised as a volume in the Reclam series. In New York I was able to find a drawing of GEORG TRAKL by OSKAR KOKOSCHKA, which is published here for the first time (for further details and Kokoschka's comments on the drawing turn to the index of illustrations.

Only the large bibliography of German literature in exile being prepared by W. STERNFELD in London at the request of the *Deutsche Akademie für Sprache und Dichtung* (German Academy of Language and Literature) in Darmstadt, which also contains my aforementioned material, will show how many thousands of books and brochures were published outside the Nazi Reich on every continent in spite of all the difficulties. The *Deutsche Bibliothek* (German Library) in Frankfurt has made a very promising start collecting and integrating the entire literature of exile, and the *Schiller-Nationalmuseum* (Schiller National Museum) in Marbach is doing the same for all of Expressionist literature.

The frequently asked question of how the Expressionists developed after 1922 and why this community of poets split up into such contradictory, mutually antagonistic individuals or groups cannot be answered here (due to lack of space). The split into the political sphere, into the religious sphere, into so-called "pure art," into folk art, into classical art, the turn by some poets to more traditional and more widely appealing forms of the novel, drama, and comedy, all of this was a consequence of the disillusionment that set in after 1920 when Expressionism failed to achieve what it hoped to, and the ardently desired transformation to a renewal of the human being and of society did not materialize, and it was also a consequence of the influence of the rapidly growing parties of the right and left. Almost all Expressionist poets later turned to simpler, more conventional forms. It is indicative that in their more mature years the two poets who were initially deemed the wildest and most unrestrained, BECHER and BENN, made use of classical stanzas, most often in the form of rhymed quatrains, although there was a total dissimilarity in style and content and the values attached to them.

After I eventually put the bio-biographical appendix in its final form and looked it over, I was seized with awe, horror, and admiration. I was now certain that I had the right and the duty to undertake this labor of thanksgiving and commemoration. In all likelihood no essay will be able to convey all that these concise, sober-dry biographical data and the lists of works with their places and dates of publication evoke in the consciousness and judgment of the thoughtful reader. Here it is, a generation of refugees, exiles, and transients, of martyrs and silent sufferers, of fighters and tenacious survivors, of those who died young and those who aged in suffering — surely a generation like no other anywhere, any time before it in world literature.

But an objection will be raised: in 1933 seven of the twenty-three were no longer living and some others remained in Germany at that time. Let us look at the three groups:

Those already dead in 1933: GEORG HEYM had drowned in the Havel River in January, 1912 while ice-skating, after he was visited by dark presentiments and visions; ALFRED LICHTENSTEIN, ERNST WILHELM LOTZ, ERNST STADLER, AUGUST STRAMM had been killed in the early days of the First World War; GEORG TRAKL had committed suicide after the battle of Grodek while in a despairing state of semi-unconsciousness; LUDWIG RUBINER was carried off in 1920 by the postwar influenza epidemic.

Those who stayed in Germany after 1933: JAKOB VAN HODDIS, mentally ill in private care or in institutions since 1913, was carted off by the authorities in order to be murdered; THEODOR DÄUBLER, after decades of a life of wandering, mostly in dire poverty, and already severely sick in 1933, died in the Black Forest, deserted and lonely, in 1934; GOTTFRIED BENN, a Nazi supporter in the beginning, was very soon attacked in the most brutal way and had himself and his work proscribed in 1936 — he never recovered from this "double life," not even in the last years of his fame; WILHELM KLEMM, who had been silent as early as 1922 because it was deemed unacceptable for a co-owner of highly respected publishing houses to have written and published Expressionist poetry, was politically persecuted under the Nazis and excluded from the *Schrifttumskammer* (Chamber of Writers); KURT HEYNICKE sought a compromise in his *Chorische Spiele* (Choral Plays) but they were soon labeled undesirable, and he took refuge in light and amusing novels.

All the others, however, were banned, banished, burnt: WALTER HASENCLEVER, after many years of wandering about, killed himself by taking an overdose of veronal in a French internment camp in 1940 as German troops were approaching, because he knew what was in store for him; ALFRED WOLFENSTEIN, after five years of a nomadic existence underground, committed suicide in 1945 in a Paris hospital; ALBERT EHRENSTEIN died in the deepest misery in New York in 1950 after two decades of vegetation and a long illness; ELSE LASKER-SCHÜLER died in Jerusalem in 1945 in a poverty to which she had been inured all her life; KARL OTTEN went blind in exile in London, but continues to publish poems and novels and supports the cause of the companions of his youth in large anthologies of drama and prose; FRANZ WERFEL succumbed to a heart attack in California several years after an adventurous flight across the Pyrenees, as did PAUL ZECH on a street in Buenos Aires after ten privation-laden years of roaming around South America. RENÉ SCHICKELE, who always lived and wrote between Germany and France, died in despair in the south of France in 1940, just as his last book was being destroyed in Amsterdam by the Nazis. IWAN GOLL, who fled to New York as France was being occupied, developed leukemia and wasted away. Only two returned, to East Germany, to Berlin: RUDOLF LEONHARD, who had escaped a number of times from French internment camps and prisons and had lived underground, arrived in poor health, only to die three years after his return; and JOHANNES R. BECHER, after having spent ten years in Moscow and Tashkent, admitted at the end of his *Poetische Konfession* (Poetic Confession) in 1955, when he was the highest cultural official and the most celebrated poet of the German Democratic Republic: "So very much have I loved you [poetry] that I did not even reject that which was repugnant to me from the depths of my soul and undertook some things that not only dirtied my hands, but also injured my soul — and thereby, too — my love for you."

Forty years ago when I called these poets a "band of yearning damned souls," I did not know how very much this characterization, at the time meant symbolically more than anything else, was destined to become horrible reality. In pondering the fate of the twenty-three, the reader, deeply moved, will at the same time marvel at the fact that all these poets, whether at the battlefronts of the First World War, or in persecution and exile, in homelessness and despair, in sickness, in incommunicability and misery, continued to write and to compose poetry wherever they were on this planet, from Russia to southernmost Tierra del Fuego, persecuted and proscribed in their native land, in constant flight and in hiding in France, starting all over again in England and America in the most wretched jobs. And it should never be forgotten: the poets described here stand for ten times, one hundred times their number.

# Before

(Berlin, Autumn 1919)

*T*he editor of this book is an enemy of anthologies — that is why he is editing this collection.

You will not find here — as has been the wont with previous anthologies — many poets who just happen to have lived at the same time, arranged in alphabetical order with a few poems each. Nor will you find a compilation of poems all of which are linked together by some common theme (love poems, for example, or the poetry of revolution). This book does not have the pedagogical ambition of offering prime examples of good poetry. It does not, in the fashion of our grandfathers' upright era, weave lyrical blossoms or poetic pearls into a garland.

On the contrary: this book does not just call itself "a collection." It *is* collection!: collection of strong emotions and passions, collection of an epoch's longing, happiness, and torment — our epoch. It is the collected projection of human movement out of time into time. Its purpose is not to show skeletons of poets, but rather the frothing, chaotic, bursting totality of our times.

Lyrical poetry has always been the barometer of psychic states, of the stirrings and agitations of humanity. Prophetically it proclaimed future events..., the shifts in society's moods, the ups, downs, and ups again of its thinking and longing. This has been so clearly felt in Germany that the culture of entire epochs has been characterized by the nature of their creative writings: Sensitivity, Storm and Stress, Romanticism, Young Germany, Pseudo-Medieval Romantic Poetry.

The human sciences of the waning 19th century — irresponsibly applying the laws of the natural sciences to intellectual phenomena — were content to look at art schematically and see in it only what is sequential, what is successive, following the principles of historical development and influences. One's vision was causal, vertical.

The intent of this book is to put together a collection in a different fashion: listen to the poetry of our time..., listen deeply, look all around,...

not vertically, not sequentially, but horizontally; do not keep the successive parts separate, but listen instead in concert, all at once, simultaneously. Hear the harmony of poetizing voices; hear symphonically. The music of our time resounds, the booming unison of hearts and minds.

Just as there was no attempt to arrange the poems according to some external alphabetical schema, so, too, no attempt was made to base their arrangement on the chronology of the individual poems or poets, on a grouping of literary cliques, on a determination of mutual influence or formal commonalities. There was no endeavor to create a mechanical, historical sequence; intended rather was a dynamic, thematic harmony: symphony!

So, do not just listen for the individual instruments and voices of the lyrical orchestra: the soaring longing of the violins, the autumnal-lamenting melancholy of the cellos, the purple trombones of arousal, the ironic staccato of the clarinets, the drumbeats of destruction, the auspicious march of the trumpets, the deep, dark whispering of the oboes, the roaring torrents of the basses, the rapid tingle of the triangles, and the flashing beats of the cymbals in their pleasure-seeking dance of death. Rather what really matters is to sense in the noisy dissonances, the melodic harmonies, the powerful pacing of the chords, the most broken semitones and quarter tones — the motifs and themes of the wildest and most chaotic time in world history. These stirring motifs (did some internal occurrence impel them out of us or did some indifferent development cause them to re-sound tremendously within us?) vary according to the nature and volition of the poets, surging to an exploding fortissimo or ebbing into a gladdening dolce. The andante of doubt and despair rises to a liberating furioso of revolt and the moderato of the awakening, awakened heart is transformed redeemingly into a triumphal maestoso of a human being-loving humanity.

If in this book neither the voices of the poets of our time resound randomly and fortuitously nor the poetic writings of a consciously organized literary grouping or school have been collected, nonetheless, a mutuality is meant to unite the poets of this symphony. This mutuality is the intensity and the radicalism of feeling, of attitude, of expression, of form; and this intensity, this radicalism compels these poets in turn to struggle against the humanity of the epoch that is drawing to a close and ardently to prepare the way for and to demand a new, better humanity.

Therefore, expect from this book neither a complete picture of the lyric poetry of our day, nor a selection of the best contemporary poems compiled on the basis of (mendacious) absolute standards of quality. Expect, instead, poetry characteristic of the youth that has the actual right to be called the young generation of the last decade because it has suffered the most from our age, protested the wildest and cried out with passionate fervency for a more noble, more humane human being.

Accordingly, it was imperative to leave out not just all the epigonic and eclectic poets, not just the countless poets engaged in putting into conventional rime feeling that originates not in the heart but in convention, but also to exclude those very talented poets who, intentionally positioning themselves beyond or above the age, mold beautiful and great feelings into aesthetically perfect forms or into classical verses. Also necessarily excluded were all those whose poetry is verbal arts and crafts, beautifully wrapped conviction, history in rime, as well as those who merely sing of or provide a happy accompaniment for contemporary events, specialized minor talents, and all those who stand between the generations or lack the courage to create independent forms. But like the epigones of the older poetry, the imitators of the newest poetry could not be included, those who deem themselves new and young when they programmatically imitate problematical models.

Deciding which poets are to be included in the multifaceted mutuality of today's younger generation cannot be a matter of ascertaining the birth dates of individual poets, nor can it be a question of objectively critical analysis; it must, in the end, come down to a decision based on intuitive feeling and personal judgment. Precisely because this personal decision was necessary, the editor is justified in emerging from his anonymity and for purposes of further clarification saying a few words about himself so as to be able to come all the quicker to some general formulations.

In the last ten years I have read almost all published books of poetry as well as very many unpublished ones. It did not seem like an easy task to identify from these innumerable works the poets who make up that actual generation of our epoch. But as I went through the hundreds of volumes of poetry once more in the midst of this bustling city, I was finally able, with an almost automatic certainty, to bring together the poets who belong essentially to this generation (even if they were not themselves aware of this mutuality). Once this delimitation was completed I saw two possible ways to organize the collection: I could either include as many poets of this generation as possible, so that each would be represented by just a few poems, or I could select as few poets as possible and let each one appear with as many poems as possible. I opted for the second principle because it would provide not only a complete picture of the era but also as thorough a delineation as possible of the talent, uniqueness, breadth of the individual poets (so that, even though the poems of each individual poet are scattered throughout the entire book, the reader can form a unified image of each poet with the help of the alphabetical index, and thus be able to evaluate the poets separately). And so, after long consideration, from the large band comprising this generation which often proclaimed itself a common phalanx I chose for the book the most independent and characteristic poets so that there could arise that multiplicity of themes and forms out of which the spiritual symphony of the fragmented totality of our times radiates in unison.

Certainly one could argue that two poets are outside this generation. But ELSE LASKER-SCHÜLER is the first poet to let the human being be all heart — and yet she expands this heart up to the stars and to all the brightnesses of the East. And THEODOR DÄUBLER cannot be numbered among those who merely sing of the cosmos; rather, he imbues the world so very much with spirit and idea that he transforms nature and humanity once more into bursting immaterial life; he discovers profound possibilities for language that are not only new but also throw light surprisingly deep into the essence and inner connectedness of things.

The selected poems of these nearly two dozen poets fit together quickly, almost by themselves, in accordance with a few large themes, into that symphony that was called *Menschheitsdämmerung*. All of the poems in this book spring from a lament for humanity, a yearning for humanity. The human being per se, not his private concerns and feelings, but humanity is the actual unending subject. These poets sensed early how the human being was sinking into the twilight [Dämmerung]..., sinking into the night of decline..., in order, however, to emerge again into the brightening dawn [Dämmerung] of a new day. In this book the human being turns consciously from the twilight of a past and present imposed on, encircling, and engulfing him toward the redeeming dawn of a future that he creates for himself.

The poets in this book know as I know: it holds our youth; lives beginning joyfully, overwhelmed early on, destroyed. What was known not at all or just vaguely in humanity's latest years, what could not be read in newspapers and treatises: it became word and form in this generation with an unconscious certainty. What was not scientifically ascertainable about the human being — here it stepped into the light with prophetic truth and clarity.

Therefore, this book offers no pleasant and comfortable reading material, and the objection can easily be raised that the last decade has produced some poems that are more mature, more accomplished, of better quality. But can a poetry that gives form to the suffering and passion, will and longing of those years and that burst forth from a humanity bereft of ideas and ideals, from indifference, decay, murder, and aggression — can such a poetry display a pure and clear countenance? Must it not be chaotic like the times out of whose rent and bloody soil it grew?

An accomplished philologist would be able to put together in mosaic fashion a complete profile of this poetry just from quotations out of this book. But what everyone will know when he has read this book should not be stated in advance. Likewise the individual poets should not be characterized one by one; for most of them are too rich and multifaceted to deserve to be saddled forever with a few constricting catchwords. But I will attempt a crosscut through these poems so that from the cruel wound inflicted by this cut the essentials will flow, all those elements that unite them into the poetry of this epoch.

The young people of this generation found themselves in a time from which every trace of ethos had disappeared. In each and every situation they had to maintain their self-control. The aggregate of hedonistically pleasurable things had to be as extensive and varied as possible; art was measured completely by an aesthetic yardstick, life completely by a materialistic, statistical yardstick; and the human being and his spiritual activity seemed only to exist in order to be observed psychologically, analytically, to be defined in accordance with historical maxims. When one of the young poets tried to penetrate more deeply from the surface into himself, he was crushed beneath the burden of the surrounding world (WALTER CALÉ). To be sure, there was a recognition of the need to get away from a realistic description of the surrounding world, from the capturing of fleeting impressions — but the result was merely an extreme differentiation and sublimation of dissected pleasures, and this in turn destroyed the sense of pleasure (HARDEKOPF, LAUTENSACK).

Felt more and more keenly was the impossibility of a humanity which had made itself totally dependent on its own creations, on its science, on technology, statistics, commerce and industry, on a rigidified communal order, on bourgeois and conventional practices. This recognition signifies at the same time the start of the struggle against the times and against their reality. An effort was launched to dissolve the surrounding reality into non-reality, to cut through appearances to the essence, to embrace and annihilate the foe in an assault of the spirit, an attempt made to defend oneself against the surrounding world with the weapon of ironic superiority, to toss about and muddle up its appearances in grotesque fashion, to float lightly through the heavy waters of the labyrinth (LICHTENSTEIN, BLASS) — or to elevate these appearances to the realm of the visionary with the help of cabaret cynicism (VAN HODDIS).

Nevertheless, the over-stimulated and over-sensitive nerves and souls of the poets were already clearly perceiving on the one side the dull advance of the proletarian masses robbed of love and joy, and from the other side the imminent collapse of a humanity that was as arrogant as it was indifferent. From the bursting blossom of civilization the stinking breath of decay wafted toward them and their presentimental eyes already saw as ruins an unsubstantially bloated culture and an order of humanity built up on the mechanical and the conventional. An enormous pain welled up — earliest and most clearly in those who died in this age, from this age: HEYM (using RIMBAUD and BAUDELAIRE as exacting models) hammered visions of death, of misery, of decay in crushing verses; TRAKL, ignoring the real world, slipped Hölderlin-like into the endless blue stream of a deadly decline that an autumnal brown strove in vain to frame; STADLER, plagued with longing, spoke and wrestled ardently with God and the world, like Jacob with the angel; LICHTENSTEIN whipped in painful lightheartedness the figures and moods of the city into bitter-funny concoctions, already possessed of the bliss-imparting certainty that "immense above everything, my human countenance wanders"; and LOTZ, under clouds, from the distress of bourgeois existence, called out for glory and revolt. More and more fanatically and passionately thundered lacerating plaint and accusation. The despairs of EHRENSTEIN and BECHER tore the dismal world apart at its center; BENN mocked the rotting effeteness of the human cadaver and praised the vigorous primitive instincts; STRAMM severed his passion from the deceptive image of appearances and associations and pressed pure feeling into booming one-syllable words, thundering single blasts. The real struggle against reality had begun with those terrible eruptions whose aim was to destroy the world and at the same time create a new world from the human being.

The attempt was made to recognize, to rescue, and to rouse the humane in the human being. The simplest feelings of the heart, the joys that goodness creates for the human being were praised. And feeling was allowed to flow over the earth's surface into every earthly creature; spirit wrested itself from the rubble and glided through every occurrence in the cosmos — or it plunged deep down into the appearances of things in order to find in them their divine essence. (In this way the youth of HASENCLEVER, STADLER, WERFEL, SCHICKELE, KLEMM, GOLL, HEYNICKE is connected with the art of the elders WHITMAN, RILKE, MOMBERT, HILLE.) Ever more clearly was seen: the human being can be saved only by the human being, not by the surrounding world. It is not institutions, inventions, derived laws that are the essential and determining factor, but rather the human being! And because deliverance cannot come from the outside — from that direction there was a presentiment of war and destruction long before the World War —, but only from the strengths inside the human being, there took place the great turn towards the ethical.

While during the World War the discerned collapse was taking place in reality, poetry had already once again stormed ahead of the times. From the eruptions of cursing there burst forth the cries and demands for revolt, for decisive action, for an account of responsibilities, for renewal (BECHER, RUBINER, HASENCLEVER, ZECH, LEONHARD, HEYNICKE, OTTEN, WERFEL, GOLL, WOLFENSTEIN), not out of any pleasure in revolting, but in order to destroy totally through revolt what destroys and what has been destroyed, so that what heals could unfold. Appeals resounded for youth to band together, to set out as a spiritual phalanx. It was no longer what individuates but what is common to all human beings, not what separates but what unites, not reality but spirit, not the struggle of all against all but brotherliness that was praised. The new community was called for. And as these poets thundered lament, despair, agitation wildly and unisonally, they were equally united and forceful in proclaiming in their songs humaneness, goodness, justice, camaraderie, every human being's love for every other. All the world and God receive human countenance: the world begins in the human being, and God is discovered as brother —, even the stone figure descends as a human being, the city of torments is turned into a beatifying temple of the community and triumphantly the redeeming words ascend: we are!

Everyone knows how tremendously wide is the arch from CALÉ's despair "And there is no bridge from human being to human being"..., from WERFEL's "Strangers are we all on earth"... to BECHER's "No one a stranger to you,/ Everyone close to you and brother"... KLEMM's "We came as close to each other as only angels can come"... HEYNICKE's "But a smile constructs an arch from me to you"... "We bestow on each other the I and the Thou —/ eternally we are united by the word:/ HUMAN BEING."

It seems that retrospective depiction has always overestimated the direct influence of poetry on the real events pertaining to an era or a nation. The art of an era is not the cause of events (as has been assumed, e.g., all too strongly for the poetry of revolution in any given era), but it is a prognosticating symptom, spiritual blossom from the same humus as the later real events — it is itself already era-event. Collapse, revolution, reconstruction were not caused by the poetry of this generation; but it did sense, know about, demand these things. The chaos of the times, the shattering of old forms of community, despair and longing, avidly fanatical searching for new possibilities of life for humanity are revealed in the poetry of this generation with the same uproar and the same wildness as in reality..., but mark my words, not as a consequence of the World War but already before it began and, with greater and greater intensity, while it was going on.

And so, to be sure, this poetry is, as a number of its programmers demanded (and how misunderstood this cry was!): political poetry, for its theme is the condition of contemporary humanity, which it laments, curses, disdains, destroys while at the same time seeking in terrifying outbursts the possibilities of future change. But — and only in this way can political poetry be at the same time art — the best and most passionate of these poets fought not against the external conditions of humanity but against the condition of the mutilated, tormented, bewildered human being himself. The political art of our time must not be a versified editorial, rather its purpose is to help humanity perfect and realize the idea of itself. The fact that at the same time poetry, too, played a part in countering the insanity of *Realpolitik* and the degeneracy of the social order was only a self-evident and small service. Its greater super-political importance lies in the fact that with glowing finger, with rousing voice it pointed at the human being himself over and over again, that it recreated in the realm of the spirit — spurring on to realization — the lost ties among and between human beings, the link between the individual and the eternal.

Accordingly it is only natural that these are the words that are most frequently found in it: human being, world, brother, God. Because the human being is so totally starting point, central point, aiming point of this poetry, there is little room in it for landscape. The landscape is never painted, depicted, celebrated; instead it is completely humanized: it is horror, melancholy, confusion of chaos, it is the shimmering labyrinth from which Ahasuerus longingly seeks to extricate himself; and forest and trees are either places of the dead or hands that are groping toward God, toward infinity. With enormous speed this poetry moves from fanatical battlecry to the sentimental, from anarchist raving to the didactics of the ethical. There is little of joy and happiness in it; love is pain and guilt — work turns into torment that destroys feeling; even the drinking song is muffled confession of guilt; and lighter, cheerier tones resound only out of the yearning for the paradise that is lost and yet lies before us.

Never before were aesthetics and the principle of *L'art pour l'art* as disdained as in this poetry, which is called the "newest" or "expressionist" because it is eruption, explosion, intensity — has to be in order to burst that hostile crust. For this reason it eschews the naturalistic depiction of reality as technique, no matter how palpable this degenerate reality was; instead, it creates with enormous and vigorous energy its own means of expression from the motive power of the spirit (and in no way attempts to avoid misusing them). It catapults its world... in ecstatic paroxysm, in excruciating sadness, in sweetest musical song, in the simultaneity of feelings poured out helter-skelter, in a chaotic shattering of language, in most gruesome derision of human mis-life, in flagellantly screaming and enraptured longing for God and the good, for love and brotherliness. Thus social aspects are not presented in realistic detail, are not depicted objectively as, e.g., slum art (like the kind in vogue around 1890), but they are always totally directed toward the universal, toward the great ideas of humanity. And even the war that crushed many of these poets is not told in a matter-of-fact realistic way; it is always there as vision (and to be sure long before the war started), smolders as a universal horror, expands as the most inhuman of evils which can be done away with only through the victory of the idea of the brotherly human being.

The fine arts of these years manifest the same themes and characteristics, manifest the same bursting of the old forms and the traversal of all formal possibilities right up to the consequent total dissolution of reality, manifest the same breakthrough and breakout of what is human and the same faith in the loosening, binding power of the human spirit, of the idea. It did happen that some attempts and some degenerations turned into empty forms, formulas, consumer-oriented phrases at the hands of imitating incompetents. And not only do pathos, ecstasy, and the grand gesture burst out and upwards but they frequently cave in convulsively because they cannot be realized as form. Time and again, however, there blows into the tremendous eruption of feeling the spirit, purifying and cleansing; there rings out from the decay the call to the mutuality of what is human; there hovers over the aimless chaos the song of love.

And time and again it must be said that the quality of this poetry rests in its intensity. Never before in world literature did there resonate as loudly, piercingly, and stirringly cry, crash, and longing of an age as from the wild band of these forerunners and martyrs, whose hearts were pierced not by the romantic arrows of Amor or Eros but by the tortures of an accursed youth, a detested society, the murderous years they were forced to endure. From sheer earthly torment their hands stretched into the heavens whose blue they did not reach; they hurled themselves, spreading their arms longingly, upon the earth, which burst asunder beneath them. They appealed for community but they found no common ground; they trumpeted into the tubas of love so that these sounds made the heavens quake, but did not penetrate to the hearts of human beings through the din of battles, factories, and speeches.

Certainly the music of this poetry will not become eternal like the music of God in the chaos. But what would the music of God be if it were not answered by the music of the human being, which longs eternally for the paradise of the cosmos.... Of the many, many poems of this generation almost all will have perished with the subsiding storms of its epoch. Instead of a few great, glowing, warming stars their numbers will appear to posterity like the Milky Way twinkling with innumerable little stars and pouring a pale-clear glow into the billowing night.

None of these poets flirts with immortality, none wraps himself in a mantle of triumph with an aloof heroic gesture, none desires to soar away with noble bearing as an Olympian; and when these poets psalm, groan, lament, scream, curse, call, hymn in their extravagant prolixity, their excessive fortissimo — they do not do so out of arrogance but out of need and humility. For slavish crawling, inactive waiting are not humility; rather it is humility when someone steps before God and the human being and publicly gives testimony, bears witness and makes demands, and his weapons are only his heart, his spirit, and his voice.

As someone who has stood in their midst, who has felt bound to many of them through friendship and to all of them through love, I come forward and cry out: let it suffice, you who were not sufficient for your own selves, for whom the old human being was no longer sufficient; let it suffice, because this riven, eruptive, churning poetry must not be sufficient for you! Let it not be enough! Rather help, all of you, to create a simpler, clearer, purer reality, leading the way toward the will of humanity. For that moment will, must come when from Beethoven's symphony, which gave us the rhythm of our youth, there suddenly rises in the wildest chaos of raging music the *vox humana*: Friends, not these sounds! Let us intone other and more joyful ones!

You young people, however, who will grow up in a freer humanity, do not follow these whose fate it was to live in terrible awareness of a decline in the midst of an unsuspecting, hopeless humanity, and at the same time to be burdened with the task of having to maintain faith in the good, the future, the divine that wells from the depths of the human being! As surely as the poetry of our age had to travel down this martyr's path, just as surely shall the poetry of the future manifest itself differently: it will have to be simple, pure, and clear. The poetry of our age is at once an end and a beginning. It raced through all possibilities of form — it is again permitted to have the courage of simplicity. The art that was rent asunder by the passion and torment of the most accursed of earthly ages —, it has the right to find purer forms for a happier humanity.

This humanity of the future, when it reads the book *Menschheitsdäm-merung* ("You terribly noble monument to the time of chaos"), may it not damn this band of yearning damned souls for whom nothing was left except hope in the human being and a faith in utopia.

# Reverberation

(Berlin, April 1922)

*T*his book, put together in the autumn of 1919, found a rapid and
ready acceptance by an age whose essence it depicted. The printings
had to follow one another in rapid succession..., and now, almost three
years later, in the spring of 1922, when it is time to get out the twenty
thousandth copy of *Menschheitsdämmerung*, the question arises whether I
should revise the work: throw out what has moldered, incorporate what
has since been written, let new themes resound, strive for a different
grouping, a different structure.

I have decided to leave the work as it is. Not only because critics of all
persuasions and opinions expressed the idea that the main value of this
book lay in its uniformity, in its symphonic effects; not only because
readers felt — and this was intended — that here was a self-contained
document of the roused feelings and the poetic form of expression of a
contemporary generation. But, looking at our age and our poetry critically,
I have to come to the realization that *Menschheitsdämmerung* is not just a
self-contained but also a concluded, concluding document of this epoch.
Plainly speaking: since the conclusion of this lyric symphony no poetry has
been written that would of necessity still have had to be included.

Anyone divesting himself of revolutionary furor who looks at the
present with open eyes, knows that these years have been more significant
for the collapse of the old than for the awakening of the new, regardless
of whether we are speaking of events in the political sphere, in community
life, in the economic sphere, or in art. To be sure, a great deal is happen-
ing..., but what is happening is only the dissolution process of Europe's
slowly but inexorably collapsing past. The things that we deem new and
confusing are always merely the elements of the old hastening to their
death in concentrated and undue fashion. The foundations of the real
future are not yet apparent.

This is also the case in the area of art. Whatever seemed so novel and pregnant here was in essence a form of destruction of the old, from the figure-dissolving cubism of painting to the ecstatic one-word lyric. Whether the artists themselves felt that their work was more oppositional than creative or whether it just happened that their powers were not sufficient to fashion something mature and of future value — only ten years after the powerful and violent emergence of this young generation a general stagnation in the domain of art can be witnessed.

Of the twenty-three poets in this book seven are no longer among the living. The others have in the last few years produced either nothing at all of significance, or, in any case, nothing that stands out from their previous achievements as new or qualitatively better. They repeat themselves or they grope their way painfully. Even when, speaking objectively and matter-of-factly, one takes into account the unwholesome conditions that make production infinitely difficult for poet and publisher, one must have the courage to say that the young poetry of our time is in danger of becoming fruitless and unfruitful.

What can be said about the small group of poets in this book holds in increased measure for the large number of poets of their generation. Many have died..., many have vanished into bourgeois life, absorbed into a practical profession or skeptical idleness..., and the countless others are content — sometimes more pallidly, sometimes more over-excitedly — to sigh, to stammer, to scream for the thousandth time what the leading poets had already set down in their books in the second decade of this century. Now, just a short time later, it is with solemn awareness that I have to say "set down," because more swiftly than any other has this generation gone into literary history, become historical; its poems have been frozen into paradigms, into models for those who come after it.

The poetry of these young writers died an early death, for neither the poets who led the way nor those who followed after them were able to develop this work further. It seems to be a law of the spirit in Germany that every artistic movement forthwith awakens a counter-movement, for already efforts which follow the classical and romantic models are beginning to triumph. For many a reader this book, whose poetry was meant to be a fanfare and a beacon and was able to have this effect for a short time, will already seem like a herbarium. It is true: some things are dead forever..., some things no longer kindle enthusiasm..., some things are transition and confusion..., a number of things, however, are so perfect and so beautiful that they are absolutely unique poetic creations..., some good things have found their way into school texts. Everything, however, is testimony to the fire of an internal and external movement that is now all but burnt out. The fire of this generation had been lit by its opposition to the past, to its corruption, and was able for some moments to light the way into the future, but not to inflame humanity to great deeds or great emotions.

So, let it be said again, this book has become — more than I could ever have foreseen while putting it together — a concluding work — and therefore it shall remain as it was then: a testimony to the deepest suffering and the deepest happiness of a generation that fanatically believed and wanted to make others believe that, if everyone willed it, paradise would have to blossom from the ruins. The trials and tribulations of the postwar period have blown away this belief even if the will to change still lives in many. Of the small band of poets in this book nothing is left except their common cry of decline and future happiness. And yet several, e.g., in addition to DÄUBLER and ELSE LASKER-SCHÜLER, the dead HEYM and the living WERFEL, are already beginning to tower above their time.

Powerfully, but not all-powerfully have the events of a decade plowed apart the souls, spirits, and external circumstances of our contemporaries. But the great, universal, new poetry, longed for by many as a staff and guide, has not sprung forth, neither from the descendants of the old bourgeoisie nor from the advancing masses of proletarians, neither from the glitter of the newly blest soaring unrestrainedly over the earth's surface, nor from the torment of the newly created proletariat. In the darkness of the youth who are now growing up there are hardly any little lights on the poetic horizon.

Let us, therefore, cherish the memory of a band of poets who at least enthusiastically wanted great things and a better future and confidently believed that they were the vanguard of a new epoch of humanity. They should not be derided and they should not be blamed for having been only a rebellious remnant that turned from the twilight of doom to the glowing of a putative dawn — but had to grow weary before they had a chance to emerge purified into the light at the head of their contemporaries.

# Kurt Pinthus

# The History of *Menschheitsdämmerung*[1]

*I*n the forenoon of November 8, 1918 all units of the Fourth Army
Corps stationed in Magdeburg elected me, a noncom, to the Soldiers'
Council as their spokesperson, and in the afternoon of the same day, as I
stood on the balcony of the old Baroque government building overlooking
a broad Cathedral Plaza, I announced the end of the war and the
beginning of the republic to thousands of soldiers, workers, townspeople.
In my capacity as a soldiers' councillor I had to negotiate with a people's
delegate named Dr. Landsberg in Berlin; at the same time at the *Hotel
Koschel* where I was staying I ran into some of my good friends, several of
whom I had not seen in years, like the publisher Ernst Rowohlt, to whom
I had been lending my support in Leipzig since 1909, right after he started
up his auspicious publishing house, the poet Walter Hasenclever, who was
likewise a member of the circle that met in Wilhelm's Wine-Cellar, which
had been the rendezvous of Expressionist writers and artists between 1910
and 1914, the poets Theodor Däubler and Albert Ehrenstein, Else
Lasker-Schüler and a bed-ridden Oskar Kokoschka still suffering from a
lung wound inflicted by a Cossack's lance and a shot past the labyrinth of
his ear. This *Hotel Koschel* is one of the few buildings on Motz Street that
survived the Second World War; it is now called the *Hotel Sachsenhof*
(Saxon Court) and ought to list on a plaque the bearers of the many
names resplendent in the history of literature and art that found lodging
there during the second and third decades of our century. In that
November all of us were without money and rather worn-out from the
long war, but hoped that the revolution would realize those ideas and
demands which a rapidly swelling number of authors sprouting from the
small pre-war literary assault detachments in Berlin, Leipzig, Munich,

[1]Originally published as the introduction to *Gedichte der Menschheitsdämmerung.
Interpretationen expressionistischer Lyrik*, ed. Horst Denkler, Munich: Wilhelm Fink
Verlag, 1971.

41

Prague, Vienna and other cities had proclaimed in countless poems and manifestos, in dozens of journals and book series.

We can see from Paul Raabe's thorough and fundamental work, *Die Zeitschriften und Sammlungen des literarischen Expressionismus* (The Journals and Collections of Literary Expressionism) (Stuttgart, 1964) that in this decade more than a hundred publishers were receptive to Expressionism and that between 1917 and 1919 the number of Expressionist journals increased from seven to forty-four. This is not the place to depict and to fathom this unusual phenomenon of a poetic-literary mass production and its causes, as well as its sudden decline, tied in with the unfinished revolution and the disappointment of these bands of authors and artists. But this fact had to be mentioned in order to understand how painful it must have been for Ernst Rowohlt, who had published the first books of Expressionist writers like Heym and Kafka, to find himself, a discharged flying officer with only a uniform to his name, in the midst of this tumult of hundreds of authors with no possibility of participating as a publisher in the literary life around him, while established publishers were pouring out huge numbers of works and entire series of books. Most painful of all was the fact that Kurt Wolff in Leipzig, whom he had taken into his newly established publishing house as a financially strong silent partner ten years earlier, but to whom he had to make over his briskly burgeoning enterprise because of incompatibility, had experienced the swiftest and most luxuriant of blooms — by skillfully publicizing lesser known but estimable older authors, and especially by publishing young or still unknown authors who were presented as a display of so many faces in a new kind of book series (forthwith frequently imitated) called *Der jüngste Tag* (Judgment Day) — with the result that the Kurt Wolff Publishing House was now regarded as the collecting vessel, as the veritable publishing house for Expressionist literature.

Even after Rowohlt's departure I had stayed on with this publishing house as literary advisor or chief reader and in December, 1918 I went back to my job in Leipzig. In the wake of the pioneering journals of Expressionism *Der Sturm* (The Storm) (since March, 1910) and *Die Aktion* (Action) (since February, 1911) the *Weissen Blätter* (White Pages) had been published as the classical journal of Expressionism since September, 1913 (by the *Verlag der Weissen Bücher* [Publishing House of the White Books], a branch of the Kurt Wolff Publishing House), but on account of its pacifist leanings under the resolute editorship of René Schickele it had to be transferred to a Swiss publisher. Now when the war was over the most beautiful journal of the publishing house — and no doubt the most beautiful of the period around 1920 altogether — was founded, to which I gave the name *Genius*. Here for the first time, gorgeously printed in quarto, the new literature was combined with Expressionist but also with classical art in the form of numerous inserted or bound original illustrations and large reproductions partly in color. Initially I edited the literary component and wrote the "Address to the Citizens of the World" for the first issue, just as I had already published the no doubt earliest comprehensive programmatic essays on Expressionism during the war: written on the breaks in my compulsory military service, these essays, entitled "On the Newest Literature" and "Address to Young Writers," appeared in the publishing house's widely circulated almanacs *Vom jüngsten Tag* (Of Judgment Day) (1916) and *Die neue Dichtung* (The New Literature) (1918).

These historical remarks will, I hope, facilitate the depiction of how *Menschheitsdämmerung* originated and also perhaps an understanding of this anthology as a whole and as a document of the times. — In the early spring of 1919 I took up residence for a time at an inn called "Zur Felsenburg" (At the Sign of the Mountain Fortress) where my friends Walter Hasenclever and Oskar Kokoschka were staying. It was located in [the resort village of] Weisser Hirsch overlooking Dresden and run by a "Mother" Nachtweih. This somewhat dilapidated, old-fashioned little hotel, with a restaurant on the ground floor and surrounded by stunted trees and brush, had once provided a home for other writers and actors who stayed there after the first night of Hasenclever's *Sohn* (Son) behind closed doors at the Albert Theater in Dresden on Sunday, October 8, 1916, at 11:15 A.M. *Der Sohn* was the first Expressionist drama to appear (several days after a performance in Prague) on a German stage, and the young Ernst Deutsch created the excessively emotional but at the same time sharply dialectical Expressionist style of acting. Hasenclever had come to Dresden from the Macedonian front, where he was serving as a mess orderly thanks to some string-pulling by Lieutenant Kurt Wolff, and refused to return to the theater of war after the extraordinary success of a play performed before the leading men of the theater in Germany. We came up with a solution: Hasenclever identified himself with the title-role of his play; he wanted to murder his father (with whom he actually was on bad terms). We rehearsed him in this role so meticulously that, when brought before the doctors, he was actually committed to the sanatorium of Dr. Teuscher, where he stayed until the military issued a general order discharging all mentally not quite normal soldiers from the army. After he was allowed to leave the sanatorium he moved into Mother Nachtweih's "Felsenburg." It is hard to tell whether he duped the doctors or they were in on it. Hasenclever's medical records are on deposit at the *Klassische Gedenkstätten* (Classical Memorial) (Goethe and Schiller Archives) in Weimar. They make entertaining and instructive reading; I get the impression that the doctors played their role just as skillfully as their patient, who published in the one year (1917) of his medical imprisonment a pacifist version of *Antigone*, obviously caricaturing Emperor William II in the figure of the tyrant Creon, as well as the very rebellious book of poetry *Tod und Auferstehung* (Death and Resurrection) containing his most famous poem, "Der politische Dichter" (The Political Poet). The Expressionist poet Hasenclever had now consciously turned into the political poet, the kind called for by Heinrich Mann and Kurt Hiller.

And so in that restless spring of 1919 we occupied four rooms on the second floor of the "Felsenburg," two of which were Kokoschka's — one was his studio. His pictures dried outside on the balcony: "They are alive," he said to me, "and need air, sun, and rain." In the evening the three of us usually sat around the circular table in Kokoschka's room, and leaning against the wall as a guest was a figure enveloped in cigarette smoke and thin as a rake, and for these two reasons barely visible: Iwar von Lücken, a poet who remained pretty much unknown. But on the green sofa there sat another, an even more eerie motionless figure wrapped in a blue coat, a snow-white life-size doll, the exact reproduction of a beautiful woman, the once beloved Alma Mahler, who was married to the architect and founder of the *Bauhaus* (House of Construction), Walter Gropius, while Kokoschka was serving in the war, but who was now living with Franz Werfel, her husband-to-be, whom she followed into a Hollywood exile in 1940 that was fatal to the poet. Now and then we could hear the post-revolutionary din and the muffled sound of shooting coming from the city below. I recounted how in the city I had seen the Social Democratic minister of war of the Republic of Saxony thrown over the railing of the Augustus Bridge into the broadly flowing Elbe; the head of the minister as he tried desperately to swim to shore became the target of his political opponents standing and shooting on the bridge and along the banks, until the head disappeared in the river.

At that time Kokoschka painted the woman-doll in the blue coat who had to be treated like a living person, lying there on the sofa of his studio, staring into nothingness with wide-open eyes. Later the painting was put in the Dresden Museum and slashed by an unknown individual who sensed its eeriness; the later restoration was a failure. Today Kokoschka, who soon became a professor at the Dresden Academy, does not know anymore whether the restoration was carried out by him or by one of his pupils. Auctioned off in Switzerland by the Nazis in the late 1930s as "degenerate art," the "Frau in Blau" (Woman in Blue) now hangs, after its adventurous experiences, in the Stuttgart Museum. But the eyes of the woman are shut. Back then in 1919 Kokoschka presented me with a large pen-and-ink drawing as a rough sketch for the "Woman in Blue"; it accompanied me to America and thirty years later back to Europe — but here the eyes are wide open, just as I remember them when they were being painted, and just as I saw them frequently in New York as a living reality in Alma Mahler's house, when we spoke of those, our times, people, endeavors, and experiences.

These reminiscences of Dresden are recounted in order to give some idea of the atmosphere out of which the poems, the paintings, the music of the period around 1920 arose, out of which also *Menschheitsdämmerung* arose. But the book itself issued less from this incredibly wild world of so many persons who felt related and bound to one another and more from a realer, more fervidly active world which, strangely enough, opened itself up to me from Mother Nachtweih's "Felsenburg." The boy-friend of the doughty woman was a sergeant who in that post-war period of food shortages frequently brought with him all kinds of meats and poultry, in the consumption of which we were allowed to participate. We frequently noticed, however, a little gentleman with a reddish face seated in epicurean absorption at an adjoining table polishing off portions of these meaty meals accompanied by spirituous liquors of every variety. One day, as we were discussing some problems in art, this gentleman addressed us from his table after finishing his meal: "Gentlemen, I find your conversation very interesting; as I hear, you are involved in matters of literature and art; I too am closely connected with this area, albeit not in a creative way. I am *Kommerzienrat* (commercial councillor) Bettenhausen and I own the newsstands at most of the railroad stations in the Kingdom, now the Republic of Saxony." We entered into a very lively discussion and *Kommerzienrat* Bettenhausen confessed to us that his family had put him in the strictly vegetarian Lahmann Sanatorium, which was very close to the "Felsenburg," because he loved good food and good alcohol too much, and that was why he occasionally escaped from the compulsory fare so that he could have his enjoyable fill of forbidden things here.

Finally he related rather timidly that as a very young man working in Constantinople he had, mind you, once engaged in writing poetry and had a book of lyrics printed with the title *Bülbül*. "Ah," I interrupted him, "that means 'the nightingale,' doesn't it?" "Right, but how come you know that?" "It is the only Turkish word that I know." By and by I asked him if he might be interested in a new publishing firm, if he might even want to help finance it. His answer: "Why not ... who is the publisher?" When I mentioned Ernst Rowohlt's name, he immediately asked, "Is that the same young man who got his publishing firm off the ground so fast in Leipzig ten years ago?" When I said yes and informed him that right now Rowohlt was engaged in establishing a new publishing house in Berlin but was still in need of some money he asked if at some time he could talk over the matter with Rowohlt. "He'll be here anyway in the next couple of days," I replied and headed for the telephone to call up Rowohlt, who had in the meantime rented a large apartment five flights up along the *Lützowufer* (Lützow River Bank) by the *Potsdamer Brücke* (Potsdam Bridge) (it goes without saying that there was a wine tavern downstairs). There he was sitting in those empty rooms without any furniture with his first secretary, Miss Ploschitzky, who was also destined to remain his last until he had to send her to America in the 1930s while the Nazis were forbidding him to publish and he moved to Brazil.

Rowohlt of course appeared the next day, Bettenhausen was called over, the huge Rowohlt and the little *Kommerzienrat* were left alone. After this we saw only dishes and bottles being taken up to them, and soon Rowohlt's roaring laughter shook the house. I never found out how many ten-thousand mark bills Rowohlt got from his noble patron. I call him "noble" because I found out much later that he did not want interest or any share of the profits from Rowohlt, who became one of Berlin's most productive and most widely talked about publishers within a few years, a popular figure surrounded by legends, whereas Kurt Wolff, who had moved to Munich, grew smaller and smaller, giving up his business in the late 1920s. As early as August 24, 1921 he had written to Franz Werfel: "I feel more and more strongly what I already had to tell you in person here in Munich: that your generation, which I can also call mine, has no promising young authors to follow in its wake; at all events, even though I have given my utmost attention to the matter, I cannot catch sight of anybody far and wide and have concluded that German literature has at the present time reached an indescribably sterile level."

Back then in the spring of 1919, in the morning after the talk between Bettenhausen and Rowohlt, a small group of happy people drove from the "Felsenburg" up to Oberbärenburg near Kipsdorf in the *Erzgebirge* (Ore Mountains) and rented rooms at the *Hotel Friedrichshöhe* (Frederick's Heights). This Oberbärenburg was Hasenclever's favorite place for years whenever he needed peace and quiet to work on his plays and later to translate and publish the Nordic mystic Swedenborg. But this time it was a matter of having some boisterous fun. Even the new reader of the Rowohlt Publishing House had come from Berlin, Paul Mayer, a quiet, gentle person, who spoke in a polished style and was so small that Rowohlt was in the habit of placing him on the palm of his right hand and pressing him against the ceiling, which he then called "the stunt."

Since I have always loved life and nature more than talking and theorizing about literature, I made off; and while my broad-shouldered, good-hearted, but noise-loving friend Rowohlt was brewing his notorious *Feuerzangenbowle* (red-wine-and-flaming-rum-punch), I went walking in the woods by myself. And as I wandered about in the solitude and stillness, all of a sudden the idea for *Menschheitsdämmerung* struck me like a flash: to put together a collection of the heretofore insufficiently known characteristic poems of the characteristic poets of my generation, not, as is the rule, in the chronological or alphabetical sequence of the poets or with a definite theme like nature, revolution, love, war, and peace, but rather as a portrait of the times, no: as an analysis of the times, no: as a symphony of the times, these times encompassing the decade 1910 — 1920. But what I saw physically in front of me, so to speak, during my stroll has been told much better than I can do it today in my first introduction to *Menschheitsdämmerung*. Here I want to speak not about the *poems* of *Menschheitsdämmerung*, but about its *history*.

Rowohlt said to Hasenclever and me: "Of course, the first thing I have got to do is publish books by the two of you." When I told him about my idea for *Menschheitsdämmerung*, he was enthusiastic, as he always was when he heard about a new or a new kind of idea. It was the idea for this book that now impelled me to go to Berlin — but it was also the many authors who lived in Berlin or went there frequently, acquaintances and friends of mine. These authors, whose writings I knew from the mass of publications of the last ten years, whose manuscripts I had selected for publication from the piles of other manuscripts or of whose poems I had written critiques. For *Menschheitsdämmerung*, i.e., for the poetry of Expressionism, I had to select from all of these books and from the small volumes in the various book series the most characteristic poets employing the most multifarious forms of expression, and then from the poets selected take, in turn, those poems suitable for the realization of my vision, for the construction, the composition of the symphony entitled *Menschheitsdämmerung*.

During the early summer of 1919 I moved into the so-called *Garten-haus* (garden house {translators' note: a euphemism for the part of a tenement house accessible only through a courtyard and thus considered inferior}) of a building that a friend of mine from my university days owned in Potsdam's *Privatstraße* (Private Street), one of the quietest side streets very close to one of the noisiest places in Berlin, the *Potsdamer Brücke* where *Potsdamer Straße* and *Lützowufer* intersect, but where the building that contained the new professionally furnished offices of the Rowohlt Publishing House as well as the private apartment of the boss happened to be located. The entire operation was already in full swing, so that I was immediately able to carry out another project that I had proposed to Rowohlt: one of those now so popular book series, the very first one of which I had initiated with Kurt Wolff in May, 1913 as *Der jüngste Tag* (Judgment Day). For this new Rowohlt series, which was to consist of pamphlets that were both revolutionary and a guide to the future, I had come up with the distinctive title *Umsturz und Aufbau* (Revolution and Reconstruction). I edited the first number, a selection from the rebellious writings of Georg Büchner: *Friede den Hütten! Krieg den Palästen!* (Peace to the Huts! War on the Palaces!), thus utilizing the title of the author who died in exile at the age of twenty-three. The second little volume was entitled *Der politische Dichter*, a selection from Walter Hasenclever's political poems and prose manifestos. It was followed by *Kampf gegen die Waffe* (Fight against the Weapon), written by my friend, the poet Rudolf Leonhard, then Karl Marx, *Zur Judenfrage* (On the Jewish Question), edited and introduced by Stefan Grossmann, who edited as well: *Der Hochverräter Ernst Toller. Die Geschichte eines Prozesses. Mit einer Verteidigungsrede von Hugo Haase* (The Traitor.... The Story of a Trial. With a Speech for the Defense by...). Paul Mayer edited a selection of Georg Herwegh's poems: *Reißt die Kreuze aus der Erden!* (Tear the Crosses out of the Ground!); Johannes R. Becher entitled the collection of his own poems *Ewig im Aufruhr* (Eternally in Revolt).

For younger readers it should be noted (older readers should be reminded) that all of the authors and editors mentioned here had to go into exile: Karl Marx, Georg Herwegh, Georg Büchner, Stefan Gross-

48

mann, Paul Mayer, Kurt Pinthus, Rudolf Leonhard, Ernst Toller, Johannes R. Becher, Walter Hasenclever. One exception: the Socialist parliamentary deputy Hugo Haase was shot to death on the steps of the parliament building.

Of the writers of this "series of pamphlets" alive at the time the following are in *Menschheitsdämmerung*: Walter Hasenclever, Rudolf Leonhard, Johannes R. Becher. Now they are no longer alive, like all the rest of the twenty-three poets of *Menschheitsdämmerung*, with the exception of Kurt Heynicke who, at the age of eighty, after all sorts of detours and wrong turns, and shortly before these observations were being put to paper, published yet another volume of Expressionist poems. In the First World War the following were killed: Alfred Lichtenstein, Ernst Wilhelm Lotz, Ernst Stadler, August Stramm, Georg Trakl (by his own hand); back in January, 1912 Georg Heym had fallen through the ice while skating and had drowned. Jakob van Hoddis elapsed into insanity early on and was murdered by the Nazis. The following died in Germany — between the First World War and 1933: Ludwig Rubiner; — between 1933 and the present: Johannes R. Becher (1958; he returned from exile in May, 1945), Gottfried Benn (1956), Theodor Däubler (1934), Wilhelm Klemm (1968). The following died in exile (or of its effects) after 1933: Albert Ehrenstein, Iwan Goll, Walter Hasenclever (by his own hand), Else Lasker-Schüler, Rudolf Leonhard, Karl Otten, René Schickele, Franz Werfel, Alfred Wolfenstein, Paul Zech.

Each person, following his individual bent, can draw his own commentary from this list of destinies. Concerning the lives and works of each of the twenty-three poets, the bio-bibliographical appendix in *Menschheitsdämmerung* provides information; concerning the idea of the whole and of the structure, concerning principles of selection and above all concerning my analysis and my assessment of Expressionist poetry, the three introductions to *Menschheitsdämmerung* do the same.

Let us turn once more to the time *Menschheitsdämmerung* came into being. After I had decided on the poets who were to be included, I dictated a letter to Miss Ploschitzky in the Rowohlt Publishing House addressed to all those whom I had been unable to contact in person or over the telephone, asking them whether they would agree to the inclusion of their poems in the planned anthology and leave the selecting to me; I also requested an autobiography from each poet. I dealt in the same fashion with the relatives and friends of those poets who had died or been killed in action. In every instance I enclosed a brief description of the idea and structure of the book. No one turned me down, although several provided only the date of birth as their autobiography or two to three lines about their various places of residence; but even these very brief data could be informative, e.g., Albert Ehrenstein: "On the 23rd of December, 1886 the Viennese earth happened to me." Gottfried Benn: "Born in 1886 and grew up in villages of the province of Brandenburg. Inconsequential development, inconsequential existence as a physician in Berlin." Ludwig Rubiner "does not wish any biography of himself," but then he justifies this wish with political arguments.

Now I began to compose the symphony of poems, of some hundreds of poems by these twenty-three poets in accordance with the four main motifs which became the titles of the four parts or symphonic movements of the book: "Crash and Cry," "Awakening of the Heart," "Call-to-Action and Revolt," "Love to Human Beings" (whereby the word "love" can be taken both as a substantive and as the imperative form of the verb {translators' note: "Love the Human Being"}). Many more critics than expected have over the course of decades sensed, emphasized, and characterized the musical structure according to main themes, secondary motifs, variations, fugal elements. Some observers have tried to draw a parallel between the structure of the book and Beethoven's Ninth Symphony, which I did not intend at all, or at least not consciously. When in 1953 I went back to Berlin for the first time after fifteen years of American exile to give some lectures at the Free University on "New Findings in Theater Studies," the professor of literature Kunisch said to me: "I just assigned the theme of *Menschheitsdämmerung* as a doctoral thesis to a student who is also studying music history." The student, who was surprised that I was still alive, visited me in my hotel and had already discovered all sorts of things that I had never been consciously aware of, e.g., the fact that each of the four parts concludes with a poem by Werfel. And as a matter of fact I now saw for the first time in these four poems by Werfel the intended intensification from the cry of desperation: "Not Us" to the realization "For I Am Still a Child" to the longed-for ideal "The Good Human Being" right up to the triumphant finale of the "Song of Life": "But beyond all words/ I proclaim, human being, *We are!!*"

I have often been asked why I included so many poems by Werfel, twenty-seven to be exact, more than by any other poet. In 1911 Werfel had been the first to emit, nay, to trumpet abroad, a fully new tone in an age dominated by George, Rilke, and Hofmannsthal, and who in a very early poem "To the Reader" had sounded the most important and later frequently repeated and varied motifs of Expressionism. Let me cite here the most significant lines from the poem, the beginning: "My only wish is to be related to you, O human being"... and the last lines: "Therefore I belong to you and to everyone!/ Do not, please, do not resist me!/ Oh, if one day it could be/ That we, brother, would fall into each other's arms!" Everything else between beginning and end follows the then much discussed structural device of simultaneity. It seems to me that today the significance of the first three volumes of poems by Werfel for Expressionism and for that period are no longer or have not yet been recognized: *Der Weltfreund* (The World Lover) (1911), *Wir Sind* (We Are) (1913), *Einander* (Each Other) (1915, in the midst of the war). Henschel, the student, took great pains as a literary and music scholar to analyse and classify each and every poem of *Menschheitsdämmerung* not only from a literary but also a musical standpoint and in such a way as to demonstrate the aptness of the subtitle: "Symphony of the Newest Poetry." He also provided examples from music and appended the main musical motif of a composition by the young Beethoven discovered later on, a cantata on the early death of the enlightened Emperor Joseph II with the word motif by the composer, "Then the human beings, the human beings emerged into the light," a motif which remained so deeply imbedded in Beethoven's memory that he lets it ring out again many years later in the opera *Fidelio*, as the chains fall from Florestan, now freed from prison.

I shall say only little about the technical difficulties connected with putting together the first edition of *Menschheitsdämmerung*. I had proposed inserting a likeness of as many of the twenty-three poets as possible based on works of Expressionist painters and graphic artists that had been created, if at all possible, at the same time as the poems. The publisher was in a hurry, but nevertheless it was possible to get hold of fourteen portraits, most of them by that ecstatic painter-friend of our generation, Ludwig Meidner, but also some by Kokoschka, Lehmbruck, Chagall, Schiele, and others, as well as self-portraits of Else Lasker-Schüler and Wilhelm Klemm.

The permission of the publishers of the twenty-three poets also had to be obtained. Only a handful of publishers of Expressionist literature were involved, mainly Kurt Wolff, who magnanimously gave me permission to print anything by his authors I wanted to. Just as obliging was Franz Pfemfert, whose *Aktion* (Action) had published contributions by me. I think that Rowohlt, an overpowering user of the telephone all his life, rounded up all the other publishers like Herwarth Walden's *Sturm*

(Storm), Erich Reiss, A.R. Meyer, Insel Publishing House *et al* in the shortest span of time. I had the feeling that all the poets and publishers were delighted to be appearing in *Menschheitsdämmerung*, for it is no secret that publishers look upon poetry as a so-called hard-to-sell commodity, and at the time it was especially difficult to market Expressionist poetry. As an octogenarian the poet Wilhelm Klemm sent me a photograph of himself and on the back he expressed his gratitude to me, for without "those nineteen poems of his [sic] that appeared in *Menschheitsdämmerung* nobody would have given a hoot about him [sic]". Rowohlt already enjoyed a reputation as an adept and energetic propagandist and had announced an initial press run of 5000 copies, unusually large for a book of poetry.

The poems chosen for *Menschheitsdämmerung* were typeset from the pile of poetry books sent to the firm of Pöschel and Trepte in Leipzig, the galleys arrived, I cut them and arranged them in the order composed by me. And now a nerve-racking job began. The first days of autumn were already gone and Rowohlt wanted to bring out the book before Christmas. And so night after night the two of us, already old buddies but still regarded as representatives of the young or new generation, sat completely alone in the offices of the publishing house high over the *Potsdamer Brücke*, above the din and lights of the heart of Berlin, and we pasted and pasted, like the girl at the beginning of Strindberg's *Dream Play*, which served as a model for the Expressionists with its negation of space and time. We pasted all the beautiful or wild poems on individual sheets, but each of these sheets could only be pasted with lines of poetry plus headings in the same amount of space as the final printed page would later comprise. Never could two or four lines of a poem be carried over to the next page, never at the end of a poem could there be an empty space left on the page that did not leave enough room for the heading and start of a new poem. And yet the poems that belonged together were supposed to stay together. Just take a look, e.g., in any edition of *Menschheits-dämmerung* at the variations on forest and tree in part two or on the poems of revolution in part three. Poems were shifted back and forth, over each other, beneath each other, a few pages ahead; practically every poem was fought for, because all too frequently the impatient Rowohlt wanted to leave out a poem that did not immediately fit into the right group. Once toward morning I fell out of my chair from exhaustion. But finally everything was done, with a bibliographical section and indexes — and when the first copies arrived in November, 1919, but postdated 1920, the two of us practically fell out of our chairs, for there on the bright stiff-paper binding and on the main title page the subtitle was glaringly printed as: "Symphonie jüngster Lyrik" (Symphony of the Newest Lyric Verse) instead of "Symphonie jüngster Dichtung" (Symphony of the Newest Poetry), and all the clear, sharp poet-portraits were printed in a blurry and muted halftone instead of as line etchings.

I can no longer recall whether Rowohlt was able to halt production right away so as to have the title corrected and the pictures redone with the more effective technique; in any case these changes were made for the second edition (6 to 10 thousandth copy), which had to be rushed into print, as was the third edition, (11 to 14 thousandth copy), dated 1921. For the book of which it had been least expected had become the first bestseller of Rowohlt's second publishing house. Then in the first half of 1922 the fourth edition (15 to 20 thousandth copy) appeared, to which was added a brief second preface, entitled "Nachklang" (Reverberation), wherein the end of Expressionist poetry was declared. I realized "that *Menschheitsdämmerung* is not only a comprehensive, but also a conclusive and concluding document of this era ... and for this reason it should remain as it was then." This is still true today and it was true when, forty years after its appearance, the book came out as a paperback. It goes without saying that, like every activity of its editor, it was forbidden right after the Nazis seized power.

In these remarks nothing is being said about Expressionism, nothing about Expressionism as art or form or tendency; the only thing being discussed is the book *Menschheitsdämmerung*, to whose poems the volume offered here {translators' note: *Gedichte der "Menschheitsdämmerung". Interpretationen expressionistischer Lyrik* (Poems of.... Interpretations of Expressionist Poetry), ed. Horst Denkler} is devoted. So let me backtrack by saying that *Menschheitsdämmerung* was not only a bestseller with 20,000 copies in print within two-and-one-half years, but that numerous critiques and discussions appeared in journals and newspapers, ranging from praise and honest analyses to clearcut rejection, especially in publications with a religious or reactionary slant, or even to vile diatribes as a book by lunatics or revolutionary wreckers. I had a Leitz file full of critiques and letters concerning *Menschheitsdämmerung*; it fell into the hands of the Nazis, as did my entire collection of letters, when I was foolhardy enough to return to Berlin from my emigration in 1938, pull a disappearing act, and ship by hook or by crook all my other collections, a library of 8,000 books, journals, manuscripts and notes, in clippings, carbons, and author's copies, everything that I had previously published, to New York in 40 boxes, from where everything, augmented, was recently brought back to Germany and donated to the new German Literary Archives in Marbach. But I recall that the most cheering and most positive letter back then came to me from Stefan Zweig, with whom I was not personally acquainted and who had written an essay entitled "The New Pathos" in 1909 which anticipated the literature of the period 1910–1921; the most insightful critique was written by Oskar Loerke in the *Neue Rundschau* (New Review), and the silliest letter was sent by a student who, after asking all sorts of questions, finished by saying he did not want to conceal from me that he was going to prove *Menschheitsdämmerung* is a work of the devil.

Toward the end of 1940 Ernst Rowohlt had gone back to Berlin from Brazil by way of France as an ordinary seaman on a blockade runner; upon his return Erich Kästner greeted him with words that have since become famous: "I notice that the rats are boarding the sinking ship." After the war he lost no time in building up his third publishing house with the help of his oldest son, Ledig-Rowohlt. His son came to New York in 1949 to study the already flourishing American paperback business, so that Rowohlt was able to bring out the first paperback series in Germany, the RoRoRo series, in 1950. We had renewed our old friendship by mail, and when I was back in Europe in 1953 for the first time, I visited, after a touching welcome with roses and a huge bowl of cold duck, the publishing house which was once again swelling to astonishing proportions. Said Rowohlt: "The literature of our younger days is gone for good, no one will publish Expressionist authors anymore, I have sold cheap or given away the rights to all my prewar authors." However, the rediscovery of Expressionist art and literature through exhibitions, reprints, and research had already begun. I remember having seen in the Charlottenburg Palace in Berlin in 1953 a small exhibition at which the Parisian *Fauves* were compared with the painters of the Dresden *Brücke* (Bridge), both of whom had exhibited their exuberantly colorful paintings for the first time in 1905 without being aware of each other's existence. Every time I traveled to Germany my reunion with Rowohlt called for a celebration, in Hamburg or at his old converted water-mill in an isolated valley of the Hunsrück region. But in 1958 he suddenly said to his son and to me: "And now we will publish *Menschheitsdämmerung* as a paperback." We thought he was kidding, and when we realized that he meant it we tried to talk him out of the idea, for a paperback in the RoRoRo series has an initial printing of at least 20,000 copies.

Rowohlt had by now become "Papa," the name generally conferred on him by the literary and publishing world; he had remained the venturesome and rosy giant who relished life, but on occasion he sported a gray beard, which made him look incredibly like his author Hemingway. I had to sign a contract immediately to bring out a new edition of *Menschheitsdämmerung*. Papa agreed to all my conditions. I had never had any problems with the contributors of *Menschheitsdämmerung* — between 1920 and 1922 one or the other would request now and then that I replace one of his poems with another in the next edition; thus, Iwan Goll soon gave me another of the four versions of his famous "Panama Canal." My first stipulation for the new edition was that *Menschheitsdämmerung* be reprinted in its entirety, without any omissions or additions, but that it contain all the poems that had ever appeared in the four press runs of the original edition. Second, because the subtitle could no longer be called "Symphony of the Newest Poetry" forty years after the initial publication, for the contributors were now old or almost all dead, the subtitle was to be called "A Document of Expressionism," which is precisely what the book had become in the meantime. And third, a new preface was to precede the complete reprint of the two prefaces of 1919 and 1922, and the bio-bibliographical section was to be brought as up-to-date as possible. This last point caused time-consuming difficulties, for as a result of the havoc wrought by the Nazis and the war the fortunes of the poets had been so buried in oblivion, their works so forgotten and dispersed that it was practically impossible, especially with New York as a base, to gather together the material. The first large Expressionism exhibition in Marbach and its exemplary catalogue by Paul Raabe and H.L. Greven, which contained a great deal of new, i.e., old-unknown information, the first reference book on Expressionism, did not come until two years later, in 1960. In 1959 the only authors of *Menschheitsdämmerung* still living were Kurt Heynicke, Karl Otten, and Wilhelm Klemm, each of whom sent a new and detailed autobiography. The autobiographies and biographies of all twenty-three poets in the original edition were kept intact but were put in *italics* and placed in front of these three new autobiographies as well as all other new and supplementary biographies.

Again Rowohlt pressed, as in 1919, for he wanted the paperback edition to come out in a hurry; and when the book appeared in September, 1959 as No. 55/56 in "Rowohlt's Classics of Literature and Science" without my getting a chance to see the proofs of the bio-bibliographical appendix, the shock was almost as severe as when the original edition came out in 1919: this appendix that had been so painstakingly put together was teeming with misprints. Luckily the shortcomings could be rectified and the material complemented immediately, for the first edition of 20,000 copies was out of print in just four months, and by January, 1960 a second edition of 10,000 copies was already on the market. Papa had been right. Once again *Menschheitsdämmerung* became a bestseller and has remained so to this day. The 85 thousandth copy was published in October, 1970. But because in the 1960s the interest of the public and the scholars in Expressionism had shown a rapid increase and a great many reprints, extensive selected editions, complete editions, and even critical editions of Expressionist poets were appearing, I re-edited the entire bio-bibliographical appendix and so, beginning with the 51 thousandth copy in September, 1964 *Menschheitsdämmerung* appeared as the "revised edition with a considerably enlarged bio-bibliographical appendix." This appendix has now grown from the 19 pages of the original edition to 54 pages. The number of poems comes to 275 {translators' note: the number comes to 278, if one counts Hasenclever's entry entitled "Poems" not as one poem but, in accordance with the intention of the poet, as four separate poems}.

The poet-portraits, too, were increased to 19. I should like to make special mention of one of these pictures. I had read that there was no portrait ever made of Georg Trakl while he was alive. Living in New York was the widow of Oskar Kokoschka's former Viennese tailor Knize who had later come into fashion in America as a maker of elegant men's apparel and perfumes. In his early years Kokoschka had paid for his suits with paintings, and over the years Mr. and Mrs. Knize had enlarged their Kokoschka collection. In this collection of Mrs. Anni Knize's I found a drawing by Kokoschka which depicted Trakl. I was somewhat skeptical and so I put the question to my old friend Kokoschka. Kokoschka wrote back: "I drew Trakl at the time I was working on my "Windsbraut" (Tempest [literally: bride of the wind]), when he frequently watched me painting and happened to write a poem which contained the word *Windsbraut*, whereupon we both agreed to give the picture this title." The poem is called "Die Nacht" (The Night) and the relevant passage reads: "Golden blaze the fires/ Of the nations round about./ Over blackish cliffs/ Plunges, intoxicated with death,/ The glowing tempest...." This letter of Kokoschka's proves Trakl's frequently disputed connection with Expressionism. The painting "Die Windsbraut," which hangs in Basel, shows Kokoschka as a self-portrait soaring horizontally across the painting with a woman in his arms. It is the same woman whom he later painted as "Frau in Blau," as I related earlier.

Papa Rowohlt lived long enough to participate in the dedication of the large new headquarters of his publishing house in Reinbek near Hamburg as well as to experience the success of the new *Menschheitsdämmerung* — to be sure, he could no longer see and read the book because his eyes had become too weak as the result of an eye hemorrhage. He liked it when I read to him and so I, the older man, read the new preface to him in his villa in Hamburg in the autumn of 1959, remembering the time and the nights when the book, pasted together by the two of us, was brought into existence in the offices of his publishing firm exactly forty years earlier, and thus actually the joint work of two friends whose friendship was now 50 years old. In the late summer of the following year we met again in the Hunsrück and at the place of Mr. Wehr, his vintner, in neighboring Bernkastel-Cues, where we sat in the garden and drank huge quantities of Rowohlt's favorite beverage, a punch with whole peaches. The marveling circle of guests was told stories from those Leipzig days around 1910, and Rowohlt sang his somewhat weird songs. This was his last drink, his last song. It had been too much of a good thing. During the night Rowohlt, who suffered from heart trouble, had a seizure. When I went to Reinbek several months later he was in the hospital, where he died in the beginning of December after his last wish had been fulfilled: "a small glass of double-strength bock beer."

With that the story of *Menschheitsdämmerung* has actually come to an end. But in addition to the original *Menschheitsdämmerung* and the paperback edition there is also a third *Menschheitsdämmerung*, about which nothing is known in the Federal Republic of Germany. Expressionism in literature, painting, and music was attacked, rejected, and proscribed for decades in the Communist countries — except for a brief period when Lunacharsky was Lenin's minister of education and the arts — for being formalist, late-bourgeois decadent, and anti-revolutionary. The most significant Marxist literary historian, Georg Lukács, who was awarded the Goethe Prize of the City of Frankfurt in 1970, had published an article entitled "Greatness and Decline of Expressionism" in 1934 in the first number of the first volume of *Internationale Literatur*, a journal started by the German emigré community in the Soviet Union. The purpose of the article was to destroy German Expressionism on the basis of an inflexibly exaggerated Marxist theory advanced by Lukács, "because they [the Expressionists] could not however detach themselves ideologically from the soil of imperialist parasitism, because they took part in the ideological decline of the imperialist bourgeoisie uncritically and without resistance, and even for a time were its pioneers...." In September, 1937 Alfred Kurella (under the pseudonym of Bernhard Ziegler) intensified the attack when he flatly assailed Expressionism as a precursor of Fascism in *Das Wort* (The Word), the second journal of the emigré community in Russia. In the subsequent issues of *Das Wort* up to July, 1938 these articles were mainly responsible for unleashing a debate for and against Expressionism, in which no fewer than 15 German authors took part, among them Ernst Bloch, who scored a decisive victory over his erstwhile university friend Lukács as well as over Kurella, besting them equally in argumentation and style.

Lukács had, as Bloch charged, directed his polemic less at Expressionist poems than at programmatic articles, especially at articles written by me as well as the introduction and poems of *Menschheitsdämmerung*. But Lukács had to live to see not only himself branded for a time as a counterrevolutionary, but also Expressionism tacitly tolerated or permitted in the long run in Communist countries and *Menschheitsdämmerung* published with both prefaces and all poems intact in the German Democratic Republic, a state considered to be especially in tune with radical Marxism.

For, several years ago, the Philipp Reclam, Jr. Publishing Firm in Leipzig (the Reclam family itself emigrated to Stuttgart and established the now flourishing "Reclam Publishing House" in that city) applied to Rowohlt for a license to reprint *Menschheitsdämmerung*. Referred to me, I gave the Leipzig people my consent provided that in the reprint nothing would be left out and nothing would be added; this stipulation applied to the 275 poems as well as the two introductions and the bio-biographical section. The Leipzig publishing firm accepted my conditions and had only one counter-condition: that an article with a Marxist basis be included in the book. Hereupon I insisted that this Marxist contribution could be published only after I had perused it and given my permission. I found nothing objectionable in the respectful and insightful essay by Professor Mittenzwei. The GDR edition of *Menschheitsdämmerung* was, so I was informed, sold out within a few days. Whether subsequent editions have appeared or been permitted to appear, I do not know.

What is more: the *Aufbau* (Reconstruction) Publishing House, the official state publishing house of the GDR, so to speak, which also publishes the works of Lukács, recently began bringing out a series of nicely printed and well-edited volumes bearing the overall title

*Expressionismus.* Two volumes of Expressionist drama have appeared and a few months ago a 700-page book entitled *Expressionismus Lyrik* came out. This large-scale and commendable anthology of Expressionist poetry includes all twenty-three poets who are in *Menschheitsdämmerung*, but in addition another thirty-eight poets. A postscriptum refers to *Menschheits-dämmerung*, "which was published exactly fifty years ago," to "that collection of poetry which is generally designated as <u>the</u> document of the Expressionist era." But "today, from a critical distance of fifty years, the historicizing discarded by Pinthus seems to be necessary in compiling an anthology of Expressionist poetry."... It endeavors however, "not to turn the poetry into an object lesson in history, not to discard Pinthus's symphony, but to compose it anew, to 'elevate' it. Combining history with motif and theme seemed the most suitable way to achieve our goal." Thus this anthology is also arranged according to main themes, but its sub-motifs are ordered in historical sequence. The work itself is edited by Martin Reso in collaboration with Silvia Schlenstedt, the author of the epilogue, which — its fundamental Marxist position notwithstanding — differs completely from earlier attempts at comprehending and assessing Expressionist poetry and poets, and is superior to all other Marxist as well as most Western analyses.

As in Germany, *Menschheitsdämmerung* has also become a subject of literary teaching and research in the USA. Hans Magnus Enzensberger told me after his lecture in New York how closely related his generation feels to mine. When the Bavarian Broadcasting Corporation announced a program entitled "Dawn of Humanity, Literature and Arts 1910–1914" for its series "End and Turning-Point," I called up the producer to ask him whether the general listening audience could really be expected to know what "Dawn of Humanity" signifies. Whereupon he asserted the phrase had been incorporated into the German vocabulary. In fact I did discover that it is to be found not only as an entry in the literary reference books but also in the general encyclopedias, e.g., in the nine-volume Paperback-Duden. I do not wish to say any more things in praise of a book, as the editor of which I have been cited for so many decades. And so I would like to conclude with the remarks of two men whose political views are not the same as mine.

Ernst Bloch ended his previously mentioned defense of Expressionism in 1938 as follows (to this day he has the article printed in his works): "Its problems will remain memorable until they are superseded by solutions better than those of the Expressionists... the heritage of Expressionism is not yet over, for it has not yet even begun." Was not Bloch's "principle of hope" one of the main motifs of Expressionist poetry? Was not the expansion of the metaphor into the infinite, "omnipresence and simultaneity" in poetry, one of its contributions?

What has meant the deepest satisfaction for *Menschheitsdämmerung* and for me is the fact that at the beginning of an article entitled "Expressionism without End", published in, of all places, the leading monthly in the GDR, in the *Neue Deutsche Literatur* (New German Literature) on December 12, 1969 (vol. 17, no. 2), Kurt Batt, one of East Germany's most recognized critics, not only calls *Menschheitsdämmerung* an "exemplary selection of characteristic poems worth handing down," but proclaims: "The fame and influence of this literary movement were based, not least, on *Menschheitsdämmerung*; indeed, it may be seriously doubted whether without this anthology Expressionism would be seen as what it is in the consciousness of posterity."

# Crash and Cry

## JAKOB VAN HODDIS

### END OF THE WORLD

The burgher's hat flies off his pointed head,
Everywhere the air reverberates with what sounds like screams.
Roofers are falling off and breaking in two,
And along the coasts — the paper says — the tide is rising.

The storm is here, the wild seas are hopping
Ashore to squash thick dikes.
Most people have a cold.
The trains are dropping off the bridges.

## GEORG HEYM

### UMBRA VITAE

People are standing forward in the streets
And gazing at the huge portents in the sky,
Where the comets with the fiery noses
Sneak menacingly around the pointed towers.

And every roof is crowded with star-gazers
Who thrust enormous tubes into the sky,
And magicians growing out of attic holes,
Aslant in darkness conjuring a heavenly body.

Suicides walk about at night in great hordes,
Looking for their lost selves just ahead of them,
Stooping south and west and east and north,
Sweeping the dust with their arm-brooms.

They are like dust, it keeps for yet a while.
Their hair is already falling on the paths they tread.
They run so they can die, and die fast,
And are lying in the fields with their dead heads,

Still twitching sometimes. And the animals of the fields
Stand round them blindly and butt their horns
Into their bellies. They turn up their toes,
Buried beneath sage-brush and the briar.

The seas however stagnate. The ships
Hang in the waves, rotting and morose,
Scattered about, and no current is moved.
And all courtyards of the skies are sealed off.

The trees do not change seasons
And stay eternally dead in their finality.
And across the decaying paths they spread
Their long finger-hands woodenly.

Whoever dies sits up straight trying to get up
And just as he has uttered one more word,
All at once he is gone. Where is his life?
And his eyes are shattered like glass.

Shadows are many. Cheerless and hidden.
And dreams that drag past silent doors.
And whoever wakes up, depressed by the light of mornings,
Must rub heavy sleep from gray eyelids.


WILHELM KLEMM

MY AGE

Song and giant cities, dream-avalanches,
Faded lands, poles without glory,
The sinful women, perils and heroism,
Spectral brewings, storm on iron rails.

In cloudy distances the propellers drum.
Nations melt away. Books turn into witches.
The soul shrinks to tiny complexes.
Art is dead. The hours move in swifter circles.

O my age! So indescribably mutilated,
So without star, so existentially poor in knowledge
As you no other age seems to have been.

Never before did the sphinx raise its head so high!
But you see to the right and left of your path,
Dauntless in the face of affliction, insanity's abyss weeping!


JOHANNES R. BECHER

DECAY

Our bodies are decaying,
Interring us as they sing:
Intoxicated evenings we,
Buried in nocturnal storm and sea.
Hot blood dries up,
Festering sore trickles away.

Mouth ear eye veiled by
Sleep dream earth the wind.
Lividly sluggish worms'
Narrow-winding movement.
Pounding of rolling storms.
Eyelashes blood-red long.
...*"Am I crumbling wall,*
*Pillar by the wayside that is silent?*
*Or tree of grief,*
*Bent over the abyss?"*...
Sweet smell of things decomposing,
Filling up room house head.
Flowers, fluttering blades of grass.
Birds, gushing songs.

*"Yes-, rotted trunk..."*
Mold groans moans.
Beneath flight of teeming heavens

Dreadful sound is heard:
Kettle-drum. Tuba booming.
Thunder. Wildly blazing light.
Cymbal. Percussive sound.
Shrilling of drums. That shatters.-

I who gave myself to you,
Wide world, readily entrusting myself,
Behold, my poor body is decaying,
But my spirit perceives my homeland.
Night, your slumber consoles me,
Mouth rests deeply as well as arm.
Bright day, you dissolve me
In unrest totally and sorrow.

That I cannot find a way out,
Alas, so woefully split up!
Now aperture, now blind and blindfold.
That no kiss will cure me!
That I cannot find a way out
Is probably my fault and mine alone:
Wild river, blood and fire-wind,
Ignominy, impatience.

Day, you sharp bitterness!
Night, grant dream and counsel!
Filth distortion cut and rip —
Cool resting-place...
Everything must still be far away,
Far, oh far away from me —
Blossom forth in starshine,
Homeland, over me!

Someday I shall be standing in the road,
Pensive at the sight of a great city.
Surrounded by the blowing of golden winds.
Light falls dimly through the flight of clouds.
Enraptured forms, veiled in white...
My hands touch
The sky, replete with gold,
Opening like wonder-doors.

Meadows, woods come into view.
Waters roll along. Bridges.

Arches. Course of unending rivers.
Ridge of gray mountains.
Red thunder swells dreadfully.
Dragons spewing earth.
Gaping jaws, the sun roars.
Indignation laughter screaming.

Darkening. Taste of earth and blood.
Tangling throngs. Carnage far and wide...
..."*When will you appear, eternal day?*
Or is there no great rush?
When will you blow, resounding bugle?
You cry of the floodtide of heavy seas?
From thicket, marshland, grave and briars
Summoning the sleepers?"...


GEORG HEYM

THE GOD OF THE CITY

On a row of houses he sits squarely.
The winds camp blackly about his brow.
He gazes full of rage to where in distant loneliness
The last houses stray into the countryside.

Eventide makes Baal's red belly shine,
The big cities kneel around him.
Tremendous numbers of churchbells
Well up to him from a sea of black steeples.

Like a dance of Corybantes the music of the millions
Thunders noisily through the streets.
The chimneys' smoke, the clouds from factories
Waft up to him like the scent of incense turning blue.

The tempest smolders in his eyebrows.
The dark evening is stunned into night.
The storms flap their wings, gazing like vultures
From his head's hair which stands on end in anger.

He thrusts his butcher's fist into the darkness.
He shakes it. A sea of fire races

Through a street. And the fiery smoke roars
And consumes it, till late the morrow dawns.


JOHANNES R. BECHER

BERLIN

The South will bleed to death in the sun's hours.
The god of deeds, provoked to anger, struck from lava crypts.
The mountains' flaming ring circles the land.
Then we set out blackly, a thin procession of the dead.

The South is destined for the sleep of eternal mourning.
We have burnt up the barques of our dreams.
We signal the still harbor with our torches,
Which the mother-hand of darknesses obliterates.

The South's breath clings to our crooked backs
With winds mild and the funereal droning of hollow bells.
Be saddened! The evening's red mist-gnats
Assail you singing. Let us pass by!

Mules break hard rocks loose from the ridge's jagged edge.
Avalanches cover us with love's white fan.
Wild streams bolt high above the bridges' cables.
Geysers burst from the quivers of crumbling rock formations.

In the morning we sank into the crevices' green chambers.
At noon we plunged into the glacier-mill's vortex.
The landslide's club-hammer zoomed down on us.
The winter's storm tore us from a cozy hiding place.

The tender miracles waited in cavernous holes.
With switches we stroked refreshment from the stones.
We crashed with damp bushes' splotchy abrasions.
We died in the chalices of the little gentians.

We thawed as the shepherds greeted and the flocks
Bleated. From the blooming soil's warm leek
A slanting scarlet beam sucked us into sparkling gardens.
A whirl-breeze brought us the spoils of our new homeland.

66

From snow-covered roofs the sea's shining vastness radiates.
Virgin forests have grown tall in smokestacks and rafters.
A sooty grove of fumes shades the walls.
The craters' cones shrivel, sloping ash-peaks.

The meadow-lands dance about like teeming plazas.
Sunsets weep in the canyons of long streets.
A welling whirling throng makes a mad dash for the sky
Midst the misery of basement-tunnels and the din of warehouses...

Berlin! You web-monster of a white metropolis!
Orchestra of the aeons! Field of iron battle!
Your iridescent serpent-body was chafed as it rattled,
Roofed over with the refuse and rot of running sores!

Berlin! You rear up with the cupolas' fist,
Around which the tempests' swarms fashion dirty clods!
Europe's faint heart trickles in your talons!
Berlin! In whose breast the brood of fevers dwells!

Berlin! Your groans rattle dreadfully like thunder!
The hot air oppresses the weak lungs.
The sludge of humans surges round your worm-eaten ankles.
Your head is decked with a garland of blue scars!

We live in a deserted cell with the moon,
Which saunters down on the narrow ridge of roofs.
The days' gray froth storms to starry coasts.
On back stairs a girl was stabbed horribly.

We hang about the splendiferous government buildings.
We have bombs ready for the cars that come and go.
The blond muse meanders along the canal,
Mercury light from shops pale-violet snows down on her.

Fog-vapors press wet compresses onto pavements.
Early morning subway trains puff on sluggish embankments.
The old whores with the frayed mugs,
They slink into the pale and dishevelled morning...

O city of hurts in the despair of dark times!
When do the dead trees become green to the sound of music?
When, hills, do you ascend in a dress of white veils?
Icy surfaces, when do you spread out your pinions of silver?

67

The prophet burns at the crackling stake.
The churches' towers soar gauntly like gallows.
His hair flax. His body stands on brass feet,
Cudgelled in an oven as hot as a glowing colossus of ore.

And his voice swells immensely like the water's roaring,
Then, at a sacred signal, the fire's torment is extinguished.
A pale ship that casts off from the shore,
Hoists its frame and escapes into the night.-

The day will come!... The poet summons it,
So that it will travel to you more swiftly from its fountainhead!
The fire's spirit has become the generations' judge of the dead.
The beggars' croaky barrel-organs will drag it to the surface.

The day will come!...The celestial legions,
They will swarm out of the clouds' gap with a flourish.
The houses' coffin-boards will slam shut with a bang.
Will smash you to pieces. Explosions will hallelujah.

The day will come!... When with a cry of anger
The godhead, outraged as of old, will blast open the mite-infested crust.
On a horizon of fragments a fat shark will be swimming,
The feed of bloody corpses dangling from his jagged jaws.


ALFRED WOLFENSTEIN

CITY DWELLERS

Windows are as close
As the holes in a sieve, houses push
And grab each other so firmly that the streets
Appear as grayly swollen as strangled bodies.

Firmly hooked into one another
The two façades of people sit
In the streetcars, where gazes project crampedly
And desire juts into desire.

Our walls are as thin as skin,
So that everyone is involved when I weep,
A whisper penetrates like shouting:

And as though silent in a hidden cave
Untouched and unregarded
Each of us is yet far away and feels: alone.


JAKOB VAN HODDIS

THE CITY

I saw the moon and the cruel
Aegean Sea's thousandfold pomp.
All my paths wrestled with the night.

But seven torches were my escort,
Glowing through clouds, prepared for every victory.

"Can I succumb to nothingness, can I be tormented
By the wicked wind of cities, of vast cities?
Because I shattered the dreary day of life!"

Long-forgotten journeys! Your victories
Flared out too long ago. Ah! High-pitched flutes
And violins intone my grief in vain.


ALFRED WOLFENSTEIN

ANIMAL HOUSE

I glide, fenced in on all sides by the dark animals,
Back and forth through the roaring house past the burst of bars,
And look far into their eyes as though far out at sea
Into their freedom... which the beautiful creatures never lose.

The harsh beat of a congested city and humanity keeps time
With my toes, but solitudes stride slackly
In the tiger's knee, and its tree-striped flanks
Are wedded not to any street but to the earth itself.

Ah, their pure hot souls are felt by my will
And I dissolve, filled with more desire than a woman.
The jaguar's lightning flashes, yellow out of its assault-night-body,
Bathe in light my snow-face and tiny pupil.

The eagle perches like statues still and ostensibly heavy
And upwards upwards in tremendous motion!
His buoyancy moves into me and harnesses me to his steerage —
I remain still, I am of stone, only he is flying.

The elephants' gray ice-blocks tower,
Mountains, now inhabited only by giant spirits:
I am throned around by the force and fire of the universe
And I remain locked up in their free orbit.

ALFRED LICHTENSTEIN

DUSK

A plump kid is playing with a pond.
The wind has gotten caught in a tree.
The sky looks hung over and pale,
As though it had run out of makeup.

Stooped down crookedly on long crutches
And chattering two cripples creep across the field.
A blond poet may well be going crazy.
A little horse is tripping over a lady.

A fat man is glued to a window.
A youth wants to visit a soft woman.
A gray clown is pulling on his boots.
A baby-carriage screams and dogs curse.

ERNST STADLER

CLOSING TIME

The clocks strike seven. The stores are now closing all over the city.
Out of already darkened hallways, through narrow alleyways from swanky
    lobbies the salesgirls press forward.
Still a little blind and as though numbed from being shut in for so long a
    time
They step, gently aroused, into the voluptuous brightness and soft openness
    of the summer evening.
Grouchy streets light up and all of a sudden beat more spirited time,
All sidewalks are crammed full with colorful blouses and girlish laughter.
Like a lake through which the strong flow of a young river burrows,
The entire city is awash in youth and homecoming.
Among the indifferent faces of the passers-by a multifarious destiny has been
    placed —
The excitation of young life, brightened by the fire of this evening hour,
In whose sweetness all things dark become light and all things heavy melt
    away, as though life were easy and free,
And as though there were not waiting, separated by just a few hours, the
    dreary monotony
Of the daily drudgery — as though there were not waiting a coming home
    to the back lanes of filthy suburban houses wedged between bare
    tenements,
A frugal supper, the oppressiveness of the common living room, and a small
    bedroom shared with the little brothers and sisters,
And brief sleep, which the dawn's first light chases out of the golden land of
    dreams —
All this is now far, far away — covered by evening — and yet already there
    and waiting like a wicked animal all set to pounce on its prey,
And even the most happy, who lightly and with slender stride
Trip along on their sweetheart's arm, carry with them in the loneliness of
    their eyes a distant shadow.
And sometimes, when for no reason the girls cast their eyes down upon the
    pavement while conversing,
It happens that a scary face with a mocking grimace obstructs their
    lightheartedness.
Then they snuggle up closer and the hand that grips the boyfriend's arm
    trembles,
As though already behind them were the old age that will drag their lives
    toward obliteration in the darkness.

## THEODOR DÄUBLER

### DIADEM

The arc lamps coronate sunsets,
Their lilac shining will outlive the night.
They hover like ghosts over the noisy crush.
There must be glazed fruits from other worlds!

Does not the trickling down of their light soothe the din?
I find it hard to comprehend the essence of these lamps.
The stars seem smart, the moon likes to get angry.
Why do you turn pale beneath diadems of stars?

Wilhelm Lehmbruck · Theodor Däubler

## Theodor Däubler

### Broken-Winged Attempt

The moon wanders through deserted streets,
Its light is doubtlessly falling through pallid panes.
I would not like to tarry in this street,
I cannot stand it when houses mutely turn pale.

But what is moving steeply on the terraces?
I imagine there the strangest goings-on,
As though circles were trying bodily to describe themselves,
I surmise sounds without making them out.

It may well be that a white bird will appear,
Strive to soar up almost like a kite,
But at the same time slowly bend down.

How blind, how strange this moon-animal seems to me,
It knocks on panes, breaks the silence
And then lies dead in groves beneath figs.


## Georg Heym

### The Demons of the Cities

They wander through the night of the cities,
Which cower blackly beneath their feet.
Like sailors' beards there hover about their chins
The clouds black from smoke and soot.

Their long shadow pitches on the sea of houses
And extinguishes the rows of street lights.
It creeps along the pavement like a heavy fog
And slowly gropes its way forward from house to house.

One foot planted on a city square,
The other kneeling on a steeple,
They tower where the rain falls blackly,
Blowing the pipes of Pan into the cloud-storm.

The ritornello of the sea of cities

Encircles their feet with sad music,
A great requiem. Now muffled, now piercing,
The tone that ascended into the darkness keeps changing.

They wander along the stream that, black and broad
As a reptile, its back stained yellow
By the street lamps, twists sadly
Into the darkness that blackly covers the sky.

They lean heavily on the side of a bridge
And stretch their hands into the swarm
Of humans, like fauns that bore their arms
Into the mud at the edge of swamps.

One of them stands up. In front of the white moon
He hangs a black mask. The night,
Which drops like lead from the gloomy sky,
Presses the houses deeply into a shaft of darkness.

The cities' shoulders snap. And a roof
Bursts, from which a red fire flushes.
They sit straddle-legged on its ridge
And scream like cats against the heavens.

In a room full of darknesses
A woman giving birth screams in her labor.
Her strong body towers immensely from her pillows,
About which the huge devils hover.

Trembling she clings to the labor-bench.
The room sways round her from her screams,
Then the fruit appears. Her womb gapes red and long
And bloodily it tears in two from the fruit.

The devils' necks grow like giraffes'.
The baby has no head. The mother holds
It in front of her. Along her spine
Frog-fingers of fright gape as she drops back.

But the demons grow to colossal size.
Their temple-horns shred the sky red.
Earthquake thunders through the cities' womb
About their hoofs blazed round by fire.

GOTTFRIED BENN

LITTLE ASTER

A drowned beer-truck driver was lifted on the slab.
Someone had stuck a dark-bright purple aster
between his teeth.
As I proceeding from the chest
under the skin
with a long knife
cut out tongue and palate,
I must have nudged it, for it slid
into the adjacent brain.
I packed it into his chest cavity
between the wadding
as he was being sewn up.
Drink your fill in your vase!
Rest peacefully,
little aster!


JAKOB VAN HODDIS

TRISTITIA ANTE ...

Snowflakes fall. My nights have
Become very loud, and their shining too fixed.
All risks that I deemed glorious
Are now as unfavorable as the winter wind.

I almost hate the bright ardor of the cities.

When in times gone by I lay awake and the midnights
Slowly blazed down — till the sun came —
When I took the splendor of the white whores,
To find out if meager splendor would finally bring me relief,

There never was this garishness or this grief.

ERNST STADLER

DAYS

O vow of sin! All you imposed pilgrimages into ravished beds!
Stations of abasement and of concupiscence at accursed places!
Shelter of dirty chambers, cooking-stove in the room where the left-overs go
    bad,
And the smoky oil-lamp, and over the wobbly dresser the mirror in pieces!
You crushed bodies! You smiles, forcedly carved into painted lips!
Poor, unkempt hair! You words from which life slipped away a long time
    ago —
Are you again around me, do I hear you mentioning my name?
Do I, from shame and fear, again feel only the one urge consuming me:
To spit upon the self-assurance of the pious, the dignity of the righteous,
To give myself, to dedicate myself to what is cheerless, unsure, already lost,
To feel, singing rapturously, the ignominy and the stupor of the defeated,
To burrow my way into the core of life as though into earth's cavities.


ALFRED WOLFENSTEIN

DAMNED YOUTH

Away from home, away through streets,
Unknown to you and every place,
Just like the sky swiftly and loftily
Through strange noises and without a word!

How nice alone, and this excites
And nobody here who paws me,
Who full of family ties dumb and dense
Wallows odiously in my breast!

This isn't home, here it's up and at 'em,
Not love laid on thick, only fighting and dealing!
Ah, the street flows exuberantly
Into others in a mighty course.

Ah, horseless things flash by brusquely
And the mush of the crowd bubbles blackly
And houses stream lashed on
By light, ringing, hissing, shouting.

76

The stones move with deceptive calm,
Hacked by the blows from an army of shoes,
On the pale heads the street lights
Sore from rapid blazing shower sparks.

Here countenances strange like animals
And eyes as if wedged in ice
And eyes that look only at themselves,
Here countenances inhibited by nothing!

You who are godless, reduce my head to dust —
You who are dehumanized, reduce my heart to dust —
Me who am without a home, without a path
You, O street, daze! daze!


PAUL ZECH

FACTORY STREET BY DAY
(1911)

Nothing but walls. Without grass and glass
the street moves down the motley belt
of façades. No trolley track hums.
Always the pavement glistens water-wet.

If someone brushes against you, his gaze coldly cuts you
to the quick; his hard steps hew
fire from the steep fence, tower-high,
even his short breathing makes clenched clouds.

No penitentiary cell clamps
in ice all thinking as firmly as this walking
between walls that look only at each other.

Whether you wear royal purple or hairshirt —:
always pressing down with gigantic heaviness
is God's anathema: *clockless shift*.

PAUL ZECH

SORTING GIRLS
(1911)

Fungus-scaled walls, dark corner by the canal,
overroared by the rotatory screeching of impetuous cranes:
blind windows' half-light creeps into a factory hall.

Pale girls, already too ripe for dream and tear,
stared at by privation's dry mange
and on calluses proliferation of plans lost without trace,

pale girls behind walls, by the canal, half blind,
pale girls, alas, what do you know of enchantment and the trees
of a wind in gardens that are like evening.

Waters that foam round the pointed keel of tugs
have never sung of streaking regattas, never of the moon
that drips on isles of love, and never of piers that border bathing
      beaches.

Water that washes round window-hatches and coolly inhabits the
      premises
breathes the smell of tar and carcass and tanner's lyes,
and never yet have the shrieks of shipwrecks spared you tenderly.

Over the tangled bales of metals that are only good
for scrap you hang your ossified faces:
blunted will in your hands and dulled whiteness in your eyes.

Sometimes a song that interweaves with the noise of the wheels
bursts from mouths that suffer from decaying teeth...
a song bursts — and you, Mary, do not hear it?

By the windows however shadows
sway maliciously like the nights that entwine
the straw of your bedsheets with wilted blossom-redness.

And you recoil and with frenzied coarseness fiddle
with your breasts, with your thighs' crumbling ruins,
and your eyes suck in flashes from somewhere.

No thing appears to you as hated
as the sham supertough bearing of a very young foreman;
not the syphilitics and not the boozers in factory-cafeterias.

Cocooned into the clockwork's narrow ring:
oh, of what use are poisons leached from shreds
of a youth that went by fruitlessly!

While your brothers keenly whet unfulfillment on revolt,
and sisters across the canal twirl pinkly in a dance,
you have to sic fierce thoughts on metals.

And only once there falls from blood and snow a wreath
into the grayly matted strands of your parted hair,
when you, sweetly intoxicated by the sparkling of the monstrance,
may press your lips to the hems of cassocks.

Ludwig Meidner · Paul Zech

PAUL ZECH

MILLING CUTTERS

White hard-steel teeth flash imperiously
from the maze of wheels. Mills operate profoundly,
they pour onto the brick-paved ground
the cloudbursts of curled copper shavings.

The glacial coolness of gigantic bulbs
illumines flesh-naked beings who, drenched in oil drops,
work the combs; while the shears, automatically stuffed,
thinly twine the bars.

The clenching of a fist now and then and a curse,
foreman's whistles, disgusting stench of burning
abruptly licking upward along muscles: to kill!

And it happens that the bearded faces turn red,
that eyes become like cut glass
and sharply, intently gaze inward.


ALFRED LICHTENSTEIN

FOG

A fog has so softly destroyed the world.
Bloodless trees dissolve in smoke.
And shadows hover where screams are heard.
Burning creatures vanish like a breath of air.

The gas-lamps are caught flies.
And each one flickers that it might still escape.
But lurking from the side and gleaming high up in the distance
Is the poisonous moon, the fat fog-spider.

But we who in our infamy are fit for death,
Defiantly trample through this desolate splendor.
And mutely stick our white eyes of misery
Like spears into the bloated night.


ALFRED LICHTENSTEIN

THE RAMBLE

Hey, these solid rooms
And the barren streets
And the red domestic sun,
The atrocious displeasure of all
Books glanced through ages ago,
These things I can't stand anymore.

Come on, we've got to leave
This city far behind.
Let's lie down
In some soft meadow.
Threateningly and yet so helplessly
We shall raise against the absurdly huge,
Deadly blue, bare sky
Our fleshless, apathetic eyes,
Our cursed eyes,
And our hands puffy from crying.-


THEODOR DÄUBLER

IF I HAD A BIT OF LUCK

If I had a bit of luck, everything would be different!
If a mild blue breeze would propitiously swell my sails,
The spirit of a bold explorer would suddenly flash through me,
And I would have to wear myself out in an endless quest for more and more.

If just some little thing were different: if I had a bit of luck,
I would not dream, gripped by the power of passion, on into the cold and
     naked night,
For in woman I would feel I had returned to the very ground of my being:
If ever I were rid of my dread, I would not have watched through any storm!

If I knew why I am pious, scared of life, and singular,
If I could surmise why green luck flourishes nowhere near me,
This little existence would suddenly make an awful lot of sense!
Nowhere would I find a purpose and yet I would die of sorrow.

Hear me nevertheless, earth: I too am a child of yours!
Ah, earth, I love you. Love is my earthly song.
Earth, love your son like the plant, like the animal!
Earth, why am I poor in love and frightened to death here?

If I had a bit of luck, I would keep this luck pure!
Thus my vision is often wildly bent on carnal pleasure.
Everything in me remains an essay. No venture ever succeeds.
If I sing this, then I think that my heart is breaking.


ALBERT EHRENSTEIN

THUS DOES THIS DEAD TIME SNOW ON ME

Expect nothing from me.
I have never had sun,
I brought the stones my sorrow.
I expected happiness from animals.

The desire of common hookers skipped past me,
And I never heard that German phrase: I love you!
They crane their groundlessly conceited brows toward the salesman,
The woman yawns at me maliciously: I distress you.

Thus does this dead time snow on me.
Unthankfully she drinks the wine and whatever else is proffered,
My yearnings are allowed to flag;
Concerned about her flesh, she observes with sudden chaste alacrity
The long boredom of proprieties.
: Female becomes time.

AUGUST STRAMM

UNFAITHFUL

Your smile weeps in my breast
The bitten-to-pieces-in-ardor lips chill
On the breath foliage-decay odors!
Your gaze encoffins
And
Hastens thumping words on top.
Forgetting
The hands then crumble!
Openly
Your dress-hem woos
Flapping
Thither hither above!


THEODOR DÄUBLER

WHAT?

Is it really true,
In every voice,
No matter how soft it sounds,
God is calling in his anger
Spontaneously and marvelously:
If THIS gets through to you,
My fellow human, then glow!

What, eh what? I do listen!
Listen to many a life,
Am always close to the wind,
Wind my way back to the nihil,
So that I can raise myself:
Strive, as a part of God,
To tremble freely in his presence!

Storms embrace me,
Hug all of us and cry:
"When no one was yet like me,
I remained so still in you;
When we created ourselves,

83

We became wind and animal
And had to be gradated."

Wind gusts, happen!
Heights, become aware of your height!
Then I shall howl after you. I the spirit.
Then I shall tug at every thicket,
And woe: woe if I should flee!
Then you that turn to ice
Would not know that you are cracking.

Human beings, do pull yourselves together:
Listen to the raging voices:
Help me, comprehend a cry!
A panting sweeps through the souls!
You will not quench the divine wrath:
Ah, if only a single one became free,
Then we would have to aspire, have to glow!

Chaos no longer confuses.
It could be we were never together.
How heavy the spirit becomes for every sea,
And for the spirit how empty creation!
Fleeing we must damn ourselves:
But always be born virginally:
Together everything proceeds from its roots.


THEODOR DÄUBLER

LONELY

I call! My voices are all echoless.
This is an old forest devoid of sounds.
I am breathing, yet nothing at all stirs or sounds.
I am alive, since I can still listen and get angry.

Is this no forest? Is this the glimmering of a dream?
Is this an autumn that goes on wandering in silence?
It was a forest! A forest filled with an old primordial force.
Then a fire broke out which I saw clambering ever closer.

I can remember, remember, merely remember.
My forest was dead. I whispered to strange linden trees,
And a spring gushed within me.

Now I stare into the dream, this rigid forest-phantom.
But my silence is, alas, totally unbounded.
In no forest can I find that echo-silence.

ALFRED LICHTENSTEIN

SUMMER RESORT

The sky is like a blue jellyfish.
And round about are fields, green meadow-hills —
Peaceful world, you big mouse trap,
If I could just get away from you... oh, if I had wings —

You throw dice. You booze it up. Babble on about the nations of
        tomorrow.
One and all exercise their jaws contentedly.
The earth is a rich Sunday roast,
Properly sopped in sweet solar sauce.

If only there were a wind... and it would tear apart this placid world
With iron claws. That would delight me.
If only there were a storm... it would have to shred
The beautiful blue eternal sky into a thousand pieces.

ALFRED WOLFENSTEIN

NIGHT IN THE VILLAGE

Before the tortuous darkness
My mouth groans, groans.
I, uneasily accustomed to noises,
Stare probingly in all directions:

Mountains hairy with trees
Loom in dark desolation,
And what their roads are up to
No light tells me, nor any cries.

85

But to be just slightly misled
Is what my ear wishes, wishes,
If only the buzzing of a bug
Would conjure up a car.

If only a window over there were inhabited,
But in the vaulted house
Nothing but stars and hollow moon
— I cannot take it —

I cannot take it, overpoweringly encompassing my sleep,
Alien, alien and close —
Swelled even closer by the lake,
It lies there in silence.

But do not deem me weak,
Because I — who was just this moment hating the city —
Am now fleeing the countryside —: it is only the night,
Only for you, for this night was I not prepared —

The way you, dead or a thousand times unknown,
Reach around my black bed,
Nowhere breached by a human hand,
Ungodly fear.


GEORG TRAKL

DE PROFUNDIS

There is a stubble-field on which a black rain falls.
There is a brown tree which stands there by itself.
There is a whispering wind which circles empty cottages —
How sad this evening.

Beyond the hamlet
The gentle orphan still gathers scanty ears of grain.
Her eyes graze round and golden in the twilight
And her womb awaits the heavenly bridegroom.

While returning home
The shepherds found the sweet body
Decomposed in the thornbush.

I am a shadow far from dark and gloomy villages.
God's silence
I drank from the fountain in the grove.

Cold metal appears on my brow.
Spiders seek my heart.
There is a light that goes out in my mouth.

At night I found myself on a moor,
Covered with filth and the dust of stars.
In the hazel-bushes
Crystalline angels were heard again.


GEORG TRAKL

REST AND SILENCE

Shepherds buried the sun in the bleak forest.
A fisherman hauled
The moon from a freezing pond in a hirsute net.

In blue crystal
The pale human being dwells, his cheek leaning against its stars;
Or he inclines his head in crimson slumber.

But always the black flight of birds moves
The beholder, the sacredness of blue flowers,
The nearby stillness thinks forgotten things, extinguished angels.

Again the brow grows dark in moon-pale stone;
A radiant youth
The sister appears in autumn and black decay.

## WHISPERED INTO THE AFTERNOON

Sun, autumnally thin and timorous,
And the fruit falls off the trees.
Stillness dwells in blue spaces
For a long afternoon.

Dying sounds of metal;
And a white animal collapses.
Brown girls' coarse songs
Are blown away with the falling of leaves.

Brow dreams God's colors,
Feels insanity's soft wings.
Shadows twirl around the hill,
Blackly hemmed in by decay.

Twilight replete with rest and wine;
Mournful guitars flow.
And at the soft lamp within
You stop off as in a dream.

Based on a drawing by Oskar Kokoschka · Georg Trakl

ALBERT EHRENSTEIN

DESPAIR

For weeks and weeks I have not spoken a word;
I live a lonely, barren life.
Not a star is twittering in the sky.
I would so very much like to die.

The confinement depresses my eyes,
I crawl into a corner,
I would like to be as small as a spider,
But nobody squashes me.

I have not done bad things to anyone,
I have helped every good person a little.
Good fortune, you are not destined for me.
They do not want to bury me alive.


ALBERT EHRENSTEIN

SORROW

How I am hitched
To the coal-tenders of my grief!
Repulsively, like a spider,
Does time crawl over me.
My hair is falling out,
My head is turning into a gray field,
Across which the last
Reaper is swinging his sickle.
Sleep encases my bones in darkness.
I have already died in my dreams,
Grass sprouted from my skull,
My head consisted of black earth.

ALBERT EHRENSTEIN

ON THE HARDHEARTED EARTH

I cheer the smoke of a locomotive,
I enjoy the white dance of the stars,
The hoof of a horse gleaming brightly,
I enjoy a squirrel dashing up a tree,
Or a lake of cold silver, trout in a brook,
Chattering of sparrows on a dead branch.
But neither friend nor foe blossoms for me on this earth,
On remote paths I tread through the field.

I trampled under foot the commandment
"Strive, O human being, to be joyous and to give joy to others!"

Gloomily I have been sauntering round myself,
Avoiding both the maidens and the men,
Ever since my tender blood-weeping heart
Was crushed in the dust by those I esteemed.
Never was my lonely and wretched self favored
With the love of women, to whom I was grateful for their very breath.
I, the chilly mortal, will go on living this way. For a long time to come.
On remote paths I sob through the wilderness.


GOTTFRIED BENN

THE YOUNG HEBBEL

You carve and form; the pliant chisel
in a fine soft hand.
With my brow I beat out the form
on a block of marble.
My hands create for bread.

I am still very distant from myself.
But I do want to become Me!
I am carrying someone deep in my blood
who is crying out for his self-created
divine heavens and human earths. —

My mother is such a poor woman
that you would laugh, were you to see her.
We live in a cramped shed
built at the edge of the village.
My youth seems like a scab to me:
beneath it a wound
from which blood seeps forth daily.
As a consequence I am so disfigured. —

Sleep I do not need.
Food just enough to keep me from croaking!
Unrelenting is the struggle
and the world is bristling with sword points.
Each one hungers for my heart.
Each one I, weaponless, have to
melt in my blood.


ALFRED WOLFENSTEIN

THE GODLESS YEARS

Music I do not want to make, but rather to stride
And show my strides.
Music is not produced by the firmly compacted galloping
Of armies of souls that battle
For my center.

And even if there be no ground anymore, no dream to stride,
You shall yet take note of my standing firm,
Like a mountain I will not allow myself to slide,
Still on such friendly terms with possibilities,
No fate is to rob me of my courage.

At the sharp edge of expanses sucked dry,
On nothing but my quivering pointed toes,
Grown up, seeing only my seeing,
Thrown out of the first garden and with no second
Music save my waiting —: note my standing firm.

ALBERT EHRENSTEIN

## THE WANDERER

My friends are as reeds in the wind,
On their lips their hearts sit,
Chasteness they do not know;
I would like to dance on their heads.

Girl that I love,
Soul of souls you,
Chosen one, luminously created one,
You never looked at me,
Your lap was not ready,
My heart burned to cinders.

I know the teeth of dogs,
Wind-in-your-face Street is where I live,
A sieve-roof is over my head,
Mildew has a good time on the walls,
Friendly cracks are there for the rain.

"Kill yourself!" my knife says to me.
I am lying in filth;
High above me, my enemies are riding over
The lunar rainbow in state-coaches.


KURT HEYNICKE

## RAISE YOUR HANDS

Raise your hands,
countenance,
nameless from the beginning,
over my head
which is moist from wine and laughter!

I plunge into sparkling hours,
rouse my blood into blooming women,
and sway along into singing violins —
see —
all hours are waning,

I could be young,
and my heart a summer —
but deep within me a thought sobs —
faraway
restrained weeping rises from the dark
and embraces my youth...
This is eternal:
The No.

If I had all my wishes,
my shoulders would rise in indifference,
my lips would be scorn:
I am a wanderer
and must not tarry...


FRANZ WERFEL

STRANGERS ARE WE ALL ON EARTH

Kill yourselves with vapors and with knives,
Hurl horrors, patriotic slogans,
Throw your lives away for a piece of earth!
The beloved is not yours to keep.
All lands turn to waters,
Beneath your feet localities melt away.

Let cities make themselves taller,
Ninevah, God's defier made of stones!
Alas, there is a curse in our pilgrimaging...
Fleetingly must what is firm fall down before our eyes,
What we hold can no longer be held,
And in the end we have nothing left but weeping.

Mountains are patient and plains...
Are amazed at how we shift up and down.
Every place we have moved to starts to flow.
Whoever still says "mine" to life is deceived.
Guilty are we and indebted to ourselves,
Our portion is: debt, to discharge it!

Mothers live only to disappear from us.
And the house is there only to collapse.

93

Blissful glances, only to vanish from us.
The very beat of our hearts is on loan!
Strangers are we all on earth,
And the things to which we link ourselves die.


WALTER HASENCLEVER

STEP OUT OF THE ARCHWAY, APPARITION

Step out of the archway, apparition without name!
Come, you mysterious early urges!
Return, Sunday! Sleep with me, rose
on the white dress of my first love!
And when I rode away from you on a horse
Duskily into the darkness of the sea — what was I!
A beam of light, a piece of my earth,
An adventure, colorful, scorched and happy-go-lucky.
My old house, ah, he who would experience your peace!
Oh, don't tell me that on the exotic islands
Monkeys now screech and parrots whine —
I could travel endlessly again!


WILHELM KLEMM

PHILOSOPHY

We do not know what light is
Nor what the ether and its oscillations are —
We do not understand growth
And the elective affinities of the elements.

Hidden from us is what the stars signify
And the solemn march of time.
The depths of the soul we do not comprehend
Nor the acts of folly in the course of which nations annihilate
        each other.

What coming is, what going is remain unknown to us.
We do not know what God is!
O vegetable creature in a thicket of conundrums,
Of all your marvels the greatest is hope!

AUGUST STRAMM

MELANCHOLY

Striding striving
Living longs
Shuddering standing
Glances search
Dying grows
The coming
Screams!
Deep down
Growing mute
We.


ALBERT EHRENSTEIN

PAIN

God, you old Epimethean,
Why did you bore your tooth
Into me?
Melancholy besets me still, still,
My laments resound without surcease
When I recall slowly decaying times
And the insatiable thighs
That do not want to satiate me.
Behold, things are kind and want to console me,
The trees turn green all over again,
Indefatigably the clock tells me the time,
And nightly the most wretched of creatures,
Some old bugs, pay my bed a visit,
Taking pity on my being all alone.
But what does a woman know about feelings and decency?!
Never shall I believe in muses.
My verse carries no weight,
: With a supply of humans transitorily closer to her
She bustles along.
God, never yet have I implored you,
Pride does not pray,

Now I beseech you:
Protect my heart from love,
My immortal soul
Has suffered enough.


ALBERT EHRENSTEIN

I AM TIRED OF LIFE AND DEATH

So what if big auto-bumble-bees are buzzing,
And airplanes are living in the ether,
The human being lacks a steady world-shaking strength.
He is like mucus spit on a rail.

And if the clamp around the most distant distance is loosened,
Earth-clamp that has not yet let go of us,
One day a holy world-policeman standing on the corner will direct us
To the shortest routes to the nearest nebula,
        — The most mortal of all things is remembrance,
        The goddess that wipes away the dust;
Beautiful tree-frogs grew up as she dozed
And then they died.
The raging rivers drown helplessly in the ocean.
The Sioux Indians never experienced Goethe in their war-dances,
And a mercilessly eternal Sirius never experienced the sufferings of
        Christ!

Never flashed through with feelings,
Unfeeling for one another and rigid,
There rise and set
Suns, atoms: the bodies in space.

## August Stramm

### Desperate

Above a piercing stone smashes
Night granulates glass
The times stand still
I
Stone.
Afar
You
Glaze!


## Wilhelm Klemm

### Lights

Lights burn on wax-wafting candles,
Quiet gathering of white, slender apostles,
Peaceful flames of the spirit on narrow heads,
Flames that lick softly in the breath of night.

Lights burn. Blazing sacrificial fire
In the cathedral of the night. Storm signal, what do you want to
        announce?
Conflagration, flame-horned beacon,
Oh, how your racing heart inflames me!

Lights fade. Like miners' lamps slowly
Dwindling in gloomy galleries, like last sparks
Smoldering dreamily in smoke and black ruins.
Memory whose memory fades.

Lights go out. Night and forlornness
Come bursting in. Our hearts shudder more deeply —
Blind angels travel upward in bewilderment —
Endless wing-flapping and whimpering.

KURT HEYNICKE

GETHSEMANE

All human beings are the Savior.
In the dark garden we drink the cup.
Father, let it not pass.
We are all of one love.
We are all deep sorrow.
All want to redeem themselves.
Father, your world is our cross.
Let it not pass.

Based on a drawing by Adolph de Haer · Kurt Heynicke

## ALBERT EHRENSTEIN

### INESCAPABLE

Who knows if
Living is not dying,
Breath strangulation,
Sun the night?
From the oaks of the gods
The fruits fall
Through pigs to become faeces,
Out of which the scents
Of roses rise
In an appalling cycle,
Corpse is embryo,
And embryo is pestilence.


## GEORG HEYM

### WAR
### (1911)

Risen is he who was long asleep,
Risen from the vaults deep down below.
In the twilight he stands, huge and unknown,
And the moon he crushes in his black hand.

Into the evening noise of the cities it falls far and wide,
Frost and shadow of an alien darkness.
And the marketplaces' round whirl coagulates into ice.
It grows still. They look round. And no one knows.

In the streets something touches their shoulders lightly.
A question. No answer. A face goes pale.
In the distance a peal of bells quivers thinly,
And the beards quiver round their pointed chins.

On the mountains he is already starting to dance,
And he cries out: All you warriors, up and at them!
And there is a resonance when he turns his black head,
Round which hangs a noisy chain of a thousand skulls.

Like a tower he stamps out the last glow,
Where the day is fleeing, the streams are already filled with blood.
Countless, the corpses are already laid out in the reeds,
Covered in white with death's strong birds.

Across country into the night he chases the fire,
A red hound with the screaming of wild mouths.
Out of the darkness the night's black world leaps,
Its rim lit up frightfully by volcanoes.

And the dark plains are strewn far and wide
With the flickering of a thousand tall pointed caps,
And everything in flight on the teeming roads below
He shoves into the fire-forests, where the flame roars along.

And the flames burn and devour forest after forest,
Yellow bats clawing jaggedly at the leaves,
Like a charcoal-burner he strikes his poker
Into the trees so that the fire will roar properly.

A large city was swallowed up in yellow smoke,
Hurled itself mutely into the abyss's belly.
But gigantic over glowing ruins he stands
Who thrice brandishes his torch at the wild heavens

Above the storm-torn cloud's reflection,
In the dead darkness's cold wastelands,
So that with his conflagration he can wither the night far and wide,
Drop pitch and fire down on Gomorrah.


ERNST STADLER

SETTING OUT

Once before fanfares rent my impatient heart till it bled,
So that, rearing like a horse, it furiously bit at its bridle.
At that time marching drums beat the attack on all roads,

And the most glorious music on earth for us was the hail of bullets.
Then, suddenly, life stood still. Roads led between old trees.
Chambers enticed. It was sweet to tarry and to stay too long,
To unchain the body from reality as though from rusty armor,
To nestle voluptuously in the down of soft dream-hours.
But one morning the echo of bugle calls rolled through the misty air,
Whistling hard, sharp, like the stroke of a sabre. It was as if lights suddenly
    shone out in the darkness.
It was as if trumpet blasts blared through the bivouac dawn,
And the sleeping troopers jumped up and struck the tents and harnessed the
    horses.
I was locked into a column that charged out into the morning, fire over helmet
    and stirrup,
Forward, the battle in eye and blood, with reins held out.
Maybe in the evening victory marches would sound round us,
Maybe we would be lying somewhere stretched out among dead bodies.
But before being snatched away and swallowed up
Our eyes would glowingly drink their fill of world and sun.


WALTER HASENCLEVER

THE CAMPFIRES ON THE COAST
May 1914

The campfires on the coast are smoking.
I have to hurl myself down in deep torment.
Leopards scent my face and hiss.
You are close to me, brother, death.
Muddled, Europe is still twitching in the wind
Of ships on the fabulous ocean;
Through the enormous fear there breaks forth
The scream of a mother for her little child.
My horse died tonight in my hand.
How you have abandoned me, creature!
From the cadaver the alien land rises
Up to another sundial.

ALBERT EHRENSTEIN

THE NIGHT-PRISONERS
(Written on June 29, 1914)

When I was totally annihilated.
Before night and hell and plague and earth
Passed away in the darkly raging expanse,
Things seemed
To pour comfort over my grief.
The light came,
Silver sea gulls soaring in the clear sky,
And the hills of the sun, wooded ore,
The lakes and ponds of the grassland,
Roads into lovely country
And ruins decaying in the evening.

Hands over my eyes, I warded off, retreating:

"The black snail of death crept
Across my path. I too once smelled
White-scented clover and loved the clouds suffused with light.
I took delight in the singing of the wheels
Of the long-axled wagons,
I took delight in the monotonously swaying poplars along the way,
I took delight in the rails restlessly gliding past
And reflashing the sun.
I took delight in the dust-white brooks
Of my country roads.

But I saw the night-prisoners:
The scouts of the Evil One contemplating dark things.
But I saw simple farmers,
Brightly colored scarecrows in the field,
Gaze in wonder at the express train
That strews soot and ashes over their green acres,
But I saw the last monkeys of Europe freeze and expire on Gibraltar,
But I saw Indian dancers, gifted with the gait of gazelles,
Dancing before the champagne and scum
Of monocled youths,
But I saw elephants that can break through jungle reeds
Bending down for the crumbs of a child,
But I saw dreadnoughts drown,
Swarmed round by killer torpedo-sharks,

But I saw — and tears streamed down from the day —
But I saw poor soldiers on a Sunday of liberty
Crouch rigidly on scaffolding
As a signal for high-sailing fliers,
But I saw a kestrel,
Used to grazing in the ether,
Burrowing into the sand of a Breslau cage,
— And I have to escape from the sweat of these nocturnal days!
I am not one of the corpses washed round by dreams,
In the thick of sleep.
When sultriness oozes down from the veiled atmosphere,
When treetops groan into each other, tempest-tormented,
When the godhead's dragon
Comes rolling through the heavens,
I no longer want the bitter wetness of thunderstorms,
The acid of clouds,
I want the flash of lightning into me!"

The heavy angel of death grew before me:
"At last you remember me,
You loved me in days gone by.
Wooing keenest pleasure.
So become what you are,
On this earth that feeds on you!"

The grinder's hands reached into my dust,
Swirling away I, torn loose, disappeared
Into the newly greening foliage.


FRANZ WERFEL

WAR

On a storm of false words,
Your head bedecked with empty thunder,
Sleepless from lies,
Girded with deeds that only do themselves,
Boasting of sacrifices,
Disagreeably abominable for the heavens —
Thus do you voyage,
Age,
Into the noisy dream

That with frightful hands God
Tears from his sleep
And discards.

Scornfully, pitilessly,
Mercilessly do the walls of the world tower up!
And your trumpets
And dreary drums,
And the frenzy of your marches,
And the brood of your horror
Surge childishly and tonelessly
Against the relentless blue
That smites the armor
Around the eternal heart,
Boldly and easily encompassing it.
Benignly in the terrible evening
Were shipwrecked men rescued.
The child placed his little gold chain
In the dead bird's grave,
The eternal, unknowing,
The heroic deed of the mother, it is still stirring.
The holy one, the man,
He sacrificed himself with exultation and shed himself.
The wise one, storming, powerful,
Behold,
Recognized himself in the enemy and kissed him.
Then the heavens broke loose
And could not contain themselves in their wonderment,
And were thrown into confusion.
And onto the roofs of human beings,
Enthusiastic, golden, soaring,
The godhead's formation of eagles
Flew down.

At any little act of kindness
God's eyes fill with tears,
And any little act of love
Rolls through the universe.

But woe to you,
Tramping age!
Woe to the miserable thunderstorm
Of vain talk!
Essence is untouched by your cavalry charge,

And by the disintegrating mountains,
The panting roads,
And the deaths, thousandfold, incidental, worthless.
And your truth is
Not the dragon's roar,
Not the garrulous community's
Venomous, vain right!
Your truth alone,
The foolishness and its harm,
The wound's edge and the failing heart,
The thirst and the slimy drinking trough,
Bared teeth,
And the brave fury
Of the malicious monster.
The poor letter from home,
The running-through-the-streets
Of a mother, who wisely
Does not comprehend all that.

Now that we have let go of everything
And have flung away our hereafter,
And have given ourselves over
To misery, possessed by curses...
Who knows about us,
Who about the infinite angel
That above our nights
Between the fingers of his hands
Sorely sheds those enormous tears,
Weightless, unbearable, dropping down?!
                    Written on August 4, 1914


ALBERT EHRENSTEIN

THE GOD OF WAR

A stream ripples serenely,
At eventide the field bleeds,
But stretching up my wildly overgrown bestial head,
Enemy of humankind,
I, Ares,
Cracking weak chins and noses,
Wringing church towers from sheer rage,

Smash to bits your earth.
Desist from calling the God who does not hear.
This you will not be able to question:
A little sub-devil is ruler of the earth,
Folly and madness serve him.
I stretched the hides of humans on stakes around the cities.
I who loaded the loose-hinged gates of old fortresses
On my demon shoulders,
I pour out the arid time of war,
Stick Europe in my war-sack.
Your blood blossoms red
Round my butcher's arm,
How I enjoy the sight!
The enemy flames up
In the rain-bitter night,
Shells hack your women to pieces,
Over the ground
Are strewn the testicles
Of your sons
Like the seeds of cucumbers.
Not to be averted by your child-hands
Death touches your masses.
You give blood for muck,
Riches for want,
Already the wolves are throwing up
After my feasts,
Your rotten carcasses must overfatten them.
Is something left over
After dysentery and plague?
The desire howls out inside me
To finish you off totally.


KURT HEYNICKE

THE IMAGE

World,
how you stumble!
Past my extended hand,
colorful and blood-infested,
world!

A cry plunges from midnight toward midnight,
a cry, O world,
your cry!

Your mothers' cry,
your children's cry —
armies vacillate by the red wall,
smoking and groaning, the golden land sinks,
armies vacillate and rise and go —
eternally armies,
armies of warriors,
armies of mothers,
armies of humans!

Stumbling, falling, breeding and standing!
Hands fight and bleed and plead,
hands, bodies and faces
yellow in the poisonous light of days
crash, O world!

I do not want to stand by the walls!
O my brothers!
I want to perish!


ALBERT EHRENSTEIN

THE BERSERKER SCREAMS

The world I would like to tear to shreds,
Burn it to ashes piece by piece
With my frame of mind, fervid as life
And strong as death.

I have possessed land,
And sea too, how much!
I have devoured humans,
And know no goal.

And new sinews grow,
And new strength rages.
Forward with a thousand axles,
Before the plague robs me of West and East!

WILHELM KLEMM

BATTLE AT THE MARNE

Slowly the stones begin to stir and to talk.
The grasses harden into green metal. The woods,
Low, dense ambuscades, devour distant columns.
The sky, that chalk-white mystery, threatens to burst.
Two colossal hours dwindle into minutes.
The empty horizon bellies out and up.

My heart is as big as Germany and France together,
Pierced by all projectiles of the world.
The battery raises its lion's voice
Out over the land six times. The shells howl.
Stillness. In the distance the fire of the infantry seethes,
For days, for weeks.

AUGUST STRAMM

GUARD DUTY

A star startles the tower cross
The nag gasps smoke
Iron clanks drowsily
Mist brushing past
Shudders
Gazing shivering
Shivering
Stroking
Whispering
You!

AUGUST STRAMM

PATROL

The stones are hostile
Window grins treachery
Branches strangle
Mountains bushes leaf swishy
Shriek
Death.

AUGUST STRAMM

ASSAULT

From all corners fears urgencies shriek
Screeching
Life
Whips
On
Before
Itself
Gasping death
The heavens shred
Blindly the horror butchers about wildly.


ALFRED LICHTENSTEIN

THE BATTLE OF SAARBURG

The earth goes moldy in the mist.
The evening weighs down like lead.
Electrical cracking tears about
And whimpering everything breaks in two.

Like old wretched rags the villages
Smoke on the horizon.
I lie God-forsaken
In the rattling fire trenches.

Many little hostile copper birds
Whiz round heart and brain.
I brace myself upright into the grayness
And face the murdering.

Max Oppenheimer · Alfred Lichtenstein

ALBERT EHRENSTEIN

## THE POET AND THE WAR

I sang the songs of a vengeance that slashes red,
And I sang the stillness of a lake surrounded by a cove of
    woods;
But no one joined me,
Erect, alone
Like the cicada that sings itself,
I sang my song for myself.
Already my tiring footsteps are fading
In the sands of toil.
My eyes are dropping out from sleepiness,
I am weary of the bleak fords,
Of the crossing of streams, girls, and streets.
At the abyss I do not think of
The shield and the spear.
Fanned by birch trees,
Shaded by the wind,
I fall asleep to the sound of the harp
Of others
For whom it purls joyfully.
I do not stir,
For all thoughts and actions
Cloud the purity of the world.


PAUL ZECH

## MUSIC OF THE STARS

You in the caves of dejection, facing the wires
of hostility, exposed to every blow —:
listen to how in the shell-mown
treetops music of the stars is swelling;

how with the increasing darkness
of the horizon and the din
from battlement flanks of other earths
God is constructing an organ house.

And when at last you raise your dusky eyebrows,
smash to pieces shield and sword,

then that uniform, gray with age,
drops off you. You stiffen yourself, unburdened

by the happenings of the day,
at the edge of the trenches like a tree.
Your very being, travel-shy but a few hours ago,
now branches out into space.

You are now silver mesh in the floral array
made of star and wind and leaf,
are curtain of a gateway
that has no exit.

You are caught
and somewhere in the light
have dissolved without a trace.
You do not sense your own self.

You but sense that notes and only notes
are being strung around you, until the chain sounds,
that the psalm of light sings your praises
and those of the brother-army of the dead,

from voice of forest and voice of stars
the great fugue of the Creator thunders,
around which the barracks of the world
whiz as a dead new moon.

In the end God alone is the
palpitating pulse in the universe...
Far over wind and waters his
Primeval eternalness hammers like wings of metal.

## THE HOMELAND OF THE DEAD

### I

The winter morning dawns late.
Its yellow turban rises over the horizon
Through thin poplars that swiftly
Stretch a black band across its brow.

The reed of the lakes whistles. The wind's path
Churned it up at the light's first glare.
The north storm stands in the field like a soldier
And loudly beats a roll on its drumhead.

A skeletal arm swings a bell loudly.
Down the road comes death, the coarse boatman.
Around his yellow horse-teeth
The white beard's scanty tangle gathers.

An old woman with a large belly
Who is carrying the little corpse of a child.
Like a rubber hose it sucks her breast
That thumps against her without milk and flaccidly.

Several beheaded men, whom he culled
From their chains in the darkness of a cold stone cell.
Their heads in their arms. The morning light in the ice
That glaciated their necks with red glass.

Through the clear morning and the winter day
With its blueness, where like the rose-scent
Of yellow roses the sun sways
In the dreamy air above field and grove.

The golden day's bridge stretches far
And resounds with the sound of a huge lyre,
In their mourning garb the poplars rustle
Down the road, where far off the evening

113

Is already flooding the land with silvery brooks,
And the distant expanse is burning boundlessly.
The twilight rises alongside the procession
Like a dark fire that races toward the heavens.

A grove for the dead, and laurels, tree beside tree,
Like green flames that the wind fans,
They flare immensely into the firmament,
Where a pale star is already flapping its wings.

Like huge geese the gaggle of vampires
Sits on the column shaft and freezes in the frost.
They test the strength of their iron claws
And their beaks on the crosses' rust.

The ivy greets the dead at the gate,
The colorful wreaths beckon from the wall.
Death unlocks. They step forward shyly,
Turning their heads in their hands in embarrassment.

Death steps up to a grave and blows into it.
Skulls fly out of the earth's bowels
Like huge clouds from the coffins,
Skulls enveloped in beards of green moss.

An old skull flutters out of the tomb,
Vibrant with a fiery-red head of hair
That the wind high up in the air
Loops into a fiery necktie round its chin.

Out of a black mouth the empty grave smiles
At them in a friendly way. The corpses faint
And fall into the wide-open maw.
The grave's slab mutely locks them in.

## II

Eyelids caked with ice, ears stuffed up
With the dust of years, you rest your time away.
Only now and then are you still summoned by a dream that
        knocks
At your dead eternity from faraway,

In a heaven as pale as snow
And quite petrified with the train of years.
On your collapsed tombstone
There will be a lily that mourns for you.

The March night's storm will bedew your sleep.
The huge moon that steams in the East
Will gaze deep into your empty eyes,
In which a huge white worm wiggles.

Thus do you keep on sleeping, rocked by the soft flute sound
Of forlornness, in the slow death of the world;
As over you a large bird flies
In black flight into the yellow sunset.


FRANZ WERFEL

THE RIDE

As my dream impelled me,
I found myself, on a most beautiful afternoon, wandering
Down the hill, which was hovering and flapping its wings.
At my feet lay
The land in golden finery,
The land in rustling swathes of ripened crops.

I came as if set free from dire distress,
Like someone who has discarded the shirt of illness
And can carry himself more breezily and adroitly
Than before; — in pore and vein enthusiasm
Pounds the thin blood that does not subjugate him.

And so I walked serenely
Into the valley of harvests that was swelling with grain and sun.
Ears of grain heavy and full swayed about chest and hip,
They nearly overgrew my hasty ridge.
But the dream was easy on my soles,
I barely saw the many flighting birds overhead.

Here the birds no doubt had a meaning...
And suddenly the earth was heavy on my soles, as heavy
As though a mighty metal were at work from below;

My knee, my pulse, they faltered forth and back.
I spoke to myself: if magnetic metal is rooting my steps to the spot,
Why do these birds fly beneath the universe, screeching, chattering?...

But this I saw: everywhere
The harvest lay squashed and crushed,
As though devastated by a torrent of rain, a shower of hail. —
And in the gold of the receding day
All about me in the grain I saw many dead men stretched out,
They had on their Sunday best, but their heads were already covered with
     black spots.

— They have been lying here a long time —
I thought and closed my eyes. But as though through a crack
I saw the many black heads, saw many a gleaming set of teeth,
On distended vests many a shiny silver chain:
These neither thieves have snatched away nor the big magpies —
So I said — the magpies that screech so loudly above this region.

I could not shake the spell
From my shoulders. No matter how hard I struggled, I had to look...
The roots of my eyebrows froze and stung me.
The dead lay stiff in the late light.
My body felt like a cumbersome sack.
But suddenly it was as though I were riding, as though someone were
     carrying me piggy-back.

Someone was carrying me piggy-back,
My thighs were firmly pressing a pair of brittle shoulders.
A shock of colorless hair fluttered in front of me.
Only now and then a countenance, black as lacquer,
Turned toward me with effort and asked: Was I riding comfortably...
The dead man who carried me, he was grinning wryly, like a good-natured
     servant.

On him I rode and rode.
He was as fleet of foot as the rare racehorse
That does not snort or pant.
But suddenly his step became unsteady and much slower.
He stopped and turned his wretchedly corroded countenance toward me...
But to me it seemed as though my own image, rotting away, appeared in a
     mirror.

He flapped his mouth
And spoke: "You my brother, it is sufficient,
Sufficient that God felled and struck me dead for you.
I took your lot upon me. You, though, are healthy.
But tell me now: is this arrangement just,
That you are my rider and master — and I your horse and servant?

Climb down from your saddle right away,
Free my neck from your thighs!
I know, good brother, it is all the same to you.
Your eyes are moist from pity, your heart is soft.
Am I not rotting for you, blackened by worms, bleached by winds?
Please! You carry me part of the way! I am so light, so light."

But I let out a powerful laugh
And spurred his body with my shoe.
"I'm not getting down. Go faster! Giddap! Go faster!
And no matter how much you may mirror for me my own form,
And even though my own face may crumble away in your countenance,
I am your rider, dead brother, and I won't let you go!

I understood deeply
That I was plunging to the depths of anxiety! It chokes,
This fear that is never a guarantor of grace.
From now on I feel a hand on my throat eternally.
I ride because I am being ridden! Wildly aware of this never-ending distress,
I am its master and the rider even of my own death!"

And laughing I tore a switch
From the hazel-bush, and I hit
The dead man's flanks lightly. He heaved a sigh and carried
My weight, mulishly at first, but then at a sharp trot,
And was finally willing to obey my serene power.
So I rode into the evening and forest encircled us.

And this forest — it was
The harp of my life stretched across the sunset.
And I gripped the reins with my big hands,
And named the triumph and named the danger!
The dead man's step whispered, gently the oaks whispered too,
But I rode my death and sang the rapture of this ride.

## MAN AND WOMAN WALK THROUGH THE CANCER WARD

The man:
This row here is decayed wombs
and this row is decayed breast.
Bed stinks next to bed. The nurses change hourly.

Come, just lift this blanket.
Look at this lump of fat and putrid fluids,
this was once important to some man
and was also called ecstasy and home. —

Come look at this scar on the breast.
Do you feel the rosary of soft knots?
Go ahead and feel, The flesh is soft and doesn't hurt. —

This one here is bleeding as though from thirty bodies.
Nobody has this much blood. —
As for this one here, they first had to cut
a child from her cancerous womb. —

They let them sleep. Day and night. — To the new ones
they say: here you will sleep yourself back to health. — Only on Sundays
for the visitors do they let them be somewhat more awake. —

They still eat but not much. Their backs
are sore. You see the flies. Sometimes
the nurses wash them. The way benches are washed. —

Here the graveyard swells around each bed.
Flesh is made level with the soil. Glow is expended.
Fluid gets ready to flow. Earth beckons. —

GEORG HEYM

THE MORGUE

The attendants creep softly on their soles
Where through the sheets there is a white glittering of skulls.
We who are dead gather for the final journey
Through deserts wide and sea and winter wind.

We are enthroned high up on bare catafalques,
Hideously covered with black rags.
The plaster falls. And from the ceiling's beam
A Christ stretches large hands toward us.

Our time is over. It is consummated.
We are finished. See, we are now dead.
The night already dwells in our white eyes,
Never again will we look upon a sunrise.

Step back from our majesty.
Do not touch us who already behold in the broad winter
The land before which stands a shadow
Whose black shoulder towers in the graying twilight.

You who are shrunken like dwarfs,
You who lie shriveled on our laps,
We grew over you like broad mountains
Into eternal death-night, like great gods.

We are ludicrously fenced about with candles,
We who were dragged from dark corners early in the morning
Still grunting, our breasts already stained blue,
Breasts that the bird of the dead flew over at night.

We kings who were cut down from trees,
From the whirring air in the bird-kingdom,
And many a one who already glided through tall reeds,
A white animal, with eyes round and soft.

Rejected by autumn. Rotten fruit of the years,
Dissolving into the gutters' hole in summer,

We, over whose bald heads
The white spider of the July heat slowly crawled.

Are we resting in the mute tower, forgotten?
Will we be a wave of Lethean waters?
Or will the storm drive us around wintry chimneys,
Riding like jackdaws on the fire's glow?

Will we be flowers? Will we become birds,
In the pride of the blue skies, in the anger of the wide seas?
Will we wander deep in the earth,
Moles mute in dead solitude?

Will we dwell in the ringlets of the morning,
Will we blossom in the tree and slumber in the fruit,
Or as blue dragonflies on the sea anemones
Quiver in a bay of silent waters at noon?

Will we be like a word heard by nobody?
Or a whiff of smoke that flutters in the evening sky?
Or a sobbing that suddenly disturbs happy people?
Or a candle in the night? Or a dream?

Or — will nobody come?
And will we slowly decompose
In the laughter of the moon
That dashes high above the clouds,

Crumble away to nothing,
— So that some day a child
Can squeeze and crush our greatness
In its paltry fist?[1]

We nameless, poor unknowns,
We died alone in empty cellars.
Why do you call us when our light has burned out,
Why do you disturb our happy gathering?

See the one over there out of whose decomposed mouth
Gray laughter merrily bursts,

---

[1] Translators' note: in the original edition of *Menschheitsdämmerung* this and the
previous stanza are a single strophe.

Who arches his long tongue over his chest,
He is laughing at you, this huge pelican.

He will bite you. For many weeks
He was a guest of the fish. Do smell how he reeks.
See, a snail has made its home in his hair,
It is waving its little horn at you in mockery.

— A little bell — . And they move out.
The darkness creeps in on black hands.
We rest alone in the vast house,
Countless coffins stacked against high walls.

Why does he not come? We have on cloths
And shoes for the dead. And we are fed.
Where is the prince who walks ahead of us,
Whose big flag leads the procession?

Where will his loud voice drift for us?
Into what twilight does our flight take us?
To face forsaken and in loneliness
The scorn and deceit of what empty heavens?

Eternal stillness. And life's residue
Erodes and decomposes in black air.
The wind of death that leaves our door,
Its dark lungs filled with the dust of the grave,

It breathes out heavily where the rain swooshes down,
Monotonous, faraway, music in our ears
That darkly listen into the night to the storm
That calls sadly and sonorously in the house.

And decay's blue glow of glory
Ignites on our countenances.
A rat hops about on bare toe-bones,
Just come, we will not disturb your hunger.

We moved out, girded like giants,
Each of us clashed like a Goliath.
Now we have the mice for companions,
And our flesh has become the scrawny maggots' path.

We Icarians who on white pinions
Once raced in the storm's blue light,
We still heard the huge towers' singing
As we zoomed backwards into black death.

On the faraway plane of lost celestial realms,
Over the wide seas where faraway the waves flew,
We flew proudly in the sunset's conflagration
With huge sails that storm and weather bent.

What did we find in the gleaming of the celestial limits?
An empty nothing. Now our bones dangle,
The way a beggar by the side of the road
Makes a penny flap in his empty hands.

Why is the lord still waiting? The house is full,
The chambers round the caravansary,
The marketplace of the dead that resounded with the noise of
        bones
Like the blaring of cornets into the wilderness.


ALBERT EHRENSTEIN

JULIAN

Sun, golden discus of the titan Helios!
Helios, you who, wading knee-deep in the gray universe,
Hurls the golden disk!
Did I not climb up the mast of prayer
Toward the distant sky,
Did I not weep, and were my tears
Not obedient to you?
In sacrifice I shed my blood,
This inconsolable reddish-sobbing poppy.
Light: in prayer I gazed at you
Until in the sun's yellow web my eyes died.
Now no silver point sinks from the night,
Flutter-light of no star.
From a rotted, topless, soil-poor trunk
A branch stretches me out
On decayed, dew-freezing bark:
The bare wood's last, autumn-lost leaf.

122

GEORG TRAKL

## TO ELIS THE BOY

Elis, when the blackbird calls in the black forest,
This is your decline.
Your lips drink the coolness of the blue rock-spring.

Forgo, when your brow bleeds quietly,
Ancient legends
And the dark interpretation of birds in flight.

But with soft steps you walk into the night
That hangs full with purple grapes,
And you move your arms more beautifully in the blueness.

A thornbush sounds
Where your moon eyes are.
Oh, how long, Elis, since you passed away.

Your body is a hyacinth,
Into which a monk dips his waxen fingers.
Our silence is a black cave,

From which at times a gentle animal emerges
And slowly lowers its heavy eyelids.
Upon your temples black dew drips,

The last gold of expired stars.


GEORG TRAKL

## ELIS

### 1

Complete is the stillness of the golden day.
Beneath old oak trees
You appear, Elis, someone peaceful with round eyes.

Their blueness mirrors the repose of lovers.
At your mouth
Their rosy sighs became silent.

In the evening the fisherman hauled in his heavy nets.
A good shepherd
Leads his flock along the forest's edge.
Oh! how right, Elis, are all your days.

Along the bare walls
The olive tree's blue stillness sinks quietly,
An old man's dark song dies away.

A golden boat
Rocks your heart, Elis, against a lonely sky.

2

Soft chimes sound in Elis' breast
In the evening,
When his head sinks into black pillows.

A blue deer
Bleeds quietly in the thornbushes.

A brown tree stands there, lifeless;
Its blue fruits have dropped from it.

Signs and stars
Quietly sink out of sight in the evening pond.

Behind the hill winter has arrived.

At night
Blue doves drink the icy sweat
That trickles from Elis' crystal brow.

Always there is the sound
Of God's lonely wind along black walls.

ELSE LASKER-SCHÜLER

SENNA HOY

Ever since you were buried on the hill
The earth is sweet.

Wherever I now go on tip-toe,
I walk over pure paths.

Oh, your blood's roses
Gently saturate death.

I no longer have any fear
Of dying.

On your grave I am already blooming
With the flowers of the climbing plants.

Your lips have always called me,
Now my name no longer knows the way back.

Every shovelful of earth that covered you[1]
Also buried me.

Therefore it is always night around me,
And stars are already in the twilight.

And I am incomprehensible to our friends
And have become a total stranger.

But you are standing by the gate of the most quiet city
And are waiting for me, you great-angel.

---

[1]Translators' note: *Menschheitsdammerung* has "ich" ("I"), a misprinting of "dich" ("you").

ELSE LASKER-SCHÜLER

MY MOTHER

Was she the great angel
Who walked beside me?

Or does my mother lie buried
Beneath the sky of smoke —
Nothing will ever bloom blue over her death.

If only my eyes could shine brightly
And bring her light.

If my smile were not swallowed up in my countenance,
I would hang it over her grave.

But I know a star
On which it is always day.
I want to carry it over her earth.

Now I will always be completely alone
Like the great angel
Who walked beside me.


JAKOB VAN HODDIS

THE ANGEL OF DEATH

I

To the roll of drums the wedding procession marches,
In a silken sedan the bride is borne,
Through red clouds the flight of white steeds
That impatiently gnaw golden bridles.

The angel of death waits in heavenly halls
As the wild suitor of this tender bride.
And his wild dark hair falls down
Over his brow, on which the morning dawns.

126

Eyes wide-open and glowing with pity,
Staring at new delights as though in despair,
A terrible hope that never dried up,
A dream of days that he never knew.

## II

He comes out of a cave where as his lover
A boy embraced him with wondrous tenderness.
He flew through his dream as a butterfly
And let him see oceans as the bridegroom's morning-after gift.

And the skies of India, where on feverish days
The hoary ocean races into yellow bays.
The temples where the priests strike their cymbals,
Dancing around hearths where a maiden is burning.

She is but softly sobbing, for the singing of the multitude
Shows her the idol that thrones on clouds.
And wears skulls as thigh rings,
And recompenses for the torment of the flames with black kisses.

Intoxicated beings dance naked between swords,
And one of them stabs himself in the chest and falls.
And while the thighs are in bloody motion,
The boy sees temple, dream, and world sink away.

## III

Then he flew over to an old man
And approached his bed as a green parrot.
And caws the song: "O shameful Susanna!"
That long forgotten litany of youth.

The old man stares at him. From eyes glassy-dull
A spark still flashes. A last malicious smile
Twitches round his toothless mouth. The room's bleakness
Is abruptly shaken by a loud death rattle.

## IV

The bride is freezing quietly under her light dress.
The angel says nothing. The air moves as though sick.
He falls on his knees. Now both tremble.
From the ray of love that broke through the heavens.

Trumpet-blare and dark thunder laugh.
A veil flew over the aurora.
As she in her tender and delicate movement
Offered him her mouth to kiss.

Ludwig Meidner · Jakob van Hoddis

GEORG HEYM

OPHELIA

I

In her hair a nest of young water rats,
And the ringed hands on the river
Like fins, thus does she drift through the shadow
Of the great primeval forest that rests in the waters.

The last sun that strays in the dark
Immerses itself deep in the casket of her brain.
Why she died? Why she drifts so very much alone
In the waters that tangle fern and weed?

There is a wind in the dense reeds. Like a hand
It shoos the bats.
With dark wings moist from the waters
They are like smoke on the water's dark course,

Like night clouds. A long, white eel
Glides over her breasts. A glowworm shines
On her brow. And a willow weeps
Its foliage down upon her and her mute misery.

II

Grain. Green crops. And the midday's red sweat.
The field's yellow winds sleep quietly.
She comes, a bird that wants to fall asleep.
The swan's pinions roof her in white.

Her blue eyelids softly throw a shadow down.
And as she hears the scythes' shining melodies
She dreams the eternal dream
Of a kiss's crimson in her eternal grave.

Drifting past, drifting past. Where on the banks
The noise of cities booms. Where through embankments
The white stream forces its way. The reverberation rings out
With a vast re-echoing. Where the sound of crowded streets

Comes echoing down. Bells and ringing.
Screeching of machines. Struggle. Where from the West
Clouded panes are menaced by the setting sun's dull red,
In which a crane with gigantic arms threatens,

A mighty tyrant, with black brow,
A Moloch round whom the black servants kneel.
Burden of heavy bridges that cross over
Like chains on the stream, and harsh proscription.

Invisibly she floats in the river's entourage,
But where she drifts, the human throng is startled
Far and wide by a dark grief with huge pinions
That throws its shadow broadly over the banks.

Drifting past. Drifting past. When to the darkness
The westerly high day of late summer sacrifices itself.
Where in the dark green of the meadows stands
The distant evening's tender tiredness.

She who is submersed is carried far away by the stream,
Through many a winter's doleful port.
Down through time. Away through eternities
That make the horizon smoke like fire.


ALBERT EHRENSTEIN

THE ETERNAL SLEEP

I was the silver-shanked cup-bearer
And served the wine that transports us out of this world.
Have I already whirled away from the joyous dance of the times,
Has delight already turned about and changed
To sorrow?

Revolving, the rich year lies
At my sandals,
But I must walk, hounded and sore,
Across fields of stubble on bare feet.

In the flowing of the water I see the thirst,
In the shining of the sun night without stars.

Pleasure lost me my whole body,
Horae were turned into Cereses.
Forests of remembrance, so deadly silent,
Came and toad-calls.

What do you women want, poor and naked,
Pain, love-wrinkles around your young eyes?
I have no use for your light landscape,
The wind-swayed slumber-grass.
I hear your hair turning gray!

I? Who am I?
I am a block of time
That crumbles away and falls back into the sea.
I am a whimper-wind that clouds puddles,
I am the lightning that vanishes as it flashes,
I am the snow that comes and melts away,
I am the wake of the oar as it loses itself in the pond,
I am the seed in the womb of a whore!

So you too, forgo the royal gesture,
You are good old death,
I am a little heap of earth.
Oh, come soon and blend me,
Earth into the earth.

FRANZ WERFEL

DRINKING SONG

We are like drinkers,
Bent calmly over our murder.
In shadowy evasion
We totter drowsily.
What sort of secret here?
What is knocking from below?
Nothing, no secret here,
Nothing is knocking here.

Let us live!
So that we can draw strength from ultimate vanity
That gets us very drunk and muzzy!
Leave us the fine lie,
The home that takes good care of us!
How we live?
We don't know...
But we utter to and fro
A word that slips from the tongue.

We do not want to see the arms
That rise from the black river at night.

Are deep woods within us,
Belltower over treetops?
Away, away!
We live back and forth.
Hand us the flagon full of black sleep!
Let us just live,
And let us drink, drink!

But if all of you were to keep watch!
If I were to keep watch over my murder!
How my feet would flee!
I would not be here under the elm trees.
I would be in no place.
The trees would turn brown,
The rocks would stand like hangmen!
Into every fire I would hurl myself,
To burn up more painfully!

We are drinkers over our murder.
Words tuck us in warmly.
Dusk and gazing into the lamp!
Is there no secret here?
No, nothing here!
Then come and sing, all of you!
And you women with the castanets, dancers!
Join us! We know nothing.
We want to fight and play.
Let us drink, just drink!

GEORG TRAKL

HELIAN

In the solitary hours of the spirit
It is beautiful to walk in the sun
Along the yellow walls of summer.
The footsteps ring faintly in the grass; yet always
The son of Pan sleeps in the gray marble.

Evenings on the terrace we got drunk on brown wine.
The peach glows reddish in the foliage;
Soft sonata, joyful laughter.

Beautiful is the quiet of the night.
On a dark plain
We encounter shepherds and white stars.

When it has become autumn,
The grove appears in sober clearness.
Soothed we stroll along red walls
And the round eyes follow the flight of the birds.
In the evening the white water sinks into funeral urns.

In bare branches the sky celebrates.
In pure hands the farmer carries bread and wine
And the fruits ripen peacefully in a sunny pantry.

Oh, how earnest is the countenance of the cherished dead.
But righteous contemplation gladdens the soul.

Powerful is the silence of the devastated garden,
When the young novice wreathes his brow with brown foliage,
And his breath drinks icy gold.

The hands touch the age of bluish waters
Or on a cold night the white cheeks of the sisters.

Hushed and harmonious is a walk past friendly rooms,
Where there is solitude and the rustling of the maple,
Where perhaps the thrush still sings.

Beautiful is the human being and luminous in the darkness,
When in astonishment he moves arms and legs,
And in crimson sockets his eyes roll calmly.

At vespers the stranger fades into the black destruction of November,
Beneath rotten branches, along leprous walls,
Where earlier the holy brother walked,
Immersed in the soft string music of his madness.

Oh, how solitary is the end of the evening wind.
Dying the head bows down in the darkness of the olive tree.

Shocking is the decline of the generations.
In this hour the eyes of the gazer fill
With the gold of his stars.

In the evening chimes sink that will sound no more,
Decayed the black walls in the plaza,
The dead soldier summons to prayer.

A pale angel
The son enters the empty house of his fathers.

The sisters went far away to white old men.
At night the sleeper found them beneath the columns,
Returned from sad pilgrimages.

Oh, how their hair bristles with filth and worms
When he stands therein on silver feet,
And deceased they emerge from bare rooms.

O you psalms in fiery midnight rains,
When the servants flailed the soft eyes with nettles,
The childlike fruits of the elder
Bend in astonishment over an empty grave.

Yellowed moons roll quietly
Above the fever-linens of the youth
Before he follows the dead silence of the winter.

A sublime destiny broods down the Kedron ravine,
Where the cedar, a tender creature,
Unfolds beneath the blue eyebrows of the father,
Across the pasture a shepherd leads his flock at night.
Or there are screams during sleep,
When a brazen angel confronts the human being in the grove,
The flesh of the holy one melts away on a red-hot grate.

Around the mud huts the crimson vine entwines itself,
Resonant sheaves of yellowed grain,
The humming of bees, the flight of the crane.
In the evening those risen from the dead meet on rock paths.

Lepers gaze at their reflections in black waters;
Or weeping they open their filth-covered garments
To the balmy wind that wafts from the rosy hill.

Slender maidens grope their way through the streets of the night
In hopes of finding their shepherd-lovers.
On Saturdays soft singing sounds in the huts.

Let the song also commemorate the boy,
His madness and white brows and his decease,
The decomposed one who opens his eyes bluishly.
Oh, how sad is this re-encounter.

The stairs of madness in black rooms,
The shadows of the ancestors in the open door,
When Helian's soul looks at itself in the rosy mirror
And snow and leprosy drop from his brow.

On the walls the stars have gone out
And the white configurations of the light.

From the carpet bones of the graves rise up,
The silence of broken crosses on the hill,
The incense's sweetness in the crimson night wind.

O you shattered eyes in black mouths,
When in placid insanity the grandson
Ponders in solitude the darker ending,
The silent god lowers his blue eyelids over him.

ALBERT EHRENSTEIN

THE GODS

Fettered, we are surrounded
By devils that constrain us bestially.
I curse myself who came
Before the earth received light.

No sail blooms for us in the wind.
Storm came up. Friends,
Hair badly cut, feet frozen,
Work abandoned, mind soldered to body,
Guarding stables they smell horse droppings at some nocturnal hour.
Or fallen silent in their mutilation,
Their unrecognizable hands puffed round by mourning coat-sleeves,
They hobbled on crutches along the wall,
Until the earth swallowed them up.

Lamenting I left them;
Nobody loves me on earth,
So I am not eager to shed my blood,
No one is pleased with the donation.
A creature of pain fashioned from affliction and horror,
I was no longer comforted by the meadow,
Home's tender blade of grass;
In my dream I fled into the jungle.
Not here, not there!
A royal tiger on Java,
Strong and its own god,
— Crumpled I perished beneath its paws.
Last breath escaped. The soul rose. Not high.
Whizzing over pale bogs,
In the black swarm of shadows,
Far from the glorious
Shores of God
It beheld only the gods.
I flew closer to the whirring roundelay,
Lifted myself up to my God in prayer:

"Phoebus Apollo,
The day dances around you ninefold with rosy muses,
Why do your destiny-laden shoulders clash?

No one has offended Chryses.
Do your gilded priests insult you?
If half-poets have contaminated poetry, news-hounds the newspaper,
Spare the innocent people,
Pass mercifully through your kingdom,
Do not smother us in pestilence and yellow decay!"

In answer a discordant mountain song pressed in on me from all sides:
"You like to talk about happiness,
And live abraded with desire,
Yet if you have been much loved and regaled,
It was through the opening in women.

You dwarfs are whirled round by the wind
Until you are shattered on a rock,
You reel, drunk and blind,
Precipitated from ashes to ashes.

Above the shipwreck of earthly powers
We gods float blissfully,
After battlefield horrors a fire-black coldness avails you,
We are joy, we are meaning.

You who have lost God and word,
The heart for deeds,
Condemned to do battle,
You struggle along your greedy way,

Fools, minions of merchandise!
Over the cliffs of time
Hemorrhage rolls red,
You should kill yourselves, barbarians!"

Then I beheld everything turned to stone.
Venerable Zeus is still pursuing the cow-woman,
In honor of Odin's one eye the monocle burrs in the field.
Saw Mohammed, far from the peak of victory,
Tired from the journey up the mountain that keeps receding.
Rigidly nailed to the cross,
Jesus Christ is guarding the wood.

In vain was the prayer of the thirty righteous.
Out of the murder-nights of the North
Came the sounds of ceaseless lamentation,

Misery hacked my heart,
Israel whines in the winter,
The Eternal One
Circumcises his people.

Against the inexorable thornbush the soul hurled itself,
In hopes of being wedded to wrath in sacrifice:
"In the marble quarries of Carrara
Your people deemed itself born,
Then it became a curbstone for dogs,
Chosen! Chosen!

You sent it
To be cut up by the scythe-chariots of your anger!
In you it is brought to an end,
Who gave birth to a monster like you?"

He did not accept me,
From the inscrutable mist-nirvana
The greeting of the walking Buddha reached me at dawn:

"You who rule: live, you know me not.
Whatever egos sees its own face.
Die all the way to your innermost heart!
Life is dirt, earth pain.
Space is, oh, affliction,
Time itself illusion,
In the world's confusion
Blessed be death."
The devil spoke with conceited cunning:

"Oh, how easily even this blueness dissipates!
You gods are not versed in miracles.
None is master of his edifice,
For the holy place keeps withering away.
On the heads of the ascetics insects couple!
If the eternal is unattainable for you cavemen,
Do not gnash your teeth before the gods hoping for earthly help. The
temporal watchword germinates as well in your brains.
In the cock-fighting of the nations
Many a fatherland puffs up.
There is nothing enticing about anonymously ululating
The arch-yelling of the battlefield in a stupefied forest of armies.
The spirit plants deeper pains in heroes' teeth.

A woe upon the mitre-helmets!
Scrape off the Jesuit cannon-Christians
Their blood-suppurating scabs!
Do not wander young across the meadow
With the worn-out shadows!
When death ceases to be of consequence for you mortals and only then,
Breathe, Assassins, the amuck air
In battles with the real barbarian czars:
The money princes of the entire world.
Terrestrial lords who thirst for supremacy
Must have their glow
Quenched with their own blood.
If the Brownings and the bombs are successful,
Fewer hecatombs by the military will ensue."

And were I to rescue myself from this precipitous dream,
I, I too, I have murdered!
Bitter things are eaten by human beings.

FRANZ WERFEL

WHY MY GOD

Why, my Lord and God, did you create me
Who flared up, ignorant candlelight,
And exist now in the wind of my guilt,
Why did you create me, my Lord and God,
For the vanity of the word
And so that I write this,
And bear presumptuous pride,
And in the remoteness of my own self
Loneliness?!
Why did you create me for this, my Lord and God?

Why, why did you not give me
Two hands filled with help,
And eyes, prevailing double star of consolation?
And an Aprilian voice, raining music of kindness,
And a brow over which hangs
The sweet lamp of humility?
And one step through a thousand streets,
To carry at eventide all

Bells of the earth
Into the heart, into the heart of suffering to the end of time?!

See, so many little children
Are at this moment feverish in their evening-beds,
And Niobe is stone and cannot weep.
And a dark sinner stares
Into the dimensions of his sky.
And at night every soul falls
From the tree, a leaf in the autumn of the dream.
And they all crowd round a warmth,
Because it is winter
And pain's warm time.

Why, my Lord and God, did you not create me
As your seraph, golden, welcome,
Laying the crystal of my hands on fever,
Going in and out of doorway-sighs?!
Greeted and named:
Sleep, tear, home, kiss, companionship, childhood, motherly?!
And so that I rest by the hearth,
And am encouragement, and the balm of your house,
Just flight and errand, and know nothing of myself,
And in my locks the early dew of your countenance!

Ludwig Meidner · Franz Werfel

FRANZ WERFEL

## NOT US

I listened into the top of the tree; — and the foliage was saying:
    Not — yet!
I put my ear to the ground; — and there is a tapping beneath plant
    and dust:
    Not — yet!
I saw myself in the mirror; my mirror image sneered:
    Not — you!
    That was my judgment.
    I repudiated my song,
    And the demanding heart that would not be content.
I stepped out into the street. The evening rush was already underway.
On the brows of the passers-by I saw the words: not us.
But in every gaze I secretly read a praise
And knew: I too, deformed by loud delusion,
Will be begun again, because a womb holds me anew
As it does every being around me. Then I praised death,
And weeping I lauded every seed in the world.

# Awakening of the Heart

ALFRED WOLFENSTEIN

## THE HEART

Forgotten lay the heart inside our breast,
How long! A pebble for the will to toy with,
Touched heedlessly from time to time
By water-cooled, glistening hands.

Hermetically turned in upon itself, so little,
Unwanted in the cities' stony perfection
And on Mammon's throne of steel, not needed
To control the cogwheels' motions.

But some day this soulless spin will end,
The source of light is not outside us,
The radiant sky is merely a reflection of the morning
Bursting forth from within the human being —

The heart — a tiny sun, yet so brilliant
That stars are named after its rays,
This little heart shines with immeasurable clarity
From the firmament of the human soul!

O forehead, bear the imprint of this heart,
Thoughts, resound more deeply with its beat.
The heart integrates the might whole!
In the universe it shines as the day of the human being.

FRANZ WERFEL

FAT MAN IN THE MIRROR

O God, this is not me staring from the mirror,
This creature, hairy-chested and unshaven.
　　　Today the sky was so blue
　　　That Nanny took me for a promenade
In the park.

The sailor suit has not yet flown away
Into the securely locked chest of dead mementos.
　　　Taken off just now,
　　　It hangs there motionless,
Small and tired, on the door.

And afternoons, was there not in the kitchen
The wintry smell of coffee, loud ticking of the clock?
　　　He stood there, delightfully entranced
　　　After strolling nimbly on the ice
With his little brother.

And today, as always, that woman scared me
With tales of Kakitz, the park constable.
　　Often, at an ungodly hour,
　　I hear in the distance
This devil dragging his sabre through the night.

The faithful servant, why is she not here yet?
My face is heavy with approaching sleep.
　　If only she would come
　　And take away the lamp
That softly hums above my head!

Alas, no soothing sound of soft footsteps in the evening,
No Babi to put out the lamp and take it with her.
　　Nothing but that fat man
　　Staring helplessly at me until,
Deeply shocked, he steps out of the mirror.

PAUL ZECH

FROM THE WINDOWS OF A BOILER ROOM

Already the glowing fire has ferricly unscrewed me
from the day. The scant moment of garden bliss:
Half dream, half back into reality.
And yet I was covered with leaves of azure.

This blue moment, this act of kindness toward God and children,
was all too brief, it was an act of theft against the blood
with which I have to serve in hard shoes
a master so that his wealth may increase.

He wants from me no less than my very being,
my breath, my muscles, and my brain.
Is all I have left red hatred
in my heart, and the veins on my brow?

I am faceless, a cogwheel in the factory:
what choice do I have but to keep paying off
the company notes that I rashly signed.
I do not have any strength left to fight back.

The fire blazes, the boilers swell
to monstrous brutes in this underground world.
But for one hour, in the vault of this hellish place,
they leave me alone and no one screams for me.

A window-hole cut into the night:
I squeeze my face into the opening and feel
my eye made softer by a throng of sensations,
by wafting breaths of air, and cooling drops.

Is it you, forest, that I always traversed
when night erected a wall around the trees?
I know only that I owned you once,
my fists filled with the blossoming green of May.

Now the moon unlocks your infinite depth
and treetops shimmer white and free of care.
And as at one time I shuddered at the sight
of an eye, immense and black like that of a god:

so now I stand in awe of the dark and glassy waters
that carry toward me the essence of this earth.
A carefree youth as well, the one I never had,
only a father's whip-happy hey you.

The waters flow and rush and have an invisible scent
and flush the evil away: now you are old!
Tree branches grab me by my ruffled hair,
and fluffy leaves have power over me.

The boiler fires are all extinguished
in me now. The hard calluses, they are gone.
Cosmic music thunders through the house.
I cannot see the wheels because of the stars.

This is not real... yet it is my world
filled with lights and glorious deeds,
issuing as if from me and surrounding me
to let me rest inviolate, on an island.


ALFRED LICHTENSTEIN

WALK

The evening comes with moonlight and silken darkness.
The roads grow tired. The narrow world grows wide.

Opiate winds comb the fields.
I stretch out my eyes like silver wings.

I feel as though my body were the entire earth.
The city begins to glow: the thousand streetlamps blow about.

Now the heavens, too, piously light their candles.
... Immense above everything: my human countenance wanders.

ERNST WILHELM LOTZ

SONG OF GLORY

Enveloped in blue cloth and red collar,
I was a standard bearer, a young officer.
But those days that sometimes loom dreamily into my nights
Are not mine anymore.

In marching order we trudged over stony roads,
Intimate with clouds of dust and the green wind.
I rode through stunned villages, through streams and towns
And life was a blond blast.

The bivouac fires glowed like stars in the valley,
And had turned the sky into their mirror.
The enemy's alarm signals threatened from black mountains,
And fireballs crackled as they burst into darkness.

But then, tanned by hot summers and hardened by winter wars,
I found myself in huge offices that smelled of dust.
There I had to bend my back into a sickle,
And meticulously enter neat rows of figures into ledgers.

And somewhere, green coasts plunged into distant seas,
The fragrance of palms wafted from the harbor,
White caravans rested at desert cisterns,
The heads of the faithful turned piously toward the East.

On oceans the large hulls of ships glided by,
With flying fish swirling coolly above them,
And brilliant horizons of vast prairies
Circled teams of horses harnessed for long journeys.

In the thick of Cameroon's unfathomable singing forests,
Engulfed by the murderous fumes of the jungle floor,
Trembling natives were lashed into obedience by the whips of
        white men
And threatened darkly by the cannibals of the broiling forests!

America's big cities bustled at break of day,
Gigantic cranes were lowered, screeching hoarsely,
Into the bowels of ships, to stow the cargo,
And trains thundered inland from the piers.———

Thus I was close to all zones of the earth,
Lush islands beckoned from neighboring desks.
I felt the spin of the smoking globe under me,
Hurling itself around the sun with maddening speed.————

Then I threw those ledgers at the boss
And stormed out the door with intemperate laughter!
And chattered days and nights away in coffee houses,
Discussing the universe with smug, complacent friends.

And one night I fell back onto my pillows,
Crushed by a fearful and tremendous pressure.—
Then I saw: that, through clouds of darkness
A star-silent future was billowing ahead of me.


FRANZ WERFEL

THE BEAUTIFUL RADIANT HUMAN BEING

Friends who converse with me, and who are
Usually ill-humored, beam with pleasure
When they walk in the beauty of my features
Arm in arm, ennobled figures.

Alas, my face can never retain dignity,
Nor limit itself to being serious and calm,
For a thousand smiles unfold their wings and fly
Perpetually towards its celestial image.

I am a parade on sunny plazas,
A summer festival with women and bazaars,
My eye will break from its own radiance.

I want to sit down on the grass
And join the earth in its journey towards evening.
O earth, evening, happiness! O the joy of being alive!

ERNST WILHELM LOTZ

## I FLASH ON THE GASLIGHT...

I flash on the gaslight.
Unrolling amazement bounces off the four walls of the room.
I stand, a thin shadow, in the middle,
Hands clenched into small fists in my pockets,
And I am overwhelmed:

The walls bulge out, swelled by the roar,
While canvasses by millennial masters roar from all sides,
Attracting the music-making thoughts of hallelujah spirits!
I see myself in that room, helplessly floundering,
Groaning softly and trembling slightly
In the presence of such massive waves of sound
And such a battle of clouds sure of victory!

O works that challenge God!
A slight stroke of the brush shatters and blinds me
With an effortless blow and easy-going strength.

My breast rebels against this raging.
Deeply I breathe in the air of the walls
— This flood, this heat! —
And expel it, coughing and spitting:
Blood! Blood!

And I sink into ice-blown nights.
And know that death is reaching out for me down there.—
But high above me swirls a confusion
Of beating hooves and bodies and sun-like pomps and powers.


WALTER HASENCLEVER

## GASLIGHT HUMS

Gaslight hums. I know that I exist,
And my soul is clinging to the desk.
I am writing a poem. Where will I land!
In the haze of large, loud cities
My many embodiments meanwhile found themselves.

Already I tumble along hard dark paths
Into raging madness, to the tomb.
A nerve in my brain has snapped,
Now prey hisses around me, ready to bite like vipers —
But then I dance — and I can breathe again.
When masquerades resort to frenzied folly,
Our hearts will find their way back to the jungle.
But our souls, although they may disperse,
Will slowly float toward Elysium.

WALTER HASENCLEVER

THE NIGHT SINKS UNSHATTERED

The night sinks unshattered into oblivion.
Experiences crumble off you like crusts.
The day prepares, with barrel, lantern, cart,
To harness one-eyed horses waiting to be fed.
Beloved women! Where would you dream today!
In what beds darkly spend yourselves.
Die out, last candle, you that are still burning!
I want to surround myself with joyful kindness.
Whoever is faithful will return from twi-realms
To a like fate, one which he knows.
He will no longer be deceived by the idle suffering
Of him who loses nothing and keeps nothing.
Whoever is faithful will be part of what is most human
And thus be fulfilled in the eternal world.

WALTER HASENCLEVER

OFTEN, AT SEXUAL PLAY...

Often, at sexual play in strange zones
Our heartbeat stops. Yet time circles on.
Grant, great earth, more powerful sensations,
That we, who dwell only in the unfulfilled,
Do not become lonely because of transitoriness!
For he who loves himself must destroy himself
And wait in alleys, longing for feasts;

151

His ear can hear the shrill cries of the night,
And many a human eye will see him.
The emptiness of chambers and obscenities
Throttles him. His thirst suffocates in the blaze.
Then sleep rescues him. Bury the dead!
Uncharted land still entices in the East.


## WALTER HASENCLEVER

### COME BACK TO ME, MY REASON

Come back to me, my reason, massaged to bits in blood;
Gather and secure what you have set loose,
And when I love, preserve my equilibrium,
Or passion will kill me as the plague would.
I want to be with you now, travel with you;
We will circle round each other like two globes,
And float from a lighted space into the dark.
Kill what brings you pleasure before it can consume you!
Sell your woman, you will get over it.
Do not be perturbed by loathing or the pains of love —
The skies are swept by winds and rose-hued dawn,
The windows clatter, and the trains go by.


## GOTTFRIED BENN

### EXPRESS TRAIN

Brown as cognac. Brown as leaves. Reddish brown. Malayan
    yellow.
Express train Berlin-Trelleborg and Baltic Sea resorts.—

Flesh walking naked.
Tanned by the sea right to the lips.
Mellow in anticipation of Hellenic bliss.
In harvest-nostalgia: the summer so far advanced!
Next-to-last day of the ninth month already!—

Stubble and a last almond pants in us.
Efflorescences, the blood, the wearinesses,
The proximity of dahlias confuses us.—

Male tan hurling itself upon female tan:

A woman is something for one night.
And if it was good, for one more!
Oh! And then this being by yourself again!
These silences! This being driven!
A woman is something with a scent.
Unspeakable! Languish! Reseda.
Therein the South, shepherd, and sea.
A promise of happiness on every slope.—

Female light tan tumbling against male dark tan:

Hold me! Dearest, I am sinking!
My neck is so tired.
Oh, this feverish sweet
Last scent from the gardens.—


## RENÉ SCHICKELE

### UPON ENTERING THE PORT OF BOMBAY

Is not the vista opening up before us
Woven entirely of transparent mist,
Breakers, bays, wide beaches —
And lifted towards the firmament,
And amidst a rose-colored glow
Half transformed into a cloud of spray?
Is this not the city open to the skies,
The one where scarlet flowers dwell?

Ocean flooding into sun-drenched waterways,
Where palaces melt rosily into the waves.
Is this not the golden trace,
Almost imperceptible in the blue,
A mere quivering image of the dwellings
They build for themselves —
Those who walk on the path of light,
Serene wanderers through the eons?

## WALTER HASENCLEVER

### THE PRISONER

No one who cruises the suburbs at night
Knows whom he loves, what woman he fancies.
Sometimes the sound of a café waltz
Brings back memories that delight and wound him.
Up surges the melody of happy youthful days,
Visions and fame, and first newspaper words;
Black fountain of painful magic power
Appears in the West, in the same old place.
There a heart lives that, allied with many,
Fathomed fate more deeply;
A heart boundlessly blazing: world —
That now is troubled as it rises to our lips.
The bars are still midnight-crowded,
Howling philistines whom we slowly kill.
Will the eternal city flush our faces?
Let us stride away in openness from the flatlands!
In the fog the muffled flight of subterranean trains
Is already glowing from our anxious brains.
Then a sudden flash makes our senses spin,
Morning is here — the morning over Berlin.
All of you who are in danger or in the agony of love:
Be on the lookout for the white horses.
The cycle closes around phantom and year;
Heady sensuous times, you too, how wonderful.
The mind, escaping the sweet present,
Rises east toward the city of light,
Which resounds, gigantic, in glorious symphony
Through the bodiless ether.
The hackney stumbles at the place where we often knelt
In homage to a lady of mystery,
Until a sudden glimpse of her stockings
Tore the illusion, permitting easy lust.
As we stepped into the corridor, tired
Yet wide awake, ready for slumberland:
What thoughts we had when at somebody's door
A solitary little lamp shone forth.
The blinds are bathed in a blue radiance;
Pointed patterns dance crazily through the brain.
The transparencies that rivaled clouds and stars
Are long gone... yes, you, too, are far away.

Soon the night will die in the rose-colored firmament,
Already birds are approaching us on their southerly flight;
Where are you, nation, that calls out my name?
The cloud is aflame — the morning over Berlin.

FOR KURT PINTHUS

RENÉ SCHICKELE

THE BODYGUARD

And there are hours, too, when I feel as if under a curse,
Although I know that an aura of my blood emblazes me,
Wherever I move and wherever I rest,
Like a great and glorious inner glow.
It contains everything that my ancestors,
Soldiers, farmers, sinners or worshipers,
Handed down to me, tempered through their lives,
So that I can feel it in my blood today.

And yes, I sense it as armor, shield and rampart
And fortress that protects me on all sides.
And yet it is there to filter creation's chaotic abundance
Through a net that seemingly consists of blood and motes in a
    sunbeam,
So that my eyes will perceive only
What will nurture them through the ages,
And what will take root in my heart:
Seeds whose growth it will have the strength to bear;

And all that will anchor it more deeply in a beginning
Of which I know nothing, save that at one time
A fiery will surged which then,
Propagated from mouth to mouth, at last reached the one who I
    am now.
And they are with me, those who save me from the gravest harm!
I ride with a host of heavenly hussars,
If I lift my hand, a thousand hands will wave,
And if I halt, the ghost riders will halt, too.

In my sleep I sense them bivouacking around me,
There they lie, their horses' reins secured,
They breathe and stir as I do, are slight and heavy,
And sometimes, as one of them draws nearer to the other,
There is a clang, whose echoes
Reverberate through my body like the falling
Jets of water at a fountain in a vestibule.
That's when I feel the hearts of mothers tremble!

This is the time when, wild and sweet, love overflows
In me and every living being,
When rocket after rocket shoots into the sky,
In the darkness every clock stops.
And translucent oceans mirror brilliant stars,
Fruits open brazenly to show their cores,
A radiance beams from me to the most distant lands,
And waves from me pound the most distant shores.

So, though there are hours when I feel as if cursed,
I know, in spite of all: an aura of my blood,
Wherever I am, sleeping or awake,
Emblazes my actions with a glorious inner glow.
It contains everything that my ancestors,
Soldiers, farmers, sinners or worshipers,
Realized in life with all their heart for my protection.


WALTER HASENCLEVER

THE ACTOR
To Ernst Deutsch

Break loose, predator, from the chains of doubt!
Backdrop falls. The dawn of cities
Trickles from the wound torn open by your passion.

You love in clouds. Die in beds.
Music stirs up the riot of your strength.
You will save the hymnic power of that spirit

Which creates your body through the word.
I greet you from the drumming hurricane.
You, brother of my ecstasy, my dreams.

156

As you soar through the imagined realms,
Circling gigantic orbits of dark peoples:
I feel that I was born to be one with you.

You live! So the deeds were not in vain.
There breathes around the cradle of our Horae
The selfsame womb of women and of mothers.

Flare up, teardrop, from the gates of the grave,
Atlantean region's unbridled route.
Oh sweetness, to be able to move human beings so!

The curtain plunges. We are leaving.


FRANZ WERFEL

HECUBA

Sometimes she traverses earth's night.
She, the heaviest, most dejected of earth's hearts.
Slowly she drifts under leaves and stars,
Through passages and doors and human breathing,
Old mother, most wretched of all mothers.

Once there was so much milk in these breasts,
There were so many sons to care for.
Woe and gone! — Now she drifts across the earth at night,
Old mother, once the center of the world, burnt out
Like a cold star that just rolls on.

Under stars and leaves she drifts across the earth
At night through a thousand darkened rooms
Where the mothers are asleep, young women,
Drifts past the cribs
And the bright, rounded sleep of children.

Sometimes, she stops at the head of a bed
And looks around with so much sadness,
She, but a waft of air so shaped by pain
That pain itself first finds embodiment in her
And the light weeps in dead lamps.

And the women climb out of their beds,
While she drifts on — with bare and heavy steps...
For hours they sit beside their sleeping children,
Staring slowly into the dimness of the room,
Weeping in uncomprehended sorrow.


GOTTFRIED BENN

CARYATID

Free yourself from the stone. Burst open
The hollow that enslaves you! Rush
To the fields! Scoff at the cornices ————:
See: through the beard of drunken Silenus,
From the eternally intoxicated
Turmoil of his loud, unique blood,
Wine drips into his genitals.

Spit at this mania for pillars: worked-to-death
Hands of old men trembled them
Towards overcast heavens. Topple
The temples to appease your yearning knees
That crave the dance.

Spread yourself. Deflower your festoons. Oh, bleed
Your soft floral bed away through gaping wounds.
See Venus with her doves girding with roses
Her hips' love gate —
See this summer's last blue breath
Floating on oceans of asters toward distant
Tree-brown shores; dawning
See this last happy-deceitful hour
Of our southernness,
High-vaulted.


ALFRED LICHTENSTEIN

GIRLS

They cannot bear the evenings in their rooms.
They sneak out into deep starry streets.

158

How soft the world is in the streetlights' wind.
How strangely life dissolves in its hum...

They walk past gardens and houses,
As if drawn by a radiance far ahead,
And they look at every lecherous man
As if he were a sweet lord and saviour.


JOHANNES R. BECHER

FROM THE POEMS FOR LOTTE

When I but think you
: Most heavenly harmony :
Arms wave flags,
North marches off with fanfare.

When I but feel you
: Palms and oases :
Wind applies balsam coolly,
Angel choirs trumpet.

When I am you, yours
: Giant and thunderstorm :
Chaste and humble-pure,
Free behind cage bars.

And certain of victory
: Human being with God's power :
Refuge after storm and fissure.
Body suddenly erect.

On to the firmament!
One with the stars.
Yes, conqueror, when
I am yours... celebration in song.

ERNST WILHELM LOTZ

## WE FOUND GLORY

We found glory, found an ocean, studio, and us.
At night, a crescent sang in front of our window.
We scaled the ladder of our voices,
And traveled hand in hand.
Along your tresses, a festive brightness in the morning,
Kisses soared crazily,
Injecting ripe insanity into my blood.
Then we thirsted frequently at wounded wells,
The towers blew steel-like in the land.
And our thighs, hips, and predator-loins
Stormed through all regions, greening with scent.

Ludwig Meidner · Ernst Wilhelm Lotz

ERNST WILHELM LOTZ

AND BEAUTIFUL PREDATOR SPOTS...

Is it really you?
Grandly at night, from the universe that is a mirror,
Your wavering image resounds through my soul.
The stars traverse your breast, playing harp music.
But you...

Perhaps you are glistening, spent, in a white featherbed,
Locked in a heavy dream.—

Or perhaps a young lover
Is tracing sensuously, with inquisitive finger,
The firm round globes of your breasts.
You are both very hot.
And beautiful predator spots adorn your backs.


ELSE LASKER-SCHÜLER

A SONG OF LOVE
(Sascha)

Since you left,
The city is dark.

I gather the shadows
Of the palm trees
Beneath which you strode.

I always have to hum a melody
Which smiles as it gets caught in the branches.

You requite my love —
To whom shall I speak of my joy?

To an orphan or to a bridegroom
Who will sense the happiness echoing through my words.

I always know
When you are thinking of me —

Then my heart becomes a child
And cries out.

At each doorway along the street
I linger and dream

And help the sun paint your beauty
On all the walls of the houses.

But I wane away
Thinking of you.

I wind myself around slender pillars
Until they sway.

Burnet grows everywhere,
The blossoms of our blood;

We sink into sacred mosses,
Made of the fleece of golden lambs.

I wish that a tiger
Would stretch its body

Across the distance that separates us,
Like a bridge to a nearby star.

On my countenance
Your breath lies in the morning.


ELSE LASKER-SCHÜLER

MY LOVE SONG
(To Sascha, the heavenly prince)

On your cheeks rest
Golden doves.

But your heart is a whirlwind,
Your blood rushes, like my blood —

Sweetly
Past raspberry bushes.

Oh, how I think of you —
Just ask the night.

No one can play so beautifully
With your hands,

Build castles, as I can,
With your golden fingers;

Fortresses with high towers!
Wreckers are we then.

When you are with me,
I am always rich.

You embrace me so
That I see stars bursting from your heart.

Your bowels
Are iridescent lizards.

You are entirely of gold —
All lips stop breathing.


ELSE LASKER-SCHÜLER

AN OLD TIBETAN RUG

Your soul, in love with mine,
Is entwined with it in the rug's Tibet.

Rays of light embracing, amorous colors,
Stars that courted each other across the skies.

Our feet rest upon the sumptuous expanse
Of thousands upon thousands of loops.

163

Sweet lama-prince on your muskplant throne,
How often has your mouth touched mine, your cheek my
    cheek;
For how long have we woven, knot by colorful knot, the
    carpet of our love?


AUGUST STRAMM

BLOSSOM

Diamonds wander across the water!
Arms outstretched
The dull dust reaches for the sun!
Blossoms sway in hair!
Pearly
Complex
Veils weave!
Sweetly smell
White opaque pale
Veils!
Pink, timidly muted, tinged
Spots quiver,
Lips, lips,
Thirsty, pursed, hot lips!
Blossoms! Blossoms!
Kisses! Wine!
Red
Golden
Inebriating
Wine!
You and I!
I and you!
You?!

AUGUST STRAMM

MIRACLE

You stands! You stands!
And I
And I
I wing
Spaceless, timeless, weightless
You stands! You stands!
And
Fury births me
I
Birth myself!
You!
You!
You banishes the time
You arches the circle
You besouls the mind
You glances the glance
You
Rotates the world
The world
The world!
I
Rotate the universe!
And you
And you
You
Stand.
The
Miracle!


ERNST STADLER

EARLY IN THE MORNING

Early in the morning the silhouette of your body stands darkly in
        the dim light
Of drawn blinds. I feel, lying in bed, your face, holy-wafer-like,
        turned toward me.

165

When you slipped from my arms your whispered "I must be off"
    only reached the farthest gates of my dream —
Now I see, as if through veils, your hand gently smoothing down
    the white shirt over your breasts...
The stockings... now the skirt...the hair pinned up... already you are
    a stranger, made up for the day, the world...
I quietly open the door... kiss you... you nod, already far away, a
    farewell...and you are gone.
I hear, in bed again, your nimble footsteps growing ever fainter on
    the stairs,
Once more captivated by the fragrance of your body streaming
    warmly from the pillows through my senses.
Morning brightens. Curtains blow. Young wind and sunlight want
    to enter.
Noises swell... music of the early hours... gently lulled by morning
    dreams I fall asleep.


WILHELM KLEMM

CONFESSION

The sashes of the sky flare up,
The evening gathers its majestic trains.
The view recedes with the setting sun,
An immense mystic eagle flies by.

Drops of blood start speaking,
A sound like blurry, quivering mist.
The blue lagoons of peace
Open vistas of a thousand golden islands.

On the scales of my will
I weighed the silver band of eternity,
But each of your kisses outweighed it.
I love you, and let the rest be death!

AUGUST STRAMM

TWILIGHT

Light awakens dark
Dark fights shine
Space explodes the spaces
Shreds drown in loneliness
The soul dances
And
Sways and sways
And
Trembles in space
You!
My limbs seek each other
My limbs caress each other
My limbs
Sway sink sink drown
In
Immensity
You!

Light fights dark
Dark devours shine!
Space drowns in loneliness
The soul
Whirls
Struggles
Halt!
My limbs
Reel
In
Immensity
You!

Light is shine!
Loneliness slurps!
Immensity streams
Rends
Me
In
You!
You!

AUGUST STRAMM

EVENING STROLL

Through softly clinging night
Our steps move silently
Our hands palely fear for cramping horror.
The light stabs our heads sharply into shadows
Into shadows
Us!
High above the star glistens
The poplar hangs upward
And lifts the earth up after it
The sleeping earth hugs the naked sky
You gaze and shudder
Your lips steam
The sky kisses
And
The kiss gives birth to us!


JOHANNES R. BECHER

EVENING PRAYER FOR LOTTE

I

The guards have barely started snoring —
And already I am weaving in you:
O fruit! O spring gardens!
Like the mildest of zephyrs.

Beloved, I am wasting away
In blackness and fallower dreams.
May your countenance shine forth
Some day in splendor across the universe.

Beloved, I am turning into
A deep dark-foliaged forest.
You, though, you — may your realm be
High above the cold tower of night.

In burnt-out craters
I would melt in red-hot misery.
You dart from stone-clouds,
Most heavenly of angel-messengers.

II

Beloved, where are you playing sweet music?!
I walk with unsure step.
And am the forest-tormented one
Whose eternity has slipped away.

He must devour the night
Stone by heavy stone,
Clenching claw-like fists,
A wallowing loathsome brute.

O zenith of our spirit!
Wondrous manifestation!
Who we are... you alone know:
Fallen angels. Yes.


KURT HEYNICKE

IN THE MIDDLE OF THE NIGHT

Your love is a white deer
that flees into the midnight of my longing,
a tree of tears stands in the forest of my dreams of you,
now you are there —
the moon throws me fulfillment from the vessel of its
          radiance —
I love you,
you,
I will place the scent of carnations in front of your
          chamber
and scatter narcissi on your bed.
I will come to you, silver like yourself,
and arch over you,
a sacred grove
over the altar of your pious soul.

## DOCTOR BENN

I cry —
My dreams fall into the world.

Into my darkness
No shepherd ventures.

My eyes do not show the way
As stars do.

I am a constant beggar in front of your soul;
Do you know that?

If only I were blind —
Would then imagine myself lying inside your body.

All my blossoms I would pour
Into your blood.

I am multirich,
No one can pluck me;

Or carry my gifts
Home.

Very tenderly I will teach myself to you;
Already you know what to call me.

See my colors,
Black and starlit

And I do not like the cool day,
It has a glass eye.

Everything is dead,
Only you and I are not.

ALBERT EHRENSTEIN

## FORSAKEN

Wherever I go
My heart hurts,
She has left me.

Wherever I stay,
Wherever I roam,
I cannot grasp it.

My beloved, you my woe,
You my child, you my deer,
Have you actually left me?


ELSE LASKER-SCHÜLER

## A SONG

The waters in the back of my eyes,
I must cry them all.

I want to soar up all the time,
Fly away with the birds of passage;

Breathe freely with the winds
Of the airy expanse.

Oh, I am so sad ————
The face in the moon knows it.

That is why much velvet devotion
And the approaching dawn surround me.

When on your heart of stone
My wings broke,

The blackbirds fell like weeping roses
From tall blue trees.

All this muted chirruping
Wants to become jubilant again

And I want to soar up
And away with the birds of passage.

Else Lasker-Schüler, self-portrait

ELSE LASKER-SCHÜLER

FAREWELL

But you never came with the evening —
I sat waiting in a mantle of stars.

...Whenever there was a knock on my door,
It was the pounding of my own heart.

Now it hangs on every doorpost,
On your door as well;

Fire-roses fading among ferns
In the brown of the garland.

I colored the sky blackberry for you
With my heart's blood.

But you never came with the evening —
...I stood waiting in golden shoes.


ELSE LASKER-SCHÜLER

RECONCILIATION

A large star will fall into my lap...
We will hold vigil this night,

Pray in languages
Which are incised like harps.

We will be reconciled this night —
So much of God overflows.

Children are our hearts,
They want to rest in sweet tiredness.

And our lips want to meet in a kiss.
Why do you hesitate?

Does my heart not border yours —
It is your blood that always colors my cheeks red.

We will be reconciled this night;
When we caress, we cannot die.

A large star will fall into my lap.


WALTER HASENCLEVER

ENCOUNTER

Tell me, with sea- and cloudlike mouth,
Already gone astray in your bed's night,
Where you slept in league with him:
At what hour did you awake?

When did clock and glass on your table's edge
Start ringing out sinister notes;
When did you rise from muffled groaning,
Shuddering at the touch of a strange hand?

In that same anxious second
She unlocked her garden gate for me,
Where I stood lost in the company
Of black trees and the chorus of stars.

Suddenly to all those banished at night
I felt a closeness at that selfsame time —
And then I sensed that we knew each other
In deep allegiance forged by reality.


GEORG HEYM

YOUR LASHES, YOUR LONG LASHES...

Your lashes, your long lashes,
Your eyes' dark waters,
Let me dive into them,
Let me explore their depths.

174

As the miner descends to the shaft,
And his dim lamp swings
Above the gateway to the ore,
High up on the shadowy wall,

So I descend
Into your lap to forget
All that throbbing far above
Of brightness and pain and day.

Along the fields,
Where the wind rests, inebriated from the grain,
Thornbushes, tall and sick,
Tangle toward the blue sky.

Give me your hand,
Let us grow each into the other,
Prey to every wind,
Flight of lonely birds.

Let us listen in summer
To the organ of faraway thunderstorms,
Bathe in autumnal light
Along the shore of the blue day.

Sometimes we will stop
At the edge of a dark well,
To peer into its deep stillness
In search of our love.

Or we will step out
From the shade of the golden woods,
Grandly into a sunset
That gently touches your brow.

One day to stand at the end,
Where already the sea, in yellowish patches,
Quietly swims
Into the September bay.

To recline above,
In the house of the sparse flowers,
And down over the rocks
The wind sings and trembles.

But already from the poplar
That towers in the Eternal Blue
A brown leaf tumbles,
To rest on your neck.

Divine sadness,
Do not speak of eternal love.
Raise the flagon,
Drink sleep.


FRANZ WERFEL

WHILE YOUR BEING WAS TRANSPORTING ME INTO MORTAL ECSTASY

While your existence was enrapturing me to tears,
And I was being boundlessly enthused through you,
Was this day not being experienced by the careworn,
Wretchedly by untold millions of oppressed?

While your being was transporting me into mortal ecstasy,
There was toil about us, and the earth was full of clamor.
And there was emptiness, godlessly unwarmed creatures,
The living and the dying of the forever unfortunate!

While I was swelled by you to the point of floating away,
There were so many who were trudging in mindless drudgery,
Shriveling up at desks and steaming in front of boilers.

You who are gasping for breath on streets and rivers!!
If there be any balance in this world, this life?
How I will have to pay this debt!?


THEODOR DÄUBLER

THE BREATH OF NATURE

The breath of nature, the wind, earth's imagination,
Dreams up the clouds of the gods that blow north.
The wind, earth's imagination, creates horses of mist,
And I see gods standing on every peak!

176

I draw a deep breath and spirits swarm up from my heart.
Away and up! Who knows where a wish discerns itself!
I breathe deeply: I yearn, and universal images engrave
Themselves upon my soul that names its god.

Nature! Only that is freedom, universal love without end!
Existence, though, makes a life of sacrifice beautiful!
O nature free, our hands are the tools that fashion time,
The world, greatness, and even the heights to be surmounted!

A forest in bloom, the flaming wood that prays as if with hands,
We all feel ennobled only by the offering.
O God, O God, I, the human being, am the only one that is late.
How often have I suppressed my soul's purest flame!

In the valley smoke rises as if from an offertory cup,
So slowly, almost sacredly, above the village.
This I know, that human beings make an offering of their meal
When a deity has chosen their hearth's fire for itself!


JOHANNES R. BECHER

THE FOREST

I am the forest filled with humid darkness.
I am the forest that thou shouldst not visit.
The dungeon from which the wild Mass thunders
With which I curse God, the ancient monster.

I am the forest, the large, dank prison.
Enter me, wailing with pain, all you who are lost!
I will bed your skulls softly on rotting moss.
Sink into me, into mud and pond, all you who are lost!

I am the forest, like a coffin draped in black,
My leafy trees stretch out in odd distortion.
In my dark hell God had perished...
I am a damp wick that will never catch fire.

Listen to the murmur of the mold-lit swamps,
And the smirking drumbeats of the potsherd's rattle!
From festering bog comes the impudent trumpeting
Of a flat beetle with forked horns on black cap.

All of you, beware of me who am malicious-cold!
The crumbling ground opens up, the tangled webbing
Of my branches ensnares you, a thunderstorm
Crashes in bursting labyrinth.

But thou art the open plain... Full of song, with flowing mane,
Brushed back smoothly by pleasant breezes.
You kneel before me, grayly inundated
By tears of stinging hail from a tub of leaden clouds.

I am the forest that will only smile
When thou sendest warm winds to calm it from afar.
The noose clings more softly to bony neck,
And noxious beasts steal back into their lairs.

The dead sing, birds awaken, illuminated
By the blinding light of colorful rays.
The evil night perishes like a howling dog.
Fragrant juices boil up from open wounds.

Thou art the open plain... the lemon
Of the waning moon swings high above thy head.
Thou lullest me vagabond to sleep with heavy poppy:
Thou, a blond angel, appearing in his dream.

I am the forest... From me spring golden brooks
That rustle through the thicket hissing softly
Like snakes with elongated needle tongues. Above me
The swift procession of the lustre of the stars.

I am the forest... And your lands crackle
In the bloody hellish glow of my last conflagration.
The edges of the icy mountains melt and topple,
The oceans' liquid rocks shoot up shrilly.

I am the forest, rushing through the evening world, broken loose
From the ground, spreading smells that benumb you,
Until my shrieking flame pierces the horizon —
Which extinguishes, which covers me with a rose-colored sheet.

The meadow of flowers has become the vault of my tomb.
A multitude of colorful flowers springs from the arcades of my
    ruins.
Ever since that open plain sank down to me,
How beautiful we sound, harmonious organ music.

I am the forest... Quietly I pervade your slumbers,
Because slander and robbery and murder have been expiated,
I am no longer doom, nor sharp punishment.
My darkness will close your burning eyes.


IWAN GOLL

FOREST

I

I had to pass through thistles to reach you,
You, ensconced in the glowing cosmos
The way a patriarch is in God.

You appeared resplendent to the dusty wanderer,
Transfigured and contented,
A holy servant of the earth;
And the stranger felt even more strange.

Golden lustres dripped from evening sweetness.
Around the ladder of the sun's last rays
The rose-colored angels bustled,
And the nymphs, your daughters,
Wove their silver bodies round your lattice.

II

A violet fell
Suddenly at my feet like a blue star:
I carried it into the golden evening.

With our eyes we both
Lit up one another and blazed mightily:
We both would have liked so much to shout and kiss!

But our language was so feeble!
And love so unspeakably sad!
We withered and we died asunder.

### III

In your deep animals, though,
Darkening from moist eyes of kindred spirits,
You were my equal, forest!

Oh, to be your creature,
Nothing but a tone of the earth,
The butterfly a colorful sundrop,
And to feel slender foxes
With strong blood from nearby bushes:
To be devotion and brotherly peace!

In your deep animals you were made sacred for me.
And I gave myself up to you,
Lost my whole being in growth and fragrances.

Marc Chagall · Iwan and Claire Goll

PAUL ZECH

THE FOREST

Tear out my tongue and I will still have hands
to praise this insular existence.
It becomes one with me and fills my being,
as if from my brow the walls grew for it

where the mountains rise transparently to meet the clouds.
With a brush of collected light I want
to paint into the blue the poem that has not yet been written,
and have it branch out transparently into the entire sky.

For here is access to the boundless;
here for a second time the world became a child
from the drawn white and from the black lots.

Enter, you who are lost and blind!
If once in dreams there was loud and clear a cry
for God —: the trees are the steps to Him.


THEODOR DÄUBLER

THE BEECH TREE

The beech tree says: the foliage remains my language.
I am no tree with thoughts that speak,
I express myself in the patterns of my branches,
I am the foliage, the crown above the dust.

I am readily responsive to the summons of new warmth.
When spring arrives, I joyfully start talking,
And in my simple ways appeal to everyone.
You are amazed that at first I am rusty-brown!

My forest mood is summer-merry.
I want the fog to wind about my branches,
I like the wetness, I myself am the rain.
When the heat dies down, I blaze in emerald flames!

My winter duty then is to be grave and gray.
But first I must shake autumn from my being.
Without me it has never happened,
And I become a carpet, a meadow velvet-red.


WILHELM KLEMM

THE TREE

The heavenly is woven into the earthly.
Who loves the one cannot hate the other.
I grew steadily into my destined form.
Now I am the way you wanted me to be.

The body changes as the years go by,
The soul explores its thousand paths.
My own existence, along with previous generations,
Streams by and hardly knows the goal.

A treetop sways above my head,
Wanders back and forth on the blue celestial plain.
Windswept it yearns for distance and departure,
But in the evening calm it is content to stay where it is.


GEORG HEYM

THE TREE

Sun boiled him,
Wind dried him out,
No tree wanted him,
He was rejected by all.

Only a mountain ash,
Studded with red berries
Flaming like fiery tongues,
Gave him shelter.

183

And here he hung suspended,
His feet lay in the grass.
The evening sun sent
Blood-wet rays through his ribs,

Made the olive groves
Rise high above the land,
God in the white mantle
Showed himself in the clouds.

In the flowery depths
Singing brood of vipers,
In the silvery throats
Thin rumors chirped.

And they all trembled
Above the foliaged realm,
As they heard the hands of the Father
Brushing luminous veins.


THEODOR DÄUBLER

THE TREE

The wind plays with the thousands of wet leaves,
And they keep beckoning to other winds,
And I hear forest waltzes resounding through the shade.

My melodies sing too, for they are windwild!
And all these songs swarm, like so many tiny bees,
Around every shoot that recollects the blossoms' shimmer.

Now I, most mortal of humans, found the courage to speak for myself:
Countless branches made me conscious of primeval knowledge,
And reason shall make use of it, like the bees.

The wind stops in its course, and listens.
It overhears its roar as dream-breath in the tree.
So listen to the sound of oceans overflowing oceans!

The earth, as tree, wants to be enraptured by the tree.
The dream-experience turns into personal vision,
For dreams are able to eavesdrop on us together with our dreaminess!

Sink your roots into me, oh dream of my tree!
The songs of yearning are already nesting in my tranquility,
For the stillness sings through the roots and as far as the forest's edge.

The roots reach far down into submission!
How deep the stillness! As deep as its falling asleep!
But in its crown the tree reflects the North.

It follows the wind. It becomes what as tree it was called to be.
It thrusts love into the raging destinies.
It speaks for itself and has as dream the deep effect of a primeval tree.

O tree, I know that as thicket I ensnare myself.
You overflow with love, you are love-crazed!
You love, O tree, the "Thou" I see in me.

And "Thou," only "Thou's" I get to hear whenever I should call.
The darkness of all repose knows the "Thou" of things!
That is why the world is full of sweet words of delight.

O sun, listen to me singing in the crown:
The high North abounds with murderous reason,
But the land has gold for starry butterflies.

You presumptuous prigs, things garbed in reason,
Your celestial sign frees you from the climbing plants.
The fetters fall: the questioning fire gnaws.

Venturous snakes rise to world destinies!
The jungle shines into the sweet well-being of the universe:
The tree believes! And all the weathered treetops nod!

The tree's roots surround the essential pole of its repose.
It guards the nests and protects the pain-ego of animals,
For every leaf is the earthly symbol of great patience.

So it happens that no effecting nod is ever lost!
The animals, though, are more than moaning wind.
For they never err. They buzz around what is theirs.

Disentangle yourselves outright! The tiniest thing is world-disposed!
And listen in your tree for the morning of free oceans.
O magnificent sun, with what precision a day elapses!

The tree is tall. It has already fulfilled the honor of its essence.
High above a star-child jubilates
As he listens to the passion of becoming's severity.

How many deer have already fallen, crying!
O star-child, preserve their soul-tear
And make us harmless and gentle in our actions!

The shyness of the creatures which I sense in their tracks
Was once a leaf, an animal that was hounded to death:
And all the land flares up like a frenzied mane.

In the name of all who are desperate, world, be outraged!
Shelter, earth, each cry of death in luminous prayers:
In the name of the tree, do not tarry! The "Now!" is glowing.

The earth's fury burns through winds long gone.
It is a jungle alive with flame-naked inspiration.
Here there is no dying! The animals glow in comets!

On gigantic tails they smolder through the universe.
Cold nights they can suddenly turn into day,
For there is no conscience that has missed the road back to itself.

The travels that carry the human being premonitorily
Fill all northhoods with passionate ardor,
And animals sniff the air of young, resplendently nocturnal sagas.

Toward its own essences the highest art matures.
Life's authenticity can only be expressed ecstatically.
There, above world-inferno-madness, dawns a silent grace.

Thoughts start to hate with a chilling glow.
The tree-dream twists upwards into blue space.
Star-children sing in the flaming streets

And nest innocently in the tree's tranquil graciousness.

Theodor Däubler

## Millions of Nightingales are Singing

The stars. Blueness. Distance.
A flaming song of stars!
Millions of nightingales are singing.
Spring is flashing.
Myriads of eyelids flutter and glow.
The green happiness of spring-night revelry
Commences its nurturing resplendence.
Warm showers take their magic course:
Millions of nightingales are singing.
Do I recognize a friendly spectre?
I will try my best to communicate with it.
The slightest nod will sharpen my awareness:
Who knows when my dream-existence will be realized?
Spectres are like our gentle animals,
They can quickly sense the velvet of affection.
They rise, they glide, they drift toward us
And keep us spellbound with uncanny kindness.
I do not want to lose the quiet of swarming lights,
An ancient ordering must soon spring from gentleness.
Millions of nightingales are singing.
All through the night we are exhorted by kindred voices.
A moon seems to be glimmering mysteriously.
But too warm is the night, filled with the breath of contentment!
Myriads of lust-conscious sparks chase each other in flight,
Their seemingly aimless swarming guided by the urges of spring.
The springtide spectre, the springtide spectre haunts the hedges!
The leaf-rich forest can wander and wait for itself,
Swaying and dancing in accordance with ancient ritual;
The night laughs: the Big Dipper ventures, Libra keeps watch.
Myriads of dance-infatuated questions flash —
Millions of nightingales are singing.

AUGUST STRAMM

EARLY SPRING

Plump clouds chase each other in puddles
From fresh ruptures blades of grass scream torrents
The shadows stand exhausted
The air shrieks up
While whirling, blowing, howling, wallowing
And rents suddenly tear open
And scar
On the gray body
The silence lollops down heavily
And oppresses!
Then the light unfurls
A sudden yellow and jumps
And spots splash —
Fades
And
Plump clouds romp in puddles.


ERNST STADLER

EARLY SPRING

Late on this March night I stepped out of my house.
The streets were roused by the smell of spring and green seeding rain.
Winds sprang up. Through the bewildered hollow of houses I strolled far
Out to the open rampart and felt: a new rhythm was surging toward my heart.

In every breath of air a young becoming was unharnessed.
I listened as the strong eddies rumbled in my blood.
Fields were already stretching in readiness. Already burned into the horizons
Was the blue of late morning hours that were to lead into the openness.

The floodgates creaked. Adventure broke out of all distances.
Above the canal rippled by young outbound winds, bright spots grew,
In whose light I drifted. Fate stood waiting in wind-wafted stars.
There was a tempestuousness in my heart like that of unfurled banners.

WILHELM KLEMM

AUTUMN

The years overlap.
Callous graves stare at us.
A thin wind blows. Lands depopulate,
Thoughts filter slowly into grayness.

But the arbor is still the same.
We drink a dead wine,
And follow the motions of forgetting,
Which are sweeter than memories.

Smoke smells far away and sad.
Smells so strong you could fall asleep in it.
Who will send us home when it gets dark,
And the dogs that bark so loudly?

GEORG TRAKL

THE AUTUMN OF THE LONELY MAN

The dark autumn enters filled with fruit and fullness,
Yellowed radiance of beautiful summer days.
A pure blue steps out of the decayed covering;
The flight of birds resounds with ancient myths.
The wine is pressed, the gentle stillness
Filled with soft answers to dark questions.

And here and there a cross on a barren hill;
A herd disperses in a scarlet wood.
A cloud is wafted across the mirror of the pond;
The rustic's calm gestures rest.
Very softly the evening's blue wing
Touches a roof of dry straw, the black earth.

Soon stars nest in the tired man's brows.
Quiet contentment enters cool dwellings,
And angels step softly out of the blue
Eyes of lovers who suffer more peacefully.
The reed rustles; bony terror strikes
When the dew drips darkly from bare willows.


ERNST WILHELM LOTZ

IN YELLOW BAYS

In yellow bays we sucked in the vapory air
Of distant lands that know of cities
Where desires green, touched by madness.
We swam upstream on the fever-ship,
And sunned our bodies in the rutting
Of jungle-hot panthers tormented by the summer.
The naked mud-rings of the rattlesnakes
Twisted in agitation as we passed,
And in the drowsing villages lust gurgled.
A warm and gratified wind caressed the palms.—

I saw you white with sleep.
And when I ebbed away from you, lifted high
By my proud and fully sated blood:
O storm of nights that drew me blood-wards,
To bold and never-discovered zones:
O my voluptuous love! Stream of secrets!
Drowsing land! In the South! O summer-torment!


THEODOR DÄUBLER

WINTER

Patient is the forest,
Gentler the snow,
Loneliest the deer.
I call out. What do I hear?
The echo, step by step,
Returns to its woe,

190

Which approaches like soft footfalls.
The echo encircles me.
Why did I disturb the forest?
The snow did not answer.
Did I startle the deer?
How I rue my calling out.


## WILHELM KLEMM

### EQUILIBRIUM

The mountain range unfolds. Stony velvet
Sinks down to the shaded valley where forests spread their wings.
From peak to peak go gentle, thoughtful paths,
The silver crown of eternal snow foams up.

Loneliness stares at me with azure eyes,
The splintering rock overhangs precipices.
A chaotic wilderness of broken slabs
Thunders downward into silent damnation.

Ruin and resurrection
Extend an infinite handshake.
The waterfall descends calmly into black chasms.
A bird circles above. The fountain smiles.


## JAKOB VAN HODDIS

### IN THE MORNING

A strong wind has leaped up.
Opens the bleeding gates of the iron sky.
Strikes the towers.
Clangorous loud resilient over the city's brazen plain.

Sooty the morning sun. Trains thunder on embankments.
Golden plows of angels plow through the clouds.
Strong wind over the pale city.
Steamers and cranes awaken along the foully flowing river.
The bells of the weather-beaten cathedral peal glumly.

Many women you see and girls on their way to work.
In the pale light. Wild from the night. Their skirts flutter.
Limbs created for love.
On their way to machines and sullen toil.
Gaze into the tender light!—
Into the tender green of the trees.
Listen! The sparrows shriek.
And out there in the wilder fields
Skylarks warble.


## RENÉ SCHICKELE

### SUNSET

I climbed from the cellar
To just below the roof,
Brighter and brighter
Grew the room.
The city, usually glum,
Raised domes of gold,
And the gutters glowed
Like veins of gold.

The fields surged,
Sea into sea,
Birds alighted,
Heavy with fire,
On coral treetops.
Showers of light
Passed over the faces
Of solemn mountain peaks...

Climbing the tower
I saw the world
As it bowed to the night
And shone with desire,
Wearing a smile
That shimmered,
A fanning of the flame,
Around its mouth,

The way women of delight,
Lying uncovered,
Lost in thought for a long time afterwards,
Are filled with memories.


RENÉ SCHICKELE

THE BOY IN THE GARDEN

I will put my bare hands together
and let them sink down heavily,
when evening comes, as though they were lovers.
Lilies of the valley ring their bells at dusk,
and white veils of fragrances waft down on us
as we, close together, listen to our flowers.
Tulips shine in the day's last rays,
lilacs well up from the bushes,
a light-colored rose melts on the ground...
We all love each other.
Outside, through the blue night,
we hear the hours striking in the distance.


THEODOR DÄUBLER

DUSK

The first star is in the sky,
Creatures' thoughts turn to the Lord,
And boats set out speechlessly,
A light appears in my house.

Waves rise up in white,
Everything seems sacred to me.
What new awareness fills my soul?
You should not always be sad.

ALFRED LICHTENSTEIN

INTO THE EVENING...

From crooked mists precious items grow.
The tiniest things have suddenly become important.
The sky is already green and non-transparent
Back there, where the blind hills are gliding by.

Ragged trees are vagabonding toward the horizon.
Drunken meadows spin in circles,
And all expanses are becoming gray and wise...
Only villages are crouching brightly: red stars —


PAUL ZECH

THE HOUSES HAVE OPENED THEIR EYES...

In the evening things are no longer blind
and hard as mortar in the surging-by
of hounded hours; wind carries from the mills
cooled dew and incorporeal blue.

The houses have opened their eyes,
the earth is again star among stars,
the bridges dive down into the riverbed
and swim there in the depths, boat next to boat.

Shapes grow massively from every bush,
the treetops waft away like lazy smoke,
and valleys throw off mountains that long oppressed them.

But human beings marvel with ecstatic
Faces in the silver torrent of stars
and are like fruit ripe and sweet for falling.

GEORG TRAKL

EVENING SONG

In the evening when we walk along darkling paths,
Our pale shapes appear before us.

When we are thirsty,
We drink the pond's white waters,
The sweetness of our sad childhood.

Having faded away we rest under the elder,
Watch the gray sea gulls.

Spring clouds rise above the gloomy city
That is silent about the nobler times of the monks.

When I took your slender hand in mine,
You gently opened your round eyes.
That was long ago.

But when dark harmonies haunt the soul,
You appear, the white one, in the friend's autumnal
    landscape.


GEORG HEYM

ALL LANDSCAPES HAVE...

All landscapes have
Been filled with blue.
All the bushes and trees of the river
That swells far into the North.

Light squadrons, clouds,
A throng of white sails,
The shores of the sky behind them
Melt in wind and light.

When the evenings sink
And we fall asleep,
The dreams, the beautiful dreams,
Enter on light feet.

They make cymbals resound
In luminous hands.
Some of them whisper and hold
Candles in front of their faces.


ALBERT EHRENSTEIN

EVENING LAKE

We combed clouds, faun and fay
In love games over star and lake.
Now dusk has snowed us in, fog has parted us,
Our lily-time yellows in sorrow.

Envy-clouds, white wolves snatching at my heart,
You frightened the playful dancing-elf out of my bubble-
        dream.
My evening song drowns in the lake.

The wild night leaps upon my deer.
The stars have turned away.
Wasteland-bird hoots its : "Late, too late!"
Sadly I feel that I am perishing
In the snow.


ALBERT EHRENSTEIN

PEACE

The trees hearken to the rainbow,
Dew-spring greens into young stillness,
Three lambs graze their whiteness,
Soft-brook slurps girls into its bath-waters.

Red-sun rolls evening-downward,
Fluff-clouds die their dream-fire.
Darkness over flood and field.

Frog-roamer jumps wide-eyed,
The gray meadow hops along softly.
In the deep well my stars resound.
The homesickness-wind wafts good night.

Oskar Kokoschka · Albert Ehrenstein

RENÉ SCHICKELE

MOONRISE

Heart, buried alive, oh moon still lacking clearness,
Break through, the last light has faded in the evening wind...
Soon all my thoughts, hitherto damnable,
Will shine forth because they soar in loneliness.

Never again to cringe before alien souls!
Never again to beg for fulfillment!
Never again to perish with every desire
And to rise falseheartedly from the dead.

Vessel of hope, oh moon in clearness...
The world has lost its radiance in the evening wind.
Night has come. Now the thoughts that were pale slaves
Shine forth because they are masters of sea and earth.


GEORG HEYM

MOON

He to whom, blood-red, the horizon there gives birth,
Who ascends straight from hell's gigantic maw,
And adorns his scarlet head with black clouds,
The way acanthus silently encircles the brow of the gods,

He sets out on enormous golden feet,
Expands his broad chest like an athlete,
And he scales the heights like a Parthian prince
Whose temples are windswept by golden locks.

High above Sardis and the darkling night,
On silver towers and a sea of spires,
Where the watch waits to sound his trumpet
And call the morning in from ancient Pontus.

At his feet Asia slumbers wide
In the bluish shadow, beneath Ararat,
Whose snow-peak shimmers through the loneliness,
Till where Arabia steps with snow-white feet

Into the soft bath of oceans;
And far to the South, like an enormous swan,
Sirius inclines his head toward the waters
And with a song swims down the main.

With towering bridges, blue as shining steel,
With walls, white as marble,
Great Nineveh reposes in the black vale,
And a few torches still cast far

Their light, like spears, where darkly
Euphrates roars, burying his head in deserts.
Susa slumbers, a swarm of dreams
Whirling round her brow still hot from wine.

High up on the dome, on the bank of a dark stream,
The paths of evil stars are traced in solitude
By an astronomer clad in a white flowing robe.
He lowers his scepter to Aldebaran

Who vies with the moon for clear white brilliancy
Where the night shines eternally, and in the distance
At the desert's edge, completely bathed in blue light,
There are solitary wells, and mild winds fan

Olive groves that protect forsaken temples far away,
A lake of silver, and deep in a narrow gorge
Formed by primeval mountains, a water
Flows softly around a cove of dark elms.

E. M. Engert · Georg Heym

## GOTTFRIED BENN

### O NIGHT —

O night! I have already taken cocaine,
And distribution through the blood is in progress.
My hair grows gray, the years fly by.
I must, I must blossom
In exuberance one last time before I pass away.

O night! I do not want so very much.
A little bit of agglomeration,
An evening fog, a surge
Of space-displacement, of ego-sensation.

Touch-corpuscles, seam of red cells,
A back and forth, and with odors;
Ripped to shreds by verbal cloudbursts —:
Too deep in brains, too thin in dreams.

The stones wing down upon the earth.
The fish snaps at tiny shadows.
Yet maliciously, through all this being-becoming
The skull's feather duster staggers.

O night! I hardly wish to trouble you!
Just a little thing, a clasp
Of ego-sensation — to blossom in exuberance
One more time before I pass away!

O night, O lend me brow and hair,
Flow away around the day's unblossomings!
Be the one that freed me from my neural myth
And bore me home to cup and crown.

O, be still! I feel a slight urge to bang away:
Stars ready to burst inside me — It is no joke —:
I feel my face, I: me, a lonely god,
All my being centering around a thunder.

AUGUST STRAMM

DREAM

Through the bushes wind stars
Eyes submerge smolder sink
Whispering babbles
Blossoms crave
Fragrances spray
Showers plunge
Winds shoot rebound swell
Sheets tear
Falling startles into deep night.


ERNST STADLER

RIDE ACROSS THE COLOGNE RHINE BRIDGE AT NIGHT

The express train feels and jerks its way through the darkness.
No star dares appear. The entire world is but a narrow mine-gallery
    railed round by night,
Into which now and then haulage stations of blue light tear abrupt
    horizons: fiery circle
Of arc-lamps, roofs, smokestacks, steaming, streaming... only for
    seconds...
And all is black again. As if we were descending into the bowels of
    the night to work our shift.
Now lights stagger by... lost, wretchedly forlorn... more... and join
    together... and grow dense.
Skeletons of gray housefronts lie bare, bleaching in the half-light, dead
    — something has to happen... oh, I feel its weight
On my brain. An apprehension sings in the blood. Then suddenly the
    ground roars like an ocean:
We are flying, suspended, majestically through air wrested from the
    night, high above the river. O bend of millions of lights, silent
    sentinels
Before whose glittering array the waters slowly roll downward. Endless
    guard of honor saluting in the night!
Storming like torches! Joyous sight! Salvoes of ships across a blue sea!
    Star-studded festival!
Swarming, pushed onwards with bright eyes! Up to where the city
    with last houses bids its guest farewell.

And then the long lonelinesses. Bare banks. Silence. Night.
Reflection. Contemplation. Communion. And ardor and the
urge
To the ultimate, to what blesses. To the feast of procreation. To
ecstasy. To prayer. To the sea. To extinction.


THEODOR DÄUBLER

SURPRISE

The moon strolls through stone-pines, through wisterias!
A bluing water brings bluer leaves.
A breath of wind blurs and softens all outlines,
The rustling and scraping sound like roses climbing.

It seems that the lilacs are flaunting their blossoms.
They waft their fragrances, almost breathing, into the open.
It is as if all nature were exhaling kisses
To impart pleasure through the exchange alone.

All at once the dream-blue paleness confuses me.
Yet, suddenly I see a miracle shining forth.
In the shimmer of a crystal-clear pond
Shapes blanch and drink from bowls.

I am drawn to them, as if homeward to brothers.
I splash into the water. They meet me with laughter.
They catch my rippling rings, offer them to the more tired ones,
And suddenly maidens begin to stir.

I swim, so lightly as if on wings, to the island
And feel at once that I am in a different land.
There they say: all this was promised to us by the Savior:
We were resurrected within you yourselves, our graves!

I see ennobled farm folk laughing.
And one of them says: look around you, it's worth the effort!
It makes us happy to cultivate our mother country,
Come, let us lead the buffaloes! Go feed the cows!

I am at home and yet deem myself far away.
Perhaps in antiquity. Perhaps only at the Nile!

There they ascend into mountains. I would much like to follow,
But a priest shows me different goals.

He says: "Once we built pyramids
And made strong attempts to bury ourselves in quartz,
But then their essence became a blissful peace
Through which we could resign ourselves to existence again."

It is true, there they descend into the earth for ore.
Suddenly camels awaken on the surface.
No, they are earth-spouts gesturing toward the sky.
There is blasting underground: that is its soul!

Nile-peace and Nile-love are at work here below.
Hieratic serenity dawns through life.
The erection of stone pyramids
Belatedly returned our basal roots to us.

All around children play silver lyres:
Most of them gently tanned, black-eyed things
In softly earth-affined, moon-shimmering veils,
And light leaps over their playing fingers.

Now I am allowed to perceive, dreamlike, the empress.
She conducts her lovely son to the peasants.
She radiantly carries a lotus through the throng
Of stout-hearted people, who tremble speechlessly.

They beckon to me to approach the powerful woman.
I sense that her being is going to test me.
I summon my courage to affirm what she intends to say.
She lowers the flower and commences to speak:

"These are the symbols of regal kindness."
Now I ask, since I am blinded: "Which?"
She says: "The glowworm above the blossom,
The blueing dew-drop under the calyx!"

The princess now effects the most gracious of smiles.
It shimmers into me to join my most intimate images.
Already its clarity is able to fan off chimeras,
And softly to soothe my pain with gentleness.

Now the boats are slowly returning home.
Fishermen all around me pull shimmering nets,
Filled with catch and seaweed, from the surging waters:
And immediately throngs swarm over all open spaces.

The women appear with moon-pale sickles,
The girls frequently laden with geese.
They giggle in the darkness, start to tease one another,
But peasants now light everything up with scythes.

Sailors help with moon-white fishes
That twist, struggling, into sickles.
And everywhere forms shimmer, slip away,
And whiz in soft and pale arousal.

Yet mute shapes are still crouching along the shore.
They want to catch the moon-fish, the full-moon-fish!
Yet I am walking, slowly, not able to fish,
And I know well, there will be much more to surprise me.

On the shore of dreams the soul tells me
The song of my suffering innermost voices.
Would that the wind swell all longings,
So that my sagas might scale the breaking of their day.

Egyptian enigmas, dawn in the dreamer!
Theban maidens, enchant us again!
You symbols of rigidity, already the wind is blowing warmer,
And so, numina of the underworld, permeate our songs!

The tropic flow of fire contains itself in life.
Astral shapes, grasp each other in trees!
Let the human soul, fever's vanishing,
Flutter away, uproot itself forever in dreams.

You plants in the sacred primeval garden of peace,
Enthusiastically enlightening the efficacious realms!
The stars and fountain-enchanters await
The lotus of the soul in the dream-blue pond.

Hurricanes of the Styx, roar through the seers!
Chimeras, start nesting in broodiness!
Already children's larvae are approaching us, twittering,
As if all around us specters were hoisting their sail-egos!

You my essence, play: create images for yourself!
Scale songs for yourself in moon-spirit-zones!
You gentleness in me, become even gentler:
Disregard eons that merely accentuate.


GEORG TRAKL

SEBASTIAN DREAMING
For Adolf Loos

Mother carried the little child in the white light of the moon,
In the shadow of the nut tree, of the ancient elder,
Drunk with the juice of the poppy, the lament of the blackbird;
And silently
A bearded countenance bent over that woman with pity,

Softly in the darkness of the window; and old household goods
Of the ancestors
Lay in decay; love and autumnal reverie.

So dark the day of the year, sad childhood,
When the boy climbed down softly to cool waters, silvery fish,
Calmness and countenance;
When he threw himself stonily in the path of wild black horses,
In the gray night his star overwhelmed him;

Or when, holding the mother's ice-cold hand,
He walked across St. Peter's autumnal churchyard in the evening,
A frail corpse lay still in the darkness of the mortuary,
And that one raised cold eyelids over him.

He, though, was a tiny bird in bare branches,
The bell tolled long through the sinking light of November,
The father's silence when he, in his sleep, descended the dim winding
       stairs.

*

Peace of the soul. Lonely winter evening,
The dark shapes of shepherds by the old pond;
Little child in the hut of straw; oh, how softly
The countenance sank down in a black fever.
Holy night.

206

Or when, holding the father's hard hand,
He climbed the gloomy hill of Calvary in silence,
And in the dim craggy recesses
The blue shape of the Man passed through His legend,
The blood flowed crimson from the wound under His heart.
Oh, how softly the Cross rose up in his dark soul.

Love; when the snow melted in black corners,
A blue puff of air clung playfully to the old elder,
In the shadowy dome of the nut tree;
And softly his rose-colored angel appeared to the boy.

Joy[1]; when an evening sonata sounded in cool rooms,
In the brown wooden rafters
A blue butterfly emerged from a silver chrysalis.

Oh, the nearness of death. In a wall of stone
A yellow head bowed, silent the child,
When in that March the moon decayed.

*

Rose-colored Easter bell in the crypt of the night
And the silver voices of the stars,
So that a dark madness showered down from the brow of the sleeper.

Oh, how still a stroll along the blue river,
Pondering things long forgotten, when in green branches
The blackbird summoned an alien something to its destruction.

Or when, holding the old man's bony hand,
He walked to the crumbling walls of the city in the evening
And that one in the black coat carried a rosy little child,
In the shadow of the nut tree the spirit of evil appeared.

Groping his way over the green steps of summer. Oh, how softly
The garden decayed in the brown stillness of autumn,
Fragrance and melancholy of the old elder,
When in Sebastian's shadow the silver voice of the angel died away.

---

[1]Translators' note: Menschheitsdämmerung has "Freunde" ("friends"), a mis-printing of "Freude" ("joy").

WILHELM KLEMM

REFLECTIONS

Trees appease their hunger in silent green.
And the sky darkens in a forgotten gray.
The infinity of the grass
Is triumphant in a thousand tiny tips.

What was it that we really loved best?
The virtues have long grown pale in the shrug
Of understanding. Fame is so thin,
Does not liberate anyone. Wisdom founders

In melancholy. Memories grow dim,
Even the most beautiful. Even those of deliverance
From grief. Strangely and incomprehensibly
The distant murmur of perceptions fades away.

A mysterious love persists,
Half woman, half star,
Which trembles in unspeakable tenderness above the darkling heart
Like a drop of eternity.

While winter again travels across the land, bringing coolness,
The sky grows lonelier above the trees,
And the breast, with a sigh of relief, sets out for the West
Where the evening returns home, a hesitant dreamer.


FRANZ WERFEL

THE TEAR

Under the birdless sky of wild cafés
We often sit when the hour of melancholy hovers!
When the flight of music sweeps with rapid beats
Seagull-like
Right past our ears.

Nowhere in places where space is the prisoner of four walls
Does the plant of strangeness bloom more utterly.

If you close your eyes, the icebergs of the pole
Are colliding,
And the old fjord is sobbing.

Open yourself up now! What is happening? Open your eyes!
What is it that shatters the tumult? What makes the turmoil stop?
There at the table the lady in black,
With a sudden cry
The young woman weeps her grief into her hands.

What was aloneness now hurls itself toward each other.
And the weeping voice becomes a law that binds.
Everyone stands and weeps,
Streams sacred tears,
Even the tray in the waiter's hand is shaking.

Shards are we all and become vessels when we weep.
Whoever acknowledges the tear knows the substance of community.
Ocean are we, brothers, and travel,
Travel forever
Like barks on the vast seas of the heart.

Pain of the lonely person, you child of immortality!
The godhood's sweet blood, our tear is flowing.
Ah, we water with our tears
Eden's beds,
Paradise, brothers and sisters, will bear us fruit.


FRANZ WERFEL

SONG

Once once —
We were pure.
Sat small on a boundary stone
With many dear old women.
We were a gazing-into-the-sky,
A small wind in the wind
In front of a cemetery, where the dead are light.
Looked at a gate half in ruins,
Bumble bee sounded through hawthorn,
A cricket-evening entered the ear grandly.

A girl was weaving a white wreath,
At that moment we felt death and a sweet pain,
Our eyes turned completely blue —
We were on the earth and in God's heart.
Our voices sang without sex,
Our bodies were pure and proper.
Sleep bore us through a green passage —
We rested on love, sacred weave,
Time was like the hereafter, leisurely and long.


GOTTFRIED BENN

SONGS

1

Oh, that we were our primal ancestors.
A blob of slime in a warm bog.
Life and death, fructifying and giving birth
Would glide forth from our mute juices.

A blade of sea-weed or a dune-hill,
Shaped by the wind and bottom-heavy.
Even a dragonfly's head, a sea-gull's wing
Would be too far advanced and would already suffer too much. —

2

Despicable are the lovers, the mockers,
All despair, yearning, and whoever hopes.
We are such lamentable, pestilence-racked gods
And still we often think of the one God.

The soft inlet. The dark woodland dreams.
The stars, snowball-blossom-sized and heavy.
The panthers leap soundlessly through the trees.
All is shore. The sea calls eternally. ——

GOTTFRIED BENN

SYNTHESIS

Silent night. Silent house.
I however am of the quietest stars.
I drive even my own light
Out into my own night.

I have returned home cerebrally
From caves, skies, filth, and beast.
Even what is still afforded to a woman
Is dark sweet onanism.

I roll world. I death-rattle prey.
And nights I naked about in happiness.
No death will wrench, no dust will stink
Me, ego-concept, back into the world.


IWAN GOLL

CARAVAN OF DESIRE

Our desire's long caravan
Never finds the oasis of shades and nymphs!
Love singes us, birds of pain
Continually eat up our hearts.
Ah, we know of cool waters and winds:
Elysium could be everywhere!
But we roam, we always roam in desire!
Somewhere someone jumps out of the window
To snatch a star, and dies in the attempt,
Someone seeks his waxen dream
In the waxworks and loves it —
But a Tierra del Fuego burns in all our panting hearts,
Ah, and were Nile and Niagara to flow
Over us, we would just scream more thirstily.

FRANZ WERFEL

BALLAD OF DELUSION AND DEATH

In the great expanse of the day, —
The city went hollow, November sea, and made heavy noises
The way Sinai sounds. Crumpled into a ball by a tower,
The cloud fell. — With a stifled cuff
The hour struck my ear,
As I sat bent over myself too very much.
And I fell out of myself, rolled along, and then found myself reeling
    on top of a sleep.

How do I interpret this sleep, —
It took possession of me like no other sleep before, as I was passing
Into darkness, when a time
Struck me in the heart!
And as I surfaced
And, emerging into the dream, began to breathe,
I stepped into my old house, into the black hall, through the wintry
    gate.

Now hear this, friends!
As I stood in the black day, a light hand tapped me.
I stood rooted at the cold wall.
O, black, terrible
Remembrance, when I did not find him,
The light one, who approached me thus
And tapped me lightly with his light hand in the black day of the
    gate!

There was no glow from anywhere,
And even the swift little light that interweaves itself into artificial
    roses,
And becomes blurred and swells beneath the picture,
This little light died out.
No black angel stepped forward,
No shadow stepped, no breath stepped out of the cold stone!
But behind me in my dream the gate sank from sight with a sob.

And no word rang out.
But in my very own voice a word deep down in my Orcus called.
And I withered like a leaf in a stand of oaks.
Woe! Dry, light, and crazy,

212

I fell off myself and was moving in autumn and a strong blast.
A word and wind took me away with them,
The word that thrust through me, the word with three syllables was,
	the word was: hopelessness!

O ultimate fear and pain!
O dream of the hall, oh, dream of the house from which the women
	led me!
O bed, there in the dark, from which she dismissed me into the
	world!
I was standing in black ore,
And constrained my heart and could not scream,
And sang a — Save me — into myself.
The expanse of stone enclosed me. I heard the river rushing and
	falling, the river: Alone.

And since it was thus,
My ultimate lot became manifest to me, and I arose from the womb
	once and for all.
In the black dream of the hall the string broke with a sound.
And so I recognized
Why the hand tapped me lightly and delicately,
Grazing my brow,
And secretly taking control of my gait so that I no longer staggered
	and barely felt my own weight.

And as soon as I recognized it,
The moment that approached me, my very self was the other man,
And my very self was my death, which ruled me harshly.
And resolutely took from me everything,
And wrenched it from my hand and held it in its grasp: —
Pleasure and love, power and fame and finally, with a moan, poetic
	art.
And I stood appalled and frazzled and without delusion and open and
	totally naked.

O death, O death, I saw
Myself being truthful for the first time, without will, wish and
	pretense,
Like a drinker standing opposite himself late at night.
—— He laughs and remains far from and close to himself ——
I stood benumbed in the immediate presence of myself, alone and as
	two.
(Ah, what we say is already a lie because it speaks.)

I found myself, found I was without delusion, and died into my
  awakening.

In the great expanse of the day
I raised my head up out of the dream and gazed at my window-tree.
The city went hollow, November sea, and made heavy sounds,
The sky was still glowing, but barely.
But I went out, with big head and hat,
And walked through streets, reddish mountains and passes...
My head still foliated by the dream. Walked with dulled blood.

I walked the way the dead walk,
A departed spirit, orphaned and unseen.
I soared far and cool through homecoming and bustle,
Saw children running and saw beggars standing.
And a hunchback was holding his belly and an old woman was
  swinging her cane and screaming.
A lady was smiling slightly. A girl was kissing her own hand...
And I understood what linked them and strode through their
  alchemy.

WILHELM KLEMM

SEARCH

The spirits of refinement
Blow through the lilac paradise
Beneath the shining milk-tide of the heavens
And the thousand radiant nebulae.

The divine swarms of colors
Fill up the world's marble amphitheater.
Through chasms, silver-green,
Pale and quiet spheres soar.

Blazing beauty delicately comes to life,
Wonderful destinies are unrolled,
Torrents of arousal
Flow by in roaring passages.

A large bud appears.
Where does the ether sink?
Above flight-stars, where do you look for it,
The never-seen, the soul?

WILHELM KLEMM

APPARITION

The shadows are sitting at the banquet-table —
Float in the air like white skins in the night.
Friends, touch glasses! We have goblets that do not make a sound!
A forgotten star is sparkling in the midst of our circle.

Fool, who thinks that between top and toe
Everything called human being is contained!
The heart's unquenchable urge, the arms of the spirit
That reach out for the rings at the portals of God!

You with the fable-look, — are you breathing eternity?
And you, beautiful profile filled with melancholy, are you inclining your
        forehead,
Listening more intently into the spiral shell of the heavens?
Hercules, are you stretching your limbs on the stone benches of eternity?

What is now beginning, end, and return?
We no longer smile at this. All errors have been reconciled.
Entire worlds are falling down noiselessly
Into the dusking folds of our garments.

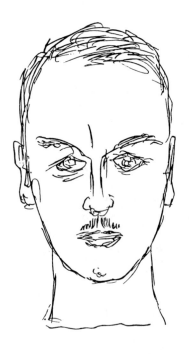

Wilhelm Klemm · Self-portrait ·
Based on a drawing from the battlefield

GEORG HEYM

WITH THE SAILING SHIPS

With the sailing ships
We roved about,
We who roamed eternally
Down through the gleaming winters.
We always got farther,
And danced in the island-studded sea,
The waters rushed far past us
And the sky was resonant and empty.

Tell me the town
Where I did not sit by the gate,
Did your foot pass through there,
You whose lock I cut?
Under the dying evening
I held the searching light
For whoever came down that way,
And shone it, alas, eternally into a stranger's face.

I called out among the dead
In the secluded place
Where the buried dwell;
You were, alas, not there.
And I walked across fields,
And the swaying trees over my head
Stood in the freezing sky
And were stripped of leaves in the winter.

Ravens and crows
I sent out,
And at dawn they scattered
Across the far-stretching land.
But in the night they fell
Like stones with a sad sound
And in their iron beaks held
The wreaths of straw and weeds.

Sometimes there is your voice,
Which passes by in the wind,
Your hand, which gently
Touches my brow in a dream;
Everything was already there ages ago.
And turns round again.
Goes about veiled in mourning,
Scatters ashes.


JOHANNES R. BECHER

LAMENT AND QUERY

Hunting grounds of the night —!
Why why must I always and ever again assault and behead myself —?
Treacherously demolish the clear straightness of my completion of a certain
       trail —
Snatch up hail and brimstone
Over the exultantly germinating innocence of my wheat—?!
Gland of the moon
You secrete magical poison-juices
Into the pure blue of my true heaven-food.
...but not in the paradisiacal region of the eternal springs do I stroll serenely...
On blood I nourish myself and on the salt of sweat.
Why why again and ever again
Disbelieving did I take myself away from you
Ophelia:
You my resin-less desert's most inexhaustible of watering places—?!
Off to you, tyrannical Lydia:
You horde of torment doubt shivers and night-mania...
Off to you, atheistic barbarians,
Big-city brutes of misery...
Most sinister of seductions:
To slurp up abyss,
To live in the cellar of rotted bones.
...For when finally will I redeeming myself strip it off this shabby felt of the
       whores...
You and you befogged me
Afra, you melancholy cage-cloud of danger,
And you devouring veins's hectic wrath-redness:
Circean Noa!
And your unfurled giant-skin's burning simoom annihilated me,
Shrill black woman!

Hah and cynically tittering
Your clashing tongue's sword
You childlike angel of death oh catamite
Brutalizes me...

Unworldly deer, O God, of your becalmed coolness
I graze
Over damp asphalt-shoreline-paths
After the horrid pressed-out thunder of a sun-sea-setting
Below the wind of death and star-milk-whirling
Mellowly in the evening.
Humbleness of ants.
Old peasant with white beard.
But the hot fairytale-honey of your undefiled lake
Trickles down from this nefarious eye's loophole.
I am rooted in the gourd of an ultimate meekness.
Your mercy's oil smooths fear-wrinkle.
Bull-neck cradles lamb and Cross
Battered helmet is called turban of your kindness.

Lamenting the acid of my scorn-laughter
And the raving funnel of my biting insurrectionist-melancholy
You, most stirring of clove-pungent harpists,
You, still soaring patiently over the untouched zenith of my murderous
        rapacity,
Smasher of cudgel-rays! Arch of gracefulness!
You, motherly escort on my seraphic childhood-journeys.
You, early sister, nightingale-rouser of the deaf despair of our sleep-poppy.
For all those who hunger and who thirst you the ever plump fire-udder.
Consoling spice you of my solitary grief-pine...
Trumpet of April as well as simple friend of my autumn-dream...
Weeper of crystal tears! Oboe-smiler!
: You sun I query
Pit of God's stomach you over my splintered and worm-eaten racks,
You, my iris's sparrow-hawk-spark and quicksilver-seeding:
When why when ———
Why why must I always and ever again assault and behead myself?!
Painfully defoliate myself with scourges and barbed comb?!
Wantonly spoil through rain the seed of my longing —?!
When finally
Will I redeeming myself strip it off this shabby felt of the whores?!
When finally will the sole festive world-sound
Of your redeeming harmonies
Burst from the vague shadows of my most futilely worn-down registers?!

When will I your obliging instrument
Sing praises with impunity
In the bleating web of grimaces?!
When will I ever-vigilant strew
The dew of divine freshness
Into your delusion-face
You who are weary of life...?!

Strolling serenely in the paradisiacal region of the eternal springs.
When will I rub out with fluff of snow mark of martyr's glaring burns!
And with trumpeting glacier-heat-rivers melt you down,
Precipitous idol-stronghold of the pyramids.
The boozer turns green from the forest-scent of my unconquerable angel.
Emptied are the countless pails of garbage.
Extirpated are slavery's eerie galleys.
Replete with steaming cow-stalls are you pitiful farms of poverty...
Lost son of insensible power you purify yourself into a shepherd of every
    transfiguration.
Then the legendary tents of your oasis-settlement stretched endlessly into time
    and space
And the sacred surfaces of our cheeks cymbaled wondrous-boldly.
The thighs of all resound and the sparse flax of their hair blusters in the storm
    of your grain.
But in the armor of the righteous
The freed slaves sit
Beneath the palms of the throne,
Between their coarse fists the earthly remains' terrible weighing-shells,
The melodic spool of judgment.


ERNST STADLER

THE MAXIM

In an old book I came across a saying,
It struck me like a blow and keeps on burning through my days:
And when I give myself over to joyless pleasures,
Exalt pretence, lies and games instead of essence,
When I complaisantly deceive myself with facile thoughts,
As if dark things were clear, as though life did not contain a thousand fiercely
    barricaded gates,
And repeat words whose range I never fully felt,
And touch things whose being never stirred me,
When a welcome dream strokes me with velvet hands,

And day and reality escape from me,
Alienated from the world, alien to my deepest self,
Then the saying rises up before me: Human being, become true to your
essence!


FRANZ WERFEL

I HAVE DONE A GOOD DEED

Heart rejoice!
A good deed have I done.
Now I am no longer lonely.
A human being lives,
There lives a human being
Whose eyes grow moist
When he thinks of me.
Heart, rejoice:
There lives a human being!
No longer, no, no longer am I lonely,
For I have done a good deed,
Rejoice, heart!

Now the sighing days are at an end.
A thousand good deeds I want to do!
I already feel
How everything loves me
Because I love everything!
I flow along filled with the joy of understanding!
You my last, sweetest,
Clearest, purest, simplest feeling!
*Goodwill!*
A thousand good deeds I want to do.

Sweetest satisfaction
Is granted to me:
Gratitude!
Gratitude of the world.
Quiet objects
Throw themselves into my arms.
Quiet objects
That in a fulfilled hour
I caressed like well-behaved animals.

My desk creaks,
I know it wants to hug me.
The piano tries to play my favorite piece.
Mysteriously and awkwardly
All chords sound together.
The book that I am reading
Turns its pages by itself.
..........................
I have done a good deed.

I want some day to stroll through green nature,
Then the trees and creepers
Will follow me,
The plants and flowers
Will overtake me,
Groping roots will already be grasping me,
Tender branches
Will tie me up,
Leaves will spray me
Gently like a thin
Sparse waterfall.
Many hands will reach for me,
Many green hands,
Completely surrounded by a nest
Of love and sweetness
I will stand there captivated.

I have done a good deed,
Filled with joy and goodwill am I
And no longer lonely.
No, no longer lonely.
Rejoice, my heart!



THEODOR DÄUBLER

OFTEN

Why does an evening valley, its brook and pines
Appear to me over and over again?
A star looks down discerningly
And tells me: Quietly depart from there.

Then I move away from good people.
What was it that could make me so bitter?
The bells start to peal.
And the star begins to tremble.


ELSE LASKER-SCHÜLER

TO GOD

You do not restrain the good and the bad stars;
All their moods are streaming.
On my brow the wrinkle smarts,
The deep crown with the gloomy light.

And my world is still —
You did not restrain my mood.
God, where are you?

I would like to eavesdrop close by your heart,
Change places with your most distant nearness,
When gold-radiant in your kingdom
Of myriad-blessed light
All the good and the bad fountains rush.


ELSE LASKER-SCHÜLER

SABAOTH
(For Franz Jung)

God, I love you in your rose-robe,
When you step out of your gardens, Sabaoth.
O you God-youth,
You poet,
I drink from your fragrances in solitude.

My first blossom of blood yearned for you,
So do come,
You sweet God,
You playmate God,
Your gateway's gold melts from my yearning.

ELSE LASKER-SCHÜLER

ABRAHAM AND ISAAC
(For the great prophet St. Peter Hille, with reverence)

In the region of Eden Abraham built
Himself a city of earth and of leaf,
And it was his wont to speak with God.

The angels liked to rest in front of his pious hut
And Abraham recognized each one;
Their winged steps left heavenly marks.

Until one day frightened in their dreams
They heard the tormented rams bleating
With which Isaac was playing sacrifice behind licorice trees.

And God admonished: Abraham!!
He broke off shells and sponge from the crest of the sea
To decorate the altar high up on the blocks.

And carried his only son tied to his back
To do justice to his great Lord —
He however loved his servant.


ERNST STADLER

ADDRESS

I am but flame, thirst and cry and blaze.
Time shoots through my soul's narrow troughs
Like dark water, forcible, swift and unrecognized.
This mark burns on my body: transitoriness.

You however are the mirror over whose orb
The large streams of all life flow,
And behind whose vital golden base
The dead things rise again shimmering.

224

My best glows and goes out — a star astray
That falls into the abyss of blue summer nights —
But the image of your days is high and distant,
Eternal sign, placed protectively round your destiny.


WILHELM KLEMM

LONGING

O Lord, simplify my words,
Let brevity be my secret.
Give me the wisdom of slowing down.
How much can be contained in three syllables!

Grant me the glowing seals,
The knots that tie together the most remote things,
Give the watchword from the secret battles of the soul,
Let the cry stream from green throats of the forest.

Fire-calls, flashed over abysses,
Messages breathed into alien hearts,
Notes in bottles on the sea of time,
Picked up after many centuries.


PAUL ZECH

I SENSE YOU

I

I sense you, I feel you, yes you, a force
that is really there, and greater than I thought.
And already you are elevating your face to me,
a face surrounded with star-leaves, its eyes a thousand years old.

And perhaps you feel: "This speck of dust in the great universe
is eager to detain me
and opines that folding his hands
will keep him from falling."

O terrible test that pierces me through and through!
I hold out and know that under my feet
the solid ground is already vanishing. My naked

struggling body whirls...
But you walk by without acknowledging me,
rejecting me by your silence.

## II

Like a drowning man I have to cling
to your hair so that you will not vanish again.
And as you cordially extend your hands to me
I was already seeing myself lying frozen on a bier.

I have bent my very self into the shape of an adversary,
in order to test my strength which pushes toward you.
But when the balance beam rises:
Will I be found too light or too heavy?

So very much is the uncertain still loud in me
that I do not even know your name,
which is familiar to every dumb animal.

I know only that I beseech you
to become for me what you are for the brute,
and that I am the last in the circle.

ERNST STADLER

DIALOGUE

My God, I seek you. See me kneeling before your threshold.
And begging admission. See, I have gone astray, a thousand paths tear me
    away into the dark,
And no one carries me home. Let me flee into the shelter of your gardens,
So that my dissipated life may find itself again in their noonday-stillness.
The only thing I always chased after were the bright lights,
Greedy for marvels till life, wish and purpose disappeared on me into the night.
Now day is dawning. Now my heart, harnessed in the prison of its deeds, asks,
Filled with fear, the meaning of the wild and wasted hours.
And no answer comes. I feel whatever carries my load of final cargo

Tossing aimlessly on the high seas in stormy weather,
And that which rocked gently in the morning, bold and delighted to be
    underway, my life's vessel, smashing
Its planks on the magnet-mountain of an erratic destiny.

Quiet, soul! Do you not know your own home?
Just see: you are in yourself. The indeterminate light
That perplexed you was the eternal lamp which burns before your life's altar.
Why do you tremble in the darkness? Are you not yourself the instrument
In which the tumult of all tones twines into a nuptial round dance?
Do you not hear the voice of innocence that sings to you softly from the
    depths?
Do you not feel the pure eye that bends over the wildest of your nights —
O fountain that sucks cloudy and clear spring waters from the same udders,
Wind-rose of your destiny, storm, thunder-night and calm sea,
You are everything unto your self: purgatory, ascension into heaven and eternal
    recurrence —
Just see, your final wish, toward which your life extended hot hands,
Was already lustrously affixed to the heaven of your earliest longing.
Your pain and your pleasure have always lain locked away in yourself as in a
    chest,
And nothing that ever was and will be that has not always been yours.


AUGUST STRAMM

OMNIPOTENCE

Searching asking
You bear answer
Fleeing fearing
You stand courage!
Stench and filth
You spread pureness
Falseness and malice
You laugh justness!
Delusion despair
You snuggle bliss
Death and misery
You warm richness!
Height and abyss
You curve pathways
Hell devil
You triumph God!

227

WILHELM KLEMM

MATURATION

I grew up into the high heavens,
Where the stars thicken into a single wall,
And saw the boundless as close
As the face of a mysterious love.

Then I sank beneath the threshold of the imaginable,
Ran silver-bright through stitches of cloth,
Became smaller than anything small —
I sought nothingness and did not find it.

I dwelt in eons of silence, where creation
Stands still; where future and past flow together
Into one, where the eternities brood
Bootlessly, and I learned to wait like God.

But then I again transformed myself into lightning speed.
I rode a thousand times faster than the light
To see the monads at play on the cutting edge of the moment,
But they, believe me, friends, were swifter than I.

And in the beauty of youth I beheld the world.
There the eternal laws were quietly triumphing!
All of that shouted with joy and dispersed.
I stood in the three realms overwhelmed.

And knew then that the soul
Wafts along alone in an unreal world.
Brotherliness surrounds me with puzzled feelings —
Where do I find, O Lord, your eternal hands!

Whether you will extend them to me or refuse to,
Your huge world is my home!
Whatever I have seen with earthly eyes,
And whatever I have lived — it has satiated me.

## GOD

I cannot say your name.
Mountains of thoughts wrap the mantle of their strength around you.
You are without depth.
If you were to tread the floor of the oceans your feet would stay dry.
If I say you
I am not I, a point on the shadow of the ineffable beings
That gave birth in your breath's tree-shaking.
I am a comma in their utterances.
But the night of your trials has roused my owlish self.
Your great light beyond all distances blinds my membranous eyes.
When I lock door and windows
And nothing is, not even nothing
When you I just as stone I
And star-cherubim I
And I you as my being dying
As my repose storm
And my thinking dream-contemplation
My will detachment
The clicking of your silver nail
Your breath beneath the blastopore
Inwardly touches my being — not-being
Behind the brow of my breast
A new heart that beats you.
Collective sparkle of the all-seeing eyeball
Pulsates around the embryo of the new human being
Whom you created Light-father in illumination.

You are where everything is
In the warm sorrow,
In the penitential robe of time
Where what is scattered gathers while fleeing,
Where no time, neither joy nor sorrow,
Only silence.
Where human being stammers his own name.
Summon up your intelligence, your faith, your health, your imagination,
    your strength, your love, your skillfulness.
Gather round yourself the feelings of your youth, the initial passionate
    fervor of your rapturous love. Arm yourself with everything that
    you are in the genuine knowledge of yourself disclosed to you
    alone, you unique being, you human being!

KURT HEYNICKE

HYMNS TO GOD

I am cast out into the world
to roll with the earth on its circular path,
I am illuminated by your flame,
Lord, I am like you!
Moving in circles I am locked in,
I am poured out into the sea,
I round my dance with the hands of unknown brothers,
your will wants to bind me to myself,
inundated by the Divine I want to find the source,
Lord, I am like you!

The nights rustle with a faraway primeval face.
Into my eyes the blue light falls.
Star of my spiritual home flooded round by radiance!
You world-bearer in the deepest stars,
I want to eliminate my sleep in your presence,
keeping watch for all eternity like the eyes of God!
You have built me high.
My head you place in your lap,
my limbs deep in the dust of the earth.

All my voices shout to you with joy,
I feel a thousand blessings swishing down,
my soul is listening at the most faraway ear in the world.
Elevated by you I kneel at the doorway to the stars:
Lord, crown me with yourself!

God,
brother, the still voice says in the night.
My brother, all truth has awakened,
from rubble and ashes a tower of flames flares up,
O brother, human beings are kneeling by your ear in a shower of
        prayers!
O human God,
Grant many sins to find you!

KURT HEYNICKE

POEM

I want to tear open my circular path,
a clear stone that breaks the golden chain,
I am not alive,
I have long been dead in the bustle of days.
My night lifts their hours high up into faraway places,
Out of blue veils white stars glow
and diamond serpents swim in sun-drenched heights.
In moonlit gardens golden colors hop about,
Their round dance is transformed into sweet evening melodies.

These are the nights
when love inundates me,
light-love, human being-love, solitudes.
These are the nights
when God makes me his guest.
This is the world
which has its home behind faraway gates.

These are the hours
that lift themselves in solitude
and their eyes high up into the source of God,
this is the life when the senses drop away,
and God alights from the most faraway constellations of the night.


RENÉ SCHICKELE

ODE TO THE ANGELS

You were the first that I saw
of the great world!
Tidings of the broad streams,
of the deep forests
and the plains in between
that with their spirit-glow
illuminate what was and is.
There love burned in full blaze,
the love of all human beings
who have ever loved,

brighter than the sun,
longer than earth and stars,
in eternity.
There you were home, from there
you came to us.
Your hands knew every place
where a heart beat.
Your wings covered every suffering.
Your brows shone
with the many secrets of the living,
which you forbearingly knew,
and with the blissfulness of the dead.
A touch of sorrow in your eyes
made you especially beautiful:
knowing about the damned.
I have seen you,
seen you in the flesh!
You were kneeling next to me in prayer,
you were standing in the room
when I woke up nights.
I sent you to protect my friends.
You sat down with legs crossed,
immensely serious like an older sister,
on my bed and shared
my first pains of love.
Like an older sister, certainly, but
you were at the same time no older than I
and my little girlfriends,
you wore your hair down
and short skirts
and offered me the taste
of your soft hands: "As much as you want!"
I placed them under me, by my heart,
and had no trouble falling asleep!

Later you were wherever
deeds were done.
Deeds of violence of every sort,
deeds that burned to heaven.
You showed yourselves to someone who was splendidly clothed
in renunciations unknown to others.
You were awesome and were tender.
You were where human beings drew
the wild sparks out of the earth,

where seeds flew across the furrows,
where the skins of fruits burst,
among swelling grape vines,
in ripe fields that rose red and heavy
beneath a wet sky
like leaven —
and in every skirt.

Surrounded by the steely glitter
you emerge from the clouds of dust
behind the automobiles,
your song is heard,
it trembles in the wind
like the high-pitched sound of a harp.
You smile at the aviators
who ascend beside you,
you are there when they return,
and your mouths are earthly red
in their presence as they rub
the light and the shock of the heavens
from their countenances with both hands,
earthly red your mouths and half-open,
and your hips are bent
so that they, still firmly secured in their seats,
can, as they heave a quick sigh of relief and joy,
see the fruits of the earth.
You are the soaring upward and across,
are everything that is stronger than death.


FRANZ WERFEL

FOR I AM STILL A CHILD

O Lord, rend me!
For I am still a child.
And yet dare to sing.
And name you.
And say of every thing:
We are!

I open my mouth
Before you would let me taste your sufferings.

233

I am healthy,
And do not know yet how old people rust.
I never clung to thick bedposts
Like women in labor.

Never did I toil through tired nights
Like cab-horses, noble in their steadfastness,
That long ago escaped from the world around them!
(From the enchanting, shattering sound
Of women's footsteps and from everything that laughs.)
Never did I toil like horses that trot into the infinite.

Never was I a seaman when the oil runs out,
When the thousand waters jibe at the sun,
When the distress-shots boom,
When the rocket rises and quivers.
Never, to placate you, did I go down
O Lord, on my knees for a final world-prayer.

Never was I a child crushed in the factories
Of this wretched age, with tiny arms, covered with scars!
Never did I suffer want in an asylum,
Do not know how mothers go blind doing fine embroidery for
        pennies,
Do not know the suffering empresses cause when they nod,
All you who are dead, I do now know how you died!

Do I know the lamp, do I know the hat,
The air, the moon, the autumn and every murmuring
Of the winds that billow out,
A countenance wicked or good?
Do I know the proud and false chatter of girls?
And do I know, alas, how flattery can hurt?

But you, Lord, descended, even to me.
And have found the thousandfold suffering,
You have given birth in every woman,
And have died in filth, in every scrap of paper,
In every circus seal you have been maltreated,
And you have been the whore of many a gallant!

O Lord, rend me!
What sense these hollow, pathetic enjoyments?
I am not worthy that your wounds should flow.
Bless me with torments, stab after stab!
I want to take in the death of the whole world.
O Lord, rend me!

Until I have died in every rogue,
Have croaked in every cat and every nag,
And, a soldier, have perished in the desert's thirst.
Until I, affrighted sinner, have sorely tasted the sacrament on
      my tongue,
Until I have stretched my devoured body from a bitter bed
To the figure that I, though sneered at, have wooed!

And when finally I am scattered in the wind,
Existing in every thing, even in the smoke,
Then flare up, God, from the thornbush.
(I am your child.)
You too, word that I speak in premonition, crackle!
Pour yourself unconsumably through the universe: We are!!

# Call-to-Action and Revolt

Johannes R. Becher

## Preparation

The poet shuns radiant chords.
He blares through tubas, beats the drum shrilly.
He whips up the people with chopped sentences.

I learn. I prepare. I practice.
How I work — ah most passionately! —
Into my still unmolded face —:
Wrinkles I engrave.
The New World
( — one like this: eradicating the old, the mystical, the world of pain — )
I etch, as correctly as possible, on it.
A sunny, an extremely structured, a *refined* landscape I envision,
An island of blissful humanity.
To achieve this, much is required. (This he has been aware of for a long time.)

O trinity of creation: experience formulation deed.

I learn. Prepare. I practice.

...soon the breakers of my sentences will be formed into an enormous corpus.
Speeches. Manifestos. Parliament. The sparkling political drama.
        The experimental novel.
Songs to be sung from tribunes.

Humanity! Freedom! Love!

The new, the Holy State
Be preached, injected into the blood of the peoples, blood of their blood.
Let it be thoroughly formed.
Paradise begins.
— Let us spread the firedamp-atmosphere! —
Learn! Prepare! Practice!

WALTER HASENCLEVER

THE POLITICAL POET

From the cisterns of underground pits
His mouth burps white steam into cities,
In the furiously sprayed-out blood of tubas
Howling over and over again work, rest, night and struggle.

With dwarfs who carry on their gigantic humps
The hardened ingrained ulcers of their burdens,
With slaves whose boils are torn open
By the lashes of the whip while oaring galleys.

His arm breaks through the massive barrages
Of armies rabble-roused to murder by the throng of nations,
Through filth and straw and rotting yellow maggots
In the prisons of all revolutionaries.

Often his ear hangs on small gabled roofs,
When from the city the big bells toll,
To endure with many heavy and bent brows
The imprisonment of poverty.

When in the movie houses misfortune shudders nightly,
Hunger goes begging behind marble halls,
Abused a child dies, and walled up
In casemates wild curses are uttered,

When defrauders throw themselves from bridges,
Instigated in the gleaming light of palaces,
When anarchists sharpen their knives,
Sealed to the deed with a dark oath,

When injustice blazing as the fire of truth
Venomously overgrows the heads of tyrants,
Till from the dragon of the earth there shoots up enormously
The lightning flash of revolt, of rebellion —

Ah then: from the tallest tower of every city
His heart will hang unfurled in the rising of the dawn;
Asphalt twilight in the sleeper's bed
Is driven away by trumpet sound: rise and kill!

Rise and kill! Assaults rage.
The chains clank down from vaulted structures.
Along river banks parliaments brood in silence.
The copula bursts. Already songs of freedom are blustering.

Unsheated rhapsody of mounted myrmidons
Gallops across holes emptied of paving stones.
Tumult increases. Obstacle waxes into mountains.
Trampled women weep behind shutters.

But from the churches the trumpets thunder,
Smash houses boomingly to the pavement.
The telegraphs whisper across provinces,
The morse key jerks in dynamite.

The last trains are backed up in the stations.
Artillery rattles forward and explodes.
Mangled masses congeal into bloody balls.
The street yawns on overturned animals.

From windows oil boils down into the avenues,
Where commandants, impaled, grow moldy.
The evening burns, over factory tops
The red flags wave from the gray heavens. —

Stop the fighting! On the other side too hearts are beating.
Soldiers, citizens: do we recognize each other?
Brotherly word amidst smoke and pain.
The procession gathers. Form ranks.

Reconciled throngs turn toward the palace,
Where finally high up on the balcony the ruler appears:
"In the presence of the dead lying here below
Remove your hat and bow your head, Your Majesty." —

Dead ashes. Night on barricades.
News of violence spreads, everything is permitted.
The thief's lantern sneaks about in suburban shops.
Looting raises its scorpion's head.

Cellar vermin crawl into the beds of the rich;
Naked beasts fall on white girls.
People sever rings from the trunks of corpses.
From the canals comes the muffled howl of anarchy.

In crude celebration the wild masses continue the dance,
Their Jacobin caps banded with blood.
Justice, law of the highest order:
You are to consummate the world which they have changed!

You freedom fighters, become freedom judges
Lest the perfidious betray your work.
From firmaments the new poet descends
To earthly and greater deeds.

In his eye, which scents the morning,
The night loses the chaos of disguise.
The muse flees. Shaken by his spirit
The earth rebuilds and becomes fulfillment.

It tears from its escutcheon the old theses
Which the privileged cunningly bequeathed to themselves.
Prairies produce bread for all beings,
Since all fruits ripen for the weak as well.

Not in the shadow of steel amphoras
Do trusts glow that hunt down their prey:
You presidents, hasten to be born,
So you can strike dead the thousand-headed moloch!

Power disintegrates. We shall unite.
We, rocking on Atlantic transports,
Emigrants for whom the clouds of home shine brightly.
Europe draws near. Iron portals are sinking.

Young men rise at universities
And sons who hate their fathers.
The shot is fired. In parched cities
Officials no longer carouse at banquets.

The people grow demoralized. They make speeches from tribunes.
Does not a pool of blood float into their assembly hall?
When will they avenge the torments of the dead?
The signal is already sounding from country to country. —

The poet no longer dreams in blue bays.
He sees bright throngs riding out of courtyards.
His heel rests on the corpses of the infamous.
His head raised high, he prepares to escort nations.

He will be their leader. He will prophesy.
The flame of his word will become music.
He will establish the grand league of states.
The rights of humanity. The republic.

Congresses will bloom. Nations will be inspired.
River banks will dwell along wide oceans.
They do not live to swallow one another:
Their hearts are sworn to brotherhood in rigid zones.

It is not wars that will do away with violence.
Give generals employment at amusement fairs.
To create a site where peace will be at home,
Assembled are the noblest and the best.

No longer is a people victorious through weapons, you know it;
For no battle will decide its course.
So rise up with the crown of your spirit,
Beloved companions, from the barren grave!


FRANZ WERFEL

FROM MY DEPTHS

From my depths I cried out to you.
For lo and behold, suddenly the metallic taste of the entire mistake was on my
      tongue.
I tasted a recognition beyond all thinking.
I felt oozing from me the evil oil with which I am heated,
Sweetish weariness played in my bones,
I had been turned into the fiddle of the entire mistake.
I felt my vibrations on a most distant dream-cape,
And wanted to rise, defend myself, win myself, protect...
But I sank back, eerily
Paralyzed into sluggishly throbbing despair.

From my depths I cried out to you.
I cried as if stepping out of sunken fevers: where am I?
I stood reeling in a swaying landscape, in the dizziness of secret earthquakes,
      and cried: where am I?
I recognized the world. It was clinging to one last twitching nerve.
I saw the mortal sweat of things. They were lashing out in jerky agony.

But like noble children who fight back their tears, they smiled humbly from
        below.
Then I shook off my solitude,
Then I abandoned restraint and room,
Then I forced my way into the halls. They roared like the bed of city-dividing
        rivers.
I was submerged in the clattering of plates, hubbub of voices, drum-betrayal of
        steps and
Typewriter ringing.

I cried out to you from my depths.
But my countenance carried its grinning around.
With my right hand I adjusted the putty of my smile.
And everyone did the same.
We sat facing one another, but our gazes were directed elsewhere.
With both hands we covered a part of our presence that we did not trust.
We spoke long strips of words...
They however were born on the palate,
And we were not able to produce gladness and pain,
As our throats made believe.

From my depths I cried out: "Where am I, where are we?"
Surrounded by unalterability, thrown into unmerciful laughter, cast upon the
        island of shipwrecked cardplayers!
Our repose is death,
Our arousal putrefaction!
We are marinated, salted, smoked with malicious disusage!
We have unlearned the resting glance,
Unlearned the lying there that gazes at the sky!
From my depths I cried out to you,
For here no will can rescue any longer, here only a miracle can rescue.
Work miracles!


KARL OTTEN

THE DAY-DOME'S PINNACLE

The day-dome's pinnacle evaporates below the cloudy breast of night.
The huge barge-like houses carry their ups and downs rudderlessly.
The iron gates of heaven screech, the choirs of cherubim boom.
Their starry lips resound twinkling brightly and the wind from their moon-
        robes

Makes the lanterns of the children flicker.

I beseech humanity, which is preparing for sleep

I beseech humanity, which the cry of the sirens is summoning into coal-thundering factories

I beseech the bearers of children and the begetters

I beseech those who are dying and divesting themselves of their earthly things

I beseech those who with dagger and crowbar are vibrating in the storms of murderer-fears

Whose bones are clattering like doors that God slams shut behind them

I beseech you who are asking your feet where they are taking you for the last time

For whom the revolver cracks, the rope stretches, poison smells sweetly, water sparkles invitingly

I beseech you who in bewilderment have been counting the bars on your cell window in the bony light of a smirking moon,

I beseech you who have been waking up for weeks and months to pulsating pus,

Who rave away your fever by beating your global skull

Against the plaster wall, against the bed posts

I beseech you for whom the world became incomprehensibly a bowl a button a steaming blood-hurricane-crater

That turns white and black and pours soup or cold water over your thin body

I beseech you sailors tossed about on salty waves in the distress of the storm

Vomiting freezing.

Into whose stiff eyelids the stars were squeezed

And in whose throats the moon is choking.


And you brothers in the trench's grave

With the mortal hunger of the thundering vaults,

Around whose bladder and testicles the barb of agony bites in the presence of intellect

Reason, health, sensuality, desire for happiness; full-blooded, clear, witty.

You soldier half dead between the trenches in stinking hissing gasses

Drowning in your blood, dying of thirst in the mud, hammered to death by your own pulse beat

More wretched than a worm a tadpole a caterpillar;

You God creating, God thinking brother,

You I beseech. All of you who raise the rifle to your shoulder, aim, and fire death, and must be unsuspecting:

I beseech all of you on this very night that begins like the first

That God created with eyelids lowered in the same way that the weeping willow

Of obstinate humility is bowed at the foot of the mountains;

All of you I beseech to forgive me my great guilt, my great guilt.

I place myself like skin, shirt, armor, and embankment
Between your soul and your lot.
I will swear off the sleep of this night
I will scourge myself and roll around in thistles
I will warn pray beg and dispute with the evil one
Like signal rockets and jets of water my imploring shall
Be in readiness. Like a valley I want to catch the mountain echo
Of your passionate fervor and distinctly, urgently
Roar back
Amplified a thousandfold
Earth's thunder against heaven's unfruitfulness.
To shake God-Father by his stiff knees
To bang furiously on all solar drums
Till he wakes up and remembers.


WILHELM KLEMM

PHANTASY

I see the spirits carousing in dark arbors
And glimmering women stretching on naked thrones.
I hear giants breaking their fetters.
Wanly the castles glimmer in which the griffins dwell.

Colossi stagger towards me. Cherubic figures,
Night in their wild eyes, blackly their feathers rustle
Skyward. Blazing banners are
Unfurled. Choruses fade away and wild combat songs.

Now then, now then, dear old heart! With countless meshes
The glimmering dreams move across the world.
Who has spun them? Who can catch their ends?
Brilliant jewelry that sinks into the infinite.

Ludwig Meidner · Alfred Wolfenstein

ALFRED WOLFENSTEIN

HAPPINESS OF EXPRESSION

Movements, flashes of the human being! Signs
Of the human being extending from eye to eyes:
At the red base of my blood commence!
Rise as though on waves of the wind.

The sea is sea incarnate to its very edge,
Yet more freely does it extend the hand
Of sails — thus from the depths
Do my sinews stretch me to the firmament.

Form! at whose long journey the emptiness
Is smashed to smithereens, O fully hoisted knee, traverse
The world, the flight of hips and shoulders
Is never adequately visible visible!

And like the red sun of morning let the mouth rise,
And proclaim the swell of feelings —
Thus the internal hazy garden
Reveals itself as blooming, and arms are like standards,

Spokespersons that elevate their message
To the sunny countenance of our brothers —
And what misery gives way? Silence gives way!
The distant human being is reached by the human being.

Just as earth, zooming, never still,
Always expresses more loftily what the depths demand,
Everything expresses everything! Akin to the Almighty
Movements, signs of the human being.


THEODOR DÄUBLER

MY GRAVE IS NO PYRAMID

My grave is no pyramid,
My grave is a volcano!
The northern lights beam from my song,
Already the night is subject to me!

245

This peace is getting on my nerves,
To freedom I am sacrificing my illusions!
The artificiality by which we maintain ourselves,
This Ararat, my ardor will cleave!

Adam is carried to his grave,
And what remains is his world-instinct.
It is constructed out of a thousand marble legends:
I myself, a shadow that hobbles to work,
Can but deeply lament my ancestor,
For thanks to me he struggles for composure in the pit.
The grave that he is constructing for himself is his belief
That transitoriness will never rob him of the archetypal self!

I feel, proud earth-father,
Your pain which bursts the laws:
You conceive a drama in the theater,
Whose thousand steps crowd around you.
You breathe freedom from the crater,
Which is frightfully compressed:
Endeavor to forgo the peace of your grave,
Then your heart's star shall light up the world!

I am myself a spark of freedom,
Equilibrium I cannot put up with!
Away with the pageantry of experience,
I hereby relinquish my grave!
In the ultrafiery potion mercy bubbles
Overabundantly into the Last Judgment.
But this I want to share with my shadow,
That I dream you, powers of the earth made free!

My grave is no pyramid,
My grave is a volcano.
My brain is a forge that sends out sparkles,
Let the task of effecting change be carried out!
No peace resounds from my song,
My willing is a world-hurricane.
Let my breathing create clear day-forms
That, no sooner espied, will cleave Ararat!

KURT HEYNICKE

SETTING OUT

The world is blooming.
Ah yes, lifted on high, O heart, awake!
The world is brightening,
The night is shattered,
Set out into the light!

Into love, O heart, set out.
May kind eyes shine from human being to human being.
Joining hands.
Mountainwards naked as gods upwards.
O, my blooming people!
Receive from my hands all the sun.
The world is brightening,
The night is smashed.
Set out into the light!
O human being, into the light!


WALTER HASENCLEVER

YOU, MY YOUNG MAN

You, my young man, I love you above all others,
You are my own image that appears to me!
I see you in many a devil's claw;
Certainly you are not happy, have wept.
You love too grievously or wait in vain,
Your father, your landlady causes you anguish,
You thrash about in an unruly life,
Your thinking becomes middle-class, your head turns bald.
Won't you follow me and hear me out!
See, I am swimming toward the same rocks.
Once on prairies, now in choirs of spirits
I want to call you and be with you!

ERNST WILHELM LOTZ

REVOLT OF YOUTH
1913

The flaming gardens of summer, winds, deep and full of seeds,
Clouds, darkly curled, and houses cut up by the light.
Lassitudes that came over us after ravaged nights,
Exquisitely cultivated, then wilted like flowers that are broken off.

And so, grown strong for new days we stretch our arms,
Shaken with incomprehensible laughter, like a force that builds up,
Like columns of troops, impatient after the alarm has been sounded,
When on high and anticipated the day blues across the East.

Dazzlingly the banners wave, we are of firm resolve,
A jolt went through us, urgency shouted, we are surging ahead,
Like a storm tide we poured into the streets of the cities
And wash away the ruins of a shattered world.

We sweep aside power and topple the thrones of the aged,
Moldy crowns we offer for sale with a laugh,
We broke down the doors to moaning casemates
And throw open the gates of loathsome prisons.

Now come the throngs of exiles, they straighten their backs,
We plant weapons in their hands that clench furiously,
From red tribunes enraged rapture blazes forth
And piles up barricades steamed round with ardent shouts.

Lit by the morrow, we are the promised illumined ones,
The hair of our heads adorned with young Messiah-crowns,
From our brows spring bright new worlds,
Fulfillment and future, days, the storm our flag!


RENÉ SCHICKELE

THE RED BULL DREAMS

Three thousand humans stood tightly packed.
There was an air of hunger, sickness and desire.
As if through cloudy vapors men's faces were staring

248

up at the tribune decorated in red high above,
faces burning, pale as death and eroded,
and, with their wild hair, half-crazed women's heads,
glances that grazed seemed to light up
in each another. They trembled and wanted to embrace.
Hot breath blew on every nape. A body was
pressed up against other bodies whose breathing
forced them apart and drew them together.
This was an apocalyptic animal, ready to fly
and gigantic, glowing with a thousand hearts.
The far-away voice engulfed in red-flaming vapors spoke:
"...no lies...no getting soft...right
of the stronger who does the labor in this world,
my work belongs to me.
No pity and no getting soft in the heart.
Long live the war!
Blood must be sacrificed to God: to our spirit
and to that of our children. All human beings are bleeding to death
daily, slowly in joy and grief,
labor is war! We will have our signals,
the long marches, the clashes,
where the human being gives birth to his secret, greater spirit,
his God, the ancient God
shouting in the thunderstorms!
It will be our war
and our own ambitious work!
No regrets!
Human beings must die as heroes,
so that others may grow in their exalted shadow,
grow away from their necessities and toward God, the spirit,
for whom we found the grand words,
the grand images
in millennial yearning...
So too in eternal minutes we shall encounter
our own victorious image.
All flesh must perish,
but this is our spirit.

Long live freedom,
which binds the powers of one human being
to those of other human beings
so that each generation
can erect its Parthenon
in open competition...

Freedom: arousing all ambition,
intensifying our enthusiasm,
filling us with strength,
making us ardently strive
for the perfection of these our hands,
of this our heart!
Long live beauty,
which arises from the longing for perfection
like a star from evening mists...
Take notice, beauty is nothing
but naturalness reflected in a smile.
They smile who can do their work.
This anyone knows
who has ever thought about his labor...

Long live God; the spirit.
Those who serve perfection shall experience the thrills
of eternity.
Long live the ambition to serve the spirit.
Accursed be who wants to lord it over us...
The slaves will free themselves!
There are enough kings in their midst,
ardent beauty, faith, morals,
and the justice that weaves our garlands.
In *our* labor we will be *our own* masters,
wild with feeling and serene.
If one of us glances at the face of another,
we mirror one another: human beings..."

Three thousand human beings stood tightly packed.
The voice in the distance broke.
Three thousand human beings shouted and wept.


KARL OTTEN

WORKER!

Worker! You forged into wheel, lathe, hammer, ax, plow,
You Prometheus without light I call upon!
You with the rough voice, with the coarse tongue.
You human being of sweat, wounds, soot and dirt
You who have to obey.

I shall not ask what sort of work you are doing.
What purpose it serves, whether it is just or unjust, pays well or badly,
Whether any amount of pay can make up for the dismal work you do.
Whether all in all money is the expression or the sop
That makes this work innocent meaningful worth the wages.
This night has lasted a long time, blackest darkness
Pressing its damp shirt over our mute mouths.
I cannot tell if you are blushing.
Nobody can gaze into your hearts.
You know in spite of everything, in spite of everything
That you are ciphers!
No matter where: in the plant in prison in sick bay in the barracks in the
cemetery,
You are there to feed a set of statistics whose sum, whose increase, decrease,
stagnation
Can be found in any newspaper.
Likewise your children, your wives, your parents, sisters and brothers.
You are better off the statistics say so:
You are freer that is the talk at the clubs
You are contented the banners and the music tell you that
You are hardworking it can be sensed from the good cloth of your suits, the
shoes of your wives.
You understand me? In your heart, deep down in the last shaft
You are awake, dissatisfied, philosophical, rebellious.
Deep in your blood is the bitterness of punishment, of meeting quotas.
You suffer in silence the enigma of this meaningful servitude,
An enigma as unutterably strange and ineffable as an angel.
Worker, proletarian, son of the factory, of the tenement, the movie house, of
Nick Carter and the bordello!
You who live on potatoes and bread, twelve people to two rooms,
Whose childhood paradise was darkened by envy and beatings
You who sought only to avenge yourself brutally and maliciously on your own
kind
You who dream of sharing, of the sea, of the Alps, the palaces and gardens of
the rich
You who are hungry for the bright lights, mirrors, curls, easy chairs and
women—
You are awaiting the day! The light! Retribution! The day when you will pay
them back:
Eye for an eye tooth for a tooth!
Radiantly it will dawn, solemnly eternal sun over yonder steeple
And your cry of victory will drown out the deepest death rattle!
You have your program you have your prophets yours is the victory!
It is inevitable since it can be calculated!

251

Calculated! And I hear your steps
Rumbling for millennia round the machine
Which is deaf to every prayer to every plea.
You say nothing and wait and let yourselves be tormented.

And while the heart was bound with ever feebler thumps
To the years as they relentlessly went by
And was beating time with wheels pistons and saws
You willingly made league with the exploiters.

And the dance of the hissing machines
Lulled you to sleep and screwed you in
The iron-fire-money-god leapt from them
Into your hearts. It is in him you put your faith.

Him you want to and will exalt
Through newspapers ciphers and wars this very god
Who now torments humanity with bloody visions
Carnage conflagration with stock exchange medals victories.
It will come to pass, oh if only tomorrow were today
That you will suddenly experience a bloodstained sober awakening
The last bit of heart, the prey of disgust
Will gush from your throats, oh terrible awakening!

You I call son of the steaming galley ship
I detain you on this island of horrors
In the sea of blood sea of fear sea of fire
In the storm of the last cries of soldiers killed in action
Of mothers sweethearts infants
Of the curses cries pleas feverish babbling
Of soldiers wounded scorched poisoned
Buried alive torn to pieces
Of soldiers made crazy by fear hunger poison —
You are a human being just like me!
You should and you can think!
You have to justify every squeeze of the lever
Every blow of the hammer, every dime earned in overtime,
Every word that you squander in lies in abuse!
Do you know that it is your duty
To be a human being, inhabitant of the earth, to have a soul, heart!
Worker, my dark brother, you do have a heart!
Your heart commits you to humanity.
From your heart all suffering spreads
Into all hearts.

Your heart is bound to all hearts in the same beat.
Your heart invigorates reconciles damns inflicts mortal wounds
Tear it out of the machine's chest cavity out of the network of wires
Hurry, blood is flowing, flowing, hurry as though
Death were drawing nigh. You can save humanity!
You son of humanity, whose calluses are licked by every buttering boss,
On your heart your goodness your being
On you alone
You son of the handmaiden, you brother of Christ
Depends whether light will penetrate this sea of blood and murderers!
Your goal your victory your happiness is within!
Within the heart, it is it is! As surely as your heart beats,
Only the heart can win
This war that has been declared on you.
Your heart is the one the pointed bullet perforates
No matter who is carrying it: it suffered and was afraid
Hoped sang was small and poor
And a human being's your brother's heart.

They gave you bread money work and sufferance —
I give you your heart!
Believe in your heart, in your feelings, in your goodness, in goodness *itself*, in
        justice!
Believe that it makes sense to believe,
To believe in the eternity of goodness,
In humanity, whose heart you are.
Only goodness shall conquer, love, gentleness
The strong unshakable will to truth
The stiff-necked resolve finally to say what one feels
And that nothing makes for greater happiness and bliss than the truth.
Be a brother to human beings! Be a human being! Be heart! Worker!


PAUL ZECH

THE NEW SERMON ON THE MOUNT
(1910)

I

You, the pale cripples gently pushed forward by children,
and you, the infirm coming from the hospital,
you, the insane picked up off the streets

253

and you who have run away from the factory;
daughters of Magdalene, Cain's robust sons,
who have strayed in from China and the Urals:

so that my words can be heard over your groans,
so that my words can penetrate the scabs on your brows,
words wild like the thundering of hot foehn winds,

and so that veins clogged up with sorrow
will open melodiously, this hour has been
once more reserved for me, before brothers in rabid blindness

hound and tear each other limb from limb like the huge dogs
of jet blowers that are set up in caverns.
And though God no longer speaks through my mouth in anger:

the Father, who has sent me, still has the same name as the world.

## II

You men, speak, are they already thundering down in smoke,
those golden palaces which were built high above blue rivers
from the bones of your forefathers? And has it burst yet,

the belly of Baal, who devoured like sweet grass
the caravans of the helpless plighted to the god?
And are the fiery flags of freedom already waving from the church spires

to the mangy inmates in their narrow cells?
And has the encrusted humiliation of your calluses
already jumped back wildly from your muscles in hatred?

Who drags an unbelieving people into the yoke of a brazen harness?
And where is the roaring battle cry that urges you on to deeds,
where does the distress-sail swell that will speed you through the ether?

The warning sign that you are writing in black with cloud-fingers,
did it stem from the five unbound wounds
of the death on the cross, which will remain unavenged

as long as this earth has not lost its appetite for human beings?

## III

And you, foliaged mothers, fruitful without sense
and stretched out eternally to conceive anew,
has your serving ever been of blessed benefit?

A kingdom? Provinces, risen grain-yellow?
And daughters: trustingly submissive like Ruth?
And have you ever in anxious nightlong

prayers lamented the spilled blood
of your husbands, and, stared at by the larvas of despair,
worked yourselves up by the hour into a vengeful rage?

God gave you the breath of psalm-green harps
to light up silvernly the frost of souls
that threw themselves remorsefully upon the nakedness of bestial things.

From your magical fingers roses
continue blooming, to appease ultimate poverty.
In order to build bridges of bold arcs

across rivers, harps must sound above rosy miracles.

## IV

Worn-down music still sways about your lips,
you children, whom I have never seen so helpless,
and so driven to tip over immediately into tears.

What was happening everywhere in the budding fields of spring:
ladybird-song and butterfly-catching
are familiar to you only from meagre picture books.

Never did bells that pealed fervidly when workers went on strike
entice you into experiencing the blissful din of a snowball fight.
Crushed feelings frequently traversed your dreams.

And when you kindle a small fire somewhere in fallow fields,
fear immediately breaks out of your mouths like bitten-up chalk,
and you always brought home dysentery and a cough.

I however want you to ripen in the sun
like a thousand stalks of grain; for my mills are practically empty
and at the crossroad's uncertain borderline of existence

sun-tanned tormentors lie in wait like an army of Huns.

V

Let deliverance break sheerly out of my mouth
and flow far out like the Atlantic,
so that, submerged on the bottom, you

can pluck up your courage for the final freedom.
My seed, once scattered in battles,
how it accumulates here as barren sand?!

Rub out of your eyes the desolate sleepless
nights of torment and become pilgrims in my procession,
which the fathers of the new tormentors already ridiculed

and priests shamelessly utilized for deceitful purposes.
You who have floated here with the dead gaze of the blind:
in me there is always high noon and flight of stars.

To overcome Sodom and Hellas, Rome,
I pour myself out hourly to everything that wants to drink.
And grandly from easterly wafting winds

I erect for you daily the final Day of Judgment.

VI

O Day of Judgment, portended by the booming of the heavens,
O fiery flash that strikes all things rotten,
O sudden bolt that shatters Baal's Tower of Babel

and clarifies into truth whatever ferments in despair:
Already I hear from the depths the stamping of curved hooves,
and scent a fire which festers yellow from black clouds

to boil away the twilight battles in the cities.
And when Elias returns in his chariot of fire,
then eyes, immensely rigid with fear,

will burst open in bright belief and plunge into the conflagration,
which burns to make fertile the soul of a new world.
And no one will settle there who is burdened with things past;

aroused to creative upswings of happiness,
God's blood, which flowed in vain once before,
will shoot through every human heart in comet leaps

and appear — threefold sun — over Canaan.


RENÉ SCHICKELE

BIG-CITY FOLK

> Yes, the big city makes you small..
> Oh, let yourselves be moved, you thousands..
> Go out, why don't you, and see the trees grow:
> they take firm root and can be cultivated,
> and each one rears itself up to the light in a different way.
> You, to be sure, you have feet and fists,
> no forest warden has first to clear a space for you,
> you stand there and create prison walls for yourselves —
> so why don't you go and create land for yourselves! Land! Get
> a move on, set out! —
>
> Richard Dehmel
> "Sermon for City Folk"

No, here you should stay!
In these depressing Mays, in bleak Octobers.
Here you should stay, because the city is the place
where the desirable feasts are celebrated,
feasts of *power*, and where the edicts that turn you pale are issued,
edicts of *power* which — whether we like it or not — drive us like machines.
Because from here the armed trains are hurled out
on murderously gleaming tracks,
conquering the land
over and over again.
Because here is the source of the will,
foaming in waves that press upon a million necks,
source which in the beat of a million backs,
in the to and fro of a million limbs
surges to the farthest coasts —

Here you should stay!
In these depressing Mays, in bleak Octobers.
Let nobody drive you out!
With the city you shall conquer the earth for yourselves.


PAUL ZECH

MAY NIGHT
(1911)

Paternosters are still rattling, window fronts are strutting
white as flamingos into the ocean of lamps.
But the waterfront lies silted up, crane next to crane,
walls grow on three sides out of the canals.

The brown hills of poverty in front of the forest of smokestacks
have forgotten that here a Vesuvius erupted...
The rooms are filled with the sounds of shouts,
in front of taverns hangs the moon, the reddish dirty joke.

And suddenly over the flat monotony of the streets
the gigantically bulging visage
is apocalyptically emblazoned with the inscription:

*"Make way on dumps, wharves and glacises,*
*make way on grass, flower bed and gravel*
*for May, which descends on our throats as a scream!"*


LUDWIG RUBINER

THE VOICE

O mouth that now speaks, swinging along in transparent swoops across the
vaulted seas.

O light inside the human being in all places on earth, in the cities voices fly up
like silver spears.

O lethargy of the rotating globe, you fight against God with legions of snarling animals, with jungles, sabres, bullets, malicious misunderstanding, murder, epidemics:

But the luminous human being bursts out of the crust of death. In the factories valves are howling across the earth. He has screamed his voice through a thousand trumpets.

A voice shot into the air, an arrow of solid steel whirring like flint glass and bursting white-hot in a glow.
A voice across America, among sweaty blacks who roll the whites of their eyes; among German refugees, bearded depressed beggars, among starving Jews darkly compressed into slippery ghettos.
A voice among worn-out workers, three million, who each year die lonely deaths because of innovative manufacturing systems,
A voice among canker-eaten women in colorful blouses who are relieved of their money by bordello bosses.
Among benumbed Chinese in the odor of hunger who wash fine linens day and night,
A voice across the Broadways, where the jobless make a grab for discarded bits of food.

A voice vibrated gently like the thin cry of rising steam before the multi-sounding water bubbles come to the boil,
It sprang like wind-sand into mute mouths, it slid like flute-energy over the stooped bones of weary haulers.

Through pitch-dark rooms sun and moon floated, the stars traversed torn patches of stinking wallpaper.
Oh, maybe the wonderlight of heaven will dawn before everyone croaks and becomes a rotting carcass!
A voice flew and sucked itself full with dirty factory-time,
Rage and hope circulated like blood, and hatred that spits its drool.
A voice whispers darkly across bad paper from bankrupted printing presses,
A voice read the whisper-word: strike! in the red shafts of the Colorado mines.

It hovers like hot smoke over pitching and tossing harbors; over distrustful saloons; in starved villages; whenever the plundered farmer sows;

In cities it shouts a clanging signal across turbulent assemblies whose entrances are watched by the police.

O mouths, out of which the voice of the human being burns!

O dry lips, sixty-years-old, sad drooping stubble-bordered, lips that open shallow because before dying someone confesses.

O wild red glow of tongue behind a black man's white teeth, the voice gurgles in joyous song.

O mouth, round resounding gateway, echo and desire, people's chorale, so that the hall swayed along.

O bitter seamstress-mouth, moaning for justice and shrilly counting dimes and the pounds on a scale.

O wrinkled speaker-mouth which opens and shuts like the eye of an owl and chooses effects.

O man in the blue shirt who hastily spreads propaganda during factory breaks.

O attentive official who sends letters and recruitment lists to all post offices.

O humble one, embarrassed heart, who would just once like to shake the hand of a good person.

O mute one, who speaks for the first time and consumes himself in one sentence, crackling.

A voice flames over Europe's hounded, over bent and taciturn coolies in the Australian bush.

O mouths, how many are waiting for you, you resound, and they too will open!


JOHANNES R. BECHER

TO THE TWENTY-YEAR-OLDS

Twenty-Year-Olds!... The crease of your coat detains
The street that has vanished into the sunset.
Barracks and the department store. And wipes out the war.
Will soon capture the gust of wind from asylums

That bends princely residences into the fire!
The poet greets you twenty-year-olds with fists like bombs,
With armored breast wherein lava-like the new Marseillaise sways!!

260

ALFRED WOLFENSTEIN

CHORUS

Touch your fingers: feel yourselves thinking,
Dabbing like violins, excitable singers,
But from the heart kettledrums throb,
More muffled wrestlers for your happiness.

Wish not to stand there, to melt while listening!
Form with your feet mountainous walking,
Struggling the earth strikes at you with its breath,
And the wafting remains wildly lodged in you.

Starry cooling, glowing of the soul,
Solitude, love, — oh, to feel both!
Walking voice ascends to voices,
Friends churn up desert in happiness.
         Based on the 2nd movement of the Symphony in A-Major


ALFRED WOLFENSTEIN

COMPANIONS!

Then freed I rushed out the door,
The warm stairwell helped by lighting up at once,
And I much preferred walking on the cobbles of the street
To crying in an eavesdroppingly small apartment!

This is the flight from relatives too close,
Who touched me before they knew me,
It is as though I were still in the hollow womb
Of parents whose pressure has not let up since birth.

But better hatred and the desert of this city
Than your love, which possesses me without reason,
We never chose each other! You suckled me,
But does this make you feel that you produced me?

No, better to be separated from the lamp's false peace of soul,
From your tight security!

261

And better into the unknown night
And without bed to stay awake in contemplation of the truth!

Here come, like the houses steep and cold,
The streetcars, stirred only by a brief stop,
Without feeling too and in a rush the dark people,
Who seek each other out to savor an exotic prey.

I wander with them as if alone —
Into dazzling cafés as if into silent groves, where
At table after table, each head sits enthroned
Like a leafless trunk, separate and never satisfied.

And see the couples going home
Without harmony in an ice-clear union,
And prefer stealing away to little stars,
Along black windows, lifeless streetlamps.

And finally I lift my true hands —
My heart expands all walls like a trumpet —
Oh, away with horny-cold solitude
And half-heartedly animated swamp-water togetherness!

Related blood from parents' night of love,
Brought close to them without our consent,
Separated blood, paired in street-love —
Oh, that both could be banished by a new cry!

A cry for friendship! That in dark rooms
The walls shall topple and the naked shall glisten
Stripped of covers stifling and invisible
And cleansed of ghostly feelings.

That *those unfulfilled* in their impoverished times
Shall waft from graves into our spirituality,
And that new beings shall now be born
With the more deep-felt gestures of blossoming hearts.

A cry for sun! Instead of using each other brutally,
To breathe prouder souls into one another —
A cry for freedom! Not to be lost in a crowd
But part of a group as in a file of soldiers — !

The plaza, filled with the quiet strong scent of lilacs,
Kindles like an echo that repeats itself,
From every street red beams dawn
Here, to paint themselves starkly into a new world.

Those are the wills, forged entirely from light,
That love each other as countenances of the will,
That is the light's opening melody,
The sweet close all-embracing companionship!


KARL OTTEN

FOR MARTINET

I

We step in front of forests over which summer roars.
Gaze down from the hill, soft with pine needles.
Under it strawberries and mushrooms lurk in all innocence.
Meadows sink at the touch of our feet, cows, goats; we lie down pairs of lovers.
We let the sky cloud over us in its blue vastness
As if it were our blood we dip into its starry folds.
We sit on a bench by the river bank, the bridge
Arches from jump to jump, thundering with carts and people.
Flashing the river sucks the land in long draughts
And smells of home, evening bells, ships, and children's songs,
Trembling we jump out of our simple sleep onto the creaking floor,
Trembling our heart listens to the strong pulsebeat of joy, to the frenziedly
      jubilant command —
The sky approaches green and set ablaze everywhere by Orion, the Bear, the
      Milky Way
Barely lit up are the ragged outskirts of my city, proud towers, townspeople's
      roofs,
Milky smokestacks — in the distance a train rushes by wailing.

II

But in the dark glow of forests, mountains, streams,
The wind of faraway places brushes past, aback behind our heads
Icy coldness wells up, pinprick pricks, conscience burns.
From clouds and pregnant moon avenger's hand bites, human-handed cyclop
Shows his pointed finger, bores into heart and kidneys!
From Orient and Occident eyes burn us to dust!
You! a cold hail-wind bellows

You! sand in teeth crunches!
You! summer rain hammers resoundingly on all your thick skins!
You! children swear, mothers keep quiet, brides-to-be babble,
You, you only one, everyone, you alone!
Only the I is at fault!
Open up, earth of summer, sky of night crash into us,
Wind of divine spring, let your wafting become acid, tannic, bite the twenty
       hides around our soul.
Sunbeam be lightning flash, it is lightning flash, spreading the flame!
Smash down on the pavement the cadaver that forgot!

### III

I have heard your greeting, brother.
Just now railway trains passed by above me,
Trains jammed with new brothers.
They waited till the brothers were nineteen so that they could be hacked to
       pieces by the book.
They lie in wait for the children, check out their joints, their muscles,
And ask will they be ready soon.
The mothers dare not watch them grow up and grow rebellious.
Would like to hide them, forbid them to leave the house,
Hypnotize them to sleep.
Two three years until — but it cannot work — things will run their course.
I crawl with all the others, it has to be that all of us crawl.
We can no longer say much, brother.
In every square, on every street the dead are loitering about,
In every house barricades of the dead,
Every river clogged up with the dead,
Sailing along in the sky like swarms of migratory birds
Beneath the blood-clouds — the dead.
Oh, that evening would never come or tomorrow!
Multiple crowds of pale skeletons from the shopwindows and streetcars,
The café gardens, the parks and churches that are overflowing with the
       inconsolable.
Through basement windows, through sewer gratings emaciated arms reach out,
       grabbing for your legs.
You step into the empty room:
Three or six or twenty are sitting there (one on top of the other) and are
       rummaging through your books
They despise you and point at you with festering fingers: you! you!

# IV

Crouching in May, blossom-springtime-splendor, lushness of decay,
Land-filter for body, soul, idea — nothing remains but the smell
Of putrefying and rotting things, slippery with blood, pus, senseless
       sweat —
Your greeting, brother, rang in my murder-poisoned, oxidized heart.
I see you waving from over there, pale, tall, gaunt with mouth wide open
Your eyes rolling, your neck is craned, and hoarse —
Shouts.
You are shouting something at us — I know, I know!
We all know, we know!
Oh shame, remorse, guilt!
You our inseparable brother, you common people bound to us as we are to you!
God swirls us round his axis on the string of time.
God, this wild animal with horns, knife in his mouth, drooling with blood,
He bangs us against each other, tears us apart, stirs up hatred, pours out
      venom, sneers.
We human beings, we idiots, we scoundrels keep silent
And let ourselves be stirred up, be provoked, be thrashed.
O God, forgive us, but your strong arm, your tremendous strength
We can no longer endure.

# V

I did not doubt that you exist,
That you worry, brother, through the night.
Golden bees hummed your thoughts,
Butterflies of the night around our patient brows
And it becomes solace-bringing night, mother-comfort, child's flower.
Your greeting has plucked me from the wheels of the machine.
(The machine: how we hate this beast, this cold iron-murder-muzzle.
Away with technology, away with the machine!
We will have nothing more to do with your accursed hellish inventions,
Your electric currents, gasses, acids, powders, wheels, and batteries!
A curse on you, you inventors, you vain, childishly bloodthirsty designers!
A curse on you, age, gloriously ludicrous, of the machine — everything factory,
      everything machine.)
I can stand on my two feet again, you open my eyes, lift my head!
You shake my hand, I recognize you!
I have told everyone about you, that you exist and that there is no longer any
      enmity.
That the enemy is an invention (machine), that the human being is the only
      truth,

That truth, hope, faith, justice *are*!
Machine is *not!* Technology is *not!* Enemy is *not!* Hatred is *not!*
It is — yes — to be *destroyed!* to be *destroyed!* to be *destroyed!*
Wipe it out, cast it from your eyes, hearts, stomachs, intestines!
Poison, poison! lies, rubbish! there are no enemies!
Only human beings!

## VI

We have crawled away from the leafy wings of the forests.
We have lain on our knees, we are still beating our breasts.
We ask you for forgiveness!
Not I alone, the dumb poet with the eyeglasses,
Staggering through the streets splattered with blood —
No, all of us, millions, remorse, shame, being ridden by guilt bangs us to the
    ground!
Oh believe us, this fluttering back and forth, this lying, cursing, pounding on
    the table,
This yelling, talking, swearing, lashing out — embarrassment, being mad at
    ourselves:
At our stupidity, our lack of faith, our cowardice, our fear.
We no longer know where we are at!
We no longer know: day, evening, yesterday, night, today? right, left?
In the delirium of our shame we feel exasperated.
O brother-hand, point out the way
So that I shall finally find you,
O brother-eye, bore through the night
Illuminate our paths.
O brother-heart, announce the hours' coming
Hour of reconciliation,
O brother-mouth, a signal, a signal!
When will your greeting sound, your song, your hymn of joy?
We await the day when the united armies of the enemies, brothers and sisters,
    parents and children,
Will finally, finally recognize each other, fall into each other's arms and tear in
    pieces the real enemy who had warmed himself at their fires!

## VII

The real enemy! There is an enemy! O day of delight, day of freedom, holy
    Russia!
Never did Europe see a more beautiful day, never our youth a more glorious
    goal!
With moon and sun, with star and rainbow

There was inscribed on the firmament:
The real enemy!
Then a hurricane of the most secret fanfares of jubilation tore
All hearts, all poor lips, ruffled up hair and hands joy enthusiasm!
All of Europe was suddenly convulsed, true ideals touched the skin of exploited
    men everywhere.
They spat out the lie, the incitement to hatred, they discarded their murderous
    blades in piles,
In this second there roared through every heart freedom, community, goal,
    closeness.
The spirit hooked into their empty lives, their lives in joyless hovels.
The glass fills, hearts mature, rage ripens.
The earth gives birth, it spreads its mountain-legs and gives birth to the
    avenger,
To Hercules, the giant, the idol of revenge!
I tell you, brother Martinet, we all want the same, we all know in what
    direction we have to march.
The true front summons, the true air victory, the holy trenches, the liberating
    drumfire!
We are one, united, we recognize our guilt, we purify our spirit!

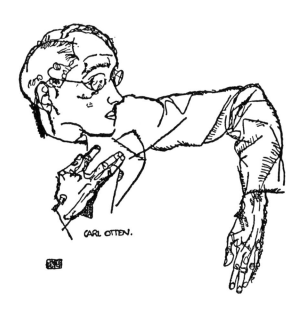

Egon Schiele · Karl Otten

KARL OTTEN

THE ENTHRONEMENT OF THE HEART

Open your heart, brother:
The book of the dawning, brother
Of the new time, brother
The mantle of fear, brother
The eye of recognition, brother!

Your heart sees enlightenment
Through your murder-blessed hands:
Pale wretched they scrape in vain
The crust of shame from the desecrated body.
Holy! holy! holy!
Ineffable, your snow-pinions
Your heavenly breath
Your death-rattling breast —
Humanity!


WALTER HASENCLEVER

JAURÈS' DEATH

His pure countenance in its white clarity
Left error's gruesome track far behind.
They murdered him, spirit of truth,
Comforter of the poor of Paris.

He was hit by the bullet whose battle
He saw coming and castigated before his country.
He who was clearing the path to peace for every human being
Was struck down by a brother's hand.

God lifted him out of the end of these times,
Would no longer let him see the despair.
His upright eye helped prepare the way.
He is close to us. He will rise for us.

JAURÈS' RESURRECTION

Weeping women in convulsions,
Children at their father's neck;
The train keeps moving
Through the cities...
Send, you spirits of the dead,
A signal of distress!
Return in the third hour,
When they scour the battlefield,
To shine light, to take pity
To strew the wreaths of hope.
No helper rises;
No humanity falls at his feet,
Laden with the guilt of legions.
In the marketplaces of the provinces
Before the ignorant, the misled
They fan the flames of eternal warfare.

To you, you beings on high,
The call goes out: help this life!
Out of caved-in trenches
The apostle's white form climbs.
They recognize him again
In the crowd.
Poor farmers kneel and adore him.
Soldiers of Europe! Devastated churches
Can no longer save your countries!
Soldiers of Europe, citizens of Europe!
Listen to the voice which calls you brother.
It comes swimming in
From singing seas,
From the wreck of ships,
Rat and mouse.
For the last time the gun barrels thunder.
Lemons blossom
At the edge of the lake.
Fall down, militaries! Bow your heads.
Call a halt, coal-mines, to the murderous day.
You princes on thrones,

Descend,
Weep by the mound of the dead;
Peace, reconciliation is dawning.

But you, a mighty people, a purified humanity:
Golden banks, magnates' estates
Will pass to you.
Leave your barracks, your galleys,
You who are narrow-chested and without dreams!
The earth lies before you.

Upwards, friends, human beings!


RUDOLF LEONHARD

THE MONGOLIAN SKULL

A Mongolian skull
lay, torn off by a shell splinter, at the edge of the trench.
The eyelids could no longer cover the white eyes,
but you could see the dry teeth showing from yellowed lips.
A soldier took it home with him.

There he showed it to a girl,
she bent over it deeply
and snatched it wildly from the man.
She placed the yellow head on a silk pillow.

It was borne by many white women
through the noise of the streets.
Children crowded round, the vehicles stopped.
Men grew silent; all joined together to take a closer and harder look.

In the somewhat slow-moving procession
a hymn was sung:
"Once expression in the eyes, blood and life, brain
and spirit and deed, and smiles, dead brow!
Now — not yet dust. Shredded hair that hung,
a white bone, soon a piece of dirt. A thing!"

The city hall tower pushed itself in front of the softly singing marchers.
A woman leapt forward, shook her hair violently, and

planted a kiss on the broad mouth of the dead head,
covered brow and eye sockets with kisses.
Everyone had to cry out.
Overhead the tocsins started ringing.


ALBERT EHRENSTEIN

VOICE OVER BARBAROPE

O you sun-golden evenings,
twilight — where is the bridge across the stream?
Mist threatens gray road under the super-night,
rail tracks buried in rubble, the fords washed away
in the torrent of all flood waters!
We reel along in the sea of blood-rain,
linger in the swamp waters of sleep
and do not know: shore.
When will the night
of your slaughter end,
which has thundered across
Barbarope, Eurasia many murderous years!?

You drown yourselves, suffocated
by the wells of your running dry,
beat of the black swan's wings
sinks exhausted into blood-river-flood tide.
Do you hear the still
pools of seeping pus bellowing heavenwards?
The sand has opened its mouth
and cannot go on.
Woe to the motherland,
gives birth to battlefields where the bones tower
— to declare war on the declarer of war.

For him the gentle fields are greening,
the green curtain's velvet flooding.
In the reverberating halls
grand-king of torments
boasts at table.

Rotting carcasses, far and wide only rotting carcasses!
Soar down, eagles, ram your talons
into the guts of the war-crowned, peace-crowing demon!

LUDWIG RUBINER

THE ANGELS

Leader, you stand there looking small, a quivering pillar of blood on the narrow
    platform,
Your mouth is an arched crossbow, you are shot off whirling.
Your eyes cast in horizontal flight luminous wings into the green,
Your wrestler-arms circle their way far into enemy territory.

You weak pillar, God's thrust has whirled your hook-nose into the trembling
    masses,
Your ears, hollow-winged, hover rosily like light birds over the leaden screams
    of the people,
The bright wings carry the throne of your head gently over stone-throws and
    gray insults,
Like cloud-plumage your head shakes down on human shoulders gold-flashing
    celestial cupolas.

O angels, you fly through blue space in the luminous ball of the head,
Eyes, you angels, you dart to the whirring brothers in the circle;
O tongue, arms, limb-pillars, angels, you entwine in each other like branches
    on a waving tree.
Leader, speak! The angels surround you on crystal mountains radiating and hot.

LUDWIG RUBINER

THINK

The night in the white prison is moon-pearl and high,
Shiny brown bars cross in front of the window into the future,
The leader lies on the uneven plank-bed,
A spying eye thin as a hair scooted through the peephole in the smooth iron
    door.
He lies there very still, so that the blood flows through the straight limbs and
    shoots back,
The tower, overgrown in brown, of the head is hurriedly ascended and
    descended by guards.
Way down below the moat of the mouth lies in dryness.
Outside the dark moving fields wait for the fire's glow.

272

O mouth, soon armed hordes will swim from you like black waves,
Brown head, you will hurl them crashing far into the countryside,
O glow of the eye, which hits its target in the blazing fire.
O cupola, in which the new houses of the earth hover, evenly enveloped in
      each other, countless, and statues, forests, languages,
                    You crystal head!
You now lie in silence within the white cube of your cell on the narrowness of
      a nocturnal plank-bed,
Fingers close by your side as in the grave tomorrow.
But your pulse-beat is already pounding softly through the wall-pipes of the
      fortress,
The warders whisper to the prisoners in violation of the rules.
Your brotherly eye circles all-seeing like a moving stone through the wakeful
      cells.
Think through every prisoner's brain, and out to the guards, past the yards, out
      into the streets!
The stone buoyed over you is swelling.
Your hair is the platform of sleepless guards,
Your trembling makes the brick walls in your blood breathe in and out,
The barred windows circling the building high up are darkly hidden from your
      gaze.
Millennia from now the fortress your image will be in every land far and near,
      your name will float like a huge fire across the skies, above your
      tremendously high head of stone.

Leader, do not sleep tonight. Just this night, keep thinking!


RUDOLF LEONHARD

THE SERAPHIC MARCH

Now peace is not to come, but war
and end without end;
let each day be a further turn
and each a step and new victory.

We shall not let the world rest:
on all European streets
on the corners of the world
with legs astraddle and firmly planted in the ether,
the brow tensed in wind and clouds, the lips contorted,
shadowed eyes, eyes of fury fixed and slanted,
let us blow, blow, blow:

into the hollow of pale hands attached to bent-up arms:
alarm, alarm!

Everyone will wound us, no one harm us:
defenseless outlawed comrades!
Without helmets, rifles and bugles,
madly believing soldiers of the future,
without the hope for which we asked,
we shall blow, blow and pray,
we knights of the spirit, we a small troop:
alarm, alarm!

The most impatient of your rescuers,
to transfigure your lives
into ethereal spheres,
we shall ceaselessly shatter your ears.

Who has poured the lumps of heavy black earth into our hair?
Weeds shoot into the air. The dark wings are felt
by us, shattered as a result of suffering your sufferings,
to be ascending slowly and smoothly and growing cool.

See how the filled spheres echo with the call!
There assembles about the place to which he who created us
Had once banished us the heavenly forms.

See, blond children are running swiftly and barefooted across radiant meadows:
we shout open the gates to the paradises!!

How ardently we grow, how poor we are,
shivering naked children,
                                    armored giants-:
alarm, alarm!


WALTER HASENCLEVER

1917

Keep awake hatred. Keep awake suffering.
Keep burning on the steel of loneliness.


274

Do not think, when you read in your paper
A human being has been killed, he is not like you.

Do not think, when you see the dreadful strides
Of a mother who carried her little ones

Out of the smoking caldron of the roaring battle,
This misfortune was not caused by you.

Approach the wretched coffin
Where a dead man's bones stare through rags.

Next to this stranger, eaten away by worms,
Fall upon your knees and be accused.

Embrace the unloved torment
Of every outcast in this sign.

Embrace a last eye that drinks from the ether,
The cry that sinks into damnation;

The burning wilderness of the screaming air,
The rude shove into the cold crypt.

If there is something trembling in your soul
That can live through this horror,

Then let it grow, let it rise up
For the storm when the old times go down.

Emerge, O human being, with the trumpet of the Last Judgment
From raging nothingness!

When the executioners drag you to the scaffold,
Hold tight the power! Rely upon God:

That amidst the murder and betrayal of human beings
The good deed will someday shine again;

That the heart's strength, noblemindedness
Will soar through the starry heavens.

That the sun, which shines on the good and the bad,
Wept through so many streams of the world,

Pulsed through the heartbeats of each of us,
Shall one day shine upon the day of righteousness.

Keep awake hatred. Keep awake suffering.
Keep burning, flame! The time draws nigh.


## FRANZ WERFEL

### CALL TO REVOLUTION

Come, deluge of the soul, pain, endless rush!
Destroy the stakes, the dam, and the valley!
Break out of the iron throat! Roar, you voice of steel!

Stupid piggishness! Life of smugness,
Away with your dead I AM!
Alas, only weeping wrenches us toward what is pure.

Never mind if the powers that be tread upon your neck,
Even if what is evil drives countless spikes into you,
Behold what is righteous rise glowingly from your cinders.

Growing recognize what is accursed!
Howling burn up in water and fire-pain!
Run run run against the old, the wretched days!!


## JOHANNES R. BECHER

### HUMAN BEING RISE

Accursed century! Chaotic! Songless!
Suspended, you human being, leanest of baits, between torment fog-madness
    lightning.
Blinded. A slave. Furrowed. Raving mad. Leprosy and acid.
With inflamed eye. Rabies in the eye-tooth. With howling fever-horn.

But
Above the cross on the neck unending ether undulates gently.
Come out of trenches, factories, asylums, sewers, the hellish dive!
Solar choirs summon the cave-blind with hymns.

And
Above the bloody abysses of the battle-waters
God's magical star sparkles in everlasting constancy.

You soldier!
You hangman and robber! And most terrible of God's scourges!
When finally
— I ask troubled and at the same time filled with frantic impatience —
When finally will you be my brother??
When
You drop altogether the murderous knife *in you*.
You turn back unarmed in the face of graves and enemies:
A deserter! A hero! Thanked! Blest!
You angrily smash into a thousand pieces the criminal rifle.
You ruthlessly shun your "damn duty and responsibility"
And refuse every exploiter, tyrant, and employer openly and with disdain your
        cheap and dastardly services.
When
Your destructive step no longer stamps mercilessly across the peaceable and
        sunny lands of an earth enlivened with creatures.
And you crush yourself in a rage in front of your glorious victims on the cross.
...then then you will become my brother...

Will be my brother:
When you kneel contritely before the lowest and worst of the executed looters.
When desperate and humiliated
You press spiny fists right through your mailed breast
Into the interior of your just awakened heart —
When overwhelmed with remorse and smashing your vows you yell out:
"See, this man too was my brother!!
Oh, what a grievous, oh my fault!!!"

Then then you will be my brother.
Then then will have come that ultimate dazzling paradisiacal day of our human
        fulfillment,
Which reconciles all with all.
Because all will recognize themselves in all.
Then the lashing storms will thaw away powerlessly before our truthful word.
The obstinate Ararat of your haughtiness will be redeemed and eagerly seat
        itself under the soft tents of humility.
The wicked onslaught, burden, and tumult of the devilish will be gone with the
        wind.
Just as the rapacious greed of the wicked, most limitless and boundless
        treachery and triumph will be vanquished without force.

Tell me, O brother human being, who are you!?
Ravager. Killer. Scoundrel and executioner.
Predator-gaze at the yellowed bones of your neighbor.
King emperor general.
Gold-glutton. Babylon's whore and ruin.
Hatred-bawling jaws. Bulging money-bag and diplomat.
Or or
*God's child!!??*

Tell me o human being my brother *who* you are!
Happily
Surrounded by the gurgling and restless ghosts of the butchered innocent and
      defenseless humans!?
Of the damned the evacuated the exploding slaves and hired servants!?
Desolate pyramid on all sides chaos graves scalp and cadaver.
The desiccated tongue of those dying of hunger and thirst is seasoning for your
      repast!?
Wretched death-rattle, last breath, raging hurricane of the embittered, are these
      the pleasant sounds of music coming to you from afar?
Or on the other hand
Does this most excruciating misery not concern you
You who are full lethargic lukewarm you who are heartlessly superior?
Is the fortress of your hardness, encircled by the roaring cyclone of the times,
      really untouched!?
Are not your proud towers crumbling away stone by stone, so that the pregnant
      donkeys can finally rest.
Your fruits are rotting: peoples soulless and brutish.
Rulers of this world, who incriminate you, only you!!!

Tell me O brother my human being who are you!?
...perfect star-pattern in the kitschy celestial wish of the poorest up above.
Searing fire-wound's cool balm-friend,
Enchantingly sweet dew on tiger-wild thornbushes.
Gentle Jerusalem of fanatical crusades.
Never ever-fading hope.
Never deceitful compass. God's sign.
Oil of the bitter bulbs of rigid doubt.
You tropical port-city of emigrant sons, of the lost sons.
No one a stranger to you,
Everyone close to you and brother.

Lost swarms of bees nesting in you.
In the southerly zephyr-sleep of your hollows there rests, entangled in the
      labyrinthian desolation of space

Singing ecstatically a beggar, the poet without possessions, Ahasuerus,
    unworldly worldly melancholic pilgrim.
The one-who-is-without-peace dives down into the slumber-arbor and oasis of
    your feet.
But the-one-who-is-luminously-never-tired climbs up the Ural-temples of your
    head:
The sources of your purity
Struggle through curse and steppes.
Into barricaded citadels
You pour spices lamb and spring-hill.
Angel you descend to where the poorest drag themselves around.
Even in the infernal regions you helper do good.
But for the wicked your youthful wing — judgment — clashes :
Blazing you snatch fruit and breath
From the rocky gorge and its foul-smelling vapors.
Scoop up heavenly blood.

...Wrathful Moloch or Eden's coast.
Poison-gas-spewer or seed of salvation.
Monster of the hyenas or zone of palms.
Christ's side-wound or vinegar-sponge.

Tell me O my brother my human being: *which one* which one of these two are
    you?!

For
Burning tides roar at you demanding a reply:
Make up your mind! Give yourself an answer!
It is an account I want and
The torn-up earth from the powerful catapult of your brain: will and fullness
    and destiny;
A sacred happy future's childlike carefree sleep urgently asks you as it dreams.
Pour yourself out! Acknowledge recognize yourself!
Give heed to yourself! Make yourself clear!
Be bold and think!

Human being: you who have turned away from human beings,
    lonely brooder, sinner tax collector brother: who who are you!!

Turn in your grave! Stretch and desire!
Breathe! Make up your mind finally! Change direction!
Citron-farm or thistle-exile.
Chosen island or sink of thieves.
Devastation-cellar. Ray-prophet and flame-Sinai.

Locomotives velocity brakes yelping.
Human being human being my brother who are you!?

Sulphur-thunderstorms nefariously fill azure space.
Your desire's horizon is grated up.
(...down into the blood! Chest open! Head off! Torn to shreds! Squashed. In
      the snout of the floodgates...)
There is still still time!
To assemble! To break camp! To march!
To step to fly to leap out of the Canaanite night!!!
There is still time —
Human being human being human being rise rise!!!

Ludwig Meidner · Johannes R. Becher

## WALTER HASENCLEVER

### ALREADY FROM RED CASEMATES

Already from red casemates
The mob is foaming forth,
Indignation whistles like a pack of rats
In the chorus of promenades.
Darkly in the hall the conductor's
Upswept arm breaks to pieces;
Along the beautifully decorated walls
The white circus light goes out.
Hatred rises from green mists:
To be there and to join in the fray.
A cripple in front of mahogany doors
Does not impede triumphant behavior —
Past the mirror of limitless happenings
Streams the semblance of the living;
After a few years of endless seeing
We shall no longer be transitory.
Strength to effect and to fulfill
In the highest spirit, which flees my countenance!
Good fortune — that we do not end in despair!
Misfortune — you Marseillaise hymn!


## ALFRED WOLFENSTEIN

### THE GOOD FIGHT

The sun comes, a fiery projectile — comes — hovers — explodes —
It strikes, oh poor earth, only the roof of the night,
And above it the stars become blue sky,
But ashen grayness rains down, onslaught and battle.

A million eyes, opened frantically,
Like counter-suns, carry the image
Of hell in their gaze! Behold every nation
Emerging red from war out of a chaotic summer.

They press themselves, drunk from poisonous streams
That sparkle blindly through this earth below,

Out of the rigid womb of their countries
For human slaughter, and smite each other in the dark.

Oh, see the sky showing forth its pure sun,
But dipping past you toward infinity,
And war and finitude and death
Climb sunlessly for you out of every dawn —

The doors creak open snappishly, into the morning
Figures stumble out over refuse and worries, —
And into a heap of city
In which even in the daytime night lies hidden.

Their pockets jingle with things old and cold,
Iron and gold digging their claws into each other,
The keys' hard bits dream
Of the doors' womb, of riches and power.

Wherever they tread, mad with hunger for their own kind,
Windows flare up instead of suns, howling
Office and storeroom creep in a cannibalic dance
Around cashbox-sparkles, furnace gratings, bookish pallor.

In their clothes, weighed down by stone-heavy lies,
Daggers wait rigidly like dogs for a signal,
And their eyes are like knives in a brow
That suddenly flash scimitar-like into the neighbor's blood.

They emerge corpulent from their park, and soon
The larger forest of their slaves grows round about them,
Herds of children gallop out of cellars
And come to a gaunt halt in the midst of smokestacks.

Then the bells drown each other out in godlessness.
On gigantic rental-convulsed shoulders the houses
Crouch and sway, with their calculated bucking they
Spitefully push and shove each other.

On tracks like desire swift and smooth
City jumps into city with the skulls of train stations,
The borders' long curved horns spike
Country against country with tips never satiated.

Oh, how much the world persecutes itself — then once more
The day's accordion of hate pushes
Its bellows and somewhere
A door knocks down just another beggar,

Just another girl is tied like a board
To the boss's lap in his private room,
And schoolchildren, wild from the green of the classroom window,
Sneak to the toilet like caricatures of freedom.

And yet O sun, — you that float black and cold
Across the earth, O shape
Of the heart: Sun! Sounds of spirit-force
Traverse your path like singing eagles —:

*Hither, all of you* that serve the soul and
Through a head resounding with art, through an inspiriting mien
Build the poor world more perfectly in your work,
In the sweep of the word, in the flight of violins —

And all of you laden with cares who work in the coal-graves,
Who work at dizzying heights on some stranger's scaffolding,
Who work naked in poverty, poison, and steam —
For the other fight! for the other fight raise head and hips!

You friends, living *everywhere*!
You who work, from out of the raging flood,
From out of the swamps of money, the abyss of war, the desert of equanimity,
From out of the wrongly divided globe of countries

*Appear!* And even if you came crawling out of mud,
Act as if you had suddenly arrived from heaven!
Shine down upon the crooked army of the wicked,
Which swells up as if stung by death —

Tumult thundering with deafening thuds —
The adversaries seek each other out, hatred and kindness,
A rain of arrows clinks, the target is hit by
Shiny missiles hurled from the clanging catapult.

The dreams bury the red face of brutality
In their white sea and breathe on
Money-armor, blasting it with angels' fire,
Their breath puts to death the hisses of greed.

From prison a head, blue as freedom, hurls
The fire of his calls at the tyrant's edifice.
The flag of smiles that flaps through every body
Is waved over the hovering throng by a lady of love.

On the stony skulls of the rich, those far removed from love,
Who everywhere construct cold tenement houses
Of chance, the youths' wrists zoom down
With stars swung high around their hands.

And tirelessly the mouths of mothers sing alarm
In children's songs fresh and stirringly warm,
The arms of mothers indestructibly
Thwart blood-drenched butchers.

You friends of friends — flowers and animals invite
Themselves into your army, an electric cord
Moves, ready to help, in spasms through the universe —
*Comrades of the earth*! God's comrades!

You friends of enemies — your hand is blow
And is also salute, soft as that of a creator!
Shaping your enemy in the struggle —! Your left hand
Clutches your own heart and molds it at the same time.

O tender beings, feverishly concerned about the smallest of things,
Beings immersed in spirit, slender as butterflies,
Yet roaming with a lion's might the densest forest
Of suffering, which is to pervade you fully —

O beautiful beings, rising from the heart's sea
On the shimmering shells, — wading up and down
Through filth and rage and sorrow — walking along
More purely on an ever new earth —

O clear beings that comprehend the ethereal head,
But, trembling deeply, sink down
Before the godhead's blue, — and yet on bended knee
Put their trust in the strong and never bowed head —:

The good charge is led by them!
And darkness shall flee. For that which has never
Been: the sun of humanity, will, born of their spirit,
Be formed by them in the heavens!

## Johannes R. Becher

### Eternally in Revolt

Eternally in revolt
Against the fortress
Of the most frenzied murderers,
Of the butchers of the lamb.
Tear tear to pieces
Powerful gusts,
Darknesses,
The profiteers' tower!
The tyrants
Have burst on thrones.
Hah already the nocturnal clouds
Of delusion have melted.
Behold too the cannibals
Of the inheritors shriveling.
No longer does the world
Give itself to the rich alone.

Forests envelop with chirping
The midday of the good.
The righteous
Are resting in God.
Horribly in the mountains
The sinners are dashed to pieces.
Slaves, rise up
From virulent gulches.
Stars are sprouting
The dead prophets,
Once crucified
By the myrmidons of Baal.
Below in the lava-crater
The hypocrites,
Their brothers' betrayers:
A ghostly dream.

Blessed are you poor,
Scattered and blinded!
For the innocent
Live without possessions.

Only the wicked
Burrow into the earth,
Unfathomably suspended
In the tormenting straits.
To span
Tides of decay...!
Into prisons
Source of the tree...!
Your buried courtyards
Are awaking!
Swept up
By the panic storm.

The squares are still
Swarming with hangmen.
Girded with knives.
Carrying rifles.
Their butts pound
The Psalters.
Bomb-storm
Impiously in space.
But soon such things will come to an end:
Then the murderers
— fevers bellowing
In the oil-belly of the tanks —
Will fall croaking
On the pavement.
Flags will unfurl
Solemnly in red.


RUDOLF LEONHARD

PROLOGUE TO EVERY COMING REVOLUTION

The swamps exhale their peace.
Again the enemy of humanity rises: time.
The cities steam, countries swell out.
Did the lightning flash back into the clouds? As yet nothing has been decided.

As yet the plains here below stare fixedly,
already thundery, already poised for the fall and the ascent.
Activity gives off the perilous scent of suffering.

Death was experienced! Already you feel the blood boiling,
so live and know that soon the flame will spew upward.

The oily stream of praise from blubbering bearded bards has floated away:
The gates of the unleashed mind yawn,
the naked youth presses forward, the emperor of our Orient,
and waves the red flag with the leopards.
Bent in the torrent, it foams across borders of the mind.
We are increasing, we are in front of battalions,
at Carmen's wedding, listen, we shall begin, we shall reward
with the serrate roaring of our fire.
The dead tumble into hillside graves.
Kneel down, you who are thunderstruck, we are laughing,
cold blooded believers we, and will spare you,
we skeptics, mutely aroused to passion.
For we are there! In choruses, wedge formations, platoons, columns
invading the lustrous land that we fill with even more lustrous shouts:

The first chorus
springs from the homes of the humbled
into the wind that grazed their brows,
and recollects:
See, my feet go where I want to go.
I bend, I kneel down childlike on the earth.
Because I know: how swiftly I am redeemed!
Because I know and am, I become quiet.
I am a human being, ready to do human things,
I can move my fingers everywhere,
though body-bound: can stroke the blood-filled temple.
Over and done with. The unfulfilled. Air and humanity still. Over and done
        with.
I stand inside humanity. Am free for freedom,
Freedom!
A second group burst into the old song
as it marched:
I do not know you.
But, brother, you walk in the same light!
I can put my arm around your waist, sister,
my hand can reach every hand.
And though we march faster with a varying pace:
All of us keep in human step!
We know that we are not alike,
but we breathe the same wind.
Because we are all on earth

and with human lips demand
that the like and the unlike be brought together!
No one is like the other,
and yet each is enriched through the other,
every You like every I says "I".
Distinguished, yet frightful in our humility,
individual, yet equal in our humanity:
Equality!
But the third group began to weep for joy:
Friends! we who appear in human form;
all of us who dare to live,
we all bear the fate of being human —
let us help each other to endure life!
Friends, let us press forward eye to eye:
against the hater, against the dead, against the enemy,
see, it works, united body to body!
All of us in the feeling of our human skin
shining far and wide over a dark earth
forming a phalanx of human beings:
Brotherliness!
Take care! There is no time for reflection:
It happened yesterday that a girl jumped from a streetcar
and slung her bare arms around my shoulder.
The world lay bare, the skies went on rumbling.
We held each other. We held ourselves in readiness,
we knew, many are ready to pave the way
for the times to come after the unfulfilled misery of these times!
Our blood sang. We strove, one chord.
Your mouth, the crown of your head — so that the flame spews upward!
We groaned as humanity screams inside us,
shouted with joy: humanity! love! and the thunder-word:
Justice!


JOHANNES R. BECHER

EROICA

But deep deep too in my desert Gobi's burning thornbush,
In breathless Mexican yew hedges
Of my ragged shores, Crete's labyrinth and island-exile,
Of my still endless Alpine slopes
There were encamped
Wildly as well as gently joined together

288

In rows
— Lambent right down to the ultimate organ of the universe,
Bodily convulsion and Dionysian orgy —
You athletic boys of Hellas.
Hymnic shepherds (Olympus your breast) radiant and narrow-hipped;
In an ore-linked coat-of-mail — paeon-tempest — eager for battle.
Through every zone's winter drought, brittle cadaver-pores, their sacred rain
      burnt with fever.
Coasts of digging Malay lips sucked you ardently into my innermost predator-
      preserve.
Abruptly out of a gigantic phallus lava-seeds shot like a cataract into my blood.
Cheek: thistle and drained
Greened softly, bedewed with a downy snow.

I roared,
A bull pregnant with visions,
With a belly filled to bursting by the humping of a demon —
Hurling destructive lightning flashes against the dreary finitude of your
      everyday landscape —
Voraciously gulping fruit seed tree and at the elegiac spring the innocent body
      of a god...
I tore, pounded and crushed and boxed —
Deluge and merciless brute —
Barbaric conqueror traversing the infested lands and infertile fields of your
      miserable earth —
I crawled panting up through the laurel groves and citron forests of the ancient
      epochs
Between and across dwarf-pine wilderness and mountain torrent
To the cheerless stinging boulder formations sparsely interspersed with the
      bluebells of the gentian
And up to the liberating womb-crater of Etna —
Empedocles feverish before the deadly lava-leap —
Corroded by sweat and the thick rage-mush of helpless fury around a crunched
      muzzle —
In desperation rearing up helplessly and brutally and for a final time against the
      impudent lashing out of the sun —

Over and over again the toughness of my animal nature
Was transformed into Asphodel-gentleness.
Over and over again the swords of my lunacy
Came to leaf with seraphic childhood-smiles.
Over and over again I was bent down, defenseless and tamed,
Into the light's last remnant, and
Onto the meagre sleep of herds

: By the aroma from the fruit of your pipes O boys;

My hooves' murder and hell-typhoon were stilled by the miracle-oil of heavenly
    doves
And the taste of bitter midday was dissolved in the jaws of corpses.
And a wicked gullet was sweetly cooled by lemons and by crystal waters.
...By the aroma from the fruit of your pipes O boys.
Harnessed to the world's singeing yoke of fate. Tormented.
The wrinkles of my wildness were blotted out. My sphere timeless and purified.
And from the portals of buried eyes a magic sparkle,
Dammed up for a long time,
Breaks out and beams back into the gorges of the world's expanses.
And from the bow of my lips, once accursed, God pronounces
His blessing on the entangled net of my boundless dreams steeped in original
    sin.

: Words inexorable,
Never again to be deleted from the neighbors' ranks.
Imperturbable center. The holy angels'
Just inheritance and sole secure possession.

*

Someday men will be over the earth
Filling its lengths and breadths.
Their heads pushing through the clouds' triangle
Into the heavens' innermost gorge.
Swans feathering the path of the glorious,
Fish rejoicing around curves of the neck.
Mother-oboes warbling you death to pieces.
Eyelashes holding sway over you sleepless suns.
Pores of the hand sowing eternal springtime.
Men girded with the rainbow. Men
Of the eastern fireball's pillar crashing.
Men of the chase around the center of the earth.
Naked and charred behind sacred plows.
Around their cottages buffalo rushing.
Dancers fluttering about the dinner table.
Men of the ray. Mountain sesame of the weak.
Men stewards of the hellish day.
Among the powerless, in the bloodbath of battles
Childlike dispensers of heavenly consolation.
Men of vengeance! Dagger into tyrants,
...their chests blooming among knives.

But around their crowns the shadow already shrinking.
The executed getting up at every wall.

*

Heroic departures! Ascensions into the heavens! Tragic failures! And electric
    spiral-leaps crosswise through sulphurous chaos.
Cyclopes! Tower builders! Working people! With trilling glacial gusts over
    southern leafy hair.
From the center of your hearts the glowing ashlar of the Styx dispersed
    sizzling.
In the white-hot focal point of your political speeches the stinking ogre of
    rottenness is finally crushed.
But your breath would draw the most irresistible barrage fire in front of the
    sanctified battlefront.
You are standing by the firing levers of wonderful artillery pieces.
And the beast in the tyrant awaits with trepidation the wild adventure of its
    last night.
For the dagger, the dagger in your fists has grown grown grown ceaselessly.


JOHANNES R. BECHER

SOUNDS FROM UTOPIA

Already they are pressing forward slowly, soon they are gliding
Up and down in the blood, gentle thrusts.
The veins resound, network of taut strings.
Bog-lake of cellos rests between mountains.

Over them the islands of the stars hang.
Decayed animals blossom out in forests.
Processions descend in songs.
The river lights up its black course.

O mother-city in the open air of morning!
Windows swing open along the rows of houses.
Out of every plaza a fountain-tree grows.
Verandas sail, moonflag-bedecked gondolas.

They herald men, elastically these sway
Through the eternally blue ravine of the streets.

Yes —: women striding! With palm-fingers.
Opened wide like calyxes of the sweetest fruit.

And friends radiate together at the gate.
How hymnic the din of crimson lips sounds.
No longer sons that ram their fathers.
Embraced they head for home, suns.

The fields would merge into the softest park.
The poorest hover there, more colorful butterflies.
Gold-sky seeps through the filter of the clouds
Toward the peoples. — Long booming chord.


KURT HEYNICKE

PEOPLE

My people,
bloom eternally, people.

Stream, stretching from midnight to midnight,
stream, large and deep from sea to sea,
from your depths springs gush forth,
feeding you from all eternity,
the people.

My people,
bloom eternally, people.
You dream yourself a future at your breast.
One day no day shall ever shatter your dream again,
the mountains of your soul will tower into the heavens
and elevate us,
us,
the people.
I am a tree in the forest of the people.
And my leaves are fed by the sun.
But my roots sleep their sleep of strength
in you,
my people.

My people,
one day all things shall kneel
before you.

For your soul shall fly away
high over smokestacks, cities into your own heart.
And you will bloom,
my people.

My people.
In you.


ELSE LASKER-SCHÜLER

MY PEOPLE
(For my beloved son Paul)

The rock is decaying
From which I spring
And sing my songs of God...
Suddenly I dash off the road
And in my very being ripple
Far away, alone across stones of lament
Toward the sea.

Have floated myself so very much away
From my blood's
New-wine fermentation.
And always, ever the echo
In me,
When the decaying rock-skeleton,
My people,
Emits a bloodcurdling cry
Eastward to God.


IWAN GOLL

NOEMI

I

I find it hard to bear the fateful inheritance of
My Bible mothers,
My prophetesses,
My queens.

There roar so mightily from out of dark centuries
The God years,
The temple years,
The ghetto years.

There ring so chaotically in my burst soul
The seasonal feasts,
The heavenly feasts,
The feasts of the dead.

There cry so deeply in my wild blood
The patriarchs,
The heroes,
The sons!
Hear, Israel, Adonai was your God, Adonai was the one and only!

## II

I am the daughter of the springtime people!
Squandering prayers and sacrifice,
I pulled the earth into my whirl.
My prayer was the human echo
Of the asphodel songs
and olive-tree symphonies.
My heaven was built in the clouds
Above the mountains blooming in white,
And the golden signs of the stars
Deeply reproduced in dark lakes.
Every man proudly carried his cedar head.
Every youth a moving acacia,
Israel as pious as a springtime hill!
The fragrance of ointments and oils compassed its limbs,
And in its large eyes
God was smiling.
Sacrifice was the language of the patriarchs,
And the angels were the reply from heaven.
Every maiden's lament like a pair of doves,
Every woman's request a blond lambkin,
And the warrior's gruff battle vow
Ascended in smoke thick from the blood of bulls.
And the dances in the sweet vineyard,
To the jubilant sound of cymbals they garlanded the year.

## III

I am the daughter of the Talmud people!
O temple, in which copper candelabras
Unfold their seven branches like trees,
Where instead of fairytale stars
Eternal hanging lamps
Disquieted the mystical night.
In golden beakers God was held prisoner.
Brocade and crimson beseemed his priests.
A dying heaven lay
Casketed in arcades of porphyry.
When Israel descended from its hills,
It smashed on rocky gorges
Its graying head of curls,
Crushed its flattened knees on flagstones.
The sun hung charred and black in the street,
Only a little lamp shone upon the temple people.
O Israel, weather-beaten mountain,
Aging glacier,
In script and drawings and cabbala
You debated coldly
The operations of heaven.
But your soul was turned to stone,
Your heart to ice!

## IV

I am the daughter of the ghetto people!
Of rasping and cadging rabbis,
Of orphan children and grave-diggers.
In dank cellars, dripping vaults,
In Spanish towers, Rumanian hovels
I have languished.
Where is Elohim,
O you Kodoshim?
Oi, oi, oi,
And where is Adonai?
At decaying altars you shake the palms,
With rotting teeth you screech your psalms of lament.
With litanies and cries
You hope to liberate God,
In sticky caftans
You imitate the gestures of your forefathers,

During bloody pogroms, in prison chains,
In the murderous quarter of cyclopean cities
You call yourselves heirs
And do not want to die!
O people of the sweet-smelling sisters and thinking brothers,
Rise again, my people and let the songs
And let the God of letters and laments
Be buried!
Hear, Israel!

## V

Hear!
You have a spirit,
You have a spirit, nourished on blood and God,
You have a spirit, welded pure in all the fires of creation,
You have a spirit, widely traveled on all the oceans and highways,
You have a spirit, encompassed by all the philosophies, poetries, geometries,
        industries of humanity,
You have the one, one and only, eternal spirit.

Hear, Israel!

Your spirit illuminate the five continents,
Your spirit master the four elements,
Your spirit conquer the three realms,
Your spirit set free the two human beings,
Your one spirit!

Hear, Israel!

With your spirit you will vivify all deaths in the world:
Your spirit is the gate to Eden,
Your spirit is the flight to Nirvana,
Your spirit is the barque to Elysium!
Your spirit! Your insight! Your omniscience!

Hear, Israel!

Your spirit is the lustrous new birth,
Your spirit is the old God,
Rejuvenated as the son of humanity.
Your spirit is life!
Hear, Israel, your spirit is your God, your spirit is the one and only!

At the new moon I will rise from the dead!
Anoint my bluish-black tresses with the oil of the walnut
And greet my beloved with a star-clear kiss.

At the new moon I will go roaming!
And across the heavens proclaim the happiness of my love,
And on earth secure the victory of my love.

At the new moon I will go dancing.
Awaken the humans from their dreams,
Over the cities light the new light.

At the new moon I will rise from the dead!
Raise the lofty spirit from the ashes like a phoenix,
Give the name insight to the old belief.


LUDWIG RUBINER

THE HUMAN BEING

In the hot red-summer, over the dust-frothing rotation of the rolling earth,
    among farmers stooped low and soldiers dulled, amidst the clattering
    hustle of round cities
The human being leapt into the air.
Oh hovering pillar, bright pillars of legs and arms, sturdy radiant pillar of the
    body, shining sphere of the head!

He hovered in silence, his breath irradiated the sprouting earth.
The sun moved in and out of his round eye. He shut his curved eyelids, the
    moon moved up and down. The gentle waving motion of his hands
    flung the orbit of the stars like the flashing thong of a whip.
The din flowed around the small earth as quietly as the moisture on a cluster
    of violets under a glass dome.

The foolish earth trembled in its blind course.

The human being smiled across the world like fiery glass caverns,
The heavens shot through him, human being, flaringly translucent, in a comet's
    tail!
Thinking, glowing spheres, boiled up and down in him.

Thinking flowed about him in a burning froth,
Blazing thinking darted through him,
Shimmering pulse of the heavens, human being!
Oh blood of God, flaming turbulent giant sea in the bright crystal.
Human being, shiny tube: globes, burning giant eyes float through him like small glowing mirrors,
Human being, his orifices are slurping mouths, he swallows and spouts the blue pounding waves of the torrid heavens.

The human being lies on the radiant floor of the heavens,
His breath gently nudges the earth like a small glass ball on the shimmering fountain.
Oh white-shining pillars, through which thinking courses up and down through the sparkling of the blood.

He lifts the gleaming pillars of the body: he casts about himself the wild whirling of round horizons as bright as the circles of snowflakes!
Flashing triangles shoot out of his head and surround the heavenly stars,
He hurls the mighty intertwined divine curves about in the world, they return to him as the boomerang returns to the dark warrior who flings it.

The human being hovers within a luminous net in flight flaring up and dying down like a pulse beat,
He extinguishes and ignites when thinking courses through him,
On his radiant body he rocks the waving motion that returns.

He turns his flaming head and paints about himself on black night the dispatched lines of light in their sinking glow:
Spheres hazily bright burst open and curve like flower petals,
        jagged planes in fire-light ball themselves shimmeringly into oblique cones, pointed pyramid pinnacles rise from yellow sparks like sunlights.

In radiant glory the human being lifts from the night his torch-limbs and pours his hands out white over the earth,
The bright numerals, oh sparkling strips like smelted metal.

But when it streams across the hot earth (which arches like a rearing animal),
Does it not later whirl back? whirl up thin and scattered, weighed down with earth-space:

Bleating of animals. Fragrance of the green trees, multi-colored dancing of pollen, colors of the sun in the rain. Long tones of music.

KURT HEYNICKE

HUMAN BEING

I am above the forests,
green and shining,
high above all,
I, the human being.
I am orbit in the universe,
blooming movement,
carried carrying.
I am sun among the orbiting,
I, the human being,
I feel myself deeply,
close to the high universe-orbiting one,
I, his thought.
My head is covered with stars,
silver my countenance,
I shine,
I,
like him,
the universe;
the universe
like me!


FRANZ WERFEL

THE GOOD HUMAN BEING

His is the power, the rule of the stars,
He holds the world in his fist like a nut,
Laughter twines immortally around his countenance,
War is his way and triumph his stride.

And wherever he is and extends his hands,
And wherever his call thunders down tyrannically,
The injustices of all creation shatter,
And all things become God and one.

Indomitable are the good person's tears,
Building material for the world and water for created things.
Wherever his good tears drop down,
Every form expends itself and shapes itself anew.

There is no fury comparable to his.
He stands at the stake of his life,
And twisting at his feet and lost
Is the devil, a crushed fire-serpent.

And when he dies, there remain at his side
Two angels, who immerse their heads in spheres
And shout jubilantly midst gold and fire,
And thunderously strike their shields together.

# Love to Human Beings

FRANZ WERFEL

## TO THE READER

My only wish is to be related to you, O human being!
Whether you are a black, an acrobat, or still resting in the depths of your
     mother's womb,
Whether your maiden song resounds across the yard or you steer your raft at
     dusk,
Whether you are a soldier or aviator filled with endurance and courage.

Did you too as a child carry a rifle in a green armsling?
When it went off, a cork on a string flew out of the barrel.
My human being, when I sing of memories,
Do not be hard, and dissolve with me in tears!

For I have lived all destinies. I know
The feelings of lonely female harpists in health spa orchestras,
The feelings of shy governesses in the homes of foreign families,
The feelings of fledgling actors nervously positioning themselves in front of the
     prompter's box.

I have lived in the woods, worked in train stations,
Sat bent over ledgers, and waited on impatient guests.
As a stoker I have stood before boilers, my face burning from the flames,
And as a coolie I ate garbage and table scraps.

Therefore I belong to you and to everyone!
Do not, please, do not resist me!
Oh, if one day it could be
That we, brother, would fall into each other's arms!

WILHELM KLEMM

INTRODUCTION

What evolves in the narrow second,
What emerges in the indifferent light
And sinks incomprehensibly in the shadows,
What wanders and changes constantly,

The return and the departure,
The new and the recurrence,
The grasping of individual forms and the forgetting;
All of this which is enclosed between beginning and end,

The agitations and the reassurances,
The desires and their fulfillments,
The finite that streams toward us as world:
I want to capture in mortal words.

So that when I read I will know doubly that I am alive.
So that you can read it, brother, human being,
So that you too will feel: yes, that is the way it is, I am like that too!
For we are all just one single living organism!


PAUL ZECH

TO MY SON
1914

The beautiful summer that jumped through your hoop,
the blue ride on a steamer and an evening walk in the woods:
are blown out like an altar candle, my son.

Your mouth that hangs heavily clouded in questions,
Your eyes that surge with a sea of torment:
I no longer find your face, my son.

The storm that breaks over the innocent games
of your child's world and forces back the hands of time:
against this storm I am pitted in the field, my son.

My arm sprained from hardship, emaciated from worry,
must brace itself for rifle and sword,
so that no one will murder what binds us, what holds us, my son.

That our bright age still loves the grim lust for war,
does not love blessed brotherhood and does not pass this love on:
where will I be absolved from this guilt, my son?

In bloodiest battle I still hear wings over me;
in my sleep they carry me away from here
like trees that flee from raging lanterns, my son.

But when she whom I left behind thinks I am in the grave,
and cries through widow nights and orphan strangeness:
grow treetop-like into the sky! Break the orbit of the stars, my son!

For you are preordained, are the last line that completes the plan;
there is no gate where we have not already been in our dreams,
where we have not seen the way to round unity, my son.

You were preordained five thousand years ago: to be
the one whose name I bite into the stone
when the pursuers strike me thrust for thrust, my son.

Yes, only then will dying become a deeply felt word.
My death will erase foe and beflagged borders,
and all life will know only "world" and "brother" —: you, my son!


FRANZ WERFEL

FATHER AND SON

As once with boundless love we
Indulged in the fun and games of eternity
For the pleasure of the blessed —
Uranus opened up the blueness of his bosom,
And united in happy childlike loyalty
We rocked our way through his breast.

But woe! The ether got lost,
World roared and body was born,
Now we are estranged.
Somber from quarrelsome noonday repasts
Glances meet like steel,
Hostile and ready.

And in the sweep of his black cape
The old man, like the young, carries
Odious iron.
The words they speak reflect the cold
Animosity of their separated ages,
Livid and emaciated.

And the son waits for the old man to die
And the aged man laughs at me triumphantly: heir!
So that the underworld reverberates.
And already in our wild hands
The hellish violence — practically unavoidable —
Of those weapons clashes.

But even we are granted evenings
At the table's sublime household peace,
Where confusion is silent,
Where in our warm-heartedness we do not prevent
Tears agitated by the surging of the selfsame blood
From welling up and falling.

How once with boundless love we
Indulged in the fun and games of eternity
We surmise in a dream.
And the nimble hand moves tremulously toward the aged hand,
And in a wonderful, quiet
Stirring of the heart the cosmos falls.


WALTER HASENCLEVER

THE OBITUARY NOTICE

When I awoke this morning from a deadening, worrisome dream,
A small, quiet angel hovered in the darkness of my room.
I read a mother's words among the announcements of death:

304

"My misled and so even more deeply loved child."
Then much sadness bent over my bed:
I know that I too, gone astray, am the child of a mother.
Then I saw the head of the other who sank helplessly into misery.
I saw him in love, drunk, sick with a terrible pestilence.
Did he not stand alone in the night and in the poorer part of town,
Did he not shed tears into the river from burning eyes?
Often he stole through alleyways where red and green glows,
Went out cheerfully at night, died tiredly in the morning.
Had to eat in houses with people hostile and unknown,
Sleep in cold rooms, freezing, without a shirt —
His mother helped with the laundry and some money;
Everything turned out well. She loved him in this world.
My brother under the stars! I have understood your poverty.
Blessed, you turned to me in this hour.
Now your smiling breath no longer streams golden and polar,
Your hair no longer kindles childlike in the fury of the storm;
Behold — in the hour of your death your mother's eternal words;
They carry you from oblivion on silver wings.
Before I open the shutters after this heavy, sad night:
My brother under the stars! How happy you have made me.


WILHELM KLEMM

THE BEGGAR

His hat was a crumbling sponge. His beard
Sintered over his gray chest,
His peg-leg frayed wide at the base,
Through his tattered clothes the stars strayed.

He wore thorns and snails in his hair,
His eyes were inflamed, his harsh
Cracked countenance bled quietly,
Metallically the flies buzzed around him.

In his bones the winters gnawed,
Eternity fermented through his bowels,
His blood was sick with rottenness, in his
Soul forests of memories petrified.

Who rocked you as a child? Who loved you?
Come, old man, I will care for you. But mutely he opens
His hands' begging abysses,
Black and empty as death, large as pain.

## ALBERT EHRENSTEIN

### HOPE

I do not have the power
To give eyes to blind stones.
Easily though to a spurned
Poor old stuffed chair
Missing a leg
I bring joy
By tenderly sitting down on it.

Be gentle, O you who are strong!
And, gathering strength in their hearts,
Human beings will, like the blessed,
Soon be detoxicated of pale-sick poverty
And in their own world,
When the gods are dead,
Find heaven.

## ELSE LASKER-SCHÜLER

### AND SEEK GOD
(To my Paul)

I have always lain before the murmuring of my heart,
Never seen the morning,
Never sought God.
Now, though, I walk around my child's
Gold-composed limbs
And seek God.

I am tired from slumber,
Know only of the countenance of night.
I am afraid of the morning,

It has a face
Like human beings who ask questions.

I have always lain before the murmuring of my heart,
Now, though, I grope for my child's
God-lit limbs.


FRANZ WERFEL

AN OLD LADY WALKS

An old lady walks like a round tower
Down the old tree-lined avenue in a storm of leaves.
Disappears panting
Where black mist blows around corners.
Will soon stand in a doorway entrance.
Slowly go up noisy steps
Damp from the lethargic staircase light.

No one helps her off with her sweater
As she enters the room.
Ah, her hands and legs soon begin to shake.
Sets about with heavy flapping of wings
To place food saved from previous days
Over the cooking stove's poor glow.
Remains alone with her body and herself.

And she is not aware, while she swallows and chews,
That sons were formed in her.
(Well, she is comfortable in her slippers.)
Whatever came out of her stands in other doorways.
She forgot the scream with which she gave birth.
Only sometimes, in the bustle of the street it happens that
A man absentmindedly gives her a friendly nod: "Mother."

But you, human being, think of yourself in her,
We have been colossal in the world
Since we broke into time.
While we dangle in the unknown,
Shadows swell out with powerful claws
That compress us to the utmost.
This world is not the whole world.

As the old woman shuffles through the room,
Ah, it may well happen that she understands.
The cracks in her face fade.
Yes, she feels herself waxing larger in all things,
And begins to fall to her knees,
When out of a lamp's faint flutter
God's countenance breaks like a colossus.


JOHANNES R. BECHER

HYMN TO ROSA LUXEMBURG

Filling you completely with strophes of olives.
May Meander's tears engulf you!
Wrapping star-nights round you for a cloak,
Intertwined with bough-tracks of hymnal scarlet blood...
O you spice of paradisiacal meadows:
You one and only! You holy one! O woman! —

I rush through the worlds —:
Once more your hand, to hold this hand:
Magical boughs on God's rose olive tree.
Divining rod for the happiness seeker.
...Into you, O most motherly of harps, trickles the sound that means home for
      all of us...
Five-pointed, dictatorially spread above our heads.
Fountain of blood from these fingers it filed through the bars of millions of the
      poorest.

I rush through the worlds —:
Once more your mouth, to feel this mouth:
Brightness-breather, butterfly-soil,
Oboes' power-stream, ambrosia-hill land,
Food of the most blessed...
Prophetic melancholy dawning on the lip-curve.
Sustaining all,
Each and every one sweetened by your kiss:
Shimmering umbel of moisture.
Mild milk for the powerless in their deadly fall,
Prodigal sons asking it questions —
! You silver-dew in the steppe-fire!

— You heaven-comfort in hell-pain!
— You smile-moon at the murder-zenith!
— You deepest crimson-respite in a countenance-cramp!
Jeremiah's cry of distress
Ecstatic upbeat.
Thunderstorm-sentences gathered in you.
Shining totally innocent
Pure virgin-white
Dove faith-sap
Holy wafer hovering high above tribune-altars.

I rush through worlds —:
Toward the ivory coasts of your ear,
To the gigantic primordial funnels, the tulip-chalice-tubes of the sibylline
      mothers,
To you, gigantic primordial funnels,
Absorbing all earthly sounds,
The childlike wish-dreams as well as the feverish fear-dreams of the most poor,
Howl of beggars and bums,
The miserably patched together tirade of the accused,
The farewell aria of a coward who was shot,
Blackberry bush warbling a fiery death,
The phraseological program-fanfare of war...
Factory sirens announcing indignation-hour.
— — — Gigantic primordial funnel:
Whispering myself deeply into it with a confession of the most ignominious
      sins,
O millions cling to it with their innermost (bursting!) avowals,
Your membrane corroded by and stained with thousands of (the most
      lacerating!) afflictions!
And and:
Made gleaming by the unending (flute and trumpet) sounds of seraphim,
Yes: for the elan of the spheres enraptured you too:
O music to music!
O melody!

Rushing through worlds —:
Your brow! O this brow!
Lily-snow-wall veiling eternal thought,
Field-furrow sheltering safe seed.
Harvest is already budding from stab and wound.
Spirit's rampart. Sacred throne.
From Orcus's depths
Typhoon-wrinkles strike,

But angels smooth you,
Relax and anoint you,
Whose heart-flame-realms contain palm forests.

Worlds, yes I rushed through worlds —:
Your eyes, these eyes,
To still crater-eye with azure light.
To immerse glacier-blueness in the dagger-hollow,
In the desolate jagged midnight,
In the cheeks' whipped-up fury,
In the moon's cooling magic.
Eyes —: scouts sent out from the ark.
Seldom did they return.
...So that they could espy their island.
Could pluck paradisiacal fruits,
Could fold wings in happiness...
— — —

Citizens! Murderers! Fist and rifle butt
Pounded your head into the filth.
! But you thunder. Your skies burst.
Your red morning dawns above all lands.

I rush through the worlds —:
Taking the broken body
Down from the cross,
Wrapping it in the softest linen.
I trumpet your triumph through the worlds:
Yours, one and only! Yours, holy one! O woman!!!

RUDOLF LEONHARD

THE DEAD LIEBKNECHT

His corpse lies everywhere in the city,
in all the yards, in all the streets.
All rooms
are weak from the outpouring of his blood.

Then for an infinitely long time
factory sirens begin
to open their booming jaws,
and send a hollow scream across the whole city.

And with a gleam
on bright
rigid teeth
his corpse begins
to smile.


IWAN GOLL

CREATION

I

Somewhere the dome of heaven shattered,
And the sun, as though wounded,
Fluttered, bleeding gold and lava,
Around the fissured earth.

Pink seas
Shone in the springtime of their waves,
Rustling palms rose up,
On coral reefs
The star-fruits ripened.

Somewhere a mountain range quaked
Down to its rigid glaciers.
And the first drop which freed itself,
A tear shed into the valley,
Was the first smile of God.

II

Sparkling trident.
The word broke from the mute ocean;
The floor of the earth shimmered darkly.

And the blue hammers of the spirit
And the flutes of the angels
Sounded across the enflamed sky.

On darkness's conquered shores
Stood the human being, an arrow in his brow,
His red mouth

Open wide like a triumphal arch:
Now and then, when it occurred to him,
He commanded the circling sun to stop.

## III

At the hill-wedding
Lilac fountains plunged into the valley,
Trees were filled with world-embrace,
And the temples throbbed in honor of spring.

Then from a dark terrestrial hut
A golden organ-storm broke:
Propped between heaven and earth,
Pillar of earthly song,
The human being stood.
Out of stony suffering,
Deep in the murmuring womb of love,
The glorious one had arisen!


ALFRED WOLFENSTEIN

COMMITMENT OF THE POET

Like a cloud enflamed, a cloud rumbling between head and earth
The speaking mouth of a human being quivers,
Lightning teeth clear
Thickets: flowers shoot up, airy and colorful.

Hear the voice, deafest sadness,
Black as underbrush beneath the ocean floor!
Begin, soundless bird, to sing in the rounded cage,
May the mouth of the human being give you more freedom through its
    singing.

But as in a dream, a dry blue sky above the roof of his thunder,
Above his own lips the poet still waits unredeemed —
Storm, gathered by the sun, does not rain up into the sun,
Above the clouds the lights keep glowing invisibly and languish.

Oh, him himself — even the thunderstorm does not make sufficiently happy!
Words, unshackled slaves, by their own weight

Flowing into the vessel of hearkening human beings,
Though risen from him, coldly abandon him like a grave.

Truth, peer from above into his soul,
Never will it become empty, proclaim that it would like to be more human,
When he calls out love in words, his brighter throat calls
Into itself a love that is even more truly generative.

When he breathes verses, his breast swells even more vitally!
So that, for shame and for joy, he would like to leave in the middle of his
        utterances
For the desert —
No, to get still nearer to human beings!

Until finally it rains from below,
Now from below: You!
Now countenances, deeply moved poems,
Strike the mover, his unveiling, like flashes of lightning!

Earth's wind extends its hands to him
Through the wide-open gate.
Speech fades into the distance, he raises his arms, now finally at the end
His heavy curtain goes up before him.


FRANZ WERFEL

SMILING BREATHING STRIDING

Draw, carry, hold
In your hand the thousand waters of a smile!
A smile, blessed moisture is spread
Over the entire countenance.
A smile is no wrinkle,
A smile is essence of light.
Light breaks through space, but is not yet light.
Sun is not light,
Only in the face of a human being
Is the light born as a smile.
From the resounding, light, immortal gateways,
From the gateways of the eyes there flowed
For the first time spring, heaven's spray,
Smile's never-burning glowing fire.

313

In the rain-fire of a smile wash your old hand,
Draw, carry, hold!

Listen, hearken, hear!
At night, the harmony of breath is abroad,
Breath, the harmony of the bosom, great.
Breath hovers
Over the enmity of dark choruses.
Breath is essence of the highest breath.
Not the wind which dives
Into meadow, woods, and bush,
Not the blowing before which the leaves turn...
God's breath is born in the breath of a human being.
From the lips, the heavy,
Secret, dark, immortal gateways,
God's breath goes out to convert the world.
On the wind-sea of breath
The nocturnal boat loaded with infinite words
Commences to spread its sails in ecstasy.
Hearken, hear, listen!

Fall down, kneel down, weep!
Behold the beloved's earthless vanishing stride!
Swing along, vanish into her striding!
Striding carries off
All things to purity, all things to the universal.
Striding is more than motion and movement,
The up and along of stellar spheres,
More than the dancing exuberance of space.
In the striding of a human being the path to freedom is born.
With the striding of a human being
God's grace and God's ways step out of every heart and gateway.
Smile, breath and stride
Are more than the light's, the wind's, the stars' path,
The world begins in the human being.
Drown in the smile, in the breath, in the stride of the beloved!
Weep away, kneel down, fall!

RENÉ SCHICKELE

HOLY ANIMALS...!

Over the millennia human beings
Have prayed: be still, violence,
All the hands and hearts that gave of themselves,
They buried violence.

Is the battle for kindness between
You and me
Before going to bed and at table,
Human animal,
Not primordially bloody and full of horror
And the anger of the proud at the lukewarm
And the ignominy of the weak, and the distress
Of the miserable poor, death in dampness,
Death in heat, and the white and red
Of a love still in the chandelier light
Of glittering drawing rooms, is not every beat
Of all our hearts: battles, victories,
Marches, wounds, ascents and descents,
Torments, fevers, jubilations, bright and dark day?

Holy animals, how great and good you appear
Wandering dreamlike through the mist of human blood!


GEORG HEYM

THE SEAFARERS

The brows of lands, red and noble as crowns,
We saw fading away in the sinking day,
And the rustling wreaths of the forests reigning
Beneath the roaring beat of the fire's wings.

To blacken the flickering trees with mourning,
A storm raged. They burned away like blood,
Perishing, already far off. As though over dying hearts,
Love's fading glow flares up one more time.

But we drifted on, out into the evening of the seas.
Our hands started to burn like candles.
And against the sun we saw our veins in them and the thick
Blood that ran sluggishly in our fingers.

Night began. Someone cried in the dark. We floated
Disconsolately out to sea with slackened sail.
But we stood on deck together in silence,
To stare into the dark. And the light went out on us.

A last cloud stayed in the distance for a long while,
Before the night began in eternal space,
Hovering crimson in the universe, like a dream with beautiful song
Above the sounding depths of the soul.


IWAN GOLL

THE PANAMA CANAL
(Initial version of 1912. Revision 1918)
[Preliminary note by the author]


*The Labor*


I


Where once the Carib dreamily floated his raft
Over the seas, where bright colored parrots
Perched in the thick tropical forest, and monkeys
Pursued each other with litanies, where the Spaniard, grand

And glistening with armor, proud after easy victory,
Kissed the earth and called it his own:
And crushed with his foot every god that rose
From the glowing fires, because he already knew Christ,

There small, black railroads
Waved the smoke's white signal flags
And gobbled wounds into the chalk cliffs.
The rigid jungle palms were felled all round,
Crane-storks winged over the dead world
With their curious necks.

## II

But where a chaos of stones lay coated with green bog,
There foul dreams gleamed around the white sun.
Tumid mosquito-multitudes
Smoldered over ditch and field,
The midday sky was hot with their swarming and humming,
The sun's every sting killed like poison.

From the swamps a pest rose
With eyes streaked greenish-brown and spat over valley and plateau
And had black teeth, and these stank so much
When they bit that its victims already felt like carrion.

From the wells and the stream-waters
A plague of rats and blindworms climbed over rails and pipes,
In the waves it was like flashing knives at play,
And they ate their fill of the bloated carcasses of horses.

## III

But the earth reared up at this outrage,
Her crusty, thirsty body squirmed torturously
Like a snake shedding its skin anew!
From the gorges oozed yellow sulphur.

The mountains, bored through with tunnels,
Fell like plaster from beams, avalanches of loam veiled in clouds —

And the cities that had sprouted like moss on the cliffs:
Cities of brick, of straw or pointed tents,
Set up around a bath house, a hospital, a temple,
Were suddenly drowned in earth.

All the workers had slurped the same ices, all had fried
Fish from the Gatun in the same pans, and they danced together on
     Sundays; —
But the vast necropolises in their midst
Soon separated them again according to the customs of peoples and
     gods.

# IV

There, gnawed by time, hollowed by blood,
Corroded by gold and torment, the canal finally made its way
Through lake and rock and chaos of sand.
Arc lamps guided it at night from ocean to ocean.

During the day however there was the din of metal and pumps and
       groans,
The echo exploded the sky like a cloud of dynamite!

The iron locks grew, each with an entrance and exit,
Every inch struck by the exacting hammer,
Monstrous floodgates carried into the deep
By small steel casings performing like titans. — —

And when these gates open,
When two hostile oceans kiss amidst jubilation —
Oh, then all peoples
Of the earth will have to weep.

### The Dedication

Everything that belongs to you, earth, will now call itself brother,
All waters, the salt and the fresh,
The cold streams and the springs that burn,
Will flow together.

And there the heartbeat of the earth will live continuously,
Where the Gulf Stream's serpent curls sun-scaled
And encircles the capes and islands of all zones
With hotly flowing blood.

Firewood from Brazil, fir trunks from the North,
And Europe's smooth, shining steel:
Ships from every dock and fjord
Are here at the canal.

Coal smoke from distant lands and mines,
Thousand-year-old forests, hard-crushed quartz,
Grows like a broad tree up to the bright clouds
From the black earth.

All masts shimmer like a bundle of spears
Over the many peaceful peoples,
And as the intoxicating song of motors and oceans is sung
The canal trembles.

The pennon-garlands hang red and green in between
Like captured birds in a great forest;
Their chirping echoes
From mast to mast.

And everyone sings the melody of his land,
Oh, the swirl of languages and sounds!
But the widely-traveled sailors and argonauts
Understand each other fully.

All human beings in port, on the docks, in the bars,
All speak to one another full of love,
Whether in a pigtail, a hat, a cap, whether with blond or dark hair,
Man is man.

Every man a brother whom one quickly recognizes,
This one's eye is made of mahogany, this one's is a brazen dagger,
This one's burns like a star on quiet nights,
This one's is a flower full of pain:

Ah, all their eyes drink brotherhood
From the infinitely deep cup of universal love:
For here all earth's strengths are like brothers,
Here on the canal.

IWAN GOLL

THE PANAMA CANAL
(Later version, 1918)

I

The centuries of the primeval forest were still lying midway between the oceans. The gulfs and coves cut out with golden spikes. The waterfalls shattered the entrenched rocks with tenacious hammer blows.

The trees swelled into the sensuous noon day. They had the red flower-spots of desire. Hemlock frothed and hissed on tall stems. And the slender liana danced with flying hair.

The parrots flitted like green and blue lanterns through the night of the brush. The rhinoceros grubbed deep in the fat undergrowth. The tiger approached it in brotherly fashion from the river bank.

The sun circled fiery in the golden sky like a carrousel. Life was thousandfold and eternal. And where death seemed to rot: new life sprang up in double brightness.

The old century still lay amidst the human beings of the earth.

II

Then came the long, slow work gangs. The emigrants and the exiled. They brought with them struggle and wretchedness.

Human beings came with gasping afflictions and struck the ringing bells of the metal.

They raised their arms as in a curse and angrily tore the sky down around their naked shoulders.

Their blood sweated into the soil. How many scrawny children, how many nights, fearful nights, were squandered in the course of such a day!

Their fists raised high like torches. Heads bursting with screams. Heaving torsos. It was work. It was misery. It was hate.

So the Spaniards once writhed at the martyr's stake. So bound Blacks once twisted as they fell to their knees.

But these were the modern work gangs. These were the holy, suffering proletarians.

They lived drearily in barracks and flimsy cabins. Smell of fried fish and the nausea of brandy smoldered in the air. Their wooden bunks were lined up like coffins in a cemetery.

On Sundays a concertina longed for Italy and the Cape. Some ailing heart sobbed itself dry for a thousand others.

They danced together with heavy, timid feet. They wanted to caress the earth that on the morrow had to cry out again under the axe. Then they slurped five cents' worth of raspberry ice.

And again the age-long day of toil came.

## III

They transformed the earth into a sickbed. Red fevers swelled from the gorges. And the clouds of mosquitoes swirled around the sun.

No tree rustled anymore. No flower bloomed in this clay-hell. No birds arched across the lost sky.

Everything was pain. Everything was rubble and sulphur. Everything was cry and curse.

The hills tore open their breasts in convulsions of dynamite. From the dripping gorges the sirens howled like wolves. Dredges and cranes scooped up the lakes.

Human beings died in this endless cemetery. They died everywhere from the same torment.

There escaped from the lips of the men a mad cry for God, and they reared up like golden pillars. There plunged from out of the women pitiful, pale children, as though they wanted to punish the earth with so much misery.

From all the corners of the earth they had come to render slavish service. All the dreamers of golden rivers. All those desperate from a life of hunger.

The upright and the honest were there, those who still believed in the pity of fate. And the dim half-wits and the criminals who buried their shame deep in their misfortune.

But the work was just an excuse. That fellow had to avenge twenty embittered generations in his heart. This fellow had to strangle a syphilitic mother in his blood.

They all screamed in their struggle with the earth.

## IV

But they knew nothing of the Panama Canal. Nothing of infinite brotherhood. Nothing of the great gate of love.

They knew nothing of the freeing of the oceans and of humanity. Nothing of the radiating tumult of the spirit.

Each of them saw a swamp dry up. A forest burn down. A lake suddenly come to a boil. A mountain range fall to its knees as dust.

But how was he to believe in the greatness of this human feat! He perceived nothing of how the cradle of a new ocean was being made.

One day however the locks opened like the wings of an angel. Then the earth stopped groaning.

She lay there with exposed breasts like all mothers. She lay there bound to the will of the human being.

The white ships climbed down the wave-steps of the ocean. The thousand brother ships from a thousand ports.

Those with singing sails. Those with smoking stacks. The pennons chirped like captured birds.

A new primeval forest of masts rustled. A net of liana was formed by the intertwining ropes and hawsers.

The Pacific Ocean and the Atlantic tumult met in a holy kiss. O marriage of the blond East and the western evening star. Peace, peace prevailed among brothers.

There at the central point of the earth, humanity stood and marveled. From the teeming cities, from the wind-blown desert dunes, from the glowing glaciers rose a single salute.

The squadron of the world's ships formed. The blue marine bands played. Joyful flags from every land waved.

Forgotten was the deadening work. The shovel of the proletarians buried. The brick barracks torn down.

The waves of freedom engulfed the black work gangs. For one whole day they, too, were humanity.

But on the very next, wretchedness threatened anew. The merchant ships, heavy with grain and oil, left their poverty behind on shore.

The next day there was again misery and hate. New bosses screamed on to new toil. New slaves cursed their lowly fate.

On the following day humanity wrestled with the old earth again.



KARL OTTEN

TO THE VANQUISHED

The bloody mud of the sucking mountains
Became your bread. The skies glued their
Poison-skins to your mask-hot blank
Faces jerk-twitching over teeth and cheekbones.

Your soles were tickled by the thunder-fist.
The thistle-spear of worn-out sagas, baseness
From ruined childhood days drove through your heart the battle
That is already thinning your empty curls.

From shot to shot surrounded by gendarmes,
Apprehended by the fear-vixen's bloodily mad grasp
Your diaphragms burst, which gathered refinement
Courage gracefulness of weapons fathers' virtues eternally-warm.

The tombs of your brothers gulp you down
Heroes of the spirit crown lily-palm saints
I kiss your defiantly fluttering hands
Promise you all glories all mercies all being.

All your sufferings: your tumble from grave to grave
Not being able to die, in spite of the fire-kiss, death
Avoids you, ice snow iron cholera dress
You like brides of the Lord — through you the mad enemy

Becomes the human being and all misery is chalked up to him!
God walks ahead of you, towards heaven goes the flight,
Mercy that sings in drops —
Every drop of blood! Every shot! Curse! Let victory be spoiled for him,

Withered in his cowardly murder-hand, which void of
The dignity of God eviscerates you like game.
You mighty in loss! You heroes: he who suffers
Is the victor! In the bosom of Abraham miraculously

I see you taking care of your good wounds
While the enemy begs for mercy and tells tales.
You, unbroken, you, untold, wedded to
The wild screaming at the stock-exchange, newspaper-venom —

Your glorious victory makes God's heart tremble!
Cast off false modesty, march out into the squares!
In the light of liberated kindness we want to praise you
No one will dare to sharpen his horns on you —

Fervently I offer my hand to the defeated soldiers!
To the friends of death, we beg you for forgiveness!
Pardon us, you who, pale with suffering, scar-disfigured
On crutches, in wheelchairs, in bed, blind and deaf, curse us!

You build up a dam with your curses and crutches
We want to wash it away with remorse kindness and prayer
We want to care for you, serve you until this hate blows away
Until we recognize each other and him who stands in the way.
O you vanquished victor, whom God's hand bathed in fire
Whiter than snow, you flame-son
We want to wait until before God's throne
Together, hand in hand,
As brothers, as brothers, yes as brothers flames of love enrapture us.

ALFRED WOLFENSTEIN

ANDANTE OF FRIENDSHIP

It is you-! And I eagerly close
My book, cut the fine intellectual tones,
Shut the door to my room, thick in smoke,
Bulging with too much embodiment.

The street now sways to our gait
Like a bird's narrow perch,
When a human mouth brings the bird to song.
The starry sky twinkles as though freed from a cage.

The night opens itself endlessly to our steps,
Into the heights towers endlessly the houses' might.
Sinking endlessly deep into trees,
The leaves gleam like stars and windows.

The meadows arc, a sky
To the earth, colorfully into the horizon's confusion,
Darkness blooms and carries — oh, how much to see!
And yet walking with earth's feet.

And what was throbbing from me has grown silent: world,
Open yourself! — oh, here it has become obvious,
What I was looking for outside in the mad void:
*The wider world, O friend, are you!*

Therefore, ethereal world, go on your way alone,
Venus and Mars and Jupiter are phantoms,
Here a star circles unencumbered by laws,
We can fly to its free realm!

You darkness through which I never broke:
Here a night sound comes to me that he spoke,
Mystery stirs his lips, sends
His hand to his brothers, brow-dazzled.

Powerfully the current quivers its way through — we hear
The many who now are present and, in choruses of equal gait,
Initiate the heavy earth
Into their clear measures.

And our knees, like columns, erect
Countless domes before us, and then sweep
Them away. For we are changing forms of air,
The great spirit's colony on earth.

Oh, that he planted *not just one* in the chaos —
How we feel it! And does not let
Laughing and crying trickle into the desert,
And catches our call in others' ears,

So that once more spreading in them
It may go on streaming in the spirit — That our growing numbers
May be no accident, a dance at a crowded ball —
How all our hearts beat for this!

Our breasts thunder from the deep beat,
And our earth's unsure supports
We dance away as though on summit peaks,
Everyone strong by himself and because of you and you.

Nonetheless, strength above all joy!
Like heaven stretching between stars,
Friendship arches *deed* — arches the deed over us!
Breathes evermore the path to a new star.

Thus, the world expands by being led through you —
Empty your space of spirits, touch
One another — and spark leaps, goes on leaping,
*Out of you*, you who stride with heads aglow!


KURT HEYNICKE

FRIENDSHIP

Friend,
when you smile,
my heart smiles,

and joy raises its torch,
our road is a smiling day!
Oh, that we are THOU to one another,
that we may carry this Thou
into every heart —
that is what unites us.

To be sure sometimes the temples' silence builds up,
and the mountains of loneliness envelop us,
oh,
deep within everyone is alone.
But a smile constructs an arch from me to you,
and the doors to the temple of the soul are wide-open.
Sacred
is the human being!
Suffering should make us kneel before each other,
joy should lift us up,
we bestow on each other the I and the Thou —
eternally we are united by the words:
HUMAN BEING.

We can be happy
always.


LUDWIG RUBINER

THE ARRIVAL

You who will never hear these lines. Wretched girls who give birth to soldiers'
    children in hidden corners,

Feverish mothers who have no milk to nurse their children.
School children forced to stand at attention with a raised index finger,
You fifteen-year-olds with black rings under your eyes and dreams filled with
    machine-gun fire,

You greedy pimps who conceal brass knuckles when you look strangers in the
    eye,
You mob, you little people who swell into raving gigantic masses when the
    miracle moves through the streets,
You who know nothing, only that your lives are all you have, your days are
    hungry and cold:

326

On you the words of the world sprinkle from the cracks in the walls, to you
they rise like incense from the haze of the asphalt.
You carry the power of the heavenly light that shone over the rooftops into
your pale blood.

You are the resounding mouth, the path of the storm, the house on the new
vaulted earth Berlin.
You more refined scholars, you who never make up your minds behind your
library tables,

You stockmarket gamblers who, with your black hats pulled back on your
necks, sweat and crack jokes in polyglot accents.
You generals, white-bearded, sleepless at your headquarters, you soldiers in the
corpse-pipes of the earth behind the fetid carrion barricades,

And you, comrade, lonely in the midst of a thousand brothers, comrades;
You, comrade, and your brothers who are finished with everything,
Poets, civil servants in debt, restless world travelers, rich women without
children,

Wise, scornful observers who prophesy the coming of war from immutable
laws: Japan-America,

You all have waited, now you are the word and the divine human being. And
the heavenly light is near.

A light flew high once brown-skinned from a South Sea gulf, but the earth was
a wild digesting animal.

Your parents all died from the light. You were begotten blind. But you rose up
out of disease and murder.

You sucked on death, and the light was your milk, you are pillars of blood and
diamonds shining like stars.

You are the light. You are the human being. For you the earth swells anew
from your hands.

You call out over the circling earth, to you echoes back your gigantic human
mouth,

You stand magnificently on a spinning sphere, like God's hair in the wind, for
all of you are the spiritual union in the glow of the earth.

Comrade, you must not be silent. Oh, if you knew how we are loved!

Millennia mixed breath and blood for us, we are star-brothers on these
heavenly earths.

Oh, we must open our mouths and speak loudly for all people until the
morning.
The least reporter is our dear brother.
The head of advertising of the large department stores is our brother!
Everyone who is not silent is our brother!

Shatter the steel casemates of your loneliness!
Oh, jump out of the violet grottos where your shadows slurp sustenance from
your own blood in the dark!

Let every opening that you make in the walls around you be your round mouth
to the light!
From out of every forgotten crack in the earth's crust force the breathbeat of
the spirit into the solar dust!

When a tree of the earth sends its sap into its white buds, let them burst with
ripeness because your mouth evokes it.

Oh, say how the beloved green-shimmering globe danced up and down across
the fire-breath of your smiling mouths!
Oh, say that it is all of our mouths that blow the earth's mountains like tufts
of wool!

Say to the worried general and the rumpled unemployed worker who sleeps
under bridges that heavenly fire issues smiling from their mouths!

Say to the dismissed minister and the freezing whore on the streets that they
must not die before their human mouths have shrilled!

Comrade, you will have a long sleep in your bed. Oh, dream how human
beings have deceived you; your friends have deserted you out of envy.

Dream how locked in you were. Dream the war, the bleeding of the earth, the
million-voiced command of murder,

Dream your fear; your lips closed tightly, your breath came short like the
trembling of leaves on frightened ornamental shrubs.

Black-oppressive dream, the past, O sleep with iron gasps!

But then you wake up, and your words shoot around the earth in comets and firebrands.

You are the eye. And shimmering space. And you build the new earthly land.

Your words scatter in prisms of the rainbow, and the night flew away like chimney soot in the light.

O human being of light from out of the night. Your brothers are awake. And your mouth, wide-open, loudly calls to earth the first divine greeting.

Wilhelm Lehmbruck · Ludwig Rubiner

ALFRED WOLFENSTEIN

THE CITY OF PEACE

The night grows dark as it moves deeper into trees,
The earth sways like skulls full of dreams,
We wander slowly, scarcely knowing why
We started out, and we wait in silence.

We lived in heavenly lukewarmness,
Colorlessly pasted onto woods and plains,
We stared quietly out of a distant landscape,
In calm bodies our wills dwelled modestly.

Our plans floated through little ponds,
Indifferent, light and lonely like swans.
Over our unsuspecting youth lay
The smooth days of an ancient time, of order.

No heart, no glance, no struggle grew in it,
From roots the landscape rose up motionlessly
Into a sheen of peace, half darkened
— And suddenly like a sheen of greatness

Our path sparkles with monsters, and torches
And weapons are pressed into our hands,
Double-edged, pressing wounds into the soul,
And we, drums beating round us, pressed, bound,

Are caught in earth's oldest destiny,
In war, — an army of spies catches our every glance,
A forest grows replete with unnatural acts of violence,
With walls that keep us gray and armed:

With barren stone-face, unapproachably evil,
In its hands a screaming noise,
Steel in its mouth and mute of heart
A specter haunts the human files.

330

Thundering destruction strikes the earth,
And nowhere is a heartbeat to be heard,
We stand in files in the army of negation
And are sent out to murder light.

But suddenly in the all-hostile land —
Whom does my groping hand touch?
Oh — a reaching out somewhat more boldly,
And then the discovery of you with me and me with you!

Human being with human being — and the world is whole again!
Violence pales, violence cowers before you,
O friend —! Barracks retreat from our heads,
From a beauty that is suddenly self-identical and self-trusting!

The earth falls, but spirits are still there
To hold it up! Come and stay near,
Over its desolateness let there be erected
The castle of peace that no one will storm again.

The city rises from the thundering tension
Of our hands! Replete with brows, heavens, energy and light,
A kiss of streets eternally embracing one another,
A delight in brightness without measure.

The sun takes wing across our city!
And never will a traitor be dark enough
To burrow beneath this peace,
No nook here will secretly forge arms.

Penetrate deeper, beam of the city, into all realms,
We nourish you, we of profoundly similar spirit,
From endless contact a sea burns
Forth, back and hotter, higher.

You, peace, struggle of the city! you red star,
Make yourself lord over war, night, cold,
Tied to us make us more deeply tied,
Loved and loving, enlighten and enkindle us!

WILHELM KLEMM

EMOTION

The cries of astonishment,
Who taught them to you, childlike heart,
And the shudders of the loneliness-hours,
Who sowed them in you, erring soul?

No matter where we are, half of the world
Lies before you, the other half behind you,
And because you are but fleeting and limited,
You cannot therefore grasp the unlimited.

But bodies flashing in the fire of God-likeness
Glow, spouses and brothers of yours!
Into your arms, humanity, beloved and
Blossoming wonder-homeland of the imperishable.


WILHELM KLEMM

FULFILLMENT

In the soul there is a rising like a sun —
The blood flows rose-red and warm,
Light are the limbs. Flooded by swift feelings
The near and the distant memories bloom.

Landscapes fly by and human faces,
The loved ones appear bathed in youth and beauty.
A thousand gleaming chambers open —
Just name the thought for which there is no answer!

We feel the key in our hearts that opens the world,
We come as close to each other as only angels can come,
Who first kiss at an infinite distance,
But then grow eternally together.

332

## PENTECOST

The angels of our mothers
have taken to the streets.
The brawling hearts of our fathers
beat more quietly.
Fiery tongues are flying
or are placed on our brows
like wreaths.

Hearing and vision know no limits,
we speak with man and beast.
Whatever we see replies "We."
The pebbles underfoot resound in song,
every pulse-beat echoes in the distance,
everything in bloom reaches out, enlivened by little flames.

Fish rock heaven on their fins
and are ringed by flashing horizons,
sun dances on the backs of dogs.
Everything is bathed in light in accordance with God's vision
and is aware of it in this singular hour
and recognizes brother and sister and sings.

Ludwig Meidner · René Schickele

RENÉ SCHICKELE

ABJURATION

I abjure:
All violence,
Every compulsion,
And even the compulsion
To be good to others.
I know:
I compel only compulsion.
I know:
The sword is stronger
Than the heart,
The blow goes deeper
Than the hand,
Violence steers
What began as good
To evil.

What I want the world to be
I must first myself become
Completely and without severity.
I must become a beam of light,
A clear water
And the purest hand,
Offered in greeting and in help.

Star in the evening assays the day,
Night maternally cradles the day.
Star in the morning thanks the night.
Day beams.
Day after day
Seeks beam after beam,
Beam by beam
Becomes light,
One bright water seeks the other,
Hands branched out
Quietly create the bond.

FRANZ WERFEL

THE MEASURE OF THINGS

Everything *is* when you love!
Your friend becomes Socrates when you give him love.
Heart, heart, how creative you are!
You float in the air! The earth becomes heavenly.
Once as a child you came to a green woodland pond.
Looked with a shudder at the mysterious algae-veil.
You stroked the pussy-willow's animal-sweet velvet —
How your boy's hand trembled in profound bliss!
In your upswing, human being, everything becomes great!
In your downswing, everything hopeless!
And only the soul that forgets itself in love
Is the measure and super-measure of all things.


ERNST STADLER

FORM IS ECSTASY

Form and bolt first had to burst,
World had to press through opened valves:
Form is ecstasy, peace, heavenly contentment,
But something urges me to plough up the clods of the field.
Form wants to lace and constrict me,
But I want to force my being into all distances —
Form is pure hardness without mercy,
But something drives me to the dull, to the poor,
And in the boundless giving of myself
Life wants to saturate me with fulfillment.


THEODOR DÄUBLER

THE MUTE FRIEND

Star misused by human beings, with all your tides
You yearn and languish palely for the moon.
We can only surmise your moon-longing
And know well that no moon-spectre has spared us.

Events that no wish has ever conceived
Well up from your depths that depended upon us,
And coax themselves on to the light moon.
Generations begin to bleed their bodies into each other
And strive to reach the star that began with death.

We dream ourselves away to a homecoming,
Where our rising will be rigid and cold.
In the dreamt slumber-ebbtide-slime
The silver embroidery of death appears;
The moon scatters the pale seeds of death:
Its compassion is already germinating in every egg.

Star misused by human beings, even the happiest child of the sun
Wants unexpectedly to be your friendly companion.
What has sprung up surprisingly quick during the day
Stays inwardly gentle and moon-like mild.

The moon let slip a word before its death,
Heard by all, but remembered by no one.
Up to the moon! Now its mouth is closed.
To the silver moon from which no syllable escapes any more.


JOHANNES R. BECHER

THE ISLAND OF DESPAIR

: — How I, cliff-ulcer, long for the sea,
Into which submerging I can sink away.
On my back nations bleed heavily.
The gentian depths, however, I love dearly:
Palaces of magical coral gifts.

Might I, freed from the ground, a ship, swing myself up,
Through the ether's brazen storms... oh, closer and closer!
Already my flesh blossoms. My joints resound.
Stars float, angels, around me. —
I can swirl easily in an eternal dance.

My mouth's sulphur smoke rose up to become a flag
That unfurling — what sweetness! — waves!!!
My forehead wall flashes balconies of light.
The craters of my eyes purest native lakes.

337

I was torn away towards the stream of grace,
Where animal praises human being. And human being fuses with
　　　　human being.
In my glow the creatures bathe.
*They are all called brothers...!!!*


IWAN GOLL

WATERFALL

Water and human being,
You are the eternal movement!
You are the drive of all drives: you are the spirit!
Here no rock stands rigid and no godhead tall:
Before your jet the blocks of granite split,
Before your voice the silence of death bursts.
O waterfall, you pearl dancer,
From your single, steep trunk of water
You bloom a million water-branches onto the earth!
You give yourself to the poisonous nettle in the roadside ditch,
You force upward the green fountain of the palms;
Forget-me-not shivers in your dew,
And the fat olive tree sucks you up with copper pumps.
You are earth's eternal lover!

In the same way I, your immortal lover, want
To stream over and inundate humanity:
Down, down out of the solitude
To melt away, foaming with love,
(By the height of the mountain peaks I estimated the depth of the
　　　　valleys)
I want to flow back to humanity,
To the dark ravines of the defeated and the enslaved,
To the gray wastelands of the careerists and the unproductive,
To the endless plains of the poor and of the louts,
To the fumy ports of the exiled and the oppressed —
Down, down, I must follow the eternal drive,
Whoever gives himself enriches *himself* most of all.
With mouth sparkling and eyes laughing I want
To squander the great love of this night,
To give and give myself because I know:
Inexhaustible are the glaciers of the earth,
Inexhaustible are the well-springs of the heart!

338

THEODOR DÄUBLER

THE SUNS AND PLANETS ARE

The suns and planets are, all of them,
The majestic givers of life in the world,
Are the lights of love in the temple
Of the godhead that swells them from the heart.

They are sheer love, compacted into deep repose,
Their light-cry is taut with primeval power,
As a surge of life it is directed into the universe:
What it reaches is held spellbound by the day!

A bond of love holds nature enchained;
The ether-threshold as well as the fire-star,
The whole world that is bedded in darkness
Seeks in itself the same center of rest.

By the love of the sun the night is lighted,
By flame and happiness the planet is enlivened,
What is rigid is destroyed by a conflagration,
From the sea a wind of love blows.

Where self-power ignites as a star,
Life is also immediately enkindled,
And when the world takes form in its creatures,
Then pain knows that it derives from happiness.

Thus, the earth must give birth to us in pleasure,
And even though our being is welded by the day,
Stars can teach us what is fundamental
And say that no bond of love is ever broken.

We see life robbing us of youth,
Old age and death frighten us,
Therefore, we want to believe in a beginning
And swear by an eternal order of things.

But rest is just its life of rest,
Nothing is different that shows change;

And even the spirit's agitation is fulfillment,
Yes, everything is nature that is silent as it speaks!

Constancy is the result of rigidity,
But the ether-rage overtakes it and wears it down,
And only the spirit remains to persevere,
Because as light it rests in its speed.

To be sure, the world seeks perpetually to preserve itself,
And it moves, therefore, around its own center,
It can huddle around itself for protection,
Yet its wish is not eternal but remote.

The world may hold together the most distant things,
But the spirit that surges from itself
Can wind such gigantic circles around itself
That its good effect is lavished everywhere.

Thus have the worlds been born perpetually.
But because the eternal wrenches itself from every goal,
Stars freed themselves from star-bonds.
Which proves the endlessness of being!

Yes, love, love wants to create worlds for itself,
Just love, without purpose and without a goal,
Always the same, it seeks always to reshape itself,
And so its eternal game remains young, too young.

For if a creator's will glowed through the universe,
*One* world only would have been constructed,
And dreamlessly spirits of bright abodes, in their pure being,
Would be permeated by its dark depths.


RUDOLF LEONHARD

EVENING SONG

As evening warmed streets already startled by light,
the woman walking next to me without brushing against me said — almost
        singing:
"Now all lives are closing in a ring,
whose center and meaning

I am.
To me have been given the faces of all who will come,
just see how they, the glowing and the care-worn,
are all revivified by the evening!

Here behind these panes people laugh and enjoy themselves.
Here blood was shed, there tears are shed.
The man over there will be bankrupt tomorrow,
the other one — do you see him — smiles and talks with his God.
That couple will soften and melt their flesh in kisses
and roll over each other like animals — as if on thick furs.
Oh, feel how all of us live on hard thrones
between the taverns and our rigid churches!

Look at this mailman. Believe me, he will have to climb many more steps,
will nod from afar to the men and girls waiting by the crack of the door,
blindly distribute joy and torment to all of them,
in ignorance climb more steps,
saying not a word.
With limber thighs and knees and his inured look,
four, five floors up into the heavens of human destinies!

I am delighted by the shining puddles between the stones
that pluck all the streetlights into shimmering bouquets,
I am enchanted by the poplars around the fountain
that draw their thin branches together;
and I am saddened by these dirty, crying children.

All the deeds that vanished with the day
evening has painted on my high held brow.
Oh, and yet to raise my head lightly into the warm evening,
and over the anesthetics in the bars and dance halls,
over you and my own torments,
to float around roofs and windows —"
I sought to look tenderly and pleadingly at her forehead;
there was a steep wrinkle between her darkened brows.

WALTER HASENCLEVER

POEMS

When death
Devours the music:
Will we recognize each other?
Do you live
In the room where men stand?
Out of the ocean rises the island,
A life that was meant for us.
Birds fly up.
Do not cry!

\*

Moon.
Gazelles call;
The desolation of the valleys, covered with snow.
Look, I am walking,
A human being of love.
A heart full of hope
Has reached me.

\*

Where are you?
A star is falling.
Your face!
You are there!

\*

When you empty the goblet
Where on yonder side
White swallows drink:
Do not forget the tear,
The kiss that you dreamt
In the heavens of the dead.
You are loved!

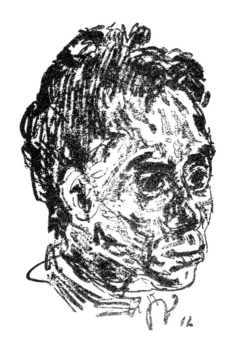

Oskar Kokoschka · Walter Hasenclever

WALTER HASENCLEVER

ON THE DEATH OF A WOMAN

When you bow at the hem of heaven,
Stripped of summer foliage:
We stay behind,
We open our eyes,
We see your eternal image.
Now you know all,
Tear and hope,
The world of suffering, the world of happiness.
Redeemed soul, beloved soul,
Our sister,
Home is there!


ELSE LASKER-SCHÜLER

PRAYER
(To my dear half-brother, the blue rider)

I am searching in every land for a city
That has an angel before its gate.
I am carrying his large wing,
Broken and heavy, at my shoulder blade,
And on my forehead his star as a seal.

And I wander ever into the night...
I have brought love into the world, —
So that every heart may bloom in blue,
And I have worn myself out keeping watch all my life,
Have wrapped in God the dark beat of my breath.

O God, close your cloak tightly around me;
I know I am the residue in the global glass,
And that when the last human being pours out the world,
You will not let me slip from your omnipotent grasp,
And a new globe shall close around me.

FRANZ WERFEL

VENI CREATOR SPIRITUS

Come, Holy Spirit, Creator!
Shatter the marble of our form!
So that a wall sick and hard will no longer
Rigidly surround the well-spring of this world,
So that together and upwards
We will rage into one another like flames!

Emerge from our wounded surfaces,
Dolphin of the ground of all beings,
You, ancient, universal and holy fish!
Come, Pure Spirit, Creator,
Towards whom we unfold eternally,
Crystal law of the world's configurations!

How very much we are all still strangers!
Just as beneath the last gown
Shadowy old men in hospital beds
Manage to hate each other right up to the last,
And each one, before he flows eastward,
Lights his evening candle alone,

Thus we are harnessed in vanity,
And crouch maliciously on our borders,
And murder each other at every table.
Come, Holy Spirit, Creator,
Rise out of us in a thousand flights!
Shatter the ice in our features!

So that in tears and an abundance of goodness
The enraptured flood may seethe up,
So that creatures remote and unreached
Will cease to crawl around each other,
So that jubilantly in look, hand, mouth and hair,
And in ourselves, we will come to know your attributes!

So that whoever falls into a brother's arms
Will lovingly hold your deep throbbing to his heart,
So that whoever is gazed at by some poor dog
Will have your wise look bestowed on him,
So that all of us, in kissing's profusion,
Will kiss only your pure and holy lips!


THEODOR DÄUBLER

THE HUMAN BEING IS A DRIED-UP BUR

The human being is a dried-up bur:
Parasite-red, the Caucasian huffs and puffs along
And assiduously builds for himself yellow-violet cities.

But his will exceeds his understanding!
Earthly exhaustion's white pinions of peace
Are our lucid gain already in life.

Work must subdue the warm body.
In the arms of relaxation do we rest:
Our first flight can succeed in a dream!

Here the soul builds itself a radiant forest home,
The pale, untouched Eden of its longing:
Though terrible, it is far from the turmoil of the earth!

Disembodied, the spirit notes the dream's defects
And then wages a battle for Christ's light,
For the spirit must make war upon earth's spectres!

In the craze of pleasure you seek no judgment.
But purified, you will step before Christ,
For grace beams into every trust.

Human beings who pray at work, facing the light,
See high up in the red sun the symbol of their world,
Their victory over the fear of the planets of the night.

Death is only fear of what is to our benefit,
The flesh is afraid of perceiving itself eternal,
But sweet hope beams over the pole.

346

The primeval fire wants to deny the end
And effects an eternity that proves itself.
Profoundly conquered are doubt's shadows:

The spirit reconciles the earth and resounds above it!


KURT HEYNICKE

SONG

In me is blue sky;
I carry the earth,
carry love,
myself
and joy.

Sun kneels before me,
the grain rises,
eternal springs flow over the loins of the earth.

Become!
Soul of the universe shouting for joy!
I am a human being in the arms of eternal becoming,
mystery is blissfully unlocked,
I am poured out brightly into my very self,
on giant blue pinions I soar toward the sun!

When the distance falls into my soul,
sweet song sings in me,
I feel
endlessly
that I am not alone...
When you are close,
brother human being,
the distance which describes an arc around us
unites our dream,
when God's countenance rises like a vault over us,
and thunderously the expanse of our thoughts
plunges across the identical prayers of our friendship...
The
circle of our hands is a longing!
Oh, let us smile above the valleys of the human beings —

like the soul of the moon
that has silvery dreams...


FRANZ WERFEL

A SPIRITUAL SONG

We dance past
A small lamp, a man.
Something tears at us,
And ultimate longing seizes us.
We will never have each other,
For formality has an imperial hold on us.
And when we are buried someday,
Dust will still be hostile to dust.

By the fence the Slovak
Spits and wipes his mouth.
Someone else raises his hoe,
And a brown dog comes nearer.
When they wash by,
Consternated by love of flesh and stone,
But when we feel bodies,
Disgust must be our response.

The promise of ultimate faithfulness
Is the light of brotherhood in our eyes,
Out of which breaks the winter blue
Of the unobstructed heavens.
May we someday find ourselves
In feelings without flaw,
Disappear through each other into each other,
May we be motion, nothing but motion and love and racing
　　　rapture.

FRANZ WERFEL

THE PASSIONATE

My God, at your right side there will be
Not only the upright and the just!
No, all those who stood at windows
On thirteen December nights. And women who took revenge
With vitriol and then turned gray in court,
All the jealous who stopped the flow of their blood,
Cried in taxi-cabs, made scenes in public!
Those who breathed deeply the air of defeat,
Singers who, with boozed
Limbs, flung themselves into death's pit,
They all will be snatched and taken up to you
And will sit, God, at your right side!

There will walk in your gardens
Not just the humble and the burdened,
No, all those who have shone and revered!
Young girls who became sick at concerts
Because their cheeks radiated too much paleness,
Looks from eyes that gave thanks —
Genuine momentary looks, elevated from time itself
To your times, to a never consumed duration,
They will go on blazing and give praise,
Airy flames walking in your gardens!

There will rest, God, in your depths
Not just those who called your name,
No, all those who could not sleep at night!
Who in the morning mounded their hearts with both hands
Like a flame, and ran
Panting, blindly, down unknown paths.
A coastal wind twitches in the letters of suicides.
The boys did not understand the ocean,
And so they burnt themselves away in hieroglyphics.
Now rusty markers rattle against the leaning
Iron crosses of the candidates for confirmation.
As much as we are here, so are we there, too —
Those who were unrestful here out of your depths,
They will find rest there in your depths.

PAUL ZECH

THIS IS THE HOUR

I

You kneel, you pray —: how this God can still
be persuaded in spite of a thousand lies
and the mockery of popes grown soft.

Your word assembles in processions,
the stream forms seven branches in space;
the virgins carry oil again in vessels.

Reed pipes echo, attracting cymbal-froth
and angel-hosts blue on golden ground.
I kiss the hem of your garment

and a dove hovers and speaks: *This is the hour!*

II

This is the hour: home everywhere
and even in the sacrament of the beloved.
Never again will a Fall of humanity

curse the earth to burning.
The You in me, the I in You
lives undivided,

still procreating, until we
have flowed forward in holy legions
as woodland or animal,

and return after millions of years.

WILHELM KLEMM

UNITY

Let fall what falls.
Even destruction is divine,
Even error and sin,
Even crime and misfortune.

When the urge to do good is in you,
Allow it to grow vigorously.
Trouble consumes itself by itself.
But lessen it as much as you can.

When the day goes to rest,
How many tarry in the lap of time!
When the earth becomes too narrow for you,
How vast the heavens are!

Around the minuteness of existence
Eternal shells vault,
They are immeasurable.
Are they not enough for you?

You can be free. Learn, therefore,
From the elements that carry you along.
You too are only a movement,
But peace is assured you.


GEORG TRAKL

SONG OF THE DEPARTED ONE
(To Karl Borromäus Heinrich)

Full of harmonies is the flight of birds. At evening the green woods
Have gathered themselves into quieter dwellings;
The crystal pastures of the deer.
Darkness soothes the plashing of the brook, the damp shadows,

And the flowers of summer that ring lovely in the wind.
Already the brow of the pensive person grows dusky.
And a little lamp, goodness, glows in his heart

And the peace of the evening meal; for sanctified are bread and wine
From God's hands, and from nocturnal eyes the brother
Gazes quietly at you so that he may rest from thorny wanderings.
Oh, to live in the ensouled blue of the night.

Lovingly too does the silence in the room embrace the shadows of the elders,
The crimson torments, lament of a great lineage
That is now piously dying in the lonely grandchild.

For ever more radiant does the long-sufferer awaken from black minutes of
     insanity
On the petrified threshold
And he is powerfully embraced by the cool blue and the glowing decline of
     autumn,

The silent house and the legends of the woods,
Measure and law and the moon-paths of the departed.


## WALTER HASENCLEVER

### YOU SPIRIT WHO ABANDONED ME

You spirit who abandoned me, whom I gain,
Who in a thousand ways waits for my work:
Vanquish me right down to the last of my senses,
Begin on another star, O journey!
I am born anew into the world
That flows from my suffering and my joys.
What I possessed I never lost,
My view has just grown larger and clearer.
I saw my brother whenever I saw the vision
Of my own heart transfiguring me;
Yet I am more than longing and lament:
I am promise! I am eternally here!

KURT KEYNICKE

PSALM

My soul is a quiet garden
I cry,
closed in by the walls of my body,
the world sits yellow before the door of my soul.

My soul is a garden,
a nightingale my longing,
the young nightingale sings songs of love,
and my heart longs for God.

God is a name,
nameless is my longing,
it has given birth to a child,
the will,
young,
a will thundered through with violence,
I must away to him.

A garden is my soul.
I do not kneel in my garden.
My arms stretch wide into the wide tapestry of blue nights,
I fly,
nameless face of the world,
I am your brother,
born out of the starry mists on the first day.

My will sprouts an altar of May and young sun,
thousands of buds burst into flames,
and my longing flutters toward your mouth in song,
God,
or mother-womb,
heart of my brother in the universe,
I cry,
for no thought sends a name,
I sing
my longing's psalm,
cradled by the harp of unending love.

FRANZ WERFEL

A SONG OF LIFE

Enmity is insufficient.
Will and deed,
An earth-conscious life,
In themselves what are they, world?
There hovers in every destiny,
In the pace of pleasure and pains,
In murdering and embracing,
*The grace of being human!*

Only that is imperishable!
Did you see the wild eyes
Of the hunchbacked peasant girls?
Did you see how they slowly veil themselves
In the fashion of ladies of the world,
Did you see glittering in them
The green of the festive platforms,
Music and lantern-night?

Did you see the beards of sick men
— You clouds above the poplar trees —,
How they remind you of God
Immersed in a storm?
Did you see the great kindness
In the dying of a child?
How the dear body
Gently slipped away from us?

Did you see the growing sadness
Of girls in the evening?
How they put their kitchens in order
And are as remote as saints.
Did you see the beautiful hands
Of furrowed constables on night duty,
As they caress their dogs
With coarse words of love?

Whoever in doing something became incensed,
Consider! Unutterably
Distant and close are we
In speech and gestures!

That we stand and sit here,
Who can grasp that without a shudder of anxiety?!
But beyond all words
I proclaim, human being, *we are!!*

# POETS AND WORKS

## BIOGRAPHICAL AND BIBLIOGRAPHICAL NOTES

IN ORDER TO PRESERVE the historico-documentary character of this new edition after 40 years, all autobiographical and biographical material from the four initial printings of the original edition (1920 to 1922) has been retained and is reproduced in *italics*. In these autobiographical or principled comments made by the poets four decades ago, nothing has been altered or left out, even if today they seem in part abstruse or the poets changed the opinions they held at that time.

Since, however, it was deemed fitting to present, although of necessity in a very concise way, the fates and works of the poets up to the time of their deaths or to the present year of 1964, a great deal had to be added. Of the 23 poets appearing in this anthology, the three who are still living as the new edition goes to press, HEYNICKE, KLEMM, OTTEN, have now contributed new autobiographies to their previous ones. The supplementary biography of GOLL was compiled by his widow, the poet CLAIRE GOLL. At the time the original edition was published in 1920 seven poets had already died or been killed in the First World War: nothing could be added to the biographies of LICHTENSTEIN, LOTZ, STRAMM, written at the time by those close to the deceased; supplements were added to the depictions of HEYM and TRAKL; new biographies have been affixed by the editor to the previous insufficient data on HODDIS and STADLER. — The editor has added supplementary biographies to the shorter or more detailed self-portrayals of the poets who have in the meantime died, BECHER, BENN, DÄUBLER, EHRENSTEIN, HASENCLEVER, LASKER-SCHÜLER, LEONHARD, RUBINER, SCHICKELE, WERFEL, WOLFENSTEIN, ZECH.

All biographical material compiled by the editor is designated by [ed.]. Anything without designation comes from the poets themselves. Anything written by others is followed by the name of the author in [  ].

In order to avoid repetitiousness in the biographical material, anything that was there in the original edition is not repeated in the newly added biographies. Hence, in order to be able to combine all recorded data and facts, both the old portrayal, printed in italics, and the new supplementary portrayal have to be read. The aim has not been stylistic ambitiousness and literary discernment in the presentation of the new material, but rather: to impart as much factual information as possible in the smallest amount of space.

The bibliographies try their utmost to list all works of the poets published in book form (no matter how rare or how forgotten). Because of limited space everything had to be left out that was published by the poets in journals and anthologies or that was published about them, as well as translations of their works into other languages, unless the poets wrote in two languages. But, of course, works of other authors edited or translated by the poets and journals or anthologies edited by them are listed. Reprints are noted only if they offer revised or enlarged texts or if there is a special reason, e.g., illustrations. More extensive selections from the works of the individual poets or collected works are listed (usually at the end of the bibliographies), as well as notations concerning literary remains.

JOHANNES R(OBERT) BECHER. *Born in Munich on May 22, 1891* as the son of the later chief judge of a provincial court of appeals, Heinrich Becher, studied philosophy and medicine in Berlin, Munich, and Jena, but gave up his studies to become a freelance writer. As an opponent of the war he joined the Spartacus League at the end of the First World War, and then the Communist Party. In 1924 the Supreme Court of Germany instituted proceedings against him on the charge of incitement to treason, committed by the publication of the collection of poems entitled *Der Leichnam auf dem Thron* (The Corpse on the Throne) and the novel *Levisite oder der einzig gerechte Krieg* (Lewisite or The Only Just War); the case was ultimately dismissed because of the Hindenburg amnesty. — He eluded a planned arrest during the night of the Reichstag fire in 1933 and emigrated first to Prague, then to Vienna and France, and, in the fall of 1935 after being deprived of his German citizenship, to the Soviet Union. He stayed in Moscow, was temporarily evacuated to Tashkent during the war, and in May 1945 returned to Berlin for good. He became president of the Cultural League for the Democratic Renewal of Germany (honorary president since February, 1948), from 1950 to 1953 vice-president, then president of the German Academy of the Arts in East Berlin, and in January 1954 minister of culture. He received the National Prize First Class in 1949 and 1950 as well as the International Lenin Peace Prize in 1952; in 1951 Humboldt University in Berlin made him an honorary doctor and in 1958 the University of Jena an honorary senator. Becher died in Berlin on October 11, 1958. He was put to rest in Dorotheenstadt Cemetery, where Bertolt Brecht also lies buried. [ed.]
Der Ringende, Kleist-Hymne (The Struggler, Kleist Hymn); Berlin, 1911. — Die Gnade eines Frühlings, Dichtungen (The Grace of a Spring, Poetic Works); Berlin, 1912. — Erde, ein Roman (Earth, A Novel); Berlin, 1912. — De Profundis Domine, Dichtung (..., Poetic Work); Munich, 1913. — Verfall und Triumph (Downfall and Triumph), 2 vols. (vol. 1: Gedichte [Poems], vol. 2: Versuche in Prosa [Experiments in Prose]); Berlin, 1914. — Verbrüderung, Gedichte (Brotherhood, Poems); Leipzig, 1916. — An Europa, Neue Gedichte (To Europe, New Poems); Leipzig, 1916. — Die heilige Schar, Gedichte (The Holy Band, Poems); Leipzig, 1918. — Päan gegen die Zeit, Gedichte (Paean against the Times, Poems); Leipzig, 1918. — Das Neue Gedicht, Auswahl 1912-1918 (The New Poem, Selections ...); Leipzig, 1918. — Gedichte um Lotte (Poems for ...); Leipzig, 1919. — Gedichte für ein Volk (Poems for a People), Leipzig, 1919. — An alle! Neue Gedichte (To All! New Poems); Berlin, 1919. — Zion, Gedichte (..., Poems); Munich, 1920. — Ewig im Aufruhr, Gedichte (Eternally in Revolt, Poems); Berlin, 1920. — Der Gestorbene, Gedichte (The Deceased, Poems); Regensburg, 1921. — Um Gott (Gedichte, Prosa und Festspiel *Arbeiter Bauern Soldaten*) (About God [Poems,

Prose and Festival Production *Workers Peasants Soldiers*]); Leipzig, 1921. — Arbeiter Bauern Soldaten, Der Aufbruch eines Volkes zu Gott (Workers Peasants Soldiers, The Awakening of a People to God); Leipzig, 1921. — Verklärung, Hymne (Transfiguration, Hymn); Berlin, 1922. — Drei Hymnen ("Vernichtung," "An die Deutschen," "Mord") (Three Hymns ["Destruction," "To the Germans," "Murder"); Constance, 1923. — Hymnen, Gedichte (Hymns, Poems); Leipzig, 1924. — Arbeiter, Bauern, Soldaten, Entwurf zu einem revolutionären Kampfdrama (Workers, Peasants, Soldiers, Outline for a Revolutionary Battle-Drama) (2nd completely revised edition); Frankfurt, 1924. — Am Grabe Lenins, Dichtung (At Lenin's Grave, Poetic Work); Berlin, 1924. — Der Leichnam auf dem Thron ("Roter Marsch," "Der Leichnam auf dem Thron," "Die Bombenflieger"), Dichtungen (The Corpse on the Throne ["Red March," "...," "The Bomber Pilots"], Poetic Works); Berlin, 1925. — Vorwärts, du Rote Front, Aufsätze und Reden (Forward, You Red Front, Essays and Speeches); Frankfurt/Main, 1924. — Penthesilea (with Ludwig Meidner), Dichtung (..., Poetic Work); Berlin, 1924. — Wladimir Majakowski: 150 Millionen, Nachdichtung (Vladimir Mayakovsky: 150 Million, Free Rendering); Berlin, 1924. — Demjan Bjedny: Die Hauptstraße, Nachdichtungen (Demyan Byedny: Main Street, Free Renderings), epilogue by L. Trotsky; Vienna, 1924. — Der Bankier reitet über das Schlachtfeld, Erzählung (The Banker Rides across the Battlefield, Story); Vienna and Berlin, 1926. — (CHCLCH) 3 As — Levisite oder der einzig gerechte Krieg, Roman (...Three A's — Lewisite or The Only Just War, Novel); Vienna-Berlin, 1926. — Maschinenrhythmen, Gedichte (Machine Rhythms, Poems); Berlin, 1926. — Im Schatten der Berge, Gedichte (In the Shadow of the Mountains, Poems); Berlin, 1927. — Die hungrige Stadt, Gedichte (The Hungry City, Poems); Vienna, 1927 and 1928. — Ein Mensch unserer Zeit, Gesammelte Gedichte (A Human Being of our Times, Collected Poems); Rudolstadt, 1929 (new edition with subtitle *Verse und Prosa* [Verse and Prose]; Berlin, 1930) — Graue Kolonnen, Gedichte (Gray Columns, Poems); Berlin, Vienna, and Zurich, 1930. — Der große Plan, Epos des sozialistischen Aufbaus (The Great Plan, Epic of Socialist Building); Vienna and Berlin, 1931. — Der Mann, der in der Reihe geht, Neue Gedichte und Balladen (The Man Who Marches in File, New Poems and Ballads); Berlin, 1932.

Neue Gedichte (New Poems); Moscow-Leningrad, 1933. — Deutscher Totentanz 1933, Gedichte (German Dance of Death 1933, Poems); Moscow, 1933. — Es wird Zeit, Gedichte (It Is Time, Poems); Moscow, 1933. — An die Wand zu kleben, Gedichte (To Stick on the Wall, Poems); Moscow, 1933. — Der verwandelte Platz, Erzählungen und Gedichte (The Transformed Place, Stories and Poems); Moscow, Zurich, 1934. — Deutschland, ein Lied vom Köpferollen und von den nützlichen Gliedern (Germany, A Song of Head-Rolling and of the Useful Members); Moscow, Zurich, 1934. — Der Mann, der alles glaubte, Dichtung (The Man Who Believed Everything, Poetical Work); Moscow, Paris, 1935. — Ausgewählte Gedichte (Selected Poems); Kiev, 1935. — Sonette und Gedichte (Sonnets and Poems); Paris, 1936. — Der Glücksucher und die sieben Lasten, Ein Hohes Lied (The Happiness Seeker and the Seven Burdens, A Song of Praises); Moscow, London, 1938. — Die Bauern von

Unterpeißenberg und andere Gedichte aus dem bäuerlichen Leben (The Peasants of ... and Other Poems from Peasant Life); Engels, 1938. — Der Weltentdecker, Ausgewählte Gedichte (The World Discoverer, Selected Poems); Kiev, 1938. — Gewißheit des Siegs und Sicht auf große Tage, Gesammelte Sonette 1935-1938 (Certainty of Victory and Prospect of Great Days, Collected Sonnets ...); Moscow, 1939. — Gesammelte Epische Dichtungen (Collected Epic Works); Kiev, 1939. — Wiedergeburt, Dichtungen (Rebirth, Poetic Works); Moscow, 1940. — Die sieben Jahre, Gedichte (The Seven Years, Poems): Moscow, 1940. — Abschied, Einer deutschen Tragödie erster Teil, 1900-1914, Roman (Farewell, Part One of a German Tragedy, ..., Novel); Moscow, 1940 (reprints since 1945, Berlin). — Deutschland ruft, Gedichte (Germany Calls, Poems); Moscow, 1942 (enlarged edition, Stockholm, 1945). — Schlacht um Moskau, Drama (Battle for Moscow, Drama); Moscow, 1942. — Dank an Stalingrad, Dichtungen (Thanks to ..., Poetic Works); Moscow, 1943. — Deutsche Sendung, ein Ruf an die deutsche Nation (German Mission, A Call to the German Nation); Moscow, 1943. — Neue Waffen, Gedichte (New Weapons, Poems); Moscow, 1943. — Die hohe Warte, Deutschland-Dichtung (The High Observation Point, Germany-Poems); Moscow, 1944 (enlarged edition, Berlin, 1947). — Deutsche Lehre, Essay (German Lesson, Essay); London, 1944. — Dichtung, Auswahl aus den Jahren 1939-1943 (Poetry, Selection from the Years ...); Moscow, 1944.

Winterschlacht (Schlacht um Moskau), eine deutsche Tragödie (Winter Battle [Battle for Moscow], A German Tragedy); Berlin, 1945, 1953, 1956. — Ausgewählte Dichtung aus der Zeit der Verbannung (Selected Poetry from the Time of Exile); Berlin, 1945. — Deutsches Bekenntnis, Drei Reden zu Deutschlands Erneuerung (German Avowal, Three Speeches on Germany's Renewal); Berlin, 1945 (enlarged edition: Sieben Reden [Seven Speeches]; Berlin, 1947). — Romane in Versen (Novels in Verse); Berlin, 1946. — Erziehung zur Freiheit, Gedanken und Betrachtungen (Education for Freedom, Thoughts and Reflections); Berlin, 1946. — Das Führerbild, Schauspiel (The Fuehrer-Portrait, Play); Munich, 1946 (new edition entitled Der Weg nach Füssen [The Road to ...]; Berlin, 1953). — München in meinem Gedicht (Munich in my Poem); Starnberg am See, 1946. — Heimkehr, Gedichte (Homecoming, Poems); Berlin, 1947. — Wir — unsere Zeit, Auswahlband in 6 Teilen (We — Our Time, Selection in 6 Parts) (with introductions by Paul Wiegler and Georg Lukács); Munich, 1947. — Wir, Volk der Deutschen, Rede (We, Nation of the Germans, Speech); Berlin, 1947. — Vom Willen zum Frieden, Zwei Reden (On the Will to Peace, Two Speeches); Berlin, 1947. — Lob des Schwabenlandes, Schwaben in meinem Gedicht (In Praise of the Land of Swabia, Swabia in my Poem); Constance and Leipzig, 1947. — Wiedergeburt, Buch der Sonette (Rebirth, Book of Sonnets); Leipzig, 1947. — Uns ist bange, aber wir verzagen nicht, Rede (We Are Afraid But We Will Not Lose Heart, Speech); Berlin, 1947. — Volk im Dunkel wandelnd, Gedicht-Auswahl (A People Wandering in the Dark, Poetry-Selection); Berlin, 1948. — Der Befreier, Rede zum 200. Geburtstag Goethes (The Liberator, Speech on the Occasion of Goethe's 200th Birthday); Berlin, 1949. — Auswahl in vier Bänden

(Selection in Four Volumes); Berlin, 1949. — Befreiung, Rede (Liberation, Speech); Berlin, 1949. — Die Faust, Gedichte (The Fist, Poems); Bucharest, 1949. — Wir wollen Frieden, Auszüge aus Reden und Aufsätzen (We Want Peace, Excerpts from Speeches and Essays); Berlin, 1949. — Die deutsche Verantwortung für den Frieden, Rede (The German Responsibility for Peace, Speech); Berlin, 1950. — Vollendung träumend, Ausgewählte Gedichte aus dem frühen Werk (Dreaming Fulfillment, Selected Poems from the Early Work); Leipzig, 1950. — Neue deutsche Volkslieder (New German Folksongs) (set to music by Hanns Eisler); Berlin, 1950. — Macht den Frieden stark! 3 Briefe den Frieden betreffend (Make the Peace Strong. 3 Letters Concerning Peace); Berlin, 1950. — Sterne unendliches Glühen, Die Sowjetunion in meinem Gedicht 1917-1951 (Stars' Infinite Glowing, The Soviet Union in My Poem...); Berlin, 1951. — Dona nobis pacem — Gib uns den Frieden, Ein Friedensbrevier (... — Grant Us Peace, A Peace Breviary); Berlin, 1951. — Auf andere Art so große Hoffnung, Tagebuch 1950 (Such Great Hope in a Different Way, Diary); Berlin, 1951. — Ein Mensch unserer Zeit in seinen Gedichten 1911-1951 (A Human Being of Our Time in His Poems ...); Berlin, 1951. — Glück der Ferne — leuchtend nah, Gedichte (Distant Happiness — Shining Near, Poems); Berlin, 1951. — Forum der Nation, Rede (Forum of the Nation, Speech); Berlin, 1951. — Verteidigung der Poesie, Vom Neuen in der Literatur ("Bemühungen" 1. Teil) (In Defense of Poetry, On What Is New in Literature ["Endeavors," Part One]); Berlin, 1952. — Schöne deutsche Heimat, Gedichte (Beautiful German Homeland, Poems); Berlin, 1952 (new edition with illustrations, 1956). — Deutsche Sonette 1952 (German Sonnets ...); Berlin, 1952. — Auswahl in sechs Bänden (Selection in Six Volumes); Berlin, 1952. — Dreimal bebende Erde, Ausgewählte Prosa aus den Tagebüchern (Thrice Trembling Earth, Selected Prose from the Diaries); Berlin, 1953. — Poetische Konfession ("Bemühungen" 2. Teil) (Poetic Confession ["Endeavors," Part Two]); Berlin, 1954. — Ein Deutschland ist, soll sein und bleiben! Rede (One Germany Is, Shall Be and Shall Remain! Speech); Berlin, 1954. — Macht der Poesie, Poetische Konfession 2. Teil ("Bemühungen" 3. Teil) (Power of Poetry, Poetic Confession, Part 2 ("Endeavors," Part 3); Berlin, 1955. — Für ein Deutschland, schön wie nie!, Rede (For a Germany Beautiful As Never Before!, Speech); Berlin, 1955. — Sternbilder auf Erden, Dichtungen (Constellations on Earth, Poetic Works); Berlin, 1955. — Vom Anderswerden, Reden, Aufsätze, Briefe (On Becoming Different, Speeches, Essays, Letters) (epilogue Alexander Abusch); Berlin, 1955. — Denn er ist unser: Friedrich Schiller, der Dichter der Freiheit, Rede (For He Is Ours: ..., The Poet of Freedom, Speech); Berlin, 1955. — Wir, unsere Zeit, das zwanzigste Jahrhundert, Ausgewählte Gedichte (We, Our Time, The Twentieth Century, Selected Poems); Berlin,1956. Sonett-Werk (Sonnet-Work); Berlin, 1956. — Von der Größe unserer Literatur, Rede (On the Greatness of our Literature, Speech); Berlin, 1956. — Das poetische Prinzip ("Bemühungen" 4. Teil) (The Poetic Principle ["Endeavors," Part 4]); Berlin 1957. — Liebe ohne Ruh, Liebesgedichte 1913-1956 (Restless Love, Love Poems...); Berlin, 1957. — Walter Ulbricht, ein deutscher Arbeitersohn (..., Son of a German Working-Class Family); Berlin 1958. — Schritt der

Jahrhundertmitte, Neue Dichtungen (Pace of the Mid-Century, New Poetic Works); Berlin, 1958. — Der Glücksucher und die sieben Lasten, Verlorene Gedichte (The Happiness Seeker and the Seven Burdens, Lost Poems); Berlin, 1958. — Als namenloses Lied, Gedichte (As a Nameless Song, Poems) (foreword Ernst Stein); Berlin, 1958. — Die sozialistische Kultur und ihre nationale Bedeutung, Ansprache (Socialist Culture and its National Significance, Address); Berlin, 1958.

Ein Staat wie unser Staat, Gedichte und Prosa vom Werden und Wachsen der Deutschen Demokratischen Republik (A State Like Our State, Poems and Prose on the Origin and Growth of the German Democratic Republic) (foreword Walter Ulbricht); Berlin, 1959. — Vom Mut des Künstlers (On the Courage of the Artist); Leipzig, 1959. — Gerichtstag über sich selbst (Sitting in Judgment on Oneself); Leipzig, 1959. — Sterne unendliches Glühen, die Sowjetunion im Dichten und Denken eines Deutschen (Stars' Infinite Glowing, The Soviet Union in the Writing and Thinking of a German) (enlarged new edition, 2 vols.); Berlin, 1960. — Du bist für alle Zeit geliebt, Gedichte (You Are Loved for All Time, Poems) (selection by J.R. Becher Archives), illustrated by Frans Masereel: Berlin, 1960. — Gedichte, Winterschlacht (Poems, Winter Battle); Berlin, 1960. — Abschied. Wiederanders (Farewell. Different Again); Berlin, 1960. — In München bin ich geboren, Erlebnis und Erzähltes (In Munich Was I Born, Experiences and Stories) (introduction by Lily Becher), illustrated by Paul Rosié; Berlin, 1961. — Ein Lesebuch für unsere Zeit (A Reader for our Time), ed. by Uwe Berger; Weimar, 1961. — Vom Verfall zum Triumph, Aus dem lyrischen Werk 1912 bis 1958 (From Downfall to Triumph, From the Lyrical Work 1912 to 1958), ed. by the German Academy of the Arts in Berlin. With 50 original woodcuts by Frans Masereel; Berlin, 1961. — Über Literatur und Kunst (On Literature and Art), ed. by Marianne Lange; Berlin, 1962.

Becher published (with others) the journal *Die Linkskurve* (Left Turn), Berlin 1930-1932, and was editor-in-chief of *Internationale Literatur, Deutsche Blätter* (International Literature, German Pages) in Moscow from 1935 to 1945. In 1949 he founded (with Paul Wiegler) the journal *Sinn und Form, Beiträge zur Literatur* (Sense and Form, Contributions to Literature). He edited the anthology *Tränen des Vaterlandes, Deutsche Dichtungen aus dem 16. und 17. Jahrhundert* (Tears of the Fatherland, German Poetry of the 16th and 17th Century); Berlin, 1954.

A complete bibliography of all of Becher's works can be found in *Sinn und Form*, Zweites Sonderheft Johannes R. Becher (..., second special issue...); Berlin, n.d.[1959].

The literary remains are kept in the Johannes R. Becher Archives of the German Academy of Arts in Becher's former residence at Majakowskiweg 34, Berlin-Niederschönhausen.

GOTTFRIED BENN. *Born in 1886 and grew up in villages of the province of Brandenburg. Inconsequential development, inconsequential existence as a physician in Berlin.*

Born in Mansfeld in the region of West Prignitz on May 2, 1886 as the son of a Protestant pastor and a mother from the French-speaking part of Switzerland. Before he was a year old, the family moved to Sellin in the region of Neumark, where he grew up until he attended Frederick Academic High School in Frankfurt on the Oder. At his father's request he initially studied theology and philosophy in Marburg, but then he switched to the study of medicine, completed his degree requirements at the Emperor William Army Medical School and after a brief tour of duty with the army he became a ship's doctor. Upon returning from a voyage to America, he served as an army doctor during all of the First World War, initially on the western front, and then at a hospital in Brussels. After the war — he had married shortly before the outbreak of the war — he opened his practice as a specialist in skin and venereal diseases, which he kept going until 1935 at Belle-Alliancestraße 12, Berlin SW 61.

After Hitler's seizure of power he at first approved of and defended National Socialism, even in his writings, but soon recognized his mistake and was at the same time attacked so fiercely by the Nazis that he chose the — as he put it — "aristocratic form of emigration" and reentered the service in 1935, carrying out the duties of a civilian official of the army medical corps (with the rank of major), initially in Hanover, then for several years in Berlin, and finally from 1943 on in Landsberg on the Warthe. He had been excluded from the Academy of the Arts and beginning in 1938 from the *Reichsschrifttumskammer* (Reich Chamber of Literature), and he published nothing from 1936 to 1948 (apart from a small private printing of poems). In the last days of the war he managed to get out of Landsberg as the Russians advanced on the city, whereas his young second wife took her life while fleeing from Berlin.

Right after the war he reopened his private practice (Bozener Straße 20), married a third time, and from 1948 on began publishing continuously poems and prose. These brought him, in his seventh decade, a late fame and many honors. As a young physician he had once received the Gold Medal of the University of Berlin, now in 1951 he received the Büchner Prize and in 1953 the Distinguished Service Medal of the Federal Republic. He died on July 7, 1956, and is buried in the *Waldfriedhof* (Forest Cemetery) in Berlin-Dahlem. [Ed.]

Morgue und andere Gedichte (Morgue and Other Poems); Berlin, 1912. — Söhne, Neue Gedichte (Sons, New Poems); Berlin, 1913. — Gehirne, Novellen (Brains, Novellas); Leipzig, 1916. — Fleisch, Gesammelte Lyrik (Flesh, Collected Lyric Poetry); Berlin, 1917. — Diesterweg, Eine Novelle (..., A Novella); Berlin, 1918. — Der Vermessungsdirigent, Erkenntnistheoretisches Drama (The Surveyor, Epistemological Drama); Berlin, 1919. — Ithaca, Dramatische Szene (..., Dramatic Scene); Berlin, 1919. — Etappe, Prosa (Communications Zone, Prose); Berlin, 1919. — Das moderne Ich, Essays (The Modern I, Essays); Berlin, 1920. — Die gesammelten Schriften (Gedichte, Novellen, Szenen, Essays) (The Collected Writings [Poems, Novellas, Scenes, Essays]); Berlin, 1922. — Schutt, Gedichte (Rubble, Poems); Berlin, 1924. —

Betäubung, Gedichte (Anesthetic, Poems); Berlin, 1925. — Spaltung, neue Gedichte (Fission, New Poems); Berlin, 1925. — Gesammelte Gedichte (1. Teil 1912-1920, 2. Teil 1922-1927) (Collected Poems [Part 1 ..., Part 2 ...]); Berlin, 1927. — Gesammelte Prosa (1. Teil Novellistische Prosa, 2. Teil Essayistische Prosa) (Collected Prose [Part 1 Novellas, Part 2 Essays]); Potsdam, 1928. — Fazit der Perspektiven, Essays (Sum Total of Perspectives, ...); Berlin, 1930. — Das Unaufhörliche, Text zu einem Oratorium von Paul Hindemith (The Unceasing, Text for an Oratory by ...); Dortmund, 1931. — Nach dem Nihilismus (Essays und Reden) (After Nihilism [Essays and Speeches]); Berlin, 1932.

Der neue Staat und die Intellektuellen, Essays (The New State and the Intellectuals, Essays); Stuttgart-Berlin, 1933. — Kunst und Macht, Essays und Reden (Art and Power, Essays and Speeches); Stuttgart-Berlin, 1934. — Gedichte (Poems); Hamburg, 1936 (Sonderheft "Das Gedicht, Blätter für Dichtung" [special issue, "The Poem, Pages for Poetry"], vol. 2). — Ausgewählte Gedichte, 1911-1936 (Selected Poems, ...); Stuttgart, 1936 (1st edition, forbidden by the Nazis, did not appear. The 2nd edition, minus the five poems deemed objectionable, appeared in the same year. This was Benn's last publication before he was forbidden to publish for good). — Zweiundzwanzig Gedichte 1936 bis 1943 (Twenty-Two Poems 1936 to 1943) (private printing, n.p., 1943). — Statische Gedichte (Static Poems); Zurich, 1948 (enlarged edition Wiesbaden, 1949). — Trunkene Flut, Ausgewählte Gedichte (Drunken Flood, Selected Poems); Wiesbaden, 1949 (enlarged edition Wiesbaden, 1952). — Goethe und die Naturwissenschaften (... and the Natural Sciences); Zurich, 1949. — Der Ptolemäer, Erzählungen (The Ptolemean, Stories); Wiesbaden, 1949. — Drei alte Männer (Three Old Men); Wiesbaden, 1949. — Ausdruckswelt, Essays und Aphorismen (World of Expression, Essays and Aphorisms); Wiesbaden, 1949. — Doppelleben, Zwei Selbstdarstellungen (Double Life, Two Self-Portrayals); Wiesbaden, 1950. — Frühe Prosa und Reden (Early Prose and Speeches); Wiesbaden, 1950. — Fragmente, Neue Gedichte (Fragments, New Poems); Wiesbaden, 1951. — Probleme der Lyrik, Vortrag (Problems of Lyric Poetry, Lecture); Wiesbaden, 1951. — Essays; Wiesbaden, 1951. — Preface to: Das Zeitalter der Angst (*The Age of Anxiety*) by W.H. Auden; Wiesbaden, 1951. — Frühe Lyrik und Dramen (Early Lyric Poetry and Dramas); Wiesbaden, 1952. — Die Stimme hinter dem Vorhang, Hörspiel (The Voice behind the Curtain, Radio Play); Wiesbaden, 1952. — Destillationen, Neue Gedichte (Distillations, New Poems); Wiesbaden, 1953. — Monologische Kunst, Ein Briefwechsel zwischen A. Lernet-Holenia und Gottfried Benn (Monologic Art, A Correspondence between ... and ...); Wiesbaden, 1953. — Altern als Problem für Künstler (Aging as a Problem for Artists); Wiesbaden, 1954. — Provoziertes Leben, Ausgewählte Prosa (Provoked Life, Selected Prose); Frankfurt on the Main, 1954. — Reden (Speeches); Munich, 1955. — Lyrik des expressionistischen Jahrzehnts, eingeleitet von Gottfried Benn (Lyric Poetry of the Expressionist Decade, introduced by ...); Wiesbaden, 1955. — Aprèslude, Gedichte (..., Poems); Wiesbaden, 1955. — Gesammelte Gedichte (Collected Poems); Wiesbaden and Zurich, 1956. — Soll die Dichtung das Leben bessern? Zwei Reden, gehalten von Gottfried Benn und

Reinhold Schneider (Is Poetry Supposed to Improve Life? Two Speeches, Given by ... and ...); Wiesbaden, 1956. — Über mich selbst, 1886-1956 (Concerning Myself, ...); Munich, 1956.

Ausgewählte Briefe (Selected Letters), with an epilogue by Max Rychner; Wiesbaden, 1957. — Dr. Roenne, Frühe Prosa (..., Early Prose); Zurich, 1957. — Primäre Tage, Gedichte und Fragmente aus dem Nachlaß (Primary Days, Poems and Fragments from the Literary Remains); Wiesbaden, 1958. — Gesammelte Werke in vier Bänden (Collected Works in Four Volumes), edited by Dieter Wellershoff; Wiesbaden, 1958-1961. — Briefe an Ernst Jünger u.a. (Letters to ... et al), selected and introduced by Peter Schifferli; Zurich, 1960. — Roman des Phänotyp. Landsberger Fragmente 1944 (Novel of the Pheno-type. Landsberg Fragments ...); Frankfurt on the Main, 1961. — Lyrik und Prosa, Briefe und Dokumente (Lyric Poetry and Prose, Letters and Documents), edited by Max Niedermayer ; Wiesbaden, 1962.

Literary remains for the most part in the possession of Frau Dr. Ilse Benn, Stuttgart (poems, prose, the musical *Die Möbelträger* [The Moving Men]).

THEODOR DÄUBLER. *Born in Trieste on August 17, 1876, lived there and later, after his 22nd year, in Naples, Vienna, Paris, Florence, Rome, Dresden, and Berlin.*

As the son of a Silesian mother and a wholesale merchant from the Bavarian part of Swabia Däubler was raised in Trieste in two languages, German and Ital-ian, and thus in two diverse cultures and between two religions. He spent his youth on the Adriatic coast he so dearly loved, in Trieste and Venice. At the age of fifteen he went to sea. Then his parents had him educated by private tutors, and one of them intensified the youth's love of classical antiquity and everything Italian.

After passing his high-school finals he moves to Vienna with his parents; here his passion for the German language and German music (through GUSTAV MAHLER) is aroused. At this point the vagabond life that he never again gave up commences. In Naples he begins his chief work, *Das Nordlicht* (The Northern Lights), goes to Berlin, to Vienna again, to Italy for several years, then in 1903 to Paris where he familiarizes himself thoroughly with the painting of the new century; he is frequently in Florence, to where he moves in 1910 to complete *Das Nordlicht*. Until the start of the First World War he wanders through the Italian cities and Sicily, decides in favor of Germany and first makes Dresden and then in 1916 Berlin the focal point of his unsettled existence. In 1919 he accepts an invitation to Geneva and ultimately in 1921 the invitation to come to Greece. He reaches Athens by way of the island of Ithaca. Greece now attains the significance that Italy once had for him. As formerly in Paris so now in Greece he lives in dire poverty; but his travel accounts, which are published in German newspapers and magazines, enable him to stay in the interior of the country for longer periods of time and to take trips to the islands of the Aegean, to Asia Minor, and to Egypt.

Severely ill, he returns to Berlin in 1926. Barely recovered, he begins anew his journeys to Italy, through all of Germany, to Scandinavia, England, France, and the Balkans. His focal point is again Berlin, where he is the recipient of great honors: he becomes president of the German PEN-Club and a member of the Academy of Arts, he is awarded the Goethe Medal and the Commander's Cross of the Greek Order of the Savior. In Italy in 1932 he is stricken with tuberculosis, but he keeps interrupting his treatment in a sanatorium near Berlin by taking trips. In the spring of 1933 he suffers a stroke; his sister brings the solitary man to St. Blasien in the Black Forest, where on June 13, 1934 he succumbed to his lung ailment. [Ed.]

Das Nordlicht, Lyrisches Epos in drei Bänden (The Northern Lights, Lyrical Epic Poem in Three Volumes) (Florentine edition); Munich, 1910 (revised and enlarged "Geneva edition" in 2 vols., Leipzig, 1921/22). — Oden und Gesänge (Odes and Songs); Dresden-Hellerau, 1913. — Däubler issue of the *Neue Blätter* (New Notes); Berlin, 1913. — Wir wollen nicht verweilen, Autobiographische Fragmente (We Do Not Wish to Tarry, Autobiographical Fragments); Munich, 1914, Dresden-Hellerau, 1919. — Hesperien, Eine Symphonie I, Gedichte (Occident, A Symphony I, Poems); Munich, 1915. — Der sternhelle Weg, Gedichte (The Starlit Road, Poems); Dresden-Hellerau, 1915 (enlarged edition Leipzig, 1919). — Hymne an Italien, Gedichte (Hymn to Italy, Poems); Munich, 1916 (second revised edition Leipzig, 1919). — Hymne an Venedig (Hymn to Venice); Berlin, 1916. — Mit silberner Sichel, Prosa (With a Silver Sickle, Prose); Dresden-Hellerau, 1916. — Das Sternenkind, Gedichtauswahl (The Star-Child, Selected Poems); (Insel Library) Leipzig, 1916. — Der neue Standpunkt, Essays über moderne Kunst (The New Standpoint, Essays on Modern Art); Dresden-Hellerau, 1916. — Lucidarium in arte musicae des Riciotto Canudo aus Gioja del Colle, Essays über Musik (... of ... from ..., Essays on Music); Dresden-Hellerau, 1917. — Im Kampf um die moderne Kunst, Essay (In the Struggle for Modern Art, Essay); Berlin, 1919. — Die Treppe zum Nordlicht, Eine Symphonie II (The Stairway to the Northern Lights, A Symphony II); Leipzig 1920. — Die Perlen von Venedig, Gedichte (The Pearls of Venice, Poems); Leipzig, 1921. — Der unheimliche Graf, Drei Erzählungen (The Sinister Count, Three Tales); Hanover, 1921. — Der heilige Berg Athos, Eine Symphonie III, Prosa (Holy Mount Athos, A Symphony III, Prose); Leipzig, 1923. — Sparta, Ein Versuch (..., An Experiment); Leipzig, 1923. — Päan und Dithyrambos, Eine Phantasmagorie (Gedichtzyklus) (Paeon and Dithyramb, A Phantasmagoria [Cycle of Poems]); Leipzig, 1924. — Attische Sonette (Attic Sonnets); Leipzig, 1924. — Der Schatz der Insel, Eine Erzählung aus den griechischen Befreiungskriegen (The Treasure of the Island, A Tale from the Greek Wars of Liberation); Berlin, Vienna, Leipzig, 1925. — Aufforderung zur Sonne, Autobiographische Skizze (Invitation to the Sun, Autobiographical Sketch); Chemnitz, 1926. — Bestrickungen, Zwei Novellen (Enchantments, Two Novellas); Berlin, 1927. — L'Africana, Roman (..., Novel); Berlin, 1928 — Der Fischzug, Acht Aufsätze aus den Jahren 1917-1929 (The Draft of Fishes, Eight Essays from the Years ...); Hellerau, 1930. — Der Marmorbruch, Erzählung (The Marble Quarry, Tale); Leipzig, 1930. — Die Göttin mit der Fackel, Roman einer kleinen Reise (The Goddess with the Torch, Novel of a Little Trip); Berlin, 1931. — Can Grande della Scala, dramatisches Fragment (..., Dramatic Fragment); Leipzig 1932.

Griechenland (Greece) (approximately 100 essays), edited by Max Sidow from the literary remains; Berlin, 1947.

Theodor Däubler — Eine Einführung in sein Werk und eine Auswahl (..., An Introduction to his Work and a Selection), edited by Hanns Ubricht; Wiesbaden, 1951.

Dichtungen und Schriften (Poetic Works and [Other] Writings) (extensive selection, also containing some materials not previously published in book form and some from the literary remains), edited by Friedhelm Kemp; Munich, 1956.

Translations: Gedichte des Boccaccio (Poems of ...); Leipzig, 1928. — Der Hahn, Übertragungen aus dem Französischen (The Cock, Renderings from the French); Berlin, 1917.

Many of Däubler's large works that were published in journals have not appeared in book form, e.g., "Delos" in *Deutsche Rundschau* (German Review), vol. 202, 1925, pp. 178-229 and 310-351. The volume *Veröffentlichungen der preußischen Akademie der Künste, Jahrbuch der Sektion Dichtung* (Publications of the Prussian Academy of the Arts, Yearbook of the Section for Literature), Berlin, 1929, contains "Mein Weg nach Hellas" (My Way to...), "Politik und Dichtung" (Politics and Poetry), "Über die Möglichkeit einer Danteübersetzung" (On the Feasibility of a Dante Translation).

Literary remains in the Goethe-Schiller Archives in Weimar and in the *Landesbibliothek Dresden* (Dresden Regional Library).

ALBERT EHRENSTEIN. *On the 23rd of December 1886 the Viennese earth happened to me.*

Born as the son of Hungarian parents in Vienna, where he studied history and philology and in 1910 "contracted a doctorate" with a thesis on "Hungary, in the Year 1790...." His literary activity began in elementary and high school; KARL KRAUS printed poems by Ehrenstein in *Die Fackel* (The Torch). He joined the Expressionist "Storm" Circle in Berlin after publishing *Tubutsch*, a self-analytical prose work illustrated by his friend Oskar Kokoschka. In Berlin he worked as a freelance writer and as a literary critic for some of Germany's large democratic newspapers. But Ehrenstein led a restless existence, was frequently on the go, not only in Europe but also in Africa and Asia, and, as he indicated, stayed in China for a time. In late 1932 he moved to Switzerland, and then in 1941 to New York. After the war he returned once more to Switzerland, but in the end he went back to New York, where the author of the most bitter poems in the German language died a bitter death on April 8, 1950 after a bitter life in poverty and after a long illness. [Ed.]

Tubutsch, Erzählung (..., Tale) (with 12 drawings by Oskar Kokoschka); Vienna, 1912 (revised edition in Munich, 1914, then in the Insel Library, Leipzig). — Der Selbstmord eines Katers, Erzählung (The Suicide of a Tomcat, Tale); Munich, 1912 (new edition as: Bericht aus einem Tollhaus, Roman [Report from a Lunatic Asylum, Novel]; Leipzig, 1919). — Die weiße Zeit, Gedichte 1900-1913 (The White Age, Poems ...); Munich, 1914. — Nicht da, nicht dort, Prosa (Not Here, Not There, Prose); Leipzig, 1916. — Der Mensch schreit, Gedichte (The Human Being Screams, Poems) (with lithography by

Oskar Kokoschka); Leipzig, 1916. — Die rote Zeit, Gedichte (The Red Age, Poems); Berlin, 1917. — Zaubermärchen (Tales of Enchantment); Berlin, 1919. — Den ermordeten Brüdern, Aufsätze und Verse (For the Murdered Brothers, Essays and Verses); Zurich, 1919. — Dem ewigen Olymp, Novellen und Gedichte (To Eternal Olympus, Novellas and Poems); (Reclam series) Leipzig, 1919. — Die Gedichte, Erste Gesamtausgabe (The Poems, First Complete Edition); Leipzig-Vienna, 1920. — Karl Kraus; Leipzig-Vienna, 1920. — Die Nacht wird, Novellen und Gedichte (The Night Is Coming, Novellas and Poems); Leipzig-Vienna 1920. — Wien, Gedichte (Vienna, Poems); Vienna, 1920, Berlin, 1921. — Die Heimkehr des Falken (The Falcon's Return Home); Munich, 1921. — Briefe an Gott (Letters to God); Vienna-Leipzig, 1922. — Schi-King, Nachdichtung chinesischer Lyrik (Shih-Ching, Free Rendering of Chinese Lyric Poetry); Vienna, 1922. — Herbst, Gedichte (Autumn, Poems); Berlin, 1923. — Pe-Lo-Thien, Nachdichtungen chinesischer Lyrik (Lo-T'ien {translators' note: public name of Po Chü-i}, Free Renderings of Chinese Lyric Poetry); Berlin, 1923. — China klagt, Nachdichtungen revolutionärer chinesischer Lyrik aus drei Jahrtausenden (China Bewails, Free Renderings of Revolutionary Chinese Lyric Poetry from Three Millennia); Berlin, 1924. — Po-Chü-I, Nachdichtung (..., Free Rendering); Berlin, 1924. — Lukian, Übersetzung (Die wahre Geschichte, Der magische Esel, Hetärengespräche) (Lucian, Translation [The True History, The Magic Ass, Dialogues of the Courtesans]); Berlin, 1925. — Ritter des Todes, Die Erzählungen von 1900 bis 1919 (Knight of Death, The Tales from 1900 to 1919); Berlin, 1926. — Menschen und Affen, Essays 1910-1925 (Human Beings and Monkeys, Essays ...); Berlin, 1926. — Räuber und Soldaten, Roman frei nach dem Chinesischen (Robbers and Soldiers, Novel Freely Rendered from the Chinese); Berlin, 1927. — Mörder aus Gerechtigkeit, Romane frei nach dem Chinesischen (Murderer out of Justice, Novels Freely Rendered from the Chinese); Berlin, 1931. — Mein Lied, Gedichte 1900-1931 (My Song, Poems ...) (with 8 lithographs by Oskar Kokoschka); Berlin, 1931. — Das gelbe Lied, Nachdichtungen klassischer Lyrik der Chinesen (The Yellow Song, Free Renderings of the Classical Lyric Poetry of the Chinese); Berlin, 1933.

Ehrenstein edited: Hölderlin's translation of the *Trauerspiele des Sophokles, Ödipus der Tyrann, Antigonä* (Tragedies of ..., Oedipus the Tyrant, Antigone); Weimar, 1918. — Christoph M. Wieland *Dschinnistan* (Jinnistan); Vienna, 1920. — Lukian *Milesische Märchen* (Lucian Milesian Tales); Weimar, n.d. [1920].

Gedichte und Prosa (Poems and Prose), edited and introduced by Karl Otten; Neuwied, 1961. — Ausgewählte Aufsätze (Selected Essays), edited by M. Y. Ben-Gavriel; Heidelberg, 1961.

Literary remains in the Jewish National and University Library in Jerusalem.

IWAN GOLL *has no native country: thanks to fate a Jew, thanks to chance born in France, thanks to a stamped piece of paper identified as a German.*

*Iwan Goll has no age: his childhood was sucked up by bloodless oldsters. The god of war assassinated the young man. But to become a human being, how many lives are required.*

*Solitary and good in the manner of the silent trees and the mute rocks: then he would be farthest from the earthly and closest to art.*

Born in St. Dié, France on March 29, 1891. Father an Alsatian, mother a Lorrainer. After his father's death in 1898, his mother moves to Metz. There Goll attends the German academic high school. Later studies in Strasbourg and receives his Ph.D. in 1912.

Finds himself in Zurich at the outbreak of the war in 1914. Associates closely with STEFAN ZWEIG, LUDWIG RUBINER, HANS ARP, etc. Makes friends there with JAMES JOYCE and later arranges for the publication of his *Ulysses* in the German language.

In 1916 becomes engaged to Claire Studer, whom he was visiting in Geneva. Lives with her in Lausanne in 1917 and in Ascona in 1918. There engages in a debate with VIKING EGGELING on the fundamentals of the first abstract film: *Symphonie Diagonale* and is active in the Eranos Group.

In 1919 Claire and Iwan Goll move permanently to Paris. In 1920 Iwan Goll is the first person in Europe to call for a superrealism — in the foreword to his *Überdramen: Die Unsterblichen* (Superdramas: The Immortals). In 1924 he launches this movement in France with his journal *Surréalisme.*

In 1939 the Golls emigrate to New York. In 1944 the first symptoms of his fatal disease: leukemia. In 1947 return to Paris. On February 27, 1950 Goll dies in Paris. In 1955 burial in the *Père Lachaise* cemetery in Paris across from Chopin's grave. [Claire Goll]

Lothringische Volkslieder (Lorrainer Folksongs); Metz, 1912. — Der Panamakanal, Dichtung (The Panama Canal, Poetic Work) (under the pseudonym of Iwan Lassang); Berlin, 1914. — Films, Gedichte (..., Poems) (under the pseudonym of Tristan Torsi); Berlin-Charlottenburg, 1914. — Elégies Internationales, Pamphlets contre cette guerre; Lausanne, 1915. — Requiem pour les morts de l'Europe; Geneva, 1916. — Requiem für die Gefallenen von Europa (Requiem for the Soldiers of Europe Killed in Action); Zurich, 1917. — Felix, eine Dithyrambe (..., A Dithyramb); Dresden, 1917. — Der Torso, Stanzen und Dithyramben (The Torso, Eight-Line Stanzas and Dithyrambs); Munich, 1918. — Der neue Orpheus, eine Dithyrambe (The New Orpheus, A Dithyramb); Berlin, 1918. — Dithyramben (Dithyrambs); Leipzig, 1918. — Die Unterwelt, Gedichte (The Underworld, Poems); Berlin, 1919. — Die drei guten Geister Frankreichs, Essays (The Three Good Spirits of France, Essays); Berlin, 1918. — Le coeur de l'ennemi, Poèmes actuels (preface and translation of 14 German poems); Paris, 1919. — Das Herz des Feindes (The Heart of the Enemy) (with Claire Goll), Übers. französischer Gedichte (Translation of French Poems); Munich, 1920. — Astral, ein Gesang (..., A Song) (illustrated by Fernand Léger); Dresden, 1920. — Die Unsterblichen, Zwei Überdramen (Der Unsterbliche, Der Ungeborene) {Translators' note: *Der*

*Ungeborene* is actually *Der Ungestorbene* (The Undead One)} (The Immortals, Two Superdramas [The Immortal One, The Unborn One]); Berlin, 1920. — Die Chapliniade, eine Kinodichtung (The Chaplinade, A Cinema Piece) (illustrated by Fernand Léger); Dresden, 1920. — Das Lächeln Voltaires. Essay (...'s Smile, Essay); Basel, 1921. — Paris brennt, Dichtung (... Is Burning, Poetic Work); Zagreb, 1921. — Lasalles Tod, Drama (...'s Death, Drama); Potsdam, 1921. Les Cinq Continents, Anthologie mondiale de poésie contemporaine; Paris, 1922. — Methusalem, Satirisches Drama (..., Satiric Drama) (illustrated by George Grosz, prefaces by Goll and Georg Kaiser); Potsdam, 1922. — Archipenko-Album; Potsdam, 1922. — Le nouvel Orphée, Gesammelte Dichtungen (Collected Literary Works) (La Chaplinade, Mathusalem, Paris brûle, Le nouvel Orphée, Astral, Assurance contre le suicide); Paris, 1924. — Der Stall des Augias, Tragödie (The Stable of Augeas, Tragedy); Berlin, 1924. — Der Eiffelturm, Gesammelte Dichtungen (The Eiffel Tower, Collected Poetic Works); Berlin, 1924. — Germaine Berton, Essay; Berlin, 1925. — Poèmes d'Amour (with Claire Goll); Paris, 1925. — Poèmes de la Jalousie (with Claire Goll, illustrated by Fouyita); Paris, 1926. — Poèmes de la Vie et de la Mort (with Claire Goll); Paris, 1927. — Le Microbe de l'Or, Roman (..., Novel); Paris, 1927. — Die Eurokokke, Roman (The Eurococcus, Novel); Berlin, 1927. — Chansons Nègres; Paris, 1928. — A bas l'Europe! Roman (..., Novel); Paris, 1928. — Der Mitropäer, Roman (The Midropean, Novel): Basel, 1928. — Die siebente Rose, Gedichte (The Seventh Rose, Poems) (illustrated by Hans Arp), Paris, 1928. — Royal Palace, Oper (..., Opera) (music by Kurt Weill); Berlin, 1928. — Der neue Orpheus, Cantata (The New ..., Cantata) (music by Kurt Weill); Berlin, 1928. — Sodome et Berlin, Roman (..., Novel); Paris, 1929. — Agnus Dei, Roman (..., Novel); Paris, 1929. — Noemi, Dichtung (..., Poetic Work) (illustrated by Jakob Steinhardt); Berlin, 1929. — Pascin, Essay; Paris, 1929. — Poèmes d'Amour (with Claire Goll), (new edition with seven drawings by Marc Chagall); Paris, 1930. — Gala, Roman (..., Novel); Paris, 1930. — Deux Chansons de la Seine; Paris, 1930. — Lucifer vieillisant, Roman (..., Novel); Paris, 1933. — Chansons Malaises, Gedichte (..., Poems); Paris, 1934. — Métro de la Mort, Ausgewählte Gedichte (..., Selected Poems); Brussels, 1936. — La Chanson de Jean sans Terre, Erster Band (..., Volume One) (cover drawing by Marc Chagall); Paris, 1936. — Deuxième livre de Jean sans Terre; Paris, 1938. — Troisième livre de Jean sans Terre (with a drawing by Galanis); Paris, 1939.

Chansons de France, in *Poet's Messages*; New York, 1940. — Landless John, translated by William Carlos Williams et al. (English and French, with 2 drawings by Eugene Berman); San Francisco, 1944. — Preface to: The Heart of Europe, Anthology of Creative Writing in Europe (edited by Klaus Mann); New York, 1945. — Fruit from Saturn, Poems in English; New York, 1945. — Atom Elegy; New York, 1946. — Le Mythe de la Roche percée (with 3 engravings by Ives Tanguy); New York, 1947. — Love Poems (with Claire Goll) (English version with 7 drawings by Marc Chagall); New York, 1947. — Traumgras, Gedichte (Dream Grass, Poems) (under the pseudonym of Tristan Thor); Mainz, 1948. — Elégie d'Ihpétonga, suivie de Masques de Cendre (with

369

4 lithographs by Pablo Picasso); Paris, 1949. — Le Char Triumphale de l'Antimoine, Sonette (..., Sonnets) (illustrated by Victor Brauner); Paris, 1949. — Jean sans Terre (selection from the complete works); Paris, 1950. — Les Géorgiques Parisiennes, Gedichte (..., Poems); Paris, 1951. — Dix Mille Aubes (with Claire Goll, illustrated by Marc Chagall); Paris, 1951. — Les Cercles Magiques (with 6 drawings by Fernand Léger); Paris, 1951. — Traumkraut, Gedichte aus dem Nachlaß (Dream Herb, Poems from the Literary Remains); Wiesbaden, 1951. — Phèdre, Oper (..., Opera) (music by Marcel Mihalovici); Paris, 1951. — Nouvelles Petites Fleurs de St. François (with Claire Goll); Paris, 1952. — Neue Blümlein des heiligen Franziskus (New Little Flowers of St. Francis) (with Claire Goll, illustrated by Francis Rose); St. Gall, 1952 (enlarged edition Darmstadt, 1957). — Malaiische Liebeslieder (Malayan Lovesongs) (translated by Claire Goll); St. Gall, 1952. — Zehntausend Morgenröten, Gedichte einer Liebe (Ten Thousand Auroras, Poems of a Love) (with Claire Goll); Wiesbaden, 1952. — Der durchbrochene Felsen, eine Dichtung (The Pierced Rock, A Poetic Work) (translated by Claire Goll); Freiburg, 1952. — Abendgesang (Neila), Letzte Gedichte, Aus dem Nachlaß (Evening Song [...], Last Poems, From the Literary Remains) (with 3 drawings by Willi Baumeister); Heidelberg, 1954. — Malaiische Liebeslieder (Malayan Lovesongs) (with 6 drawings by Henri Matisse); Tokyo, 1955. — Yvan Goll, Auswahl aus seinen Werken (..., Selection from his Works) (with 4 prefaces by Jules Romains, Marcel Brion, Francis J. Carmody, Richard Exner); Paris, 1956. — Der Mythus vom durchbrochenen Felsen, Eine Dichtung (The Myth of the Pierced Rock, A Poetic Work) (French and German, translated by Claire Goll, with 3 drawings by Ives Tanguy); Darmstadt, 1956. — Pariser Georgika (Parisian Georgics) (French and German, rendered by Claire Goll, with 2 drawings and cover by Robert Delaunay); Darmstadt, 1956. — Multiple Femme, Gedichte (..., Poems) (with 8 woodcuts by Hans Arp); Paris, 1956. — Melusine, lyrisches Drama (..., Lyric Drama) (music by Marcel Mihalovici); Berlin, 1956. — Jean sans Terre, Volls. Ausg. (..., Complete Edition) (cover drawing by Marc Chagall); Paris, 1958. — Landless John—Jean sans Terre, Englische Gesamtausgabe (..., Complete English Edition) (preface by W.H. Auden, translated by 21 English and American poets, illustrated by Chagall, Dali, and Berman); New York, 1958. — Nouvelles Petites Fleurs de St. François d'Assise (with Claire Goll, 3 drawings by Salvador Dali); Paris, 1959. — L'Histoire de Parménia, Calle Virtude de la Hanava, Dichtung (..., Poetic Work); Paris, 1959. — Herbe du Songe (translated by Claude Vigée); Paris, 1959. — Neila (deluxe edition with 4 lithographs by Joan Miró); Paris, 1959. — Duo d'Amour, Gedichte (..., Poems) (with Claire Goll, with 14 drawings by Marc Chagall); Paris, 1959. — Jean sans Terre (deluxe edition with 10 lithographs by Bernard Buffet); Paris, 1959. — Jean sans Terre, Kritische Ausgabe von Francis Carmody (..., Critical Edition by ...); Berkeley, 1962. — Four Poems of the Occult, illustrated by Léger, Picasso, Tanguy and Arp; edited and introduced by Francis Carmody: Kentfield, Cal., 1962.

Dichtungen (Literary Works) (extensive selection of lyric poetry, prose, and drama, edited by Claire Goll); Darmstadt, 1960.

Goll edited the following journals: Menschen — Clarté (Human Beings — ...); Dresden, 1921. — Surréalisme (one number); Paris, 1924. — Jeune Europe (two numbers); Paris, 1932. — Poet's Messages (two numbers); New York, 1940. — Hemisphères (bilingual, English and French, 6 numbers); New York, 1943-1946.
Literary remains in the possession of Mrs. Claire Goll, Paris.

WALTER HASENCLEVER. *Born on July 8, 1890 in Aachen, where to this day I am still in disrepute. In 1908 academic high school senior finals, then went to England and studied at Oxford. Here I wrote my first play; the printing costs I won at poker. In 1909 I was in Lausanne, then I went to Leipzig, where I met the editor of this anthology. Introduced by him to the realms of love and science, I soon surpassed the master. I traveled to Italy with him and frequented the doctors. In 1913* Der Jüngling (The Youth) *was published; in 1914* Der Sohn (The Son) *was finished in Heyst am Meer (... by the Sea). In the war I was an interpreter, a purchasing agent, and an apprentice cook. Thus did the book* Tod und Auferstehung (Death and Resurrection) *get written. In 1917* Antigone *was published, a year later* Die Menschen (The Human Beings). *In 1919 my friend ERNST ROWOHLT printed* Der Retter (The Savior), *a play banned during the war. In the summer of 1919* Die Entscheidung (The Decision) *was written.*
As a result of numerous attacks brought on by the preceding autobiography Hasenclever wrote the following for later editions:
*Now that press, profession, and professors have taken the required offence at my biography in the first edition of this book, a biography which was more than a joke and less than an intention and whose only purpose was to bewilder the reader in order to protect the author from his curiosity, I am content with stating in the new edition of this book that I was born in Aachen on July 8, 1890 and have written the following books:* [what follows are the titles of his books from *Der Jüngling* 1913 to *Gobseck* 1922.]
Hasenclever studied history of literature, philosophy, and history in Oxford and Lausanne and beginning in the spring of 1909 in Leipzig. Futile attempt to do a doctorate with a thesis on the publisher of realism, Wilhelm Friedrich, and his journal *Die Gesellschaft* (Society) based on the correspondence kept in the archives of the publishing house. Close friendship with the editor of this book and FRANZ WERFEL in an active literary circle which collected around the Ernst Rowohlt Publishing House, later the Kurt Wolff Publishing House, in Leipzig and constituted one of the groups in the literary movement later called "Expressionism." After the outbreak of the war in 1914 initially in the postal censor's office in Ghent, then an orderly in Macedonia; returns in September 1916 as an opponent of the war in order to be present at the October 8 premiere of his drama *Der Sohn* (in the title role: ERNST DEUTSCH) behind the locked doors of the Albert Theater in Dresden.In 1917 he is awarded the Kleist Prize. After his discharge from a military sanatorium on the Weißer Hirsch (White Deer) {translators' note: a spa on the edge of a plateau} near Dresden he remains in the city for several years. In the mid-twenties is sent to Paris as a correspondent for the Berlin *8-Uhr Abendblatt* (8 O'Clock Evening News). He lives there until

Hitler's seizure of power, save for several months in 1930 spent as a scriptwriter for Metro Goldwyn Mayer in Hollywood and for several longer stays in Berlin. Proscribed and expatriated, sojourns in exile: 1933-1934 southern France, 1935 an island near Dubrovnik, end of 1935-April 1936 London, 1936-1937 Nice, 1937-1939 a small estate near Florence. Because he is taken into custody during a Hitler visit to Italy he goes to London for a short time and then moves to Cagnes-sur-Mer in the south of France. Upon the outbreak of war in 1939 he is interned twice in the camp at Antibes for a short period; when the German troops march into France in May 1940 he is confined in the camp at Les Milles, where, in fear of Nazi vengeance, he departed this life voluntarily on June 21. His grave is in the cemetery in Aix-en-Provence. [Ed.]

Nirwana, Eine Kritik des Lebens in Dramaform (Nirvana, A Critique of Life in Dramatic Form); Berlin-Leipzig, 1909. — Städte, Nächte und Menschen, Erlebnisse (Cities, Nights, and Human Beings, Experiences) (poems); Munich, 1910. — Der Jüngling, Gedichte (The Youth, Poems); Leipzig, 1913. — Das unendliche Gespräch, Eine nächtliche Szene (The Endless Dialogue, A Nocturnal Scene); Leipzig, 1913. — Dichter und Verleger, Briefe von Wilhelm Friedrich an Detlev von Liliencron (Poet and Publisher, Letters from ... to ...), introduced and edited by Walter Hasenclever; Munich, 1914. Der Sohn, Drama (The Son, Drama); Leipzig, 1914 (many subsequent editions). — Tod und Auferstehung, Neue Gedichte (Death and Resurrection, New Poems); Leipzig, 1917. — Antigone, Tragödie (..., Tragedy); Berlin, 1917. — Die Menschen, Schauspiel (The Human Beings, Drama); Berlin, 1918. — Der Retter, Drama (The Savior); Berlin, 1919 (a special edition printed privately during the war for fifteen specific persons; Leipzig, 1917). — Die Entscheidung, Komödie (The Decision, Comedy); Berlin, 1919. — Der politische Dichter (The Political Poet) (poems and prose); Berlin, 1919. — Die Pest, Ein Film (The Plague, A Film); Berlin, 1920. — Jenseits, Drama (Beyond, Drama); Berlin, 1920. — Gobseck, Drama (..., Drama); Berlin, 1922. — Gedichte an Frauen (Poems to Women); Berlin, 1922. — Dramen (Der Sohn, Die Menschen, Jenseits) (Dramas [The Son, The Human Beings, Beyond]); Berlin, 1924. — Emanuel Swedenborg — Himmel, Hölle, Geisterwelt, eine Auswahl aus dem lateinischen Text in deutscher Nachdichtung (... — Heaven, Hell, Spirit World, A Selection from the Latin Text Rendered into German); Berlin, 1925. — Mord, Ein Stück in zwei Teilen (Murder, A Play in Two Parts); Berlin, 1926. — Ein besserer Herr, Lustspiel in zwei Teilen (A Gent, Comedy in Two Parts); Berlin, 1926. — Ehen werden im Himmel geschlossen (Marriages Are Contracted in Heaven) (in the first acting edition entitled Doppelspiel [Double Dealing]), Komödie (Comedy): Berlin, 1928. — Bourgeois bleibt Bourgeois (... Remains ...) (with Ernst Toller), Musikalische Komödie (Musical Comedy) (based on Molière's Der Bürger als Edelmann [The Bourgeois as Nobleman], music by Friedrich Hollaender); Berlin, 1928 [manuscript and copies missing despite premiere February 20, 1929 at the Lessing Theater, Berlin]. — Kulissen, Lustspiel (Stage Wings, Comedy); only as a stage script, Berlin, 1929. — Napoleon greift ein, Ein Abenteuer (... Takes a Hand, An Adventure) [Comedy]; Berlin, 1929. — Kommt ein Vogel geflogen, Komödie (A Bird Comes Flying, Comedy); only as a stage script, Berlin,1931. — Christoph Kolumbus oder die Entdeckung Amerikas (Christopher Columbus or the Discovery of America) (with Peter Panter, i.e., Kurt Tucholsky), Komödie (Comedy); only as a stage script, Berlin, 1932. — Sinnenglück und Seelenfrieden, Schauspiel (Sensual Bliss and Peace of Soul, Play); only as a stage script, Vienna-Berlin, 1932.

Münchhausen, Ein Schauspiel (..., A Play); as a stage script, Nice, 1934 and Hamburg, 1952; printed Reinbek, 1963 [see below]. — Ehekomödie (Comedy of Marriage) (with Robert Klein), Lustspiel (Comedy); only as a stage script, London, 1937; English version by Hubert Giffith as *What Should a Husband Do?*, premiered in London, 1937. — Konflikt in Assyrien, Komödie (Conflict in Assyria, Comedy); only as a stage script; English premiere as *Scandal in Assyria* by Axel Kjellstrom [i.e., Walter Hasenclever], translated by Gerard Bullet, London, 1939; also a German acting edition, Berlin, 1957.

Gedichte, Dramen, Prosa, Unter Benutzung des Nachlasses (Poems, Dramas, Prose, With Utilization of the Literary Remains), edited and introduced by Kurt Pinthus (contains the previously unprinted play *Münchhausen* and the previously unpublished novel *Die Rechtlosen* (The Outlawed); Reinbek, 1963.

Hasenclever edited (with Heinar Schilling): *Menschen, Zeitschrift neuer Kunst* (Human Beings, Journal of New Art), vols. 3 and 4; Dresden, 1920-1921.

The literary remains are in the possession of Mrs. Edith Hasenclever, Cagnes-sur-Mer, comprising, *inter alia*: the manuscripts of the dramas for young people *Das Reich* (The Kingdom) and *Das Königsopfer* (The King's Sacrifice) (fragment); the manuscript Der *Froschkönig, Eine Farce nach dem Märchen der Brüder Grimm* (The Frog King, A Farce Based on the Fairytale of the Grimm Brothers), c. 1930; the manuscripts of the novels: *Irrtum und Leidenschaft* (Error and Passion), 1934-1939; *Die Rechtlosen* (The Outlawed), 1939-1940. — Manuscripts of the completed screenplays: *Anna Christie* (based on Eugene O'Neill's drama), written in Hollywood for Greta Garbo and filmed; *Looping the Loop* (with Rudolf Leonhard); *Komm zu mir zum Rendezvous* (Go on a Date with Me); untitled, first words "Bei Lherminois" (Near ...). Drafts of screenplays: *Was geschah am 6. Mai?* (What Happened on May 6th?) (with Harry Kahn); *Ein halbes Jahrhundert* (Half a Century) (with Harry Kahn); *Giganten der Landstraße* (Giants of the Road) (with Franz Höllering); all after 1930. — In addition more than a thousand letters from and to Hasenclever and, along with essays on theater and literature, approximately 250 articles from the years 1924 to 1928, almost all of them from Paris and initially published in the *8-Uhr-Abendblatt* (8 O'Clock Evening News), Berlin.

GEORG HEYM, *scion of an old family of civil servants and pastors, was born in Hirschberg (Silesia) on October 30, 1887. At the age of thirteen he moved to Berlin. After he had graduated from academic high school he devoted himself to the study of law in Würzburg and later in Berlin. While skating on the Havel River he broke through the ice and together with his friend, the poet and doctoral candidate Ernst Balcke, drowned near Schwanenwerder on the afternoon of January 16, 1912; his* *grave is in the cemetery of the Luisengemeinde (*Parish of Queen Luise) *in Char-lottenburg.* [The editors of the posthumously published poems *Umbra Vitae*].

Georg Heym's only autobiographical document is contained in a letter of February, 1911 to his publisher ERNST ROWOHLT, in which he proposes that at the end of his first book of poetry, *Der ewige Tag* (The Eternal Day), "I would very much like to put the following epilogue which, I am hopeful, will have some effect: There are some friends of the arts who have the understandable desire to be informed about the person of the author to whom they may be indebted for several hours of pleasure. If there are such persons among the readers of this book, I want to provide them with a few notes.

I am currently in my 23th year. My childhood was spent in a Silesian mountain town like all childhoods, tedious and dreamy. Then I was deported across several academic high schools. Until my senior finals the threat of expulsion on account of nightly drinking bouts at the tavern and participation in forbidden clubs never left me. Then for several years I sojourned at various universities, was a member of a dueling corps. And I wound up in Berlin. This fall a poem of mine was printed for the first time in *Der Demokrat* (The Democrat). A few days later I received the following letter: 'My attention having been drawn to you by your sonnet in *Der Demokrat*, I take the liberty of asking you whether you might want to submit a manuscript to the publisher ....' This letter was followed by a second: 'I acknowledge receipt of the poems you have sent. I am prepared to undertake the publication of a volume of your poems. As royalty I offer you....' The fact of these two letters speaks for itself. A short time ago I completed my state board exams and am now ready to drift with every wave. I would very much like to see the wide world. Perhaps one of my readers will be sufficiently interested in me to make it possible for me. An understanding person will not take offense at my expressing my wish openly." — In a postcard following this letter Heym withdrew the epilogue and it remained unprinted. [Ed.]

Der Athener Ausfahrt, Trauerspiel in einem Aufzug (The Departure of the Athenians, Tragedy in One Act); Würzburg, 1907. — Der ewige Tag, Gedichte (The Eternal Day, Poems); Leipzig, 1911. — Umbra Vitae, Nachgelassene Gedichte (..., Posthumously Published Poems) (epilogue by the editors Baumgardt, Gangi, Ghuttmann, Hoddis, Jentzsch); Leipzig, 1912. — Der Dieb, Ein Novellenbuch (The Thief, A Book of Novellas); Leipzig, 1913. — Marathon (12 sonnets); Berlin, 1914. — Dichtungen (Literary Works) (containing: Der ewige Tag [The Eternal Day]; Umbra Vitae; Der Dieb [The Thief]; Der Himmel Trauerspiel [Tragedy of the Heavens]; edited by Kurt Pinthus and Erwin Löwensohn); Munich, 1922. — Umbra Vitae, Nachgelassene Gedichte (..., Posthumously Published Poems) (with 47 original woodcuts by Ernst Ludwig Kirchner); Munich, 1924. — Gesammelte Gedichte, Vollständige Ausgabe v. Karl Seelig (Collected Poems, Complete Edition by ...); Zurich, 1947. — Marathon (22 sonnets), edited in accordance with the manuscripts of the poet and interpreted by Karl Ludwig Schneider; Hamburg, 1956.

Dichtungen und Schriften, Gesamtausgabe in 4 Bänden (Literary Works and [Other] Writings, Complete Edition in 4 Volumes), edited by Karl Ludwig Schneider, Hamburg, 1960 ff.

Georg Heym's literary remains are in the *Staats- und Universitäts-Bibliothek Hamburg* (National and University Library of Hamburg) and contain, among other items, the diaries from 1904 to 1911.

KURT HEYNICKE, *born in Liegnitz in 1891, child of working-class parents, elementary school pupil, office drudge, merchant.*

*Are you smiling, human being, you who feel this blessed existence?*

*Oh, we are nothing. An animal in the stable. Only our soul is sometimes a cathedral in which we can pray to each other.*

Born September 20, 1891 in Liegnitz, Silesia. Elementary school: Liegnitz, Dresden, Zeitz, Berlin. After that office worker in an insurance company. At twenty tuberculosis. Sanatorium. Earlier attempts to write resumed after cure. First poem published by HERWARTH WALDEN in *Der Sturm* (The Storm). More poems follow. There too the first volume of poetry, *Rings fallen Sterne* (All Around Stars Are Falling). War. A soldier for four years. Even as a soldier lyrically productive (see section "Die Hölle Erde" (This Hell Earth) in *Das namenlose Angesicht* (The Nameless Countenance). After the war again office worker in a small town in the Mark Brandenburg, for the Klöckner Corporation in Duisburg, for the Deutsche Bank (German Bank) in Solingen. In between the attempt to live as a freelance writer. A stay with the poet ALEXANDER VON BERNUS at the *Stift Neuburg* (Neuburg Foundation) near Heidelberg. Here spiritual contact with STEINER's anthroposophy. In 1919 the Kleist Prize for my volume of poetry, *Das namenlose Angesicht*. In 1933 dramatic producer at the Düsseldorf playhouse of LUISE DUMONT—GUSTAV LINDEMANN, who had staged my play *Der Kreis* (The Circle) back in 1920. Two years later at the city theater in Düsseldorf; here I also directed. These years in the theater were very fruitful for me: I have written a number of plays, all of which were performed on first-rate stages.

In 1932 I moved to Berlin; here I also worked for Ufa (Universal Film Studios). At a certain point in time I felt myself drawn to the novel. I admit openly, they are novels that people in Germany designate as "entertainment." Finally I moved from Berlin to the edge of the Black Forest in the vicinity of Freiburg. I am a storyteller but I would be a bad storyteller if at the same time I did not want to entertain my readers. After the war I wrote a number of radio plays and was twice awarded prizes for them. And above all: I still write poems. I have, taking into account the human developments of a lifetime, remained a believer, as in the initial period of my poetic endeavors. [Kurt Heynicke]

Rings fallen Sterne, Gedichte (All around Stars Are Falling, Poems); Berlin, 1917. — Gottes Geigen, Gedichte (God's Violins, Poems); Munich, 1918. — Das namenlose Angesicht, Rhythmen aus Zeit und Ewigkeit, Gedichte (The Nameless Countenance, Rhythms from Time and Eternity, Poems); Munich, 1919. — Der Kreis, ein Spiel über den Sinnen (The Circle, A Play above the Senses); Berlin, 1920. — Die hohe Ebene, Gedichte (The High Plain, Poems);

Berlin, 1921 (enlarged edition Stuttgart, 1941. — Der Weg zum Ich, Die Eroberung der inneren Welt, Essays (The Way to the I, The Conquest of the Inner World, Essays); Prien, 1922. — Sturm im Blut, Erzählungen (Storm in the Blood, Tales); Leipzig and Cologne, 1925. — Eros inmitten, Erzählungen (Eros Inside, Tales); Rudolstadt, 1925. — Das Meer, Dramatische Ballade (The Sea, Dramatic Ballad); Leipzig, 1925. — Der Prinz von Samarkand, Märchenspiel (The Prince of ..., Fairytale Play); Leipzig, 1925. — Kampf um Preußen, Schauspiel (Fight for Prussia, Play); Leipzig, 1925. — Fortunata zieht in die Welt, Roman (... Goes into the World, Novel); Leipzig, 1930. — Neurode, chorisches Spiel (..., Choral Play), 1933, and Der Weg ins Reich, chorisches Spiel (The Way into the Kingdom, Choral Play), 1934, were designated as undesirable soon after their publication. — Der Fanatiker von Schönbrunn, Novelle (The Fanatic of ..., Novella); Stuttgart, 1935. — Das Leben sagt ja, Gedichte (Life Says Yes, Poems); Stuttgart, 1936. — Herz, wo liegst du im Quartier, heiterer Roman (Heart, Where Are You Quartered, Amusing Novel); Stuttgart, 1938. — Der Baum, der in den Himmel wächst, heiterer Roman (The Tree That Grows into the Sky, Amusing Novel); Stuttgart, 1940. — Rosen blühen auch im Herbst, Roman (Roses Also Bloom in the Fall, Novel); Stuttgart, 1943. — Es ist schon nicht mehr wahr, Roman (It Is No Longer So, Novel); Stuttgart, 1948. — Der Hellseher, satirischer Roman (The Clairvoyant, Satirical Novel); Stuttgart, 1951. — Ausgewählte Gedichte (Selected Poems) (also containing unpublished poems); Stuttgart, 1952. — Die Nichte aus Amerika, Lustspiel (The Niece from America, Comedy); Munich, 1957.

The following plays were performed (published in acting editions): Ehe, ein Bühnenwerk (Marriage, A Stage Play); Berlin, 1922. — Wer gewinnt Lisette, Lustspiel (Whoever Gets ..., Comedy); 1928. — Emilie, oder der Sieg des Weibes, Komödie (..., or The Victory of the Woman, Comedy); 1930. — Frau im Haus, Lustspiel (Woman in the House, Comedy). — Steckenpferd und Staatssekretär, Komödie (Hobby-Horse and State-Secretary, Comedy); 1959.

Since 1951 Heynicke has written a number of radio plays and some television plays.

JAKOB VAN HODDIS. *Born in Berlin in 1887, lives in Thuringia.*

Born in Berlin on May 16, 1887 as HANS DAVIDSOHN, elder son of a materialistic/sceptical physician and an idealistic, highly cultured mother from a Silesian estate-owning family from which FRIEDERIKE KEMPNER, an eccentric poet fond of humans and animals, also descended, he grew up a happy youth. But soon the contrasts inherited from his parents began to have an effect on him; he had to leave Frederick-William Academic High School, passed his senior finals at the municipal Frederick Academic High School, studied architecture in Munich, did practical training in construction in Berlin for half a year, but gave up the profession on account of his "small size," from which he was destined to suffer all his life. Beginning in 1907 he studied Greek and philosophy in Jena and Berlin, founded in 1909 with KURT HILLER as guiding spirit and with ERWIN LÖWENSON, DAVID BAUMGARDT, ERNST BLASS, W.S. GHUTTMANN and others the New Club, a small debating group out of which developed the

Neopathetic Cabaret, where young writers presented their works every week, among them also GEORG HEYM. His early death in 1912 severely shook van Hoddis, who felt that Heym alone was his equal.

His unrequited passion for LOTTE PRITZEL, a creator of gracile dolls whom he followed to Munich, and then for the poet EMMY HENNINGS, totally bewildered him and signs of his mental illness began to manifest themselves in 1912. Neither his conversion to Catholicism nor voluntary and involuntary stays in sanatoriums nor his friends' readiness to help was able to reassure him. He turned up and disappeared in Paris and Munich, re-emerged in Berlin in 1913, regarded his once deeply revered mother as his enemy, but in the winter of 1913/14 once more appeared at authors' readings with new poetic works. Gradually, however, his schizophrenia became so evident that he was initially put up at an asylum in Jena, and then at a teacher's home in Frankenhain near Gräfenroda in Thuringia, where he worked as a gardener. Beginning in 1922 he was cared for privately in Tübingen. — When his condition grew worse he was first confined in Esslingen (Württemberg), and finally in the asylum in Bendorf-Sayn near Coblenz, from which he was transported as No. 8 on April 30, 1942 in order — we do not know where, when, or how — to be exterminated.

Not until 1958, thanks to the edition of his preserved poetic works, collected by PAUL PÖRTNER, and the essay of his friend ERWIN LÖWENSON living in Israel contained therein (along with some other, shorter documents), could clarity be achieved concerning his dark existence and his enigmatical personality. Many of his poems and practically all of his prose are lost. [Ed.]

Weltende (End of the World) (16 poems); Berlin, 1918. — Weltende, Gesammelte Dichtungen (End of the World, Collected Poetic Works), edited by Paul Pörtner; Zurich, 1958.

WILHELM KLEMM. *Born in Leipzig in 1881, lives in said place.*

Born May 15, 1881 in Leipzig. Father a bookseller, mother from Lübeck. Educated in the classics (Thomas School), senior finals in 1900. Military service; study of medicine in Munich, Erlangen, Leipzig, Kiel. In 1905 state board exams. Junior physician in various places, ultimately at the surgical policlinic in Leipzig. In 1909, after his father's death, head of the firm of Otto Klemm; in 1912 marriage to ERNA KRÖNER, daughter of the publisher ALFRED KRÖNER, four sons by her. From 1914 to 1918 senior physician on the western front. In 1919 taking over of the wholesale book dealership of CARL FRIEDRICH FLEISCHER in Leipzig. After Alfred Kröner's death in 1921 partner and managing director in the firm of Alfred Kröner; in 1927 acquisition of the Dieterich Publishing Firm. In 1937 resignation from Kröner. Political persecution. Expulsion from the *Reichsschrifttumskammer* (Reich Chamber of Literature); in 1943 destruction of all businesses and properties; two sons killed in action. In 1945 transport to Wiesbaden via the Americans. In 1948 marriage to ILSE BRANDT from Leipzig, one daughter by her. In 1955 sale of the *Sammlung Dieterich* (Dieterich Collection) to CARL SCHÜNEMANN in Bremen. Lives at Steubenstraße 3 in Wiesbaden. [Wilhelm Klemm]

Gloria, Kriegsgedichte aus dem Feld (..., War Poems from the Battlefield); Munich, 1915. — Verse und Bilder, mit eigenen Zeichnungen (Verses and Images, With Drawings by the Author); Berlin, 1916. — Aufforderung, Gesammelte Verse (Challenge, Collected Verses); Berlin, 1917 (new edition with epilogue by Kurt Pinthus; Wiesbaden, 1961). — Ergriffenheit, Gedichte (Emotion, Poems); Munich, 1919. — Entfaltung, Gedichtfolge (Unfolding, Poetic Sequence); Bremen 1919. — Traumschutt, Gedichte (Dream-Rubble, Poems); Hanover, 1920. — Verzauberte Ziele, Gedichtfolge (Enchanted Goals, Poetic Sequence); Berlin, 1921. — Die Satanspuppe, Verse (Satan's Doll, Verses) (under the pseudonym of Felix Brazil); Hanover, 1922.

ELSE LASKER-SCHÜLER. *I was born in Thebes (Egypt), even though I came into the world in Elberfeld in the Rhineland. I attended school until I was eleven, became Robinson, lived in the Orient for five years and have been vegetating ever since.*

Else Lasker-Schüler always gave her date of birth as February 11, 1876; the register of the records bureau in Elberfeld indicates that she was born there on February 11, 1869. Granddaughter of a rabbi, daughter of an architect, she grew up there as an unruly child, married the physician Dr. LASKER, but soon divorced him and entered the wide world. She lived for the most part in Berlin. For fifty years she led the unsteady life of a poet-vagabond; she never had a home or an apartment of her own, always staying instead in cramped rented rooms. For a few years around 1900 she followed another highly gifted vagabond, the poet PETER HILLE, who died on the bench of a train station of a Berlin suburb in 1904.

She lived inside the memory of her native region and, much more still, inside the world of a fantastic Orient that gradually became her real world. Her poems and stories sprouted from this fantastic world, into which the many friends who admired her also entered (KARL KRAUS, DÄUBLER, DEHMEL, TRAKL, WERFEL, SCHICKELE, BENN, FRANZ MARC, KOKOSCHKA). In this world she portrayed herself likewise in numerous colorful images, and with many stars and flowers in her letters, which she usually signed Prince Jussuf because she identified herself with the Jussuf, Prince of Thebes, whom she had made up. For a short time around 1910 she was once again married, to HERWARTH WALDEN, the founder and propagator of *Der Sturm* (The Storm), the journal as well as the Expressionist group with this name.

In 1932 she received the Kleist Prize for, as the document reads, the "timeless values" of her poetic works, in which "there are many verses that are the equal of the definitive creations of our greatest German masters." In the following year she, as a "frivolous and morbid coffeehouse litterateuse," was forbidden to publish these poetic works. She fled to Switzerland initially, journeyed to Palestine by way of Egypt in 1934, but soon returned to Zurich, where in 1936 *Arthur Aronymus und seine Väter* (... and his Fathers) was performed, a play "from my beloved father's childhood days." In 1937 she turned up again in "das Hebräerland" (the land of the Hebrews), where she lived and suffered in poverty and desolateness until her death in Jerusalem. She died on January 18, 1945 and is buried on the Mount of Olives. [Ed.]

Styx, Gedichte (..., Poems); Berlin, 1902. — Der siebente Tag, Gedichte (The Seventh Day, Poems); Berlin, 1905. — Das Peter-Hille-Buch (The ... Book); Berlin, 1906. — Die Nächte Tino von Bagdads, Erzählungen (The Nights of Tino of Baghdad, Tales); Berlin, 1907. — Die Wupper, Schauspiel (The Wupper {translators' note: river and district}, Play); Berlin, 1909. — Meine Wunder, Gesichte (My Miracles, Visions); Karlsruhe and Leipzig, 1911 and 1914. — Mein Herz, Ein Liebesroman mit Bildern und wirklich lebenden Menschen (My Heart, A Love-Story with Pictures and Really Living People); Munich and Berlin, 1912. — Hebräische Balladen (Hebrew Ballads); Berlin, 1913. — Gesichte, Essays und andere Geschichten (Visions, Essays, and Other Stories); Leipzig, 1913. — Der Prinz von Theben, Ein Geschichtenbuch, mit 25 Zeichnungen der Verfasserin und 3 farbigen Bildern von Franz Marc (The Prince of Thebes, A Story-Book with 25 Drawings by the Author and 3 Pictures in Color by ...); Leipzig, 1914. — Die gesammelten Gedichte (The Collected Poems); Leipzig, 1917. — Gesamtausgabe in 10 Bänden (Das Peter-Hille-Buch; Der Malik, eine Kaisergeschichte; Die Nächte der Tino von Bagdad; Die Wupper; Mein Herz; Gesichte, Essays; Der Prinz von Theben; Hebräische Balladen; Die Kuppel) (complete edition in 10 volumes [The ... Book; The ..., An Imperial Story; The Nights of Tino of Baghdad; The Wupper; My Heart; Visions, Essays; The Prince of Thebes; Hebrew Ballads; The Copula]); Berlin, 1919-1920. — Briefe Peter Hilles an Else Lasker-Schüler (Letters of ... to ...); Berlin, 1921. — Der Wunderrabiner von Barcelona (The Marvelous Rabbi of ...), Berlin, 1921. — Theben, 10 Gedichte in Faksimile und 10 handkolorierte Lithographien der Dichterin (Thebes, 10 Poems in Facsimile and 10 Hand-colored Lithographs by the Poet); Frankfurt on the Main, 1923. — Ich räume auf! Meine Anklage gegen meine Verleger (I Am Cleaning Up! My Indictment of My Publishers); Zurich, 1925. — Konzert, Prosa (Concert, Prose); Berlin, 1932. — Arthur Aronymous und seine Väter, Die Geschichte meines Vaters (... and his Fathers, The Story of My Father); Berlin, 1932. — Arthur Aronymous und seine Väter (aus meines geliebten Vaters Kinderjahren), Schauspiel (... and his Fathers [From my Beloved Father's Childhood Days], Play); Berlin, 1932. — Das Hebräerland, mit 8 Zeichnungen von Else Lasker-Schüler (The Land of the Hebrews, With 8 Drawings by...); Zurich, 1937. — Mein blaues Klavier, Gedichte (My Blue Piano, Poems); Jerusalem, 1943 and 1957.

Else Lasker-Schüler, Eine Einführung in ihr Werk und eine Auswahl von Werner Kraft (..., An Introduction to her Work and a Selection by...); Wiesbaden, 1951. — Else Lasker-Schüler, Dichtungen und Dokumente (..., Literary Writings and Documents) (poems, prose, plays, letters, testimony, and recollection), selected and edited by Ernst Ginsberg; Munich, 1951. — Briefe an Karl Kraus (Letters to...), edited by Astrid Gehlhoff-Claes; Cologne, 1959. — Gesammelte Werke (Collected Works), edited by Friedhelm Kemp (Vol. 1: Poems 1902-1943; Vol. 2: Prose and Plays; Vol. 3 Verses and Prose from the Unpublished Works, edited by Werner Kraft); Munich, 1959 to 1961. — Helles Schlafen — Dunkles Wachen, Gedichte (Bright Sleep — Dark Wakefulness, Poems), selected by Friedhelm Kemp; Munich, 1962. —

Else Lasker-Schüler's literary remains are in the custody of Manfred Sturmann, Jerusalem (includes the play *Ich und Ich* [I and I]).

RUDOLF LEONHARD. *Born in Lissa (in Posen) on October 27, 1889. In an age in which it seems to me a fantastic risk to plan ahead for more than fourteen days, any sense of (though not a feeling for) the continuity of my own life has been lost to such a degree that I cannot even put together an autobiography that goes backwards. It seems to me, too, that determining and clarifying what was the right thing is an almost insoluble problem and an unadvisable undertaking. If there is anyone who might be seriously interested in this matter, I ask him to wait until after I die, when my detailed diaries will be available.*

Son of a jurist, Leonhard studied jurisprudence in Berlin, where he began the practice of law. When war broke out in 1914 he volunteered but his experiences at the front made him an ardent opponent of the war, and as such he was courtmartialed. He took an active part in the revolutionary events of 1918/19 and then lived in Berlin as a freelance writer; for a number of years he was a reader for the publishing house *Die Schmiede* (The Forge). In 1927 he moved to Paris where he also published in French.

Beginning in 1933 he was actively engaged in helping the large group of writers who sought refuge in France and he endeavored to bring together the anti-fascist elements of the emigration in an organization set up by him, the *Schutzverband deutscher Schriftsteller im Exil* (Association for the Protection of German Writers in Exile). As a member of several anti-fascist organizations and committees he was, like all emigrants, interned at war's outbreak in 1939, in his case at the camp in Le Vernet in the Pyrenees. During the collapse of France in 1940 he tried to escape to America but was caught and brought back to Le Vernet, from where he was transferred to the notorious extradition camp in Castres. Shortly before he was to be handed over to the Gestapo he managed to pull off a daring escape with several companions. He lived illegally in Marseilles, participated in the French underground movement, published during the German occupation a small volume of poems that was addressed to the German soldiers, and returned to Paris in 1944 after the liberation of France.

In October, 1947 he took part in the First German Writers' Congress in Berlin and decided to stay in Berlin permanently. But while moving he became so ill in Paris that he had to be hospitalized there for two years, having temporarily lost his sight. In 1950 he returned to East Berlin for good, constantly ailing but always active in many areas of literature and education, up to the day of his death on December 19, 1953. [Ed.]

Angelische Strophen, Gesichte (Anglian Verses, Visions); Berlin, 1913. — Der Weg durch den Wald, Gedichte (The Path through the Forest, Poems); Heidelberg, 1913. — Barbaren, Balladen (Barbarians, Ballads); Berlin, 1914. — Über den Schlachten, Gedichte (Above the Battles, Poems); Berlin, 1914. — Äonen des Fegefeuers, Aphorismen (Eons of Purgatory, Aphorisms); Leipzig, 1917. — Bemerkungen zum Reichsjugendwehrgesetz (Comments on the Imperial Compulsory Service Law for Youth); Berlin, 1917. — Beate und der große Pan, lyrischer Roman (... and the Great ..., Lyric Novel); Munich, 1918 (new editions 1928, 1948). — Polnische Gedichte (Polish Poems); Leipzig, 1918. — Katilinarische Pilgerschaft, Gedichte (Catilinarian Pilgrimage, Poems); Munich, 1919. — Kampf gegen die Waffe, Rede (Fight against Arms, Speech); Berlin, 1919. — Briefe an Margit, Gedichte (Letters to ..., Poems); Hanover, 1919. — Das Chaos, Gedichte (Chaos, Poems); Hanover, 1919. — Die Vorhölle, Tragödie (Limbo, Tragedy); Hanover, 1919. — Gedichte über das Thema "Mutter," mit 10 Radierungen von Michael Fingesten (Poems on the Theme of Mother with 10 Etchings by ...); Berlin, 1920. — Alles und Nichts! Aphorismen (Everything and Nothing! Aphorisms); Berlin, 1920. — Maria Stuart, Königin von Schottland, Sämtliche Gedichte (..., Queen of Scotland, Complete Poems) (translation); Berlin, 1921. — Spartakus-Sonette (Spartacus Sonnets); Stuttgart, 1921. — Die Prophezeiung, Gedichte (The Prophecy, Poems); Berlin, 1922. — Die Insel, Gedichte (The Island, Poems); Berlin, 1923. — Die Ewigkeit dieser Zeit, eine Rhapsodie gegen Europa (The Eternity of this Age, A Rhapsody against Europe); Berlin, 1924. — Segel am Horizont, Drama (Sail on the Horizon, Drama); Berlin, 1925. — Das nackte Leben, Sonette (Bare Life, Sonnets); Berlin, 1925 (new edition 1948). — Tragödie von heute, Drama (Tragedy of Today, Drama); Berlin, 1927. —

Comment organizer la collaboration franco-allemande?, Essay; Paris, 1930. — De l'Allemagne, Essay, 1931. — L'Allemagne et la Paix, Rede (..., Speech); Paris, 1932. — Das Wort (The Word) (attempt to compile a sentient dictionary of the German language): Berlin, 1932. — De l'Allemegne, Essay; Paris, 1933. — Confiance en Hitler?; Paris, 1934. — Führer & Co., Politische Komödie (..., Political Comedy); Paris, 1936. — Gedichte (Poems) (illegally smuggled into Germany in a reprinted jacket of volume No. 7248 in the Reclam Series); Paris, 1936. — Spanische Gedichte und Tagebuchblätter (Spanish Poems and Diary Pages); Paris, 1938. — Der Tod des Don Quijote, Erzählungen (The Death of Don Quixote, Tales); Zürich, 1938 (new edition Berlin, 1951). — Deutschland muß leben...!, Gedichte (Germany Must Live...!, Poems) (under the pseudonym of Robert Lanzer, illegally printed and distributed during the German occupation of France); Marseilles, 1944. — Geiseln, Tragödie (Hostages, Tragedy); Lyons, 1945. — Plaidoyer pour la démocratie allemande, Essay; Paris, 1947. — Deutsche Gedichte (German Poems); Berlin, 1947. — Anonyme Briefe, Drama (Anonymous Letters, Drama); Berlin, 1947.

Unsere Republik, Aufsätze und Gedichte (Our Republic, Essays and Poems); Berlin, 1951. — Hausfriedensbruch, Laienspiel (Trespass, Amateur Play); Halle, 1951. — Spielzeug, Ein Laienspiel (Playthings, An Amateur Play); Halle, 1951. — Die Stimme gegen den Krieg, Hörspiele (The Voice against the War, Radio Plays); Berlin, 1951. — Hölderlin, Étude et présentation; Paris, 1953. — Banlieue, Gedichte (..., Poems) (with watercolors by Max Lingner); Dresden, 1953.

Rudolf Leonhard erzählt, Erzählungen (... Narrates, Tales) (edited and introduced by Maximilian Scheer); Berlin, 1955. — Ausgewählte Werke in Einzelausgaben: Le Vernet, Gedichte (Selected Works in Individual Editions: ..., Poems) (preface by Maximilian Scheer); Berlin, 1961.

He also published short pamphlets, e.g., *Mensch über Mensch* (Human Being about Human Being) (1923) and *Elemente der proletarischen Kultur* (Elements of Proletarian Culture) (1924). — In addition he edited the *Ausgewählten Schriften* (Selected Writings) of Georg Forster with an introductory essay (Berlin, 1928) and the book series *Außenseiter der Gesellschaft — Die Verbrechen der Gegenwart* (Outsiders of Society — The Crimes of the Present) (Berlin, 1924 ff.). — The titles of some unpublished plays from the period 1917-1932 are *Zwillinge* (Twins), *Traum* (Dream), *Das Floß der Medusa* (The Raft of ...), *Le Bandit*. — Films: *Das Haus zum Mond* (The House at the Sign of the Moon), *Die Liebe der Jeanne Ney* (The Love of ...), *Das Tagebuch einer Verlorenen* (The Diary of a Forlorn Woman), *Don Quijote* (Don Quixote).

The literary remains are in the German Academy of the Arts, Department of Literary Archives, Berlin (East). The diaries referred to by Leonhard himself in 1919 are lost; but extant are a cycle of over 600 poems from the camp in Le Vernet written between 1939 and 1941 and in addition numerous essays and dramatic works from the last years.

ALFRED LICHTENSTEIN *was born in Berlin on August 23, 1889. There he attended Luisenstadt Academic High School. He studied law at the University of Berlin. In the summer of 1913 he obtained a doctorate at the University of Erlangen with a dissertation on theater law. In October 1913 he joined the 2nd Bavarian Crown Prince Regiment in Munich as an officer candidate and when war began went into combat with his regiment. On September 25, 1914 he was killed near Vermando-villers (in the vicinity of Rheims).* [Kurt Lubasch]

Die Geschichten des Onkel Krause, Ein Kinderbuch (The Stories of Uncle ..., A Children's Book); Berlin, 1910. — Gedichte und Geschichten (Poems and Stories), 2 vols., edited by Kurt Lubasch; Munich, 1919. — Gesammelte Gedichte (Collected Poems), critically edited by Klaus Kanzog; Zurich, 1962.

Lichtenstein's literary remains, in the keeping of Kurt Lubasch in Berlin, were destroyed during the Second World War, except for "four handwritten oil-cloth copy-books," containing most of his poems in handwritten form, which Mrs. Lubasch handed over to the Free University of Berlin upon her husband's death, as requested by him.

ERNST WILHELM LOTZ *was born in Culm on the Vistula River on February 6, 1890, lived in Wahlstatt, Karlsruhe, Plön, and attended the cadet school in Gross-Lichterfelde. At 17 he became an officer candidate in the 143rd Infantry Regiment in Strasbourg and, after attending officer candidate school in Kassel, a lieutenant in the same regiment. For a year and a half he was on active duty as an officer and then resigned his commission. On September 26, 1914 he died in combat while serving as a lieutenant and company commander in the western theater of war.* [Henny Lotz]

Und schöne Raubtierflecken..., Gedichte (And Beautiful Predator Spots..., Poems); Berlin, 1913. — Wolkenüberflaggt, Gedichte (The Clouds Our Flag, Poems); Leipzig, 1917. — Prosaversuche und Feldpostbriefe aus dem bisher unveröffentlichten Nachlaß (Prose and Letters from the Field from the

Previously Unpublished Literary Remains), edited by Hellmut Draws-Tychsen; Diessen near Munich, 1955.

Literary remains (letters and approximately 60 poems, including some translations of poems by Arthur Rimbaud and Paul Verlaine) in the possession of Hellmut Draws-Tychsen; some poems published in *Hortulus*, vol. 9.

KARL OTTEN. *Born in Aachen in 1889, studied in Munich, lived in Vienna.*
For later editions Otten added the following:
*About my life I can only say that it was dedicated to the struggle for the happiness and victory of the poor, the proletariat. And is now veiled in grief over the disgrace to which the German proletariat has been subjected through its own fault: that of being the toughest obstacle on the road to world revolution, in fact, the most bitter saboteurs of the communist idea. I admit that I have never loved the Germans, that I have hated nothing as much as the German bourgeoisie — as long as I can remember. And for just as long a time I have loved Russia and I call upon every revolutionary poet first of all to share this love. If he recognizes the Russian idea then he recognizes the mistakes of our people. The struggle for the former and against the latter will do away with the duality of the German poet, and his life will embody the synthesis of person and deed: revolutionary and poet!*

*Do not be afraid of the prisons — they are ridiculous and their closed gates triumphal arches for your courage! Rifles — they kill the body — the spirit, the sacred cause live! Never before has the object of the dark struggle of the oppressed been so clearly visible to one and all... there is only one thing: liberty and life for all eternity... or death — for all eternity! Salvation comes from the East. I have made my choice.*

Upon the editor's current request to Karl Otten for a life-history the following reply by the poet was received:

Dear Kurt Pinthus, you, a survivor of the end of the world, request another survivor to say a few words about the life of a shipwrecked man on the occasion of the second launching of our raft *Menschheitsdämmerung*, on which 23 "yearning damned souls" saw themselves exposed to the tempests of utopia 40 years ago. Words which are meant to explain and to appease the "angry young man" I was then. I could also say — to set right.

This holds true for that place in my outburst back then where I, taking seriously messianic communism, thought that I perceived in Russia and its revolution our deliverance from evil. I was not the only one who did that. Like me many persons hoped at that time, 1917-1919, that they had rendered the final great and gruesome sacrifice to everlasting peace in the spirit of Dostoevski and Tolstoi. History undeceived us and the years that then followed eclipsed the horror of the First World War. Hope and horror have thus determined my life down to the briefest utterance. There have been few peaceful stages: student years in Munich, Bonn, and Strasbourg (1910-1914); friendship with ERICH MÜHSAM, HEINRICH MANN, CARL STERNHEIM. FRANZ BLEI provided me with political and artistic direction. This truly happy epoch, for me the measure and value of the times as such, remained a guideline, a summons to reshape the human ordering of things.

Because I, filled with foreboding, saw the First World War coming and made no secret of my opposition, I was put under "preventive arrest" at the outbreak of hostilities and spent the war partly in prison, partly as a soldier in a labor company, in short, as a suspicious character whose life was hanging by a thread. In this frame of mind I wrote *Die Thronerhebung des Herzens* (The Enthronement of the Heart), from which the poems printed here were taken.

War, revolt, inflation took my breath away at first. I went to Vienna where I worked as editor and publisher of the journal *Der Friede* (Peace). 1924 — 1933 in Berlin, where novels, stage plays, and the film *Kameradschaft* (Comradeship) originated in quick succession. On March 12, 1933 I left Germany and went to Spain, out of which the Civil War drove me in 1936. In the same year deprivation of citizenship by the National Socialist regime. The next twenty-two years I spent in England doing political and literary work. In Switzerland since 1958.

Dear Kurt Pinthus, don't be mad at me for this simplification of a life-history — a survival-history —, whose gaps anyone can fill in at his pleasure or displeasure, most easily by reading my books. —

Always your old friend Karl Otten.

The poet, who had lost his eyesight in London in 1944, died on March 20, 1963 in Locarno where he had lived the last five years of his life with his wife, who was his collaborator.

Die Reise nach Albanien (The Journey to Albania); Munich, 1913. — Thronerhebung des Herzens, Gedichte (Enthronement of the Heart, Poems); Berlin, 1917. — Der Sprung aus dem Fenster, Erzählungen (The Leap out of the Window, Tales); Leipzig, 1918. — Lona, Roman (..., Novel); Vienna, 1920. — Der Fall Strauß (The Strauss Case) (criminal-psychological study); Berlin, 1925. — Prüfung zur Reife, Roman (Test of Maturity, Novel); Leipzig, 1928. — Der schwarze Napoleon (The Black ...) (biography of Toussaint Louverture); Berlin, 1931. — Die Expedition nach San Domingo, Schauspiel) (The Expedition to Santo Domingo, Play); Berlin, 1931. — Eine gewisse Victoria, Roman (A Certain ..., Novel); preprint in the *Berliner Tageblatt* (Berlin Daily News), 1930. — Der unbekannte Zivilist, Roman (The Unknown Civilian, Novel); preprint in the *Berliner Tageblatt*, 1932. — Torquemadas Schatten, Roman (...'s Shadow, Novel); Stockholm, 1938. — A Combine of Aggression, Masses, Elite and Dictatorship in Germany (sociology of fascism); London, 1942. — Der ewige Esel, Eine Legende (The Eternal Ass, A Legend); Freiburg, Zurich, 1949. — Die Botschaft, Roman (The Message, Novel); Darmstadt, 1957. — Der Ölkomplex, Schauspiel (The Oil Complex, Play); Emstetten, Westphalia, 1958. — Herbstgesang, Gesammelte Gedichte (Autumn Song, Collected Poems); Neuwied, 1961. — Wurzeln, Roman (Roots, Novel) (with a farewell by Kasimir Edschmid); Neuwied, 1963.

Karl Otten edited the following anthologies with introductions or epilogues and bio-bibliographies: Ahnung und Aufbruch, Expressionistische Prosa (Foreboding and Revolt, Expressionist Prose); Darmstadt and Neuwied, 1957. — Schrei und Bekenntnis, Expressionistisches Theater (Scream and Avowal, Expressionist Theater); Darmstadt and Neuwied, 1959. — Das leere Haus, Prosa jüdischer Dichter (The Empty House, Prose of Jewish Writers) (later only under the title: Prosa jüdischer Dichter); Stuttgart, 1959. — Schofar, Lieder und Legenden jüdischer Dichter (Shofar, Songs and Legends of Jewish Writers); Neuwied, 1962. — Expressionismus grotesk (Expressionism Grotesque); Zurich, 1962. — Ego und Eros, Meistererzählungen des Expressionismus (... and ..., Master Tales of Expressionism) (with an epilogue by Heinz Schöffler); Stuttgart, 1963. — Editor, *Albert Ehrenstein*, Gedichte und Prosa (..., Poems and Prose); Neuwied, 1961. —

Kameradschaft (Comradeship), German-French miners' film. Idea and script, 1931.

Karl Otten edited (with Julian Gumperz) the periodical *Der Gegner. Blätter zur Kritik der Zeit* (The Adversary. Pages for Contemporary Criticism); Berlin, 1919-1922, vols. 1-3.

Karl Otten's literary remains are in the possession of Mrs. Ellen Otten, Locarno, Switzerland.


LUDWIG RUBINER *does not wish any biography of himself. He feels that not only the enumeration of deeds but also of works and of dates has its origin in a haughty mistaken notion from the past kept alive by an individualistic dressing-gown artistry. He is convinced that only an anonymous and creative membership in the community is of consequence for the present and the future.*

Born June 12, 1881, died February 27, 1920 in Berlin. Rubiner lived mostly in Berlin, but also in Paris and during the First World War in Switzerland. As the most passionate champion of activism, calling for the political poet, for the "humanocentric consciousness," for a global mentality, he had, in spite of his successfully preserved anonymity, great influence on the Expressionist generation.

Die indischen Opale, Kriminalroman (The Indian Opals, Crime Thriller); Berlin, 1912. — Kriminalsonette (Crime Sonnets) (with Friedrich Eisenlohr and Livingstone Hahn); Leipzig, 1913 (illustrated new edition, edited by R. Braun and G.E. Scholz; Stuttgart, 1962). — Das himmlische Licht, Gedichte (The Heavenly Light, Poems); Leipzig, 1916. — Der Mensch in der Mitte, Aufrufe (The Human Being in the Center, Appeals); Berlin, 1917 (new edition 1920). — Die Gewaltlosen, Drama (The Non-Violent, Drama); Potsdam, 1919.

Editor of: M.A. Kusmin, *Taten des großen Alexander* (Deeds of the Great ...); Munich, 1910. — Tolstoi, Tagebuch (..., Diary); Zurich, 1918. — Kameraden der Menschheit, Dichtungen zur Weltrevolution (Comrades of Humanity, Poetic Works on the World Revolution); Potsdam, 1919. — Die Gemeinschaft, Dokumente der geistigen Weltwende (The Community, Documents on the Spiritual Turning Point in World History); Potsdam, 1919. — Voltaire, Die Romane und Erzählungen, vollständige Ausgabe (..., The Novels and Tales, Complete Edition); Potsdam, 1919.

He edited volume three of the journal *Zeit-Echo* (Echo of the Times) (Berne, 1917). For the first (double) issue, May, he wrote all contributions himself; the 2nd and 3rd issues also contain contributions by other Expressionist authors.

RENÉ SCHICKELE. *Born on August 4, 1883. Academic high school: Saverne and Strasbourg. Universities: Strasbourg, Munich, Paris. Journeys through all of Europe west of the Elbe, Greece, Palestine, Egypt, India. Wherever I happen to be, there it is always most beautiful. Now in a Swiss fishing village on Lake Constance.*

*I am a German writer of Gallic-Alemannic blood that pullulates in the forms of the German language, a description that also fits Gottfried of Strasbourg — a triple bow to my insuperable ancestor! — whom no one to be sure plans on "annexing" or "disannexing." Yesterday a German, today a French citizen: I couldn't care less. There are people (and among them I number most of my compatriots) who even want to pick and choose their executioners. My esthetic conscience does not go that far. What do I care where the conquerors push their soccer ball! To me shifting borders around is, like every other national transaction, just another game played at the stock exchange. I have nothing to do with such matters, they do not concern me. Because I have taken such heretical ideas seriously for as long as I can remember and most especially so during the war, I have a bad name among the liveried riff-raff on both sides of the Rhine. Year after year the psychologists among them expose me as an "unreliable customer" although I have never denied it. God preserve me my unreliability!*

*For all that I am part of German literature, which I — and as is gradually becoming evident: rightly — regard as a greater reality than the armored, powder-charged, polished, foam-lying utterances of the German public. None of my comrades will lose me through any fault of mine. And if the war were to start all over again and regardless of what militarisms would be relieving each other. I know: the human being, heretofore the most pathetic of animals, has recognized his situation and nothing will prevent him from striking a blow for his liberation, the likes of which no history book has yet recorded.*

The son of a French mother and a German father, the owner of a wine-growing estate in Oberrehnheim (Alsace), Schickele began his study of the natural sciences and philosophy in 1901, attending the universities of Strasbourg, Munich, Paris, and Berlin. After marrying in 1904 he became a freelance writer and traveled frequently: Greece, Italy, Asia Minor, North Africa, and India, in Paris and Berlin as a journalist, in Zurich during the First World War. Unremitting in his efforts to effect a reconciliation between Germany and France, he made his home in Badenweiler in the Black Forest in 1920, but moved to the French Riviera in 1932, living in Sanary-sur-Mer most of the time. He died in Vence on January 31, 1940. [Ed.]

Sommernächte, Gedichte (Summer Nights, Poems); Strasbourg, 1902. — Pan, Gedichte (..., Poems); Strasbourg, 1902. — Mon Repos, Gedichte (..., Poems); Berlin, 1905. — Der Ritt ins Leben, Gedichte (The Ride into Life, Poems); Stuttgart, 1906. — Der Fremde, Roman (The Stranger, Novel); Berlin, 1907 (new edition Leipzig, 1913). — Meine Freundin Lo, Novelle (My Girl Friend ..., Novella); Leipzig, 1911 (enlarged edition Berlin, 1931, new edition 1935). Weiß und Rot, Gedichte (White and Red, Poems); Leipzig, 1911 (enlarged edition Berlin, 1920). — Das Glück, Novelle (Happiness, Novella) (illustrated by W. Wagner); Berlin, 1913. — Schreie auf dem Boulevard, Essays (Shouts on the ..., Essays); Leipzig, 1913 (new edition Berlin, 1920). — Benkal, der Frauentröster, Roman (..., The Comforter of Women, Novel); Leipzig,

1914. — Trimpopp und Manasse, Erzählung (..., Tale); Leipzig, 1914. — Die Leibwache, Gedichte (The Bodyguard, Poems); Leipzig, 1914. — Mein Herz, mein Land, Ausgewählte Gedichte (My Heart, My Country, Selected Poems); Leipzig, 1915. — Hans im Schnakenloch, Schauspiel (Jack of the Midge Hole, Play); Leipzig, 1915 (new edition Munich, 1927). — Aissé, Novelle (..., Novella) (illustrated by Ottomar Starke); Leipzig, 1915. — Die Genfer Reise, Essays (The Geneva Trip, Essays); Berlin, 1919. — Der neunte November, Essays (The Ninth of ..., Essays); Berlin, 1919. — Der deutsche Träumer, Prosa (The German Dreamer, Prose); Zurich, 1919. — Die Mädchen, Drei Erzählungen (The Girls, Three Tales); Berlin, 1920. — Am Glockenturm, Schauspiel (At the Bell Tower, Play); Berlin, 1920. — Die neuen Kerle, Schauspiel (The New Guys, Play); Basel, 1920 (new edition, with preface by Schickele, illustrated by Emil Bizer; Basel, 1924). — Wir wollen nicht sterben! Essay (We Don't Want to Die! Essay); Munich, 1922. — Ein Erbe am Rhein, Roman in zwei Bänden (A Heritage on the Rhine, Novel in Two Volumes); Munich, 1925. — Das Erbe am Rhein, Erster Roman: Maria Capponi (The Heritage on the Rhine, First Novel: ...); Munich, 1925. — Zweiter Roman: Blick auf die Vogesen (Second Novel: View of the Vosges); Munich, 1927. — Dritter Roman: Der Wolf in der Hürde (Third Novel: The Wolf in the Pen); Berlin, 1931. — Symphonie für Jazz, Roman (Symphony for ..., Novel); Berlin, 1929. — Die Grenze, Essays (The Border, Essays); Berlin, 1932. — Himmlische Landschaft, Gedichte in Prosa (Heavenly Landscape, Poems in Prose) (illustrated by Hans Meid); Berlin, 1933 (new edition 1956). — Die Witwe Bosca, Roman (The Widow ..., Novel); Berlin, 1933 (new edition Hamburg, 1951). — Liebe und Ärgernis des D.H. Lawrence, Essay (Love and Scandal of ..., Essay); Amsterdam, 1935. — Die Flaschenpost, Roman (The Message in the Bottle, Novel); Amsterdam, 1937 (new edition Hamburg, 1950). — Le Retour, Souvenirs inédits; Paris, 1938. Published as Die Heimkehr (The Return Home) in a translation by Ferdinand Hardekopf; Strasbourg, 1939. — Das Vermächtnis, Deutsche Gedichte von Walther von der Vogelweide bis Nietzsche (The Legacy, German Poems from ... to ...); first edition, Amsterdam, 1940, was destroyed by the Nazis; new edition Freiburg, 1948. — Werke in 3 Bänden (Works in 3 Volumes), edited by Hermann Kesten; Cologne, 1960.

Schickele translated: Balzac, Die Lilie im Tal (The Lily in the Valley), Leipzig, 1923; Die verlassene Frau (The Deserted Woman), Leipzig, 1923; Flaubert, Madame Bovary, Munich, 1928 (new edition Zurich, 1932).

René Schickele edited the following journals: Der Stürmer, Halbmonatsschrift für künstlerische Renaissance im Elsaß (The Assailer, Semimonthly Magazine for Artistic Renaissance in Alsace); Strasbourg, 1903 (nine issues). — Der Merker, Halbmonatsschrift (The Critic, Semimonthly Magazine) (with Otto Flake); Strasbourg, 1903 (three issues). — Das neue Magazin (The New Magazine); Berlin, July to December, 1904. — Die weißen Blätter, Monatsschrift (The White Pages, Monthly Magazine); Leipzig, September, 1913 to March, 1916; Zurich, April, 1916 to December, 1917; Berne, January, 1918 to December, 1918; Berlin, January, 1919 to December, 1919.

The literary remains are in the keeping of Mrs. Anna Schickele, Badenweiler, and of the Schiller-National Museum, Marbach on the Neckar. The largest portion of the literary remains was lost during the Second World War. Extant are a diary (excerpts published in: Monatshefte für den deutschen Unterricht [Monthly Issues for German Instruction], November, 1954, edited by P.K. Ackermann; individual prose fragments.

ERNST STADLER. *Born in Colmar in Alsace on August 11, 1883, was an assistant professor of German language and literature in Strasbourg, was killed in action on the western front at the beginning of the World War.*

Born in Colmar (Alsace) on August 11, 1883 as the son of a prosecuting attorney, Stadler attended academic high school in Strasbourg, studied German and Romance languages and literatures as well as comparative linguistics there and, starting in 1904, in Munich, where he earned his doctorate with a dissertation on *Parcifal.* From 1906 to 1908 he was in Oxford as a Rhodes Scholar. Here he wrote a treatise on Wieland's Shakespeare translation with which he qualified as a university lecturer in Strasbourg in 1908. In 1910 he accepted an appointment at the *Université Libre* in Brussels and in 1914 was offered a guest professorship by the University of Toronto in Canada. But as an artillery officer he had to report for duty at the start of the First World War and was killed near Ypres by a shell on October 30, 1914. He is buried in Strasbourg. Like his friend and fellow Alsatian, RENÉ SCHICKELE, he committed himself to effecting a rapprochement of France and Germany; his reconciliatory intentions are also manifest in his activities as a translator and in his scholarly work, which centered on the interrelations of national literatures. [Ed.]

Präludien, Gedichte (Preludes, Poems); Strasbourg, 1905. — Der Aufbruch, Gedichte (Setting Out, Poems); Leipzig, 1914 (new edition by K.L. Schneider; Hamburg, 1962). — Das Balzac-Buch, Erzählungen und Novellen (The ...- Book, Tales and Novellas), translated and introduced by E. Stadler; Strasbourg, 1913. — Francis Jammes, Die Gebete der Demut (..., The Prayers of Humility), rendered by E. Stadler; Leipzig, 1913 (enlarged edition Leipzig, 1917; new edition Graz, 1949).

Dichtungen, 2 Bände. Gedichte und Übertragungen mit einer Auswahl der kleinen kritischen Schriften und Briefe (Poetic Works, 2 Volumes, Poems and Renderings with a Selection of the Short Critical Writings and Letters) (introduced, critically compared with the original text, and commented on by Karl Ludwig Schneider); Hamburg, 1954.

AUGUST STRAMM. *Born in Münster in Westphalia on July 29, 1874, attended academic high school in Eupen and Aachen. Despite an inner reluctance he embarked on a career in the postal service at the express wish of his father. After finishing his studies he became a post-office supervisor in Bremen and, later, in Berlin, where he was transferred to the Imperial Post Office Department. Moreover, he earned a Ph.D. degree from the University of Halle. As a captain in the reserves he was called up when the war broke out. During an assault in Russia on September 1, 1915, he was the last man in his company to be killed, after he had participated in over seventy battles and skirmishes. August Stramm is buried in the cemetery near Horodec* {Translators' note: also spelled Gródek [Polish]} *in Russia.* [Herwarth Walden] Sancta Susanna, Drama (..., Drama); Berlin, 1914. — Rudimentär, Drama (Rudimentary, Drama); Berlin, 1914. — Die Haidebraut, Drama (The Bride of the Heath, Drama); Berlin, 1914. — Du, Liebesgedichte (You, Love Poems); Berlin, 1915. — Erwachen, Drama (Awakening, Drama); Berlin, 1915. — Kräfte, Drama (Forces, Drama); Berlin, 1915. — Die Unfruchtbaren, Drama (The Barren, Drama); Berlin, 1916. — Geschehen, Drama (Happening, Drama); Berlin, 1916. — Die Menschheit (Humanity); Berlin, 1917. — Tropfblut, Nachgelassene Gedichte (Drop-Blood, Posthumously Published Poems); Berlin, 1919 (also published in a large-format deluxe edition). — Weltwehe, Dichtung (World-Pangs, Poetic Work); Berlin, 1922.

Dichtungen, Gesamt-Ausgabe (Literary Works, Complete Edition); Berlin, 1919 (of 3 planned volumes only 2 were published, comprising vol. 1: Die Unfruchtbaren [The Barren], Rudimentär [Rudimentary], Sancta Susanna, Die Haidebraut [The Bride of the Heath]; vol. 2: Erwachen [Awakening], Kräfte [Forces], Weltwehe [World-Pangs], Geschehen [Happening], Die Menschheit [Humanity]). — Dein Lächeln weint, Gesammelte Gedichte (Your Smile Weeps, Collected Poems); Wiesbaden, 1956 (published in lieu of the 3rd volume of the complete edition, edited and introduced by August Stramm's daughter, Inge; contains the earlier volumes of poetry: Du (You), Tropfblut (Drop-Blood) — Das Werk. Vollständige Gesamtausgabe der Gedichte und Dramen (The Works, Complete Edition of the Poems and Dramas), edited by René Radrizzani; Wiesbaden, 1963.

Literary remains in the library of the University of Münster in Westphalia.

GEORG TRAKL *was born in Salzburg on February 3, 1887. In 1913 at the age of 25 he went to Innsbruck to serve as a pharmacist in the garrison hospital, but soon gave up this and all other work and until war broke out lived in* LUDWIG FICKER'S *home.*'*In his outer life he found it increasingly more difficult to cope, while at the same time the wellspring of his poetic creativity opened up more and more deeply. Although a heavy drinker and consumer of drugs, his noble and unusually steeled spiritual composure never deserted him; there is absolutely no one who might have seen him staggering or becoming impudent while intoxicated, although his manner of speaking, normally so gentle and, as it were, encompassing an unutterable muteness, could frequently harden in a strange sort of way and come to a point in words of sparkling maliciousness when he drank wine into the late hours of the night. But from behaving in this fashion he often suffered more than his silent drinking companions, over whose heads he let fly his flashing word-daggers; for at such moments he seemed filled with a veracity that positively caused his heart to bleed. Otherwise he was a quiet person, given to taciturnity but by no means uncommunicative; he could, on the contrary, converse in the kindest and most human way with ordinary and unaffected people, as long as they had their hearts 'in the right place' — from the highest to the lowest social strata — and particularly too with children. He had by now hardly any worldly goods, owning books seemed to him more superfluous all the time, and he wound up 'selling off' his entire set of Dostoevski, whom he revered most fervently...*

*Then the war broke out and with his old rank of pharmacist Trakl was assigned to a mobile hospital at the front. In Galicia. At first he seemed unbent and wrenched from his melancholy. But then — after the retreat from Grodek — I received from the garrison hospital in Cracow, where he had been brought for mental observation, several postcards which sounded like a soul's cry for help. With quick resolve I was on my way and journeyed to Cracow. There I had my last shattering get-together with my unforgettable friend. In Cracow and on the return trip to Vienna I tried in every possible way to have him cared for at home. However, I had but just gotten back when I received the news of his death. He died during the night of November 3/4, 1914 after he had lain in agony for a whole day — presumably from the effects of an overdose of poison he had taken; but in any case his death is shrouded in darkness, because his attendant was not allowed to see him during the final hours of his life. This person — a miner from Halstatt by the name of Mathias Roth assigned to the medics — was the only one present as a mourner at Trakl's burial."* [From information supplied to the editor by Ludwig Ficker, 1919]

To this account by Ludwig Ficker, who published almost all of Trakl's poems in his journal, *Der Brenner* (The Burner), continuously from 1912 on, several data can be added. Trakl was the fourth of six children of Tobias Trakl, a dealer in iron and hardware. He attended the academic high school in Salzburg; upon completing a three-year period of practical training he studied pharmacy in Vienna and after receiving his master of science degree in pharmacology he went on active duty in the army pharmaceutical service. From May 1912 to August 1914 he lived mostly in Innsbruck; the first half year was spent as a pharmacist at the garrison hospital. In January 1913 he had himself transferred to the reserves, tried three times without success to be self-supporting in Vienna, but returned to Innsbruck each time, where eventually Ludwig Ficker took him in and cared for him. Friends made it possible for him to take brief trips to Venice, Berlin, and Lake Garda. Towards the end of August, 1914 he went up to the front in Galicia with an ambulance column. "After the battle of Grodek he had to attend to ninety severely wounded soldiers by himself in a barn, without being able to help them," whereupon he broke down. — In the fall of 1925 the mortal remains of the poet were transported to the Tyrol and buried in the cemetery in Mühlau near Innsbruck. [Ed. based on data in *Erinnerung an Georg Trakl* (Recollections of ...), Innsbruck, 1926.

Gedichte (Poems); Leipzig, 1913. — Sebastian im Traum, Gedichte (Sebastian Dreaming, Poems); Leipzig, 1915. — Die Dichtungen, Erste Gesamtausgabe (The Poetic Works, First Complete Edition) (edited by Karl Roeck); Leipzig, 1917 (subsequent editions Zwickau, 1928, Salzburg, 1938 ff.). — Der Herbst des Einsamen, Gedichte (The Autumn of the Lonely Man, Poems); Munich, 1920. — Gesang des Abgeschiedenen, Gedichte (Song of the Departed One, Poems); Leipzig, 1933 (Insel Library). — Aus goldenem Kelch, Die Jugenddichtungen (From a Golden Goblet, The Early Poetic Works) (prefaced and edited by Erhard Buschbeck); Salzburg, 1939 (enlarged edition Salzburg, 1951 ff.). — Die Dichtungen, Gesamtausgabe. Mit einem Anhang: Zeugnisse und Erinnerungen (The Poetic Works, Complete Edition. With an Appendix: Testimonies and Recollections) (edited by Kurt Horwitz); Zurich,

1945. — Offenbarung und Untergang, Die Prosadichtungen (Revelation and Decline, The Prose Writings) (with pen-and-ink drawings by Alfred Kubin); Salzburg, 1947.

Gesammelte Werke (Collected Works) (edited by W. Schneditz) Band 1 Dichtungen; Band 2 Aus goldenem Kelch, Die Jugenddichtungen; Band 3 Nachlaß und Biographie — Gedichte, Briefe, Bilder, Essays (Volume 1 Poetic Works; Volume 2 From a Golden Goblet, The Early Poetic Works; Volume 3 Literary Remains and Biography — Poems, Letters, Images, Essays); Salzburg, 1948 ff. — Historisch-kritische Gesamtausgabe (Complete Historical-Critical Edition) (edited by Walter Killy), also containing the complete literary remains and letters, is in preparation.

FRANZ WERFEL. Born in Prague in 1890, lived in Hamburg, Leipzig, and now in Vienna.

Werfel was born in Prague on September 10, 1890 as the son of a very prosperous glove manufacturer, who was so appalled by the poetry writing of the youth that he dispatched him to an export firm in Hamburg to undergo a rigorous business training after graduation from an academic high school. Upon publication of his first book of poems Der Weltfreund (The World Lover) he was asked to come to Leipzig in 1912 to accept a position with the Kurt Wolff Publishing House. Here together with Walter Hasenclever and the editor of this book he constituted a collecting center where many young authors of the Expressionist generation and older writers close to them were given a friendly reception and encouragement. From 1915 to 1917 he served as an Austrian soldier in the First World War. Then in Vienna he met ALMA MAHLER, the widow of the composer, and remained united with her until his death.

In 1925 he received the Grillparzer Prize, in 1921 {translators' note: a misprint; the correct date is 1927} the Schiller Prize. No matter where they were living, the Werfels were always the focal point of a circle of artists of every stamp. They lived in Vienna, in Breitenstein at the Semmering Pass, in Venice, made frequent trips as far as the Near East. When Hitler's troops marched into Austria in 1938 they fled to France, first to Paris, then to the southern coast. Their attempt to escape to Spain in good time was thwarted but they found refuge in Lourdes, and Werfel vowed that, if they succeeded in making their way to freedom, he would write a book about St. Bernadette. After they had made their way on foot across the Pyrenees to Spain via secret trails and had finally reached New York from Portugal in October 1940 and made their home in Hollywood-Beverly Hills, he kept his promise. In 1943 he suffered two heart attacks, and on August 27, 1945, pen in hand, reading the proofs of his Gedichte aus den Jahren 1908 bis 1945 (Poems from the Years 1908 to 1945), he was stricken with a fatal heart attack.

Der Weltfreund, Gedichte (The World Lover, Poems); Berlin, 1911 (3rd revised edition Leipzig, 1918). — Die Versuchung, ein Gespräch des Dichters mit dem Erzengel und Luzifer (The Temptation, A Conversation of the Poet with the Archangel and Lucifer); Leipzig, 1913. — Wir sind, Neue Gedichte (We Are, New Poems); Leipzig, 1913. — Einander — Oden, Lieder, Gestalten

(Each Other — Odes, Songs, Shapes); Leipzig, 1915. — Die Troerinnen des Euripides, in deutscher Bearbeitung (The Trojan Women of Euripides, In a German Adaptation); Leipzig, 1915. — Gesänge aus den drei Reichen, Ausgewählte Gedichte (Songs from the Three Realms, Selected Poems); Leipzig, 1917. — Der Gerichtstag, Gedichte in fünf Bänden (The Judgment Day, Poems in Five Volumes); Leipzig, 1919. — Der neue Dämon {translators' note: actually *Daimon*}: Sonderheft Franz Werfel (The New Daemon: Special Issue ...) (tales, poems, fragments); Vienna, 1919. — Spielhof, Eine Phantasie (Play-Court, A Phantasia); Munich, 1920. — Spiegelmensch, Magische Trilogie (Mirrorman, Magic Trilogy); Munich, 1920. — Nicht der Mörder, der Ermordete ist schuldig, Novelle (Not the Murderer, the Murdered Man Is Guilty, Novella); Munich, 1920. — Der Besuch aus dem Elysium, Romantisches Drama (The Visit from Elysium, Romantic Drama); Munich, 1920 (written 1910, first publication in the anthology *Arkadia* [Arcadia], 1911). — Bocksgesang, Drama (Billy-Goat Song, Drama): Munich, 1921. — Arien (Arias); Leipzig, 1921. — Schweiger, Trauerspiel (..., Tragedy); Munich 1922. — Die Mittagsgöttin, Zauberspiel (The Noonday Goddess, Magic Play); Munich, 1923. — Beschwörungen, Gedichte (Conjurations, Poems); Munich, 1923. — Juarez und Maximilian, Dramatische Historie (... and ..., Dramatic History); Vienna, 1924. — Verdi, Roman der Oper (..., Novel of the Opera); Vienna, 1924. — Paulus unter den Juden, Dramatische Legende (Paul among the Jews, Dramatic Legend); Vienna, 1926. — Gedichte (Poems) (contains: Der Weltfreund, Wir sind, Einander, Der Gerichtstag, Neue Gedichte [The World Lover, We Are, Each Other, The Judgment Day, New Poems]); Vienna, 1927. — Der Tod des Kleinbürgers, Novelle (The Death of a Petty Bourgeois, Novella); Vienna, 1927 (new edition with pen-and-ink drawings by Alfred Kubin, Vienna, 1928). — Geheimnis eines Menschen, Novellen (Secret of a Human Being, Novellas) (contains: Die Entfremdung, Geheimnis eines Menschen, die Hoteltreppe, Das Trauerhaus [The Estrangement, Secret of a Human Being, The Hotel Staircase, The House of Mourning]); Vienna, 1927. — Der Abituriententag, die Geschichte einer Jugendschuld (High School Class Reunion, The Story of a Youthful Wrong); Vienna, 1928. — Neue Gedichte (New Poems); Vienna, 1928. — Barbara oder die Frömmigkeit, Roman (... or Piety, Novel); Vienna, 1929. — Dramatische Dichtungen (Die Troerinnen, Juarez und Maximilian, Paulus unter den Juden) (Dramatic Works [The Trojan Women, ... and ..., Paul among the Jews]); Vienna, 1929. — Das Reich Gottes in Böhmen, Tragödie eines Führers (The Kingdom of God in Bohemia, Tragedy of a Leader); Vienna, 1930. — Die Geschwister von Neapel, Roman (The Siblings of Naples, Novel); Vienna, 1931. — Realismus und Innerlichkeit, Rede (Realism and Inwardness, Speech); Vienna, 1931. — Kleine Verhältnisse, Novelle (Narrow Circumstances/Ephemeral Love-Affairs {translators' note: title has a double meaning}, Novella) (with illustrations by A. Kubin); Vienna, 1931. — Können wir ohne Gottesglauben leben? Rede (Can We Live without Faith in God? Speech): Vienna, 1932. — Die vierzig Tage des Musa Dagh, Roman (The Forty Days of ..., Novel), 2 vols.; Vienna, 1933. — Schlaf und Erwachen, Neue Gedichte (Sleep and Awakening, New Poems); Vienna, 1935. — Der

Weg der Verheißung, Ein Bibelspiel (The Promised Road, A Bible Play); Vienna, 1935 (as *The Eternal Road* with music by Kurt Weill, New York, 1937). — Höret die Stimme, Roman (Hearken unto the Voice, Novel); Vienna, 1937 (as *Jeremias. Höret die Stimme* [Jeremiah. Hearken unto the Voice]; Frankfurt on the Main, 1956). — In einer Nacht, Schauspiel (In One Night, Play); Vienna, 1937.

Von der reinsten Glückseligkeit des Menschen, Rede (On the Sheerest Bliss of the Human Being, Speech); Stockholm, 1938. — Der veruntreute Himmel, Roman (Embezzled Heaven, Novel); Stockholm, 1938. — Gedichte aus dreißig Jahren (Poems from Thirty Years); Stockholm, 1939. — Das Lied von Bernadette, Roman (The Song of ..., Novel); Stockholm, 1941. — Eine blaßblaue Frauenhandschrift, Novelle (A Woman's Pale-blue Handwriting, Novella); Buenos Aires, 1941. — Jakobowsky und der Oberst, Komödie einer Tragödie (... and the Colonel, Comedy of a Tragedy); Stockholm, 1942. — Die wahre Geschichte vom wiederhergestellten Kreuz (The True Story of the Restored Cross); Los Angeles, 1942. — Stern der Ungeborenen, Ein Reiseroman (Star of the Unborn, A Travel Novel); Stockholm, 1946. — Gedichte aus den Jahren 1908-1945 (Poems from the Years ...); Los Angeles, 1946 (newly edited by Adolf Klarmann; Frankfurt on the Main, 1953). — Zwischen Oben und Unten, Drei Reden und Theologumena (Between Above and Below, Three Speeches and ...); Stockholm, 1946.

Werfel translated (with Emil Saudek) the following by Otokar Brezina: Wind von Mitternacht nach Mitternacht (Wind from Midnight to Midnight), Munich, 1920; Musik der Quellen (Music of the Springs), Munich, 1923. — He wrote the preface to: Schlesische Lieder (Silesian Songs) by Petr Bezruk (translated by Rudolf Fuchs), the preface to the novel: Ein Kind unserer Zeit (A Child of our Time) by Ödön von Horvath, who was accidentally killed in his Parisian exile, Amsterdam, 1938; likewise the epilogue to Karl Brand, Das Vermächtnis eines Jünglings (The Legacy of a Youth), edited by Johannes Urzidil, Vienna, 1920, and the preface to the novel by Hermann Borchardt: The Conspiracy of the Carpenters, Historical Account of a Ruling Class; New York, 1943.

Werfel edited (with Richard Specht) Verdi's letters (Vienna, 1926) and translated and adapted the texts of several of Verdi's operas, e.g., *Simone Boccanegra, Don Carlo* and *Die Macht des Schicksals* (The Force of Destiny) ("freely rendered from the Italian of F.M. Piave and adapted for the German operatic stage").

In the process of being published since 1948 are the Gesammelte Werke in Einzelbänden (Collected Works in Individual Volumes), Frankfurt on the Main, edited by Adolf Klarmann. Hitherto published, apart from reprints of the novels: *Erzählungen aus zwei Welten* (Tales from Two Worlds), 3 volumes (vol. 1 Stockholm, 1948; vol. 2 Frankfurt on the Main, 1952; vol. 3 Frankfurt on the Main, 1954), containing all stories previously published in book editions and journals, as well as some items from the literary remains, especially the novel *Cella*, not yet published in book form; *Gedichte von 1907-1945* (Poems from ...) (Frankfurt on the Main, 1954); *Die Dramen* (The Dramas), 2 volumes

(Frankfurt on the Main, 1959; *Zwischen Oben und Unten* (Between Above and Below), new edition augmented and enlarged with unpublished material from the literary remains (Frankfurt on the Main, 1964). — Also published was a selection from Werfel's complete works, *Das Reich der Mitte* (The Middle Kingdom), introduced by Adolf Klarmann; Graz and Vienna, 1961.

Werfel's extensive literary remains are in the keeping of Mrs. Alma Mahler-Werfel, New York (initial versions, fragments, and drafts), but also at the University of California, Los Angeles, and Yale University, New Haven, Connecticut.

ALFRED WOLFENSTEIN. *I was born on many days. Anyone who has for all that not come into the light of the world cannot describe his life while in the dark. That I was put into prison when I was six and later sent out into the dark forest of a lumber-yard and then back again to school (just one sample of our destiny's early command: be glad that you are allowed to exchange one nothingness for another —); that I found myself newly associating with youths whose friendship beamed away a dreary freedom from love until a youth-girl will appear; that I was propelled to Paris by lightness and back into the unstable center of Europe and into every diaspora of the world of blood and money by heaviness; that in southernmost Germany I encountered the spirit-glow of unknown workers and there on that swiftly sinking, peculiarly high island encountered the struggle that keeps on shining and germinating through eternity, the struggle in which real voices from the assemblies of the phoney revolution, voices out of the unknown, made themselves heard and in which in the face of a persecuting stupidity — brotherhood, this catch-word of the day, was for once realized in a stirring way and the murder of two inspired men of the people made me feel as though I had lost a pair of fathers: indeed all of this remains in the dark.*

*For only the lights of the world that we ourselves make to shine, exist. Biography does not exist. Every word that is not begotten is silently mutilated. Only what a human being forms has speech; in order to form the human being! The work. No one is born until he gives birth. He remains a phantom, his birth was no beginning, and there is nothing for death to finish off. That is our starry freedom — and a phoney life's ever everlasting peril. But every poetic work mocks that peril and proclaims: we ourselves beget ourselves! Only those who do not see our shapes will come to our funeral.*

Wolfenstein was born in Halle on the Saale on December 28, 1888. A short time later his family moved to Berlin, where he lived as a freelance writer upon receiving his doctorate in law. In Munich from 1916 to 1922, then again in Berlin until he fled to Prague after being warned of his imminent arrest. From here he managed to get away to Paris on an airplane during the German occupation in 1939.

When the German troops marched into France he tried to flee but was seized by the Gestapo at the Loire and imprisoned. After three months he was released from the prison in La Santé and was now compelled to live as a fugitive, hiding out for years mostly in peasant cottages and in barns along the southern coast of France. Finally he returned to Paris under an assumed name. During this period of increasing nervous exhaustion he wrote a novel about a young person of our times to whom he gave the name of his son Frank, and he worked on a selection of his poems. As Paris was being liberated, he was lying in a small hotel room with a very bad heart condition; he was taken to Rothschild Hospital. Along with his heart trouble he suffered from such severe bouts of depression that he voluntarily departed this life there on January 22, 1945. [Ed.]

Die gottlosen Jahre, Gedichte (The Godless Years, Poems); Berlin, 1914. — Die Nackten, Eine Dichtung (The Naked, A Poetic Work); Munich, 1917. — Die Freundschaft, Gedichte (Friendship, Poems): Berlin, 1917. — Der Lebendige, Novellen (The Man Who Is Alive, Novellas); Munich, 1918. — Menschlicher Kämpfer, Ausgewählte Gedichte (Fighter for Humanity, Selected Poems); Berlin, 1919. — Der gute Kampf, Eine Dichtung (The Good Fight, A Poetic Work); Dresden, 1920. — Sturm auf den Tod, Drama (Assault on Death, Drama); Berlin, 1921. — Der Mann, Fünf szenische Dichtungen (The Man, Five Scenic Poetic Works); Freiburg im Breisgau, 1922. — Jüdisches Wesen und neue Dichtung, Essay (Jewish Character and New Poetry, Essay); Berlin, 1922. — Der Mann, Szenische Dichtung (The Man, Scenic Poetic Work); Berlin, 1922. — Mörder und Träumer, Drei szenische Dichtungen (Murderers and Dreamers, Three Scenic Poetic Works); Berlin, 1923. — Der Flügelmann, eine Dichtung (The Flank Man, A Poetic Work); Dessau, 1924. — Unter den Sternen, Novellen (Under the Stars, Novellas); Dessau, 1924. — Der Narr der Insel, Drama (The Fool of the Island, Drama); Berlin, 1925. — Bäume in den Himmel, Drama (Trees into the Sky, Drama); Berlin, 1926. — Netze, Sechs Einakter (Nets, Six One-Act Plays); Berlin, 1926. — Bewegungen, Gedichte (Movements, Poems); Berlin-Wilmersdorf, 1928. — Die Nacht vor dem Beil, Drama (The Night before the Axe, Drama): Stuttgart, 1929. — Celestina, Schauspiel (..., Play); Berlin, 1929. — Die gefährlichen Engel, 30 Geschichten (The Dangerous Angels, 30 Stories); Mährisch-Ostrau and Leipzig, 1936.

Wolfenstein edited: Die Erhebung, Jahrbuch für neue Dichtung und Wertung (The Rising, Yearbook of New Creative Writing and Appraisal) (two volumes); Berlin, 1919 and 1920. — Hier schreibt Paris, Eine Sammlung von heute (Here Paris Is Writing, A Contemporary Compilation); Berlin, 1931. — Stimmen der Völker, Die schönsten Gedichte aller Zeiten und Länder (Voices of the Peoples, The Most Beautiful Poems of All Times and Countries); Amsterdam, 1938. — Wolfenstein translated: Gérard de Nerval *Erzählungen* (Tales), 3 vols.; Munich, 1921. — Percy B. Shelley *Dichtungen* (Poetic Works) and *Die Cenci* (The ...), drama; Berlin, 1922. — E.A. Poe *A.G. Pyms abenteuerliche Erlebnisse* (...'s Adventurous Experiences); Berlin, 1922; — *Die Denkwürdigkeiten der Scharfrichterfamilie Sanson* (The Memoirs of the Sanson Family of Executioners); Berlin, 1924. — Paul Verlaine *Armer Lelian, Gedichte der Schwermut, der Leidenschaft und der Liebe* (Poor ..., Poems of Melancholy, of Passion, and of Love); Berlin, 1925. — Arthur Rimbaud *Leben, Werke, Briefe* (Life, Works, Letters), rendered and edited by Alfred Wolfenstein; Berlin, 1930. — In addition: Victor Hugo *Dreiundneunzig* (Ninety-Three) and *Die letzten Tage eines Verurteilten* (The Last Days of a Condemned Man).

Alfred Wolfenstein, Eine Einführung in sein Werk und eine Auswahl (..., An Introduction to his Work and a Selection) by Carl Mumm, Wiesbaden, 1953.

The literary remains are in the keeping of Mrs. Henriette Hardenberg-Frankenschwerth and Frank Wolfenstein in London; they contain, among other things, the poem cycle *Der Gefangene* (The Prisoner), written in a French prison, and the novel *Frank*.


PAUL ZECH. *Dear reader, do not always expect serene objectivity from a self-portrait. Somewhere the reflection of the mirror always stays behind as a splotch of makeup. But basically what business of yours is the shape of my skull? Or the outline of my upper arm as it lifts itself athletically when it wants to reach God? Or even what I experience as houses whizz around me? Every life is lived a thousand times by a thousand lives. Sometimes in terza rimas. Sometimes with fists. Sometimes on woodland trees. Sometimes in a bordello. Anything beyond that is legend. I destroy it. For I am not* The Newest Poetry, *but in fact almost forty years old. And* The Forest *I described around 1904. And I am not a Vistulian (although born near Thorn), but rather a pig-headed fellow of Westphalian peasant stock. Some of my forefathers mined coal. I myself (after track and field sports, Greek, and poor exams) never got beyond the attempt (demanded by something inside me). But these two (richest) years —: Bottrop, Radbod, Mons, Lens — made me resolve: from rulers, from the hard of hearing and the blind —: to demand keenness of hearing and loving kindness for all on earth. Long before the business of November 1918 came about.*

*And yet I don't like it when you dub me* Political Poet *(in your sense). Every piece of poetic writing is political insofar as it is less than blood (in other words, irrelevant). Thus when you leaf through field, forest, evening, and dusty streets in my eight books of verse and hear of God and woman (her last!), the agrarian affiliation, the sinewy, the sooted, bawdiness and belief should thoroughly rattle you into becoming a better, a live human being.*

*Or else I deserve: to be thrown on the scrapheap. Just don't punish me: having me gather dust in museums.*

*Decide!*

*And not just for yourself!*

Born the son of a country school teacher in Briesen (West Prussia) on February 19, 1881, Zech was raised by relatives on a farm in the Sauerland near the Ruhr area. He attended school in Wuppertal-Elberfeld, discontinued his studies later out of a sense of social idealism in order to work as a hewer and foreman in the coal mines of the Ruhr and then in the steel mills of Belgium and northern France. Gradually working his way up in the industrial area, he was sent on an assignment to Paris by his union and there he made the acquaintance of some young French writers. This is the reason why he worked for decades on translations of Villon, Mallarmé, Verlaine, Rimbaud; and he also began to write on his own at the start of the new century. Later he resided mostly in Berlin, making his living from the most diverse of occupations, as an editor, an assistant at the *Volksbühne* (People's Theater), and a librarian. The thick-set man with broad shoulders and a gigantic skull was a workaholic who required but four hours of sleep; his literary output was inexhaustible.

In 1933 he was imprisoned in Spandau, and after his release in June 1933 he emigrated by way of Prague and Paris to South America, where he lived mainly in Argentina. But after some bitter years (as a door-to-door salesperson) he traveled around South America, usually by invitation. "He sails up the Amazon and its most remote tributaries," as his son Rudolf reports, basing himself on a description by his father, "and lives with wild Indian tribes. He tours Chilean copper mines with a professional interest and retraces the route of the conquistadors to the Gate of the Sun at Tiahuanaco, crosses Lake Titicaca in a rush boat and takes part in archeological expeditions to the ruins of the Incas. At one time he is out in the jungle with Brazilian butterfly catchers, a little later he is at the waterfalls of the Iguaçu River in Paraguay. We see him among the remnants of the Ona Indian tribes in Tierra del Fuego, and then taking it easy on a hacienda, questioning Indians so that he can complete his collection of old Indian stories." He was always homesick for Europe, but he was not able to go back; on September 7, 1946 he collapsed in front of the garden gate of his residence in Buenos Aires and died there in a hospital on the same day. [Ed.]

Das schwarze Revier, Gedichte (The Black District, Poems) (private printing); Elberfeld, 1909. — Waldpastelle, Gedichte (Forest Pastels, Poems); Berlin, 1910. — Schollenbruch, Gedichte (Breaking up the Soil, Poems); Berlin, 1912. — Das schwarze Revier, Gedichte (The Black District, Poems); Berlin, 1912 (considerably enlarged edition Munich, 1922). — Rainer Maria Rilke, Essay; Berlin, 1913. — Schwarz sind die Wasser der Ruhr, Gesammelte Gedichte aus den Jahren 1902-1910 (Black Are the Waters of the Ruhr, Collected Poems from the Years ...); Berlin, 1913. — Die eiserne Brücke, Neue Gedichte (The Iron Bridge, New Poems); Leipzig, 1914. — Der schwarze Baal, Novellen (The Black ..., Novellas); Leipzig, 1917 (3rd considerably enlarged edition Leipzig, 1919). — Helden und Heilige, Balladen aus der Zeit (Heroes and Saints, Ballads of the Times); Leipzig, 1917. — Vor Cressy an der Marne, Gedichte eines Frontsoldaten namens Michel Micael (Before ... on the ..., Poems of a Front-Line Soldier Named ...); Laon, 1918. — Gelandet, Ein dramatisches Gedicht (Landed, A Dramatic Poem); Laon, 1918; Munich, 1919. — Der feurige Busch, Neue Gedichte (The Burning Bush, New Poems); Munich, 1919. — Das Grab der Welt, Eine Passion wider den Krieg (The Grave of the World, A Passion-Oratorio against the War); Hamburg-Berlin, 1919. — Herodias, Dramatisches Fragment nach Stéphane Mallarmé in freier deutscher Nachdichtung (Herod, A Dramatic Fragment Adapted from ... in a Free German Rendering); Berlin, 1919. — Golgatha, Eine Beschwörung zwischen zwei Feuern, Gedichte (..., A Conjuration between Two Fires, Poems); Hamburg-Berlin, 1920. — Das Terzett der Sterne, Ein Bekenntnis in 3 Stationen, Gedichte (The Trio of the Stars, A Confession in 3 Stations, Poems); Munich, 1920. — Der Wald, Gedichte (The Forest, Poems); Dresden, 1920. — Das Ereignis, Neue Novellen (The Event, New Novellas); Munich, 1920. — Verbrüderung, Ein Hochgesang unter dem Regenbogen (Avowal of Friendship, A Hymn under the Rainbow); Berlin-Hamburg, 1921. — Omnia mea mecum porto, Die Ballade von mir (..., The Ballad of Myself); Berlin, 1923. — Kuckucksknecht, Ein sauerländisches Stück (The Devil's Servant, A Sauerland Play); Leipzig, 1924. — Die Reise um den Kummerberg, Novellen (The Journey around Mount Worry, Novellas); Rudolstadt, 1924. — Die ewige Dreieinigkeit, Neue Gedichte (The Eternal Trinity, New Poems); Rudolstadt, 1924. — Das trunkene Schiff, Eine szenische Ballade (The Drunken Ship, A Scenic Ballad); Leipzig, 1924. — Das Rad, Ein tragisches Maskenspiel (The Wheel, A Tragic Masque); Leipzig, 1924. — Steine, Ein tragisches Finale in sieben Geschehnissen (Stones, A Tragic Finale in Seven Happenings); Leipzig, 1924. — Der Turm, Sieben Stufen zu einem Drama (The Tower, Seven Steps to a Drama), Leipzig, 1924. — Erde, Vier Etappen eines Dramas zwischen Rhein und Ruhr (Earth, Four Stages of a Drama between Rhine and ...); Leipzig, 1924. — Tierweib, ein dramatisches Spiel (Animal Woman, A Dramatic Play); Leipzig, 1924. — Die Geschichte einer armen Johanna, Roman (The Story of a Poor Jane, Novel); Berlin, 1925. — Peregrins Heimkehr, Roman (...'s Homecoming, Novel); Berlin, 1925. — Das törichte Herz, 4 Erzählungen (The Foolish Heart, 4 Tales); Berlin, 1925. — Die Mutterstadt, Zwei Erzählungen (Mother Town, Two Tales); Munich, 1925. — Triumph der Jugend, Schauspiel (Triumph of Youth, Play) (with Henry Marx); Leipzig, 1925. — Ich bin Du, Roman (I Am You, Novel); Leipzig, 1926. — Rainer Maria Rilke, Ein Requiem; Berlin, 1927. — Jean Arthur Rimbaud, Ein Querschnitt durch sein Leben und Werk (..., A Cross-Section of his Life and Work); Leipzig, 1927 (enlarged edition Berlin, 1948). — Rotes Herz der Erde, Ausgewählte Balladen, Gedichte und Gesänge (Red Heart of the Earth, Selected Ballads, Poems, and Songs); Berlin, 1929. — Das Baalsopfer, Vier Erzählungen (The Sacrifice to Baal, Four Tales); Hamburg, 1929. — Rainer Maria Rilke, Der Mensch und sein Werk (..., The Human Being and his Work); Dresden, 1930. — Morgenrot leuchtet, Ein Augsburger Festspiel (Sunrise Gleams, An Augsburg Festival); Augsburg, 1930. — Neue Balladen von den wilden Tieren, Gesammelte Tierballaden (New Ballads of the Wild Animals, Collected Animal Ballads); Dresden, 1930. — Terzinen für Tino, Gedichte (Terza rimas for ..., Poems); Berlin, 1932. — Berlin im Licht, Gedichte linker Hand (... in the Light, Poems of the Left Hand) (under the pseudonym of Timm Borah); Berlin, 1932. — Das Schloß der Brüder Zanowsky, Eine unglaubwürdige Geschichte (The Castle of the Zanowsky Brothers, An Implausible Story); Berlin, 1933. — Neue Welt, Verse der Emigration (New World, Verses of Emigration); Buenos Aires, 1935. — Bäume am Rio de la Plata, Gedichte (Trees along the ..., Poems); Buenos Aires, 1936. — Ich suchte Schmid und fand Malva wieder, Erzählungen (I Was Looking for ... and Found ... Again, Tales); Buenos Aires, 1938. — Stefan Zweig, Eine Gedenkschrift (..., A Commemoration); Buenos Aires, 1943. — Die schwarze Orchidee, Indianische Legenden (The Black Orchid, Indian Legends); Berlin, 1947. — Occla, das Mädchen mit den versteinerten Augen, Eine indianische Legende (..., The Girl with Eyes Turned to Stone, An Indian Legend) (retold by Pablo Cze [i.e., Paul Zech]); Frankfurt, 1948. — Die Sonette aus dem Exil, Gedichte (The Sonnets from Exile, Poems); Berlin, 1949. — Paul Verlaine und sein Werk, Essay mit Gedichtauswahl (...

and his Work, Essay with Selected Poems); Berlin, 1949. — Die Kinder von Parana, Roman (The Children of ..., Novel) (illustrated by E. Zimmermann); Rudolstadt, 1952. — Das rote Messer, Begegnungen mit seltsamen Menschen und Tieren (The Red Knife, Encounters with Strange Human Beings and Animals) (a book of travels in South America); Rudolstadt, 1953. — Die Vögel des Herrn Langfoot (The Birds of Mr. ...); Rudolstadt, 1954. — Die grüne Flöte vom Rio Beni, Ausgewählte Legenden (The Green Flute of the ..., Selected Legends); Rudolstadt, 1956. — Die Ballade von einer Weltraumrakete (The Ballad of a Space Rocket); Berlin-Friedenau, 1958 (written in 1929). — Abendgesänge und Landschaft der Insel Mara-Pampa (Evening Songs and Landscape of the Island of ...); Berlin-Friedenau, 1959. — Die Sonette vom Bauern (The Sonnets of the Farmer); Berlin, 1960. — Die ewigen Gespräche, Deutsche Variationen nach Themen von Charles Péguy (The Eternal Dialogues, German Variations on Themes by ...); Berlin, 1960. — Venus Urania, Sieben Gesänge für Miriam (..., Seven Songs for ...); Berlin, 1961 (written in 1911). — Omnia mea mecum porto, Eine selbstbiographische Ballade (..., An Autobiographical Ballad); Berlin, 1961 (altered text with final touches of the poetic work published under the same title in 1925, designated by Zech as "final version, Buenos Aires, Argentinia, in May, 1946" — in other words, a few months before his death).

Zech translated: Leon Deubel, Die rotdurchrasten Nächte (The Red-Rushed-Through Nights) (with lithographs by W. Rösler); Berlin, 1914. — Emile Verhaeren, Die wogende Saat (The Undulating Grainfield); Leipzig, 1917. — H. de Balzac, Tante Lisbeth (Aunt ...); Berlin, 1923. — J.A. Rimbaud, Erleuchtungen, Gedichte in Prosa (Illuminations, Poems in Prose); Leipzig, 1924; Das Gesammelte Werk (The Collected Work); Leipzig, 1927; Dresden, 1930; Das Herz unter der Soutane, Prosa und nachgel. Gedichte (The Heart under the Cassock, Prose and Posthumous Poems); Lorch, 1948. — François Villon, Die Balladen und lasterhaften Lieder (..., The Ballads and Wicked Songs); Weimar, 1931; Berlin, 1947; Rudolstadt, 1953. — Stéphane Mallarmé, Nachmittagstraum eines Fauns, franz. und deutsch (..., Afternoon Dream of a Faun, French and German); Berlin, 1949. — Louise Labé, Die 24 Liebesgedichte einer schönen Seilerin (The 24 Love Poems of a Beautiful Rope-Maker); Berlin, 1949 (2nd edition, illustrated by Stratil; Rudolstadt, 1957). — Jorge Icaza, Huasi-pungo, Roman aus dem Spanischen m. Vorwort (..., Novel from the Spanish with a Preface) (illustrated by E. Zimmermann); Rudolstadt, 1952. — He published privately translations of Verlaine, Rimbaud, Villon, Baudelaire, Mallarmé and edited a two-volume Grabbe edition for the *Volksbühnenverlag* (Publishing House of the People's Theater).

The following plays were published as stage copies (in small editions): Fremdes Gesicht im Haus (Unfamiliar Face in the House), 1926; Der unbekannte Kumpel (The Unknown Buddy), 1927; Jochanaan (Johanan), 1928; Windjacke (Windbreaker), 1932; Nur ein Judenweib (Just a Jew Woman), 1934; Der Fall Robert Puhl (The Case of ...), 1935.

Zech edited the following journals: Das Neue Pathos (The New ...) (with Ehrenbaum-Degele et al), volume 1 (1913), no. 1-6; volume 2 (1914), no. 1-2;

volume 3 (1920), no. 1-4. — Jahrbuch der Zeitschrift *Das Neue Pathos* (Yearbook of the Journal *The New...*), 1914/1915, 1917/1918, 1919. — Das dramatische Theater (The Dramatic Theater), 4 numbers; Leipzig, 1924. — Weihnachtsblätter (Christmas Pages), 1918-1932, 13 numbers.

All of Paul Zech's literary remains are in the keeping of his son Rudolf Zech in Berlin and are being transferred to the Schiller-National Museum, Marbach. They contain 16 manuscripts: poems, tales, and translations from the years 1920-1935, and approximately 50 manuscripts from the years of emigration 1934-1946, some of them very extensive: novels, tales, Indian legends, poems, essays, 12 stage plays, and 8 volumes of travel diaries from South America. All these works are ready for printing; in addition there are fragments, untitled materials, last revisions.

## END NOTE

The editor owes thanks to many persons in Europe and America who helped him with all kinds of information. The list of names would become very long; for that reason I shall only make mention of those to whom I am especially indebted.

Mrs. Anni Knize in New York and Oskar Kokoschka, who have made possible the reproduction of the Trakl portrait; the (since deceased) collector Wilhelm Badenhop, Wuppertal; the writers: Kurt Heynicke, Merzhausen near Freiburg in the Breisgau; Wilhelm Klemm, Wiesbaden; Karl Otten, Locarno, Switzerland; Claire Goll, Paris; Heinrich F. Bachmair, Berlin; Henriette Hardenberg-Frankenschwerth, London; Doris Lubasch, Berlin; Alma Mahler-Werfel, New York; Hilde Guttmann, London; Paul Pörtner, Zurich; Rudolf Zech, Berlin; Helmut Henning, Hamburg; the professors: P.K. Ackermann, Boston; Alfred Kantorowicz, Munich; Edgar Lohner, Palo Alto, California; Fritz Martini, Stuttgart; Walter H. Sokel, Palo Alto, California; Karl-Ludwig Schneider, Hamburg; The Academies of Art in West Berlin and in East Berlin and that indefatigable assistant, my sister Else Pinthus.

# INDEX OF POEMS IN ORDER OF APPEARANCE

## PART I: CRASH AND CRY

## PART II: AWAKENING OF THE HEART

## PART IV: LOVE TO HUMAN BEINGS

# INDEX OF POEMS IN ALPHABETICAL ORDER OF THE POETS

## WERFEL, FRANZ

## WOLFENSTEIN, ALFRED

## ZECH, PAUL

# INDEX OF ILLUSTRATIONS AND THEIR SOURCES

Unless otherwise noted the illustrations are copied from the reproductions in the second edition of *Menschheitsdämmerung* (5th to 10th thousand, Rowohlt Publishing House, Berlin, 1920). All poet-portraits reproduced here, including those newly added, originated before 1920 in the era of Expressionism.

[1]Oskar Kokoschka writes to Kurt Pinthus concerning this: "I drew Trakl at the time I was working on my 'Windsbraut' (Tempest), when he frequently watched me painting and happened to write a poem which contained the word *Windsbraut*, whereupon we both agreed to give the picture this title." The poem is called "Die Nacht" (The Night) and the relevant passage reads: Golden blaze the fires/Of the nations all around./Over blackish cliffs/Plunges, intoxicated with death,/The glowing tempest....